In Defence of the Independence and Sovereignty of the Country

Durand Appuhamy

sarasavi Publishers
30 Stanley Thilakaratne Mawatha, Nugegoda

By the same author:-
1. Rebels, Outlaws and Enemies to the British
2. The Kandyans' Last Stand Against the British

In Defence of the Independence and Sovereignty of the Country

First Published - 2010

ISBN - 978-955-671-198-1

Typesetting by - Sarasavi Publishers (Pvt) Ltd

Cover Design by - Saman Indika Lokukaluge

Printed by Published by - Sarasavi Publishers (Pvt) Ltd
1/3 Stanley Thilakaratne Mawatha
Nugegoda, Sri Lanka

ACKNOWLEDGEMENTS

I do owe debts of gratitude and my sincere thanks to the SUNDAY TIMES, SUNDAY ISLAND, DAILY MIRROR for publishing some of the articles in this book. My special thanks and gratitude go to THE ISLAND newspaper for publishing most of the articles in this book.

My special thanks to Mr. Somachandra Wijesuriya and his staff at Sarasavi Publishers (Pvt) Ltd. for the corporation and help given in undertaking to publish this book.

The ideas or opinions expressed in this volume belong to the author and have been published as newspaper article.

CONTENTS

CFA = Ceasefire Agreement

MOU= Memorandum of understanding

ISGA = Interim self-government authority

P-Toms = Post tsunami organizational management structure

INTRODUCTION

This book contains many articles written by me and published in the local newspapers over the years. I have published these selected articles in book form, because, I believe, they deserve to be documented as they were written by "a nobody" in defense of his country, at a time, when it was not the fashionable thing to do. Even though ninety-nine percent of us are nobodies in this country, yet we are all citizens. We do not wear overtly our patriotism in our sleeves. It lies deep within us. When the country is under threat of disintegration, we suffer helplessly, moments of anxiety, trying to anticipate the fate of our country. My articles were written to dispel those anxious moments by defending our country from the perceived danger it was subjected to by our power-hungry politicians. Now that the immediate danger to our country has been eliminated, we still need to maintain vigilance to preserve our country, its sovereignty and territorial integrity from separatist political vultures, both Sri Lankan and foreign. In this respect, I hope, this book will encourage patriotic others to take up the baton to defend and preserve the integrity of our beloved motherland.

Section A of the book is devoted to moving our government to initiate talks with the British Government for a British Crown apology for the many atrocities committed by the colonial British on the Kandyan Sinhala Buddhists. I have listed in the articles the British government's public apologies to others for past mistakes and crimes committed by them. So there are no obstacles to doing the same in our case. It is now the responsibility of our government to take up this issue in earnest and pursue it to a successful conclusion.

Section B of the book contains contra-opinions to those propagated and defended by the various governments hell-bent on appeasing the LTTE and concocting a settlement with them with scant regard for the security of the country. The INGOs, the treacherous local NGOs and some foreign embassies were also engaged in this conspiracy. My articles were also aimed at rebutting the spurious arguments adduced by all those enemies to our country. I would like to think that they had some effect, I hope you will agree.

Section C is really the support a writer could give our security forces when they were reduced to an escort agency for the terrorists and their morale was shattered by the governments of the day. When everybody was shouting from rooftops that the LTTE was invincible and that the war was unwinnable, this author, together with few others, robustly argued in the English press to the contrary long before the eventual demise of the terrorists. My complete faith in the ability of our security forces to physically decimate the LTTE has been vindicated. All of us do owe lifelong gratitude to our security forces both living and dead. Without the political support and motivation infused by President Rajapakse and his brother, Secretary for Defense, Gottabaya Rajapakse, to our security forces led by able, determined and courageous commanders, this onerous job would not have been successfully completed. They too deserve our undying gratitude.

Finally, I do hope the reader will remember the date of publication of each article as he reads it, as the ideas in it were relevant to events at of the time of the article. Unfortunately, if I had described the background to each article, then the book would have become unwieldy and too long. As the background is recent history, I hope the reader will excuse me. It is not necessary to read this book from page one to the last page at a stretch. The reader can select the article he/she wishes to read and finish it in a short time as most the articles are short too. I hope you will find it easy and enjoyable reading which will inspire you to do your best for your motherland in your chosen vocation in life.

Durand Appuhamy

Millewa Niwasa,

12/283 Mirigama Road,

Dawatagahawatha, Negombo.

1

KADAHAPOLA UNNANSE, THE EXECUTED MONK

(The Sunday Island, 31st Dec. 1995)

From July 28th 1848, Matale—Gongawela, to give its Sinhalese name—and Kurunegala were under the iron grip of Martial Law declared by Governor Torrington.

This draconian law, extended beyond the duration of the rebellion, was enforced by a merciless British army, to brutally suppress the rebellion against the British, as well as to prevent it from spreading to other Kandyan provinces,

The rebellion was headed by Gonggalegoda Banda and was supported by many Kandyan local headmen.Many of them died shot on sight by the army, and their houses were burnt by the rampaging army and the looters. Purang Appu was one of the eighteen executed men after a brief trial by Court Martial. Even the only surviving signatory to the Convention of 1815, Dullawe Adigar was twice arrested for suspected complicity, but was freed, as investigation did not find any substantiating evidence against him. This was the climate of terror in which Kadahapola was tried and executed.

PARLIAMENT

The atrocities committed under the cover of Martial Law were so appalling that it was condemned vehemently in Parliament in London and by the London and Colombo press of the day. The Courts Martial were denounced as "bloody assizes presided over by demons". This oppression of people by Torringtton's policies led to the investigation of the entire administration of Ceylon by a Committee of the House of Commons, and the termination of office of both, Governor Torrington and his Colonial Secretary, Sir Emmerson Tennent.

The Court Martial

Kadahapola Unnanse was tried on the 25th August 1848, before a Court Martial consisting of five army officers, presided over by Major Franklin Lushington. Such was the indecent earnestness to try the prisoner that they cared not to appoint a judge advocate, to ensure the fairness of the trial from the point of view of the prisoner.

The Charges

The prisoner, Kadahapola Unnanse was arrainged upon the following charges:- First, for directly or indirectly holding correspondence with the rebels, and not giving all the information in his power which might lead to the apprehension of a proclaimed, The Pretender, he, Kadahapola Unnanse professing to know his place of concealment on or about the 17th of August 1848. Second for administering or conniving at the administration of a treasonable oath to one Kiri Banda on or about the 17th of August 1848. Kadahapola pleaded not guilty to both charges.

The court was packed with lawyers from KandyBar. Not one of them volunteered, when requested by Major Lushington, to conduct the defence of the prisoner. One lawyer did ask for his fees from the indigent Kadahapola before taking on his defence and declined, when the prisoner told him that he had no money. Kadahapola conducted his own defence which was totally inane and ineffective. A skillful lawyer could have exploited to good effect, the many inconsistencies and contradictions in the evidence of the two main witnesses, viz. Palamakumbure Basnayake Nilame and his son Kiri Banda. Probably, even the demolition of their evidence by a skilful lawyer might not have mattered, given the indecent haste of the Court to find the prisoner guilty, and then execute him without delay. Such at least was the sentiment of Governor Torrington.

The Nilame told the Court that Kadahapola had visited him on the 18th and had admitted to him that he knew where the Pretender was living without revealing the exact location, and that his son Kiri Banda took the oath on the Bana Potha as administered by Kadahapola.

Kiribanda spun the same story. "I swore, I knew what book it was. I swore that I would never be unfaithful to any King that reigned in this country. I meant in my heart to be faithful to the British Government, but I intended the prisoner to believe that I was faithful to the rebel King". This swearing of the oath was attested by another witness, Koodawattegedera Kangan. This was the gist and the crux of the evidence on which the prisoner was found guilty. There was no proper cross examination of the witnesses to expose the many inconsistencies and contradictions in the details of their narratives of what happened at the home of the Nilame.

Kadahapola Unnanse in his statement to the Court denied the Nilame's statement, and affirmed that he was an innocent bystander, when the oath was taken on his own initiative by Kiri Banda. As to where the rebel King lived, he was prepared to show the road which would take the Nilame to this King. The road he had in mind was the road to Colombo, where the Governor lived.

The Court found the monk guilty of both charges and sentenced him to be shot to death. Many of the lawyers who were present at the trial had grave doubts about the reliability of the evidence, and considered it a frame-up by the Nilame, to advance his career in the service of the British.

Post trial doubts

They were also probably plagued by their consciences for their failure to defend the indigent monk. These lawyers persuaded the Queen's Advocate, Mr.H.C.Selby to intercede with the Governor on behalf of Kadahapola. The Governor's fount of mercy was dry. On hearing Selby's plea "he had turned pale, and slapping his thigh with his hand said 'by God, even if all the Proctors in the place said that the man was innocent, he shall be shot tomorrow morning'. That my Lord is a matter for your consideration, I thought it my duty to let you know what I have heard" was Selby's parting reply. The Chief Justice Anthony Oliphant too was dissatisfied with the trial and wanted to approach the Governor to request at least a postponement of the execution. He was dissuaded by Selby from this mission of mercy, given the experience he had just had with the Governor.

On the 26th at 7am Captain Fenwicke escorted Kaqdahapola for his execution to Bogambara. He was shot dead in his yellow robes. The Captain reported that before his death, the prisoner had admitted that he had been with the rebel King. The Governor, who had been under attack for this execution, immediately pounced on this report as admission of guilt to the two charges preferred against Kadahapola. Whether such admission of being with the rebel merited execution was beyond Governor's thinking!

Stirring in London

When London raised the possibility of miscarriage of justice, the Governor, who had earlier prior to the trial, designated Kadahapola as a "very influential priest", now sought to make him a phantom priest, and a vagrant of no fixed address, a man of no consequence. Dunuwille, the police superintendent and Palamekumbure, drew blank in their mutually independent inquiries about the personal details of Kadahapola. The Governor used these inquiries to show that Kadahapola was not a man of any status, as if, that would exculpate him from the fact that a human life was extinguished on flimsy evidence and on charges which did not merit capital punishment. The fact, probably was, that given the terror of Martial Law, no one was prepared to risk his life by revealing his connection with the executed monk.

Another acerbic twist to this macabre episode, was the fact that the shooting of the priest in his yellow robes, was attacked in England as an outrage on Buddhism, an unnecessary insult to the priesthood, an affront to the religious feelings of the people, and as an act of wanton as well as of impolitic severity. The Governor defended himself by pointing out that a "priest is clothed in yellow robe, and that robe he wears at all times indoors or out of doors, in public and in private, whether engaged in performing the rites of his religion, or occupied with domestic affairs. The individual in question was taken in the ordinary dress of that fraternity, in that dress, he was executed".

Opinion of the Buddhist Fraternity

The Governor was supported in his view by the Nayakke Theras of Asgiri Chapter and the Anu Nayakke Thera of Malwatha Chapter. Both maintained that Kadahapola was not ordained by them and did not belong to their fraternity. They also stated in their letters that they could prove from ancient records, that the ancient Buddhist Kings had put priests to death in their robes, and that there were no complaints made by the people or priests that those executions had been unjust. The Malwatha Thera's letter ended with the following statement that, "a man having been shot in his yellow dress is no shame to us, we do not consider that any indignity to our order was intended by that circumstance"

Kadahapola's death in his yellow robes emanated a larger and a potent symbolism which appropriately fitted in with the turn of events in the former Kingdom of Kandy. Just as much as a Buddhist monk was shot to death in his yellow robes, so was the Buddhist kingdom demolished by the British within a matter of seventeen years, after they had taken it over on false pretences. Kadahapola's execution was the dramatic tangible finale of the death of the Kingdom of Kandy itself, and the loss of status of state religion by Theravada Buddhism. [Extracted from the book by the same author: Kandyans' Last Stand Against The British].

2

THE KANDYAN PEASANTRY

(The Island, 8th Jan. 1996)

The letter on the above topic published by your newspaper on the 20th of Dec. was a compelling plea for justice to a long forgotten people. It should be ringing loud and clear in the ears of all Kandurata MPs lest they make the same mistakes as the Adigars and Dissawes of 1815, and in current terms hand over to all and sundry the Kandyan lands, without the slightest consideration or regard for the descendants of the people, who fought three imperialist nations to preserve their land and their way of life.

In my view, it is neither possible, sensible nor practicable to go back to Kandyan Kingdom of old. The Kandyans gave up armed struggle for their land in 1848. Nearly five-eighth of the country which formed the Kandyan Kingdom at 1815 was merged with the rest in 1833 by the British, and the Kandyans had to seek their destiny in one land, one country and one nation. However, within this context of one nation, the fact that Kandyan lands were expropriated should not be forgotten. Therefore like in New Zealand, Australia and British Columbia, where today the original people (or the native Indians and the Aborigines) are given preference over others in matters of land and settlements, the Kandyans should be given the first choice on settlement in as well as on sale of crown lands.

To those MPs who are unaware of Kandyan history, or perhaps do not care about it, and to the general public at large, I would like to quote below the admissions of guilt made by colonial authorities on the dispossession of lands belonging to the Kandyans.

1) Governor Colin Campbell (1841-47) to Lord Stanley at Colonial Office in London. The discontent among the Kandyans is "caused by the encroachment of European settlers upon lands belonging to the natives. The former frequently endeavour to have lands

belonging to the natives put up to sales as Crown lands, and I fear they are frequently neither considerate nor conciliatory in their intercourse with their native neighbours".

2) George Ackland, whose company controlled about 35 coffee estates before the House of Commons Committee on Ceylon (HCCC). " there were instances in which lands have been taken from them (Kandyans) in which they had not a legal title, but in which it would have been policy to have conceded to them possession" In one instance 1000 acres sold to Britishers Wilson and Ritchie was claimed and forcibly occupied by the Kandyans, and the Governor was forced to return the purchase money with interest

3. Sir Emmerson Tennent, the Colonial Secretary before the HCCC. "They (the Kandyans) complain of the sale of their forests for the purpose of converting them into coffee estates.....They were in fact an easement to their paddy lands.....They have repeatedly complained of this to the Government. But it must be obvious that these are grievances to which we can apply no remedy....we cannot check coffee plantations".

4. Governor Torrington (1847-49) to Earl Grey in London. "The formation of coffee plantations, the invasion of the secret haunts of the Kandyans by the Europeans and Malabar coolies contributed not a little to disturb the habits, and interfere with the customs of the Kandyans....Abuses they have undoubtedly suffered in many instances at the hands of the newcomers". He also reported that " the coffee estates are a source of deadly hatred to the Kandyans".

5. Another coffee planter, P.D.Millie described the protests made by the Kandyans at Punduluoya when the surveyor went up there to demarcate the land for coffee cultivation. "The next morning the surveyor commenced with theodolite and chain, but the natives stood in front of the former, and threw themselves down on the ground before the course of the latter saying 'pass over our bodies, our dead bodies, before you measure and sell

our hunting grounds of our forefathers'. So without any actual violence being used, the work was stopped and the surveyor had to depart". Those Kandyans were probably the first Green Party in the world!

It was in 1925 that the Kandyan National Congress (KNC) made an attempt with great pomp and fanfare to revive the lost Kandyan identity. Mr. P.B. Nugwela (Dissawe), its President, talked of "rebuilding our nationality". Before the Donoughmore Commission, the KNC argued for a Federal set-up basing its argument on the "claim of a nation to have the right to live its own life and realize its own destiny". The KNC failed primarily because it was an elitist cabal which failed to represent the interests of the Kandyans at large, most of whom were victims of the plantation economy.

This mistake should be avoided by the present-day Kandyans who want a fair and square deal for the Kandyan peasantry. Any Kandyan organization should be supra-political commanding the support of the impoverished Kandyans and having within its fold politicians of all hues. Its sole objective should be a positively preferential deal for the Kandyans in land settlements and the sale of Crown lands. Justice demands positive discrimination in favour of the victimized Kandyans.

3

GONGALEGODA BANDA - A REBEL WITHOUT A CAUSE

(The Sunday Island, 11th Feb 1996)

The last Kandyan rebellion against the British rule over the former Kandyan Kingdom broke out in Matale in the last week of July 1848. It was reported to Governor Torrington that the rebellion was headed by a Pretender to the Throne of Kandy, and that he was on his way from Dambulla, marching with a large following to Kandy. The Governor declared Martial Law in Matale on the 29th of July, and proclaimed a reward of sterling pounds 100 (later increased to 150) for the capture of the Pretender, and used the army to suppress the rebellion most ruthlessly. The army pursued a policy of shoot to kill and widespread arson.

"Coronation" of the Pretender

According to Ambulame Unnanse, the Chief Monk of the Dambulla temple, on the 26th of July, a large party of about 800 armed persons gathered at the temple premises, and demanded from him the keys to the temple. He sent a junior monk with the keys and proceeded there later. When he went to the Maha Devale, he saw the Pretender sitting on a carpet with a pillow on his side. The brief conversation that took place was an angry phillipic against him for not coming immediately to meet the Pretender, and for not having the temple decorated for the reception of the King. As the crowd was getting ready to have their lunch, the monk diplomatically left the temple, leaving behind the other monks of his fraternity.

When he returned a few hours later, he was informed by the other monks that in his absence the Pretender had made offerings to Buddha, and had made the following declaration before the image of Vishnu Deviyo: "I do not lie, I am not an imposter. I am a grand-son of King Kirti Siri, to the truth of which, I call heaven and earth and the Kataragama God to bear witness, and if this is false, my head will burst and lightening will strike". On the arrival of Ambulame he took out a Pusskola and read it aloud—Sriwickreme Saraave Siddhi--- and demanded that the coronation ceremony be performed. He did not accept the plea of the priests, that they did not know how to perform this ceremony. However, fearing for their lives, they did conduct a Pirith ceremony. A British spy who probably was at Dambulla, did report that the priests sang the hymn of victory over a vase full of water and anointed the Pretender. The people then prostrated before their King and rose to fight against the British. The new King then commandeered the temple palanquin, and with the beat of Tom Toms proceeded to Matale. So began the rebellion of 1848.

After his arrest Ambulame made the following statement: " I do not know who was the King. He spoke Malabar (Tamil). He spoke in Sinhalese with us. He was like a Sinhalese man. He spoke like a learned man in Sinhalese, and spoke it without any foreign accent. He was of light colour.....All the people said that he had cat's eyes. He had whiskers and mustachios, the latter curled up, but no beard. He was of middle size, rather stout in figure and good looking. He appeared to be about 37 years of age, more not less. He had on his head a stripped yellow silk turban, a white jacket extended as far as his waist. He wore white cloth with gold border in a Sinhalese way. He had a ring on the forefinger of his right hand". This was an accurate description of the man as it transpired later.

The Capture of the Pretender

According to Lt. Col. Drought, who was the commander of the troops in Kandy at this time, the Pretender was caught with the help of the man-servant who supplied the daily food to the Pretender. This servant had approached Capt. Watson in Matale on the 21st of Sept. and had offered to help, provided no Europeans were included in the arrest party. Capt. Watson sent six Malays dressed as natives, two Mudaliyars and a Headman with the servant. The party left Matale, so as to arrive at the place of concealment, just at dark, which was the Pretender's dinner time. The servant went in first with the rice and curry as usual. The Malays crept in afterwards, and when in the middle of his meal, they seized him. He struck and struggled and freed himself and climbed up the side of the rock, but was soon pulled down, thrown on the ground, bound and conducted into Matale the same night.

The prisoner had hidden himself in a large cave on the side of a prominent rock in the thick jungle, about 8 to 9 miles from Matale in the Elkaduwa district. The rock was high enough to give a commanding view of the surrounding districts. There had been only one other person stationed as a watch. He appeared to have slept on his job, and awakened by the noise and commotion of the arrest, had fled the scene. Today anyone can visit this yet unexplored cave on the side of the large rock. It is in the Elkaduwa tea estate in a place known to the locals as "Thotilpullama". One can drive on the estate road up to the cave. The assent up to the cave is overgrown with shrubs. It is also an area full of poisonous snakes. Should not this site be made widely known, so that, the many visitors to Hunas Falls hotel near which this cave is situated, can pay a visit to this historical site? Archaelogical Dept. and Historical Societies, please take note.

The Pretender was tried for High Treason before the Supreme Court on the 27th of Nov. He pleaded guilty and was found guilty. He was sentenced to death with recommendation for commutation. Torrington, who was at this time under severe attack in Parliament in London commuted the sentence to transportation for life and severe public flogging (100 lashes) in Kandy preparatory to his exile to Malacca prison, so as to make a lasting impression upon the minds of the Kandyans. He died there of some disease in Dec. 1849. This flogging too was attacked in Parliament as an unnecessary and unwarranted measure of inhuman cruelty.

[Dr. K.D.G. Wimalaratne in a letter to the press on the 5th of Mar.1996 did dispute the title of this article and quoted SLNA 6/2077 to assert that the prisoner was not sentenced to death. My sources for this article were CO 54/251 and CO/252 documents at Kew archives. I have quoted his plea in full to Torrington in my book: "Kandyans' Last Stand Against The British". In that he clearly says that he was an unwilling Pretender and that at the opportune moment he deserted those who forced him to be the Pretender. It might be that he stated this to escape punishment. By this admission he had cast doubt on his commitment to fight the British on behalf of the Kandyans. It is this aspect of the man, I have tried to portray in this article. This article was not intended to belittle the heroic struggle of the Kandyans against the British which I have amply described in my book].

Who was the Pretender

Col. Drought described the man as "five feet five and a half inches in height, complexion light brown, eyes hazel, hair dark brown, beard and mustachios dark brown, marks slight scar over the left temple, age forty, well-proportioned and of intelligent countenance". C.R. Buller who was the Government Agent in Kandy, reported that the Pretender was a man named David. He was a low-caste from a village about five miles north of Colombo. He had married into a Kandyan family, and was looked down upon by the Kandyans, until Galgodde Ratemahatmaya had projected David as a descendant of one of the past kings. He was not in any way connected with any Royal families. He was set up as a mere tool by the Kandyan chiefs. This was confirmed by Panebokke Guneratne Unnanse, who was commissioned by Torrington to tour the rebel areas to ascertain the causes of the rebellion. Panebokke too reported that the imposter was David. He had taken on the name of Gongalegodda Banda, and that he was from Peliyagodda.

Gongalegoda Banda was a rebel without a cause. For, in his statement submitted to the Supreme Court on the 1st of Dec. after the trial, he did admit that a few individuals, all of whom he named, did coerce him into the role he played as the Pretender to the Kandyan throne. They dressed him in silk cloth, jacket and turban and conducted him against his wishes to Dambulla. His opposition to the looting, plunder and destruction of property in Matale and Kurunegala by his retinue had not endeared him to his followers. He had come to know that they would soon eliminate him and appoint another person. So he had deserted them, and had hidden in the cave, where he was captured.

He did implore for his pardon and the restoration of his property, and compensation for his house, which the army had burnt down. His statement did not change an iota of the sentence passed on him. So ended the last attempt to set up a low-country Sinhalese on the throne of Kandy.

4

OUR HISTORIANS ARE IGNORANT OF WHAT HAPPENED TO KANDYAN KINGDOM

(the Island, 20th Mar. 1997, A report on my submission to Sinhala Commission by Rupiuka Gunawardene and Sakuntala Perera)

There are two common histories regarding Sri Lanka. One is what actually happened in Sri Lanka and the other is what the historians say. I do not know why our main historians are ignorant as to what truly happened to the Kandyan Kingdom. There is a concept that, Sri Lankans never fought for our independence, which is a wrong concept. What actually happened was that we did fight and win our independence from them, but in the process, we were mercilessly massacred.

There is a belief among politicians and intellectuals that our people should not know our history. So there is no wonder why our people are gullible to all suggestions made by our politicians, said Durand Appuhamy, a former lecturer resident in UK.

He expressed the above idea at the Sinhala Commission chaired by S.W.Walpita, comprising, A.D.T.M.P. Tennekone, Prof. A.D.V. de Indraratna, P.D.Uduwela and Mr. Padmashantha Wickramasooriya.

"At the beginning the British church was not a party to the Convention. The chief spokesman James Steven was also the chief architect of ant-Buddhist policy in Sri Lanka. The second point I want to make is that Buddhism was brought down to the level of paganism, so that they could say that the British Government could in no way support or sustain Buddhism. What was the support they were talking about? A mere 350 sterling pounds".

"Then they had the missionaries funded, churches built from the vast amount of taxes collected from Kandyan Buddhists. The fourth point I want to make is that there was absolutely no lay organization to protect

Buddhism or the clergy or the temples, and as a result of abolishing Rajakaria, a lot of temples lost their lands. The fifth point is the lack of unity between the clergy and the laymen. They even quarreled among themselves as to whether the British should be allowed to play the part as guardian of the Temple of the Tooth Relic. Buddhism was no longer a state religion. The Buddhist way of life was completely taken away. In fact this is what is happening today with the Devolution Package, which is what happened to the Kandyan Kingdom in the hands of the British.

"The other point is regarding the Tamil labourers from India. They were migrant labourers and not permanent workers. It is my contention that they should not be given any preferential treatment. Why should all succeeding governments fall over each other to treat them so? It is unforgivable that they were given lands of the Kandyan Kingdom at the expense of the Kandyans, who were banished to Mahawelli settlements. This is actually creating a new country by bringing in new laws to ensure these lands are given to those who continuously profess their faith on LTTE's Eelam".

"The British High Commission should examine possibilities of making an apology to the Buddhists and to the Kandyans for the injustice done to them under their rule. Then the purpose of your sitting on this Commission will be fulfilled" he added.

[Author's note: My submission was more elaborate in more precise English. The reporters have captured only some elements of my submission. This newspaper report is included in this book for completeness of my campaign for the Kandyan cause].

5

KANDYANS, COLONIALISTS AND THE NEW CONSTITUTION

(The Island, 17th April 1997)

There is a legitimate and an overwhelming case for an apology by the British Crown to the descendants of the Kandyans of the former Kingdom of Kandy. This case is based on the provisions of the Convention of 1815, the subsequent deliberate flouting of those provisions by the colonial British, and the consequent irreparable loss suffered by the Sinhala Buddhist Kandyans. The Convention may be atrophied by disuse. Yet it remains valid. It has not been formally abrogated or nullified by anyone anywhere. It therefore behoves the British to examine the case for an apology to the present-day Kandyans. In this respect the honourable precedents worthy of emulation are the apologies tendered by the British Crown to the Canadian Indians and the Maoris of New Zealand.

The Convention of 1815 was an International Treaty signed by Governor Brownrigg on behalf of King George the Third and his government on the one hand, and on the other, the Kandyan Chiefs on behalf of the Kandyan people, who were then an identifiable and recognized nation, enjoying its independence and freedom without any external impositions. The Chiefs had no conditions imposed on them, nor did they undertake to fulfill any conditions. They voluntary ceded their nation to the British by this Convention. This position was acknowledged by Earl Bathurst, the Colonial Secretary at that time, as well as by his successors in that office. However, they ignored it in their actual dealings with Kandyans.

As a result of this agreement, the British gained many advantages which they did not enjoy before. They obtained sovereignty over the Kandyan territory, the power to appoint the Chiefs as well as British Agents, and the power to collect royal dues and revenues. In return, the British also solemnly undertook many obligations. All of them were deliberately reneged on, and unilaterally replaced with new onerous impositions. Thus the Treaty was broken ex parte the British, without any quarter given to the Kandyans to change their minds on the Convention they signed trusting the British. Only the British could change their minds and hearts with impunity. A change of minds on the part of the Kandyans was condemned as traitorous rebellion deserving condign punishment. In any breach of contract, the aggrieved party can obtain redress from the courts, and have the contract declared null and void. The Kandyans had no such avenues open to them. The British were the judge and the jury in this case, supported by the full might of their imperial army.

Open Rebellion

Open rebellion was the only avenue open to the Kandyans against the British usurper. This they resorted to in 1817/18 throughout their territories. Then again in Wellasse in 1820, in Matale in 1823, in Bintenne in 1824, in Badulla in 1843, and finally in Matale and Kurunegala in 1848. Their struggles were spontaneous and ill-conceived, and became unequal mortal combats with the imperial British army, which used draconian measures to slaughter those freedom-fighters. Many were massacred, many were similarly executed, and many were left to rot in jails in Sri Lanka and abroad. There were no Human Rights Organizations or Laws of Warfare then, just brutal might was always right. It is absurd that today (2009/10) the British are trying to preach Human Rights to us!

The Kandyans paid a heavy price in their struggle to regain their country and their freedom. The repressive and oppressive measures taken against them reduced them to abject misery from which they have not recovered even today.

By Clause 4 of the Convention, the Chiefs were assured of "their rights, privileges and powers of their respective offices, and to all classes of people, the safety of their persons and property, with their civil rights and immunities, according to the laws, institutions and customs established and in force amongst them". These words were only pious platitudes, as fragile as most new year resolutions.

The first infringement of the above undertaking took place when a Hadji was appointed as Headman of the Muslims in Wellasse. Brownrigg did accept that the appointment of a Muslim to what was essentially a Sinhalese office was "an encroachment on the national rights and reasonable expectations of the Kandyans by birth". Yet the appointment was confirmed, despite protests by the Kandyans. This was to be expected, as Brownrigg had already conveyed to Huskisson in 1816 that "the Chiefs' power must and ought to be circumscribed".

After the rebellion of 1817/18, many surviving Chiefs were summarily dismissed from their posts and their lands were confiscated. Many Kandyan posts were suppressed. The newly appointed Chiefs were deprived of their retinues in lieu of inadequate monetary payments. The little judicial powers they had were curtailed. They were fully subordinated to the British functionaries. Their status and position in society were degraded and denuded of all official rank and authority. They were "reduced to the ranks and office of stipendiary organs for effecting the Orders and Regulations of the British Government". They were no more the equal partners to the contract of the Convention. They were now the paid servants of the British, and as such, subject to preferment and manipulation by the British. Clause 4 was in tatters. They lost everything that they were before the Convention. The complete usurpation of the Kandyan country was made complete by Clause 7 of the unilateral Proclamation of Nov. 1818. From then on, the British Government was the " source alone from which all power emanates, and to which obedience is due".

During the rebellion of 1817/18 the civilians were not spared. They were shot on sight. Henry Marshall wrote that "no attention was paid to guilt or innocence or to degrees of guilt or degrees of misfortune. In many places, much care was taken to sweep the country bare of everything, for the purpose of depriving the inhabitants of the means of subsistence". The government in Colombo pursued a scorched earth policy. Everything was torched, including the paddy fields. Fruit trees were chopped down and their cattle impounded. The Kandyans were literally starved into submission.

Peacetime

In peacetime the people fared no better. On top of Grain Tax, they were also subject to Rajakaria rules which Major Forbes claimed, "enabled the British to exact much more, both of labour and revenue, than any native despot would have dared to demand". Thus the Kandyans were forced into sweated labour to clear their forests, to cut down their trees, to trace and to actually build the roads and bridges, at the neglect of their own health, cultivations and at the expense of their own livelihood. Their wives' meagre earnings from pounding paddy saved many road gangs from stark starvation.

The Kandyan lands were first taken over for roads and bridges. Those roads were built not for the benefit of the Kandyans. They were, in fact, the means to keep the recalcitrant Kandyans under control, as they made it easy to rush in troops and commissariat to Kandy. Later on, they were built to transport the cash crops of the planters to the ports, and their supplies back to the plantations.

Kandyan lands next fell prey to foreign planters. A potential planter, as well as any land speculator, could go anywhere in the Kandyan country, mark out a piece of land, clear it of vegetation temporarily, and have it sold to him, even without a proper survey, at five shillings an acre. In doing this he willfully ignored the ownership of such lands. Governor Campbell (1841-47) himself complained that the planters were "endeavouring to have lands belonging to the natives put up to sales as Crown lands". He also reported to the Colonial Secretary that the "system of land sales was very loose and irregular".

The first two coffee planters, George Bird and Governor Sir Barnes, had to fight in the courts for their title to lands. They eventually had to buy out many claimants. The civil court in Kandy was clogged up with land dispute cases. Many Kandyans did not have the means, or the written documents of title, and lost their lands by default to contest the sale of their lands. The Clause 4 assurance "of safety of person and property according to laws and institutions and customs in force in the country" became meaningless rhetoric, worthy of modern day Sri Lankan politics. However, due to the expropriation of Kandyan lands for coffee plantations, they became the landless, jobless and the most deprived of peasants in our country today.

One incident, as reported by a contemporary planter. P.D. Millie, is worth the mention here. On the arrival of the government surveyor to mark out the lands for sale, the people of Puduluoya surrounded his tent, and spent the night with him. The next morning, they obstructed him by throwing themselves down on the ground saying "pass over our bodies, our dead bodies before you measure and sell our hunting grounds of our forefathers". They offered no violence. The surveyor packed up left the place. In 1980s, when the Kotmale reservoir flooded the lands of the descendants of those brave Kandyans, they were denied alternative lands in their traditional homelands, allegedly at the behest of the leaders of CWC, who today rule the roost in the hill country. Their ancestors came as migrant labourers to work in the plantations. Compared to the Kandyan peasants, and to their economic/social position, when they arrived on the estates, those Indian Tamil migrants have fared very well. They have eclipsed the Kandyan Sinhalese. Their arrogation of economic and political strength has been largely at the expense and neglect of the Original people of the Kandyan districts. This is the desperate position of the Kandyans today. Which Kandurata MP would plead their case given their supine compliance to dispatch the Kotmale Kandyans to far away Mahaweli settlements?

Clause 5 of the Convention

The translation of the Clause 5 from the Sinhala version is as follows: "The Sasana of the Buddha and the Agama of Devas in which the Officials and the inhabitants of the aforesaid Rataval have faith, must be so maintained that they cannot be broken, and their ceremonies, Sangha Viharasthana and Devalayas maintained and protected". This was a guarantee in clear and unqualified terms. Yet behind it, sincerity ex parte the British, was woefully lacking. Brownrigg admitted that the possession of the Kandyan country depended on this clause, and had to accede to it to quite all uneasiness. He confessed that the words were "more emphatical than would have been my choice".

To the Kandyans, Buddhism was their state religion, patronized and protected by their kings and laymen alike from time of king Devanam Piyatissa (247-207BC). That was what they expected from the British. The British, however, had other ideas.

Even as the ink was drying on the Treaty document, Brownrigg was already engaged in 1816 in vilification and character assassination of the Buddhist monks. In his dispatches to Barthurst, the monks had become the "grand movers of plots.....deep and artful dissemblers". He distrusted the monks, so did the other governors who followed him.

The first organized attack on Buddhism came from the Weslyan missionary R. Spence Hardy. He argued that Buddhism was idolatry, that "any open or implied encouragement to its teachers or its worship was an offence in the sight of God". Dandesan Coats of the Church Missionary Society took up this issue with the Colonial Secretary, arguing that Clause 5 was a hindrance to the conversion of the natives to Protestant Christianity, and that all connections with Buddhism should be speedily and entirely dissolved. Later James Peggs, a Baptist missionary urged Lord Stanley (CS in 1843), " to resign the affairs of idols, their temples, and their lands to their own votaries". James Stephen, the Permanent Under-Secretary (1837-47), was the astute and bigoted advocate of the anti-Buddhist colonial policy. He strained the largely unwritten British Constitution itself to elicit the argument that a Christian Government run by Christians, could not support or sustain an idolatrous religion like Buddhism. According to him "the Treaty did not , and could not, mean that George the Third succeeded to the religious duty and character of the King of Kandy, and that the Defender of the Christian Faith should in the same sense become the Defender of the Buddhist Faith".

This indeed was precisely the expectation of the Kandyans, and this was the reason for their lamentation at the absence of a Buddhist king in Kandy. That such an interpretation became an untenable contradiction to the British was entirely their own fault. An honourable solution would have been for the British to hand over the country and its Buddhist religion to the Kandyans, and to have departed from the Kandyan country. Instead the British fragmented the country, dismantled its institutions and imposed their own brand of administration, law and culture on an unwilling people. British cultural imperialism was the new article of faith.

Breach of Contract

Deliberate decision to break the contract on the inviolability of Budhism came first from Vernon Smith, the political boss of James Stephen at the Colonial Office. In 1841 he minuted that "time has come when we may safely, and as good Christians, violate our agreements in Ceylon". Later Earl Grey (CS in 1846) referring to Clause 5 emphatically minuted that "I also deny that any immutable arrangement can be made by men of one generation which men of all future generations are to abide by…..the Sovereign authority of no country can be deprived of the inherent power of making from time to time such change in the laws as may be required". Had the Kandyans the same freedom of choice, they would have embraced Grey's interpretation, and opted for independence from the British. Later on Golahella RM was to ask Governor Torrington, "what good have we gained by British rule if you violate your Treaties, not only cease to protect our religion, but on the contrary, endeavour to destroy it?" Buddhism was not the only casualty under the British.

The British Protestant churches were not a party to the Convention of 1815. They had nothing to do with it. Their interests began to dominate the policy of the government, which, both in London and Colombo took on the garb of bigoted missionary on the warpath against idolatry and demonism. The government became the obedient servant of the British missionaries and sought to carry out their wishes.

Support to Buddhism stopped

Persuaded as well as scared, by the British missionary propaganda, the British colonial government stopped all support to Buddhism. The financial support was only a mere 315 sterling pounds in an annual budget of 147,000 pounds. This was a gross injustice to the Kandyans, given the fact, that the government was paying the salaries of Anglican missionaries and financially supporting the building of Protestant churches in Kandy itself. The Kandyan Buddhists were taxpayers, therefore it was inherently illogical, as well as patently unjust, to have stopped spending some of the taxes on their religion.

For more than two millennia, Buddhism had survived as the state religion of the country. Schism within the Sangha, anti-Theravada monarchs, anti-Buddhist Hindu and European foreign invaders, failed to knock it off this prime perch. This primacy of place and status of Buddhism ended dramatically, when Governor Torrington handed over the three keys (one each) to the sacred Karanduwa, to the Heads of Malwatha and Asgiri and to Dullawe the Dewe Nilame on the 2nd of Oct. 1847. The Kandyans did not bargain for this. They signed the Convention in good faith. That document is today a curiosity item and an ominous warning to our new constitution gurus, who want to alienate land together with absolute power over such land. As a result of that document the Kandyans lost everything. They lost their right to have a king of their own. They had their religion demoted to demonism, and stripped of all support and sustenance. They lost their customs and their traditional way of life. They lost their lands and their country to outsiders who today dare to demand a Tamil hill country of their own. [In the mid 1990s there were some tea estate Tamils demanding a homeland of their own].

The case outlined above is compelling evidence that the predatory depredations of the former colonial administration, led to the deplorable situation of the Kandyans. The British Government could help to mitigate this calamity imposed on the hapless Kandyans, by a formal acknowledgement of the failures of their colonialists.

In the words of the Memorialists who petitioned Queen Victoria in 1846, "the infringements of the promises and engagements, amicably made and entered into….. are contrary to British Law, are in opposition to Equity, Justice and impartiality of the British Government, and discreditable to its good faith" Surely, the Kandyans and their religion deserve an apology from the British Crown.

6

Kandyan Lands and the British

(The Island, 10th May 1997)

S. Boralesgamuwa (SB) in his letter on "The Land Policy of the British" in your newspaper of the 5th of May has got hold of the wrong end of British rule of the Kandyan provinces. He is almost 100 years too late to have quoted Sir H. Clifford, who was the Governor from 1925 to 1927. The actual expropriation of land by the Europeans took place when the coffee cultivation started to creep up the Kandyan hills in the 1820s and 1830s. This was legitimized by the Ordinance No.12 of 1840. If he had looked at the Colonial Office (CO) documents, or read the writings of contemporary authors, he would have found ample evidence of land grabbing by the planters, some of whom were the Governors, Civil Servants and Army personnel in the country.

Before I quote some of their confessions to this transgression, the helplessness of the Kandyans even to make use of the law to protect their land rights was clearly articulated by a civil servant in London itself. ...Referring to the draft of the Ordinance of 1840 he wrote, "the attempt to throw the burden of proof on the private party by demanding the exhibition of titles would scarcely be productive of any favourable results. It is difficult to conceive that, even in cases of valid titles, such instruments are taken care of by a poor and illiterate people unable to comprehend the importance of strict forms in judicial matters, and they are constantly liable to destruction or loss from all the accidents of insecurity and neglect"(CO54/171). This was a valid observation given the fact that many Kandyans did not possess written titles to their lands. The local Gansabas knew who owned what, and sorted out all land disputes most amicably during the times of Kandyan kings.

The few who possessed any titles found it too expensive to resort to courts to prove their cases. To quote Governor Campbell (1841-47), "the natives complain that Europeans frequently encroached on their lands.....but justice is in consequence of the system inaccessible to them.... They say if we go to the District Court to complain, in the first place, we must pay a sum of money to the Proctor exceeding the value of the land....even delays are endless" (CO54/229).

This was the situation which enabled any planter or even a land speculator to select the land he wanted, clear it temporarily, mark out its boundaries and have it sold to him, even without a proper survey, at 5 shillings an acre. This was the first phase of the mad scramble for land which deprived many Kandyans of their legitimate inheritances.

That Kandyan lands were expropriated was admitted to by the colonial authorities. Let me quote a few of them:-

1. Governor Campbell to Lord Stanley: The dissatisfaction among the Kandyans was caused "by the encroachment of European settlers upon lands belonging to the natives....The former frequently endeavour to have lands belonging to natives to put up to sales as Crown Lands, and I fear, they are frequently neither considerate nor conciliatory in their intercourse with their native neighbours" (CO54/196).

2. G.Ackland whose company controlled 35 coffee estates stated before the House Of Commons Committee on Ceylon (HCCC, 1848-50) that "there were great many disputes constantly between the natives and the parties applying to purchase the land... The government, unless the natives could show a title to it, was anxious to sell as much land as possible; and [did not] in all cases [show] as much leniency....towards the natives as perhaps ought to have been shown; there were instances in which lands have been taken from them in which they had not a legal title, but in which, it would have been policy to have conceded to their possession".

3. Sir Emmerson Tennent before the HCCC. "They (the Kandyans) complain of the sale of their forests for the purpose of converting them to coffee estates....They were in fact an easement to their

paddy lands….They have repeatedly complained of this to the government. But it must be obvious that these are grievances to which we can apply no remedy….We cannot check coffee plantation".

4. Governor Torrington to Earl Grey. "The formation of coffee plantations, the invasion of secret haunts of the Kandysns by Europeans and Malabar coolies contributed not a little to disturb the habits, and interfere with the customs of the Kandyans…. Abuses they have undoubtedly suffered in many instances at the hands of the newcomers…. Our coffee estates are a source of deadly hatred to the Kandyans" (CO54/250).

5. A contemporary planter, P.D.Millie in his book "Thirty Years Ago", described the protests mounted by the Kandyans of Puduluoya against this scramble for their lands, when the surveyor went up there to demarcate the land for sale for coffee cultivation. "The next morning the surveyor commenced with the theodolite and chain, but the natives stood in front of the former, and threw themselves down on the ground before the course of the latter saying 'pass over our bodies, our dead bodies, before you measure and sell our hunting grounds of our forefathers'. So without any actual violence being used, the work was stopped and the surveyor had to depart". Those Kandyans were probably the first Green Party in the world. It is their descendants who have become the landless peasants today. The same descendants were also denied suitable local land at the behest of the "new Nayakkars of Thottum", when the new Kotmale reservoir flooded their villages. Their plight cries out for justice.

If one were to travel on the highways of British Columbia or Quebec, one would not fail to see the many highway notices informing the traveller that he is in native territory, and if he wants to do anything, even pitch a camp in that land, he should first obtain a permit from the Native Office of that territory. This is how justice is being done to the Original People (Canadian Indians). It was not long ago that the Queen herself apologized to the Maoris in New Zealand for what her ancestors did to their lands. Today both USA and Australia are in the process of taking steps to restore the rights of the Original People to the lands taken from them. Only in Sri Lanka there is prevarication as well as reluctance to restore to the Kandyans their due. They should be treated preferentially and be given the first refusal in land settlements and Crown land sales. The others could then follow suit.

I hope the information I have given is sufficient to establish the deprivation the Kandyans suffered under the British.

7

A British Apology

(The Island, 24th Jan. 1998)

I petitioned the British government in March last year to consider the case for an apology to the Kandyans at the 50th independence celebration in Kandy. In response, the British High Commission promised me a "substantive reply" to my petition, which I have not received to-date. Your newspaper published my petition in full on April 17th 1997 under the title, "Kandyans, Colonialists and the new Constitution". [The Sunday Leader published the same under the title "The Crown Must Bow"on 11th Jan.1998]. I remain grateful for this favour. Given these circumstances, I think it is incumbent on me to pen a few words in reply to your two editorials on this subject, the latest being on Jan.8th 1998 titled "Kicking into our Own Goal".

At the outset I ought to declare that I do not belong to the NJC. I do not advocate a boycott of the independence ceremonies. Further, as it is beyond my powers to prevent any British participation (by Prince of Wales) in these ceremonies at the highest levels, I realize the futility of any anti-British stance. My case is rather based on history, reasoned arguments, recent precedents and the natural justice of the case.

First, let me dispose of your argument that the demand for an apology would be considered by western opinion "as being utterly ridiculous". This was not the case when the Queen herself apologized to the Canadian Tribal Chiefs, who, in their tribal regalia, attended on her at Buckingham Palace in mid-eighties. The apology was for the depredations of the colonialists on the Canadian Original People (Canadian Indians) stretching from Vancouver to Quebec. Then in 1990 the Queen again apologized to the Maqoris in her speech delivered in the New Zealand Parliament, for violating the provisions of the Waitaki Treaty of 1840.

Those apologies did not lead to shame or humiliation of the British. Nor were charges of xenophobia and chauvinism levelled against the Canadian Indians or the Maoris. Those apologies were in fact followed by efforts to compensate those people in the best way possible. As for the British, their honour and decency in the eyes of the world got enhanced by no small measure. Neither the British- Canadian nor the British- New Zealand relations suffer in any way as a result of these apologies.

On Jan. 7th 1998, Canada attempted to expiate its sins against the Canadian Indians in a three-hour long ceremony in Ottawa Parliament. During this ceremony Jane Stewart, the Minister for Indian Affairs, read a "statement for Reconciliation", in which the government expressed its "profound regret for past actions of the Federal Government against the Canadian Indians". Thus contrary to your editorial opinion, tendering an apology for one's past sins is not an "utterly ridiculous" act. It, in fact, has become the order of the day for proper internment of one's murky past.

I might also point out at this point, that last June, when President Clinton himself apologized to the African Americans for the bio-experiments conducted on them without their consent at Tuskergee, he did , in his speech float the idea, that white Americans should, in fact, apologize for the slavery of the Africans, and all the atrocities committed on the American Indians.

Thus apologies for wrongs done in the past are not prerogatives of anyone. An apology is, in fact, a noble and redeeming quality of mankind.

It is a pity that you had to drag LTTE into your arguments. The LTTE has nothing to do with this. It is a historical fact that an independent nation was most ruthlessly dismantled, and foreign imposition was forced down the throats of the unwilling Kandyans, in spite of their rebellions in 1817/18, in Wellasse in 1820, in Bintenne in 1824, in Badulla in 1843 and in Matale/Kurunegala in 1848. It is also a fact that their lands were appropriated willy-nilly by the coffee planters. It is also a fact that Buddhist religion of the Kandyans was reduced to the level of demon worship and deprived of all state support, which it had hitherto enjoyed and had been solemnly guaranteed to it. Above all, all those actions were clear infringements of the undertakings solemnly given in the Convention of 1815. It is unpardonable that every time someone speaks for the Sinhalaya, he is vilified as a chauvinist and a racist.

It is also typical of some Sinhala myopic journalists to downgrade our written history, while other nations are trying to discover, if not invent, histories of their own countries. Looking back at history is not a retrograde step. It is simply an assertion of what we were, and how we came to be what we are today. Without history, and without the knowledge of our history, we become rootless, and subject to manipulation by others. This is why many have succumbed to the fabricated history of Tamil homeland originally floated by some racist Tamil politicians.

Nelson Mandela is certainly an extraordinary man endowed with sublime fortitude and statesmanship. He certainly is a beacon for all of us to follow. Yet in his humanity, he too decided on a Truth Commission as a way of reconciling a divided nation. What we see happening before it, are the confessions of past atrocities, which were perpetrated on innocent and not so innocent persons. Those confessions were considered adequate expressions of contrition and sorrow for the crimes committed, and therefore deserving of pardon. Are these any different from normal apologies for past sins? Is my invitation to the British to apologize any different from what we see in South Africa today?

It is not necessary for the British to make any confessions. The confessions are there in writing in the Colonial Office documents, except that they are adroitly and cunningly used to defend the oppressive colonial administration. Governor Torrington's confession alone is sufficient here. In his dispatch to Lord Grey dated 14th Aug. 1848, he admitted that "it has since been ascertained that the total number killed and wounded (in the bushes of Wariapola estate in Matale) amounted to little less than two hundred" (CO54/250). Does not this deserve an apology given the fact that the victims had already surrendered to the army?

Had there been a formal acceptance and acknowledgement of the suffering, deprivation and oppression the Kandyans endured at the hands of the British, then the new nation, at independence in 1948, and thereafter, would have been compelled to take necessary measures to alleviate the abject plight of the Kandyans. The Sri Lankans as well as the world would have known that the greatest injustices were committed on the majority Sinhala community by the colonialists, that they were victims in their own country. This alone would have silenced all false propaganda by the separatist Tamil terrorists.

[An Editor's note was appended to this letter which needs to be included for the information of the readers:-

"There is a fundamental difference between the Original inhabitants of Americas, Australia and New Zealand, on whose homelands the Europeans settled and established new nations, and countries like Sri Lanka which the British conquered, administered and quit, leaving the nation intact. The devastating effects of colonialism on American Indians, Australian Aborigines and New Zealand Maoris who became subject races to the white settlers are vastly different to what happened to the peoples of countries like Sri Lanka and India where the colonialists did not settle down".

"Sri Lanka and India have now existed as independent nations for fifty years, had good relations with Britain and still have the British monarch as the head of the Commonwealth. If the injustices perpetrated by the British such as the seizure of lands of the Kandyans, were not righted for half a century, the fault lies certainly with our own politicians, who should tender apologies to their own people. There is nothing to be gained by demanding apologies for crimes committed 150 to 180 years ago, other than to cause embarrassment to two very friendly nations. Verbal bashing of colonialists in the hey- day of colonialism made sense and may have been a delightful pastime, but when done 50 years after their departure, it does smack of eccentricity or petty chauvinism".

"To look to the distant past of 180 years and cry foul while being blind to the immediate threats facing this nation will certainly not be in our national interests. As pointed out in our editorial of January 14th under the heading 'LTTE's concern for Security Nightmare', the terrorists are doing their damnedest to scare away foreign dignitaries attending the Independence ceremony, particularly Prince Charles. The Tamil Guardian published in London claims that while Nelson Mandela declined the offer to be the chief guest at the ceremonies, protests that Buckingham Palace has nominated Prince Charles to be chief guest. The British sending the heir to the British Throne could be taken as a rejection of the terrorists' cry of fake independence and acknowledgement of Sri Lanka being a sovereign and independent state. Had they rejected the invitation it would have been severe embarrassment to this nation. We urge our readers to follow Indian leaders who invited the Queen as their chief guest for their independence celebrations and like the Indians look to the future and not hark back to mistakes made in the dim distant past. This is not to down grade or forget our history but not to make our history a brake to the progress of the nation".

[My rejoinder in Nov.2009 in point form:- (a) The British took only the maritime provinces from the Dutch by force of arms. Sri Lanka was not conquered by the British. The Kandyan Kingdom was obtained fraudulently by making false promises with no intention to honour them. (b) The British did not quit for nearly 150 years and they did not leave the country intact. They divided the country into provinces for the convenience of their administration. This has become a bone of contention and many have died to keep the country an undivided unitary state. (c) As I have stated in my letter above the atrocities committed on the Kandyans and the injustices done to them were ignored and suppressed. If that had been acknowledged in the first instance, then the British would have been compelled to right the wrongs and our local politicians would have been forced to follow that good example. (d) The invitation of Prince Charles or anyone else is not the point at issue here nor the intentions of the then President for such an invitation. The issue was a superb opportunity accorded to the chief guest to put right the wrongs done and restore to the Kandyans their self respect and dignity. (e) Since the letter, the Pope had apologized to the Jews, the Spanish King had apologized to the Arabs, the German Chancellor had apologized to the Polish people and the Jews for the Nazi crimes and the Australian Prime Minister had apologized to the Aborigines. I am sure the readers will have their own comments on the editor's note, which to me, smacks of Angophilinism!! Today, 16th Nov.2009, Kevin Rudd the Australian PM has tendered his apology to the British Child Migrants to Australia. Nearly 7000 of indigent children had been shipped to Australia for a better life there. They were instead abused and exploited unashamedly. Mr. Norman Johnston, himself a former child migrant, now the President of the International Association of Child Migrants and Their Families is demanding significant reparations from the British as well as the Australian Governments. I hope he will be successful and open the door for the solution of our longstanding grievances against the British.

8

The Last days of Ehelapola in Mauritius

(The Sunday Island, 27th Sept. 1998)

Ehelapola Maha Nilame was arrested on the 2nd of March 1818, and was moved forthwith under escort to Colombo. Geo Lusignan, the Secretary to the Kandyan Provinces, minuted on behalf of Governor Brownrigg that "he is removed for a time because the government considers his presence here (in Kandy) detrimental to the public good, but it is not at all meant to charge him as a traitor" (CO54/70). Unfortunately for Ehelapola, all his protestations of innocence of any part in the Kandyan rebellion of 1817/18 and his petitions for an investigation took him nowhere. He remained a prisoner in Colombo till 1825.

Governor Barnes sought to get rid of this embarrassment by exiling him in Mauritius. Lusignan wrote on behalf of Barnes to the Governor of Mauritius that if Ehelapola was outside Ceylon, he could be given a greater degree of personal liberty without endangering the British hold on the Kandyan provinces. Accordingly it was decided to send him by the ship *Alexa nder* to Mauritius "with instructions to Major Bates to have him accommodated with a house wholly separated from the place where the other Kandyan chiefs are confined, in so pleasant and comfortable situation as due regard to economy and an attention to his not clandestinely quitting the island should allow" (CO54/88). Major Bates was further instructed to liberally provide for his table and other wants.(see table for his monthly ration)

Ehelapola arrived in Mauritius with several of his attendants, among them was Don Bastian, his interpreter. Major Bates found him a house in Pamplemouses at a monthly rent of 30 Spanish dollars. Ehelapola was said to have been "highly pleased and satisfied with it".

From the drawings and the description given of this house by Major Bates, this writer was able to identify this house as the largish rectangular one storey, near empty shell of a house, within the Botanical gardens in Pamplemouses. It still has the circular wooden staircase and the separate servants' quarters as described and drawn by Major Bates. Even today the servants' quarters look almost as exact as the drawings of Major Bates and it was confirmed to me that no building changes had been done to them to the knowledge of the personnel in the park.

This house carried the name of *Mon Plaisir*, and had been the venue of important government functions and grand farewell parties to departing governors of Mauritius. From the drawings of this house available at Port Louis museum, it was a house surrounded by trees, colourful flower beds and palmed avenues. Today it is an empty shell housing the Ministry of Agriculture for administering the Botanical Garden.

From the front veranda of the house, Ehelapola would have seen in the distance the panorama of the two mountains dominating Mauritius. One peak, known as *Le Pouce*, would have reminded him of Pidurutalagala, and the other majestically pointed peak, named *Pieter Both*, closely resembling our Sri Pada, would have evoked in him the thought that both were abodes of deities.

The house had ample supply of excellent water. The Botanical Gardens provided him many opportunities to meander there and to avail himself of its facilities for his exhilarating pastime of horse riding.

Both he and Don Bastian were accomplished jockeys and ventured out frequently on a gallop. On those occasions, Don Bastian was the butt of many jokes as "his shining jet-black hair was combed back entirely off his forehead and fastened at the top of his head with a large comb, similar to that used by females. This gave him a singular appearance, while he rode through the town with his uncovered head, great astonishment was excited in the spectators, particularly the negroes who used to say moitie homme moitie femme (half man, half woman); his attire being that of a man, his long hair confined with a comb given his face a resemblance to that of a woman", wrote Mrs Batrum, a contemporary resident at Mauritius.

The other Kandyan prisoners (Pilimatalawe, Mattemagoda etc.) were incarcerated at Powder Mills, which was about couple of miles from Mon Plaisir. So it was natural for Ehelapola to visit his compatriots at Powder Mills. Unlike Ehelapola they were prisoners, though confined under a benevolent regime by the standards of the day. One can only speculate on what transpired at those meetings. Major Bates did report that such meetings did take place.

The best description of Ehelapola's life in exile was given by Mrs. Alfred Bartrum in her book "Reflections of Seven Years' Residence at Mauritius". This book was written for her daughters Ellen and Mary in 1830. She frequently invited Ehelapola for parties at her place and also met him at parties given by others and attended the parties given by Ehelapola himself.

According to her the Englishmen paid him attention and respect. He was always entitled the Prince. Her description of him was that of a broken man. " his countenance is very mild in its expression but not intelligent, and his manner is gentle and unassuming; if one might judge from his physiognomy, I should pronounce him a person by no means likely to ferment political disturbances, or to take part in public affairs; he seemed devoid of energy, and looked like a very harmless, quiet personage".

He was fond of children especially of little Mary and her sister Ellen. In exile he wore his usual Kandyan dress. In Mrs. Bartrum's words " he wore a flat kind of hat, covered with white muslin, sometimes ornamented with gold; his hair was as white as snow, was rolled up in a ball at the back of his neck, nearly on the nape of his neck and was seen projecting beneath his hat; the rest of his dress consisted also of white muslin, and he had a necklace of lumps of gold, each the size and shape of a small hen's egg....He wore also a ring, the stone of which, apparently an emerald, was nearly the size of a half crown".

Ehelapola did not know English and he conducted his business of conversation through his interpreter Don Bastaian. In reciprocation he held a party for his erstwhile English host at *Mon Plaisir*. Everything was in English style under the supervision of Don Bastian, "who being well acquainted with the English custom had the arrangement of the whole; tea, coffee, cakes were handed about and card tables were prepared for those who wished to play cards". Maha Nilame himself took part in a game of whist.

At this party he got one of his attendants to sing the Parangi Hatana which lasted a long time and taxed the endurance of his guests and "completely tired out our patience" wrote Mrs. Bartrum. According to her, the guests restrained their smiles with great difficulty at the "horrible growl intended for a tune, and the ridiculous contortion of the singer's face".

At the ninth birthday party of Ellen, Ehelapola "favoured us with a song that evening, but we could not discover more harmony in that than in the one we had heard from his servant. He and Don Bastian were very abstemious with regard to wine, and generally refused it.... But as he was requested to drink to the health of the little girl whose birthday it was, smilingly took a glass of liquor, and made a flowery speech....wishing all happiness and good fortune to the little damsel, then taking Mary on his knees, he said she must not be left out of the good wishes showered on her sister".

According to governor Barnes, Ehelapola died on the 4th of April 1829 "in consequence of an attack of dysentery after an illness of six days during which he was attended by the Medical Officer of Mauritius" (CO54/105). He was aware of his approaching end and he made a disposition of his property by Will on the 2nd of April.

By his Will he gave Dingiriya, his slave servant his freedom, all the goods and money which belonged to him and were at Mautitius. To Kendagamuwe Nilame and Dawgadeniya Arachchy one hundred Spanish Dollars each and implored the British government to pardon them both and set them free. To Pilimatalawe, he gave all his property and money which were in the custody of the Kandy Kachchery. To Don Bastian he gave 3555 Pagodas, his Sinhalese watch and carriage and the large ring set with diamonds. He also bestowed on Don Bastian all his landed property after the death of his sister. All the linen which was his wearing apparel was to be handed over to Maligawa in Kandy.

He was cremated at St. Andre forest a quarter of a mile distance from Powder Mills where the other Kandyan prisoners were imprisoned. There is a square white monument in his honour. In the center, there is a white granite block with the inscription which reads, "sacred to the memory of Ehelapola Wijesoondra Wickramasinghe Chandrasekra Amerakoon Wahalanodianse, late First Adikar or Prime Minister of Kandy, who died 4 April 1829, aged 57 years".

From the many stubs of burnt out candles on the spot, it is apparent that even today someone lights a candle there in memory of a man whose life was only full of promise, but devoid of any achievement, and futile to the point that he lost his kith and kin, and died in exile an untried and unconvicted state prisoner ennobled unto eternity in this monument in a foreign land. Who today will dare suggest that his ashes be brought back to this country and interred with the appropriate honours due to him? I do.

[The table of monthly ration and expenses can be found in my book "Rebels, Outlaws and Enemies to the British" pages 133 and 137].

[A recent publication assigns the residence of Ehelapola to an empty piece of land near Pamplemouses and a now non-existent house. I prefer to go by the description of the house sent by Major Bates as above. Could Ehelapola have changed residence later? I do not know].

9

Development of the site of capture of the Kandyan King

(The Island, 8th Sept. 1998)

It has been reported in The Island of Aug. 31st that the government has decided to develop "Udupitiya at Bambure in Udispattuwa as a tourist attraction", as this was the " place where Sri Wickrama Rajasinghe was captured by the British on Feb. 18th 1815". The Minister of Cultural Affairs, (Mr. Luxman Rajapakse) is to allocate Rs.2 million as a preliminary grant. I welcome this gesture and hope that this programme will actually be implemented without the usual bureaucratic delays, which accompany projects undertaken by the government.

In this era, when our glorious history has not been taught in our schools, and most adults are ignorant of our history, and some professors in Colombo and USA are engaged in the malicious art of "deconstructing" our history, little mercies like the above should be welcomed and encouraged.

Given this change of attitude of at least some in the Ministry of Cultural Affairs, I would like the Ministry to consider three other sites, which are also doubly worthy of development as tourist sites. These were the places where our Kandyan patriots, who wanted to eject the British were also captured. They rose in rebellion against the British because the British had reneged on the solemn undertakings they gave the Kandyans in the 1815 Convention, had ursurped the crown, and had dispossessed the Kandyans of their lands and their heritage.

The first is Parawagamme in the south of North Central Province. It was here that Pilimatalawa and Keppitipola were captured by Lieut. O'Niel on 28th Oct 1818. The latter was executed by the British at Bogambara on 25th Nov.1818. The former was exiled in Mauritius. There is a fading pillar and an image of Keppitipola on this spot, but is little known to the general public outside the area. Those pilgrims who visit Avukana and Sessvehera would be willing to pay their respects to these two valiant Kandyans too.

The second is the place where Madugalle was captured by Ensign Shootbraid on the 2nd of Nov.1818. The exact spot is yet unknown, but was described as situated "half a mile from the village Elahera". The villagers who were scared to death by the way the Martial Law was enforced, led the soldiers "to the exact place of Madugalle's concealment, behind a rock without covering". Madugalle too was executed with Keppitipola. This place, I believe, is about a mile off the present tiny Pansala at Elahera in the jungle-covered hillock, where one can see evidence of ancient ruins, probably of the Polonnaruwa period.

The third place is the cave where Gonggallegoda Banda, the last Pretender to the Throne of Kandy, was captured by Malay soldiers in Capt. Watson's Regiment on the 21st of Sept. 1848. This place is in the upper reaches of the Elkauwa tea estate, in a place named by the locals as "Thottilpallama". There is a huge rock there giving a commanding view of the surrounding area and Matale town itself. There is an unexplored cave on the side of the rock. Gonggallegoda Banda had hidden himself in this cave. He was betrayed by the servant who conveyed to him his daily food. The threat of execution by Capt. Watson of those who knowingly withheld information on the rebels, scared the servant to reveal, as well as accompany the Malay soldiers to this cave. This site is a few minutes' drive from the Hunnas Falls hotel. Should we not expect the Ministry to keep faith by our fallen heroes?

[Alas nothing had been done by the Ministry or the relevant Provincial Councils to develop any of these places as tourist sites as at Jan. 2010].

10

That British Apology is Never too Late

(The Island, 5th May 1999)

The Sinhala Commission in July 98 published its recommendations. The third recommendation called "upon the British Government to make amends and apologize to the Sinhala people and pay substantial compensation" for breaking the solemn undertakings given in the Kandyan Convention of 1815, the consequent depredations committed on the Kandyans, the wholesale expropriation of lands, the imposition of forced labour and intolerable taxes and for causing environmental degradation and for settling of alien people amongst them. The Commission in its report has given enough cogently relevant reasons for this stance, which, one hopes, the British goovernment would now seriously consider. It is in fact, a godsend opportunity for the British to enhance their reputation, tainted though it is, with the Sinhala populace of Sri Lanka.

I raised this same issue in April 1997 with the British Government. My petition was acknowledged with a joinder that I would get a "substantive reply", which, needless to say, never came. Only a very insensitive British government could ignore the case against them.

An apology for injustices done in the past is not a demeaning act. An apology redeems the degraded humanity of the oppressor and restores the battered dignity of the oppressed. It elevates the villain and the victims to equality of status in the mutual respect for each other. It is an ennobling act of true humanity.

In the recent past there had been a spate of apologies by statesmen and politicians all over the world for injustices done by their predecessors. The Chancellor Helmut Kohl apologized to the Poles for the atrocities committed on them by the Nazis. The Japanese PM apologized to the Koreans and the Chinese for the monstrous crimes committed on them during WW2. In Canada Jane Stewart, the Minister for Indian Affairs, expressed the profound regret of her government for the past actions of the Canadian Federal Government, which had been detrimental to the Canadian Original People (Indians). In the US President Clinton apologized to the African Americans for the bio-experiments performed on some of them at Tuskergee, and at the same time, floated the idea that a national apology was due from the white Americans for the slavery of the African Americans. In Australia PM Howard apologized to the Original People(Aborigines) for kidnapping of their children to be brought up in white Australian homes. In South Africa we had the spectacle of the apologies and contritions by the tormentors of the innocent before the Truth Commission. Even the Catholic Church is now in the process of framing a document apologizing to the world for the many atrocities committed in its name in the past. In all the cases cited above, the post-apology effect was perceived to have enhanced the relationship between the parties concerned. There was a sense of great relief, which, in turn, engendered a new fruitful beginning in their relationships.

England was no exception to the soul-searching episodes. PM Blair apologized to the Irish Catholics for the "shoot to kill" policy of the previous British government. Of more relevance to the above issue was the apology tendered by Her Majesty the Queen in the mid1980s to the Canadian Tribal Chiefs at a tea party at Buckingham Palace for the depredations the colonialists committed on them and on their people. Again in 1990, Her Majesty apologized to the Maoris for violating the provisions of the Waitaki Treaty of 1840. The principles underpinning the Waitaki Treaty were similar to our Kandyan Convention of 1815, wherein guarantees were given for the protection and perpetuation of customs, traditions and the rights of the Maoris to their lands. Those guarantees were subsequently flouted by the colonial British with impunity, hence the apology backed by compensation in kind by both the British and the New Zealand governments. Both the Canadian Indians and the Maoris have obtained substantial restitution as well as compensation from their own governments. Both the Canadian and New Zealand governments played a vitally active role in securing the apology from the British. This is what one expects from our government. It should make a definitive move in this matter. Alas our governments have miserably failed even to listen to the grievances of the Kandyans let alone raise the matter with the British.

Let no one say that the Kandyans did not do anything for their cause. When they realized that their nation state was ruthlessly dismantled and foreign imposition was forced down their throats, the beleaguered Kandyans rebelled against the British in 1817/18, in 1822, in 1823, in 1824, in 1843 and finally in 1848 in Matale and Kurunegala. All those freedom fighters were mercilessly executed in a manner to strike terror in the minds of the Kandyans. Governor Torrington maintained that "the wholesome terror inspired by Martial Law" was necessary to bring the Kandyans to submission. Even the petitions the Kandyans submitted in good faith were construed as conspiracies against the British, and were ignored without any consideration, but used as weapons against them.

There were the usual Kandyan collaborators. The British took good care of them. They were showered with gold chains, gold Pagodas, gold Padakamas, land grants, official government positions and venal honours. They became pliant servants of the British and sought to promote the British interests in our country. Some of them became important and influential persons under the British administration and helped to usher in the general amnesia on the deplorable plight of the Kandyans.

There was a reawakening of the Kandyan cause in the 1920s. But by then, the British had managed to mollycoddle as well as to conquer the hearts and minds of the effete Kandyan elite by their exercise of patronage, sinecures and other handouts. Thus the emergence of the new spirit was still-born. The Kandyan cause was confined to the limbo. I have made an effort to resurrect it and hope others will take up the cause and continue the demand for an apology from the British.

What then is the relevance of raking up this shameful episode in our colonial history? It simply is justice for injustice done with impunity. It is salutary for us too to know what happened, so that we would be goaded into action to put right the wrongs done. It is also important that the world knows about the fact that enormous crimes had been committed against the Sinhalese in their own country. Perfidious treachery was committed on the Kandyan people after guarantees had been given to get control over them. Not only were those guarantees thrown overboard, the people were abused, exploited and reduced to the level of knaves and villains. History and the nation are not separable. "We are, whether we acknowledge it or not what the past had made us, and we cannot eradicate from ourselves those parts of ourselves which are formed by our relationship to each formative stage in our history" wrote Alastaire Macintyre, a British philosopher. This is absolutely true of the landless, jobless and the penniless Kandyan peasantry of today. They are the forgotten victims of a special brand of ruthless colonial British mal-administration. They need help urgently, which the British not only owe them, but also have it in their power to discharge.

In an article on injustices suffered by the Kandyan Sinhalese in The Sunday Island (4th Oct) Neville Ladduwahetty has pointed out that by the provisions of the ILO Convention 169, the Kandyan Sinhalese would be entitled to restitution, and where this is impossible , suitable compensation under appropriate guarantees.

It is partially correct to argue that as masters of our own destiny, it is incumbent upon our government to take steps to mitigate the wrongs done. This is indeed what is happening in New Zealand and Canada. However, the missing element in this argument, in the case of Sri Lanka, is the absence of the admission of guilt by the perpetrator of injustices. This is why an apology by the British is paramount to add weight and give momentum to the efforts aimed at making appropriate reparations.

It was Vernon Smith as Under Secretary in the Colonial Office in London in 1841 who admitted to the fact that the colonial government had decided to "violate our engagements" in Ceylon(CO54/193). Thus it was a deliberate decision to renege on the treaty obligations with the Kandyans. This is the floating debt they created, which the current society is entitled to collect and use it as it wills. The Roman maxim, pacta sunt servanda, which today is backed with Cruise Missiles and B52 bombers in the case if Iraq, had absolutely no meaning when it was the turn of the British to observe treaty obligations. We shall fail in our duty if we did not impress upon the British that justice has been knocking on their door for far too long. It is time to relent.

There are some who gloat over the "goodies" the British left behind when they left our shores. Those undeniable benefits are there for all to see. The fact, however, is that they were all incidental benefits. All the "goodies" were conceived and executed first and foremost for the benefit of the British and the British Empire. In case you do not accept my thesis, here is what one very influential Britisher wrote in his book. John Stuart Mill (1806-1873) was one of the philosophers who influenced the British politicians of his time. In his book, "The Principles of Political Economy" he wrote that the colonies "can not be regarded as countries with a productive capital of their own [but are] the places where England finds it convenient to carry on the production of sugar, coffee and a few other tropical commodities. All the capital employed is English capital; almost all the industry is carried on for English uses; there is little production of anything except staple commodities, and these are sent to England, not to be exchanged for things exported to the colony and consumed by the inhabitants, but to be sold in England for the benefit of the proprietors there" (Vol.3 p693). This was the case with colonial Sri Lanka. So while we are glad to have those "goodies", it precludes the British from claiming that they instituted them primarily for the benefit of Sri Lankans.

Finally, let me urge Hon. Mr. Fatchett MP, the Minister responsible for Sri Lankan Affairs in the Foreign Office, to consider seriously the Sinhala Commission recommendations and my 1977 petition to him together with my two books on British/Kandyan history which he received from me. I remain in hope that he will do the decent thing and recommend an apology by the British Crown. Let me remind him again the words of Kandyan Memorialists who petitioned Queen Victoria in 1846. "The infringements of promises and engagements amicably made and entered into is contrary to British law, is in opposition to equity, justice and impartiality of the British government, and discreditable to its good faith" Is it too much to expect the British government to do its duty by the Sinhalese?

11

Parawagamma: The Apogee of British treachery

(The Island, 5th May 2000)

The Convention of 1815 was a bona fide treaty between the British colonial power in Sri Lanka and the Chiefs of the Kingdom of Kandy. By this treaty the Kandyan Kingdom was ceded to the British. It was not conquered by the British as some assume even today. Therefore conditions and obligations were imposed on the British, which the British readily accepted and solemnly undertook to fulfill to the best of their endeavour. Today we know that the British had acted duplicitously and had no intention of fulfilling their treaty obligations and solemn promises, when they signed the treaty.

Soon it became apparent to the Kandyan Chiefs also that the British were reneging on their treaty obligations. Their powers, privileges and property rights were being gradually eroded, and the British missionaries in the island and their godfathers in London, had begun in earnest to spearhead the thrust to violate the "inviolability" of Buddhist religion (cl.5 of the Treaty). Finally in 1817, in an address to the Chiefs in the Audience Hall in Kandy, Governor Brownrigg announced his intention to frame new regulations to reform the administration of the Kandyan provinces. This power, he arrogated to himself, because the treaty itself, did not give the governor any such freedom to effect a wholesale reorganization.

The Kandyans protested in vain. The British had by now established some military strength in Kandy, and had won over some Kandyan chiefs (especially Molligoda Adikar) to their strategy of subjugating the Kandyans. The British were therefore in a position to simply ignore all representations by the Kandyans. It was no surprise therefore that the Kandyans, in their frustration, sought to evict the British from the

Kandyan provinces. The Kandyans took up whatever arms they could lay their hands on, including bows and arrows, to fight the British.

The first persons to engage in this dangerous yet patriotic combat was Madugalle Uda Gabada Nilame, Polwatte Unnanse and Maha Vidaan. They were convicted in 1816 of treasonable practices, and for "sending offerings to the temples of Bintenna and Kataragama, with prayers for the removal of the English, and establishment of a Sinhala king". Even to pray to the gods against the British was a capital offence!! This was the severity of the oppression practiced by the British. The sentence on Madugalle was intentionally made an exemplary one, in order to deter others, from further concocting any conspiratorial plots against the British. He was removed forthwith to Jaffna prison, he was given no opportunity to see his dear ones, his residence was ceremoniously and publicly burnt down. His other property was confiscated and sold. Madugalle's resolve, however, remained indomitable.

The armed struggle to eject the British from the Kandyan Kingdom began in earnest in Oct.1817 after the death of Mr. Wilson, the British Government Agent at Badulla. He was killed in a melee, when he attempted to arrest Wilbawe, the Pretender to the vacant throne of Kandy.

All the supporters of Wilbawe, ie. virtually, all the Kandyans, were condemned as "rebels, outlaws and traitors" by the British. This perverse contemptuous reference was totally misplaced. The treaty of 1815 was signed between equals. It guaranteed "to the people in general, their property and other rights, and liberty in accordance with ancient customary law and legal procedure which have continued unbroken among them" (cl.4 of the treaty). Therefore the Kandyans could not be traitors so long as they abided by their customary law and legal procedure. The British were totally guilty of breaking all treaty promises and were secretly engaged in reducing the Kandyans to vassalage. In short, they had illegally usurped the kingdom, and therefore it was a contradiction to condemn the legitimate citizens of the country as "rebels, outlaws and traitors", when they attempted to overthrow the cunning illegitimate trespasser. They were, therefore, legitimate freedom fighters. This would have been precisely how the British would have referred to their heroes, if Napolean or Hitler had obtained control of Britain by deception or conquest.

This unequal mortal combat lasted for nearly a year. Britain was an imperial power. It had a trained professional army equipped with the latest military weapons. It also had the vast manpower resources available to the British Raj in India. Nevertheless, the Kandyans with their bows and arrows and outdated weapons came within a whisker of defeating the British. Mr. Anstruther, a Colonial Secretary in Colombo, admitted to the Parliamentary Committee in London that "it was a most serious and dangerous war. The British government was nearly beat as possible". Even Governor Brownrigg, when he appealed to British India for help, admitted the disgrace that would ensue "to a great military nation in being expelled by a horde of semi-barbarians and the bad example such an expulsion would give to the Indian subjects". With the armed help he got from India he was soon able to subdue the Kandyans.

The British resorted to most atrocious measures during their campaigns. They declared Martial Law throughout the Kandyan province. They shot the Kandyans on sight and committed massacres. They burnt down houses and paddy fields. They cut down fruit bearing trees. They slaughtered all the cattle and other domestic animals. They broke down all water conserving embankments to prevent future cultivation of paddy. This caused destitution and famine for a long time, and many Kandyans perished from starvation. In short, the British shamelessly practiced a scorched earth policy. The Kandyans were starved into submission. The death toll from random executions and starvation was inestimable. One partisan pro- British observer put it down to 10,000. Given the absence of any communication, the isolation and remoteness of most Kandyan villages, this 10,000 could be considered as a gross under estimation. This episode of marauding British army, which engaged in atrocious depredation on even non-combatant civilians, demands an unconditional apology to the Kandyan Sinhala Buddhists from the British Crown. Until this is done, the British remain condemned and disgraced. One cannot tire of repeating this demand at every opportunity.

Besides Wilbawe the Pretender, the three prominent leaders of this revolt were Pilimatalawe (Jr), Monarawila Keppitipola, and Madugalle. The first two were signatories to the Convention of 1815. At the start they were able to galvanize the Kandyans to fight the British for nearly a year even without a properly trained army and appropriate weapons. They had no answer to the scorched earth policy of the British. Besides, they had neither a strategy, a campaign plan, nor were they able to give proper leadership and direction. After initial unity to fight the British, as the fight dragged on without much success, they had disagreements among themselves. The Governor's proclamation of Aug. 1818 promised pardon to all those who surrendered, death and condign punishment to others, and handsome rewards to squealers. This had the effect of isolating the three chiefs. Thus by Oct.1818, they were fugitives from British law, and took refuge in Kahalla Walawa in Parawagamma in the wilds of Nuwara Kalavaya.

There a Muslim trader/spy had identified them, and conveyed the news to Lieut. William O'Neill, who captured the two chiefs on the 28th of Oct.1818. Madugalle with some of the followers escaped to Elahera. He was captured by Ensign Shootbraid on the 2nd of Nov.1818.

When the soldiers entered the Walawa, Keppitipola had surrendered without a fight and had identified himself to prevent the trigger-happy soldiers from shooting him willy-nilly. Pilimatalawa "was lame from disease and was found lying in bed". This was the end of the 1817/18 revolt against the British. Both Keppitipola and Madugalle were executed by decapitation at Bogambara on 26th Nov.1818. Pilimatalawa was exiled to Mauritius.

Prawagamma marks the zenith of British treachery. Even in ordinary civil law, if a party to a contract breaks his contractual obligation, that person will be prevented from exercising his rights under the contract. This should have been the position of the British, but it was the age when might was right and British imperialism had no equal. The British usurped the Kandyan Kingdom and proceeded to subvert it. They shed much Kandyan blood to impose their own brand of law and order. They had neither moral nor legal right to arrest the Kandyan chiefs, brand them as traitors, let alone execute them. This was why the Kandyans always maintained that "infringements of the promises and engagements, amicably made and entered into between them, and by, Articles of Convention, is contrary to British law, is in opposition to Equity, Justice and Impartiality of the British Government, and discreditable to its good faith" (Petition to Queen Victoria, 1846).

Kahalla Walawa is no more. In the alleged place where it stood, there is now a statue of Keppitipola erected by the Tourist Authority of the North Central Province. It should be on the route of all British tourists who visit Aukana. As our history is also under attack, I hope, this article will catch the eyes of our countrymen, and they will make it a point to pay a visit while on their way to Aukana.

[How to get there: Proceed on Kurunegala/ Dambulla road to Galewela. At Galewela turn left to Andiyagala. There turn left again, go past the temple (4km) and take the first left turn. This is a dirt road and leads to a dead end (400yds). There you will find the statue. None of the roads are marked].

12

Crown appology to the Kandyans

(The Island, 18th sept 2001)

[This letter was written while on holiday in London and addressed to Mr. Jack straw MP, The British Secy. of State for Foreign and commonwealth Affairs]

I have made representations on the above topic to your predecessors. They did not respond in any way. I hope I shall have some consideration from you. As on previous occasions, I have enclosed a short article on one of the numerous massacres committed by the colonial British on the Kandyans in support of my case for a Crown Apology. There is ample evidence of the many atrocities in the Colonial Office documents at Kew, and the House of Commons Committee Report (1849 - 50). No matter where you look, you will find overwhelming of dastardly deeds perpetrates on the Kandyans in the name of the Crown, hence the necessity for an apology from the Crown itself, A mere note of regret would be travesty of genuine atonement.

The British Crown has already graciously apologized for colonial depredations to the New zealand Maoris and the Canadian Indians, All I request is that this precedent be followed in the case of Kandyans too.

This is after all the age of apologies. We have the Truth commission in South Africa. Apologies were tendered for despicable deeds, purgation was sought, and forgiveness was granted, all in public domain. Prime Minister Blair's apology to the Northern Irish Catholics was fully in tune with the prevailing mood in the world, Now we have General Massu, the French Military Governor of Algiers at the height of colonial troubles (1954 / 62), had also publicly admitted to torture and murder and had apologized. General Ausssaresses has also admitted "efficient torture. Most people cracked and talked. Then most of the time we kill them." His revelations of routine torture and murder in his autobiography, has shocked the French nation. The League of Human Rights has already filed a lawsuit against him. Quite recently, we also saw His Holiness the Pope apologizing to Ukraine's Orthodox Christians for the sack of Byzantium by the Crusaders in 1204AD. Thus remoteness of events in history is no bar to justice.

As the leader of the London University Students Union, you were responsible for carrying out "sit - ins" at LSE in 1960s. As a past union member, I did then admire your courage and determintion to win justice for the student's cause. I also did visit the "sit - ins" twice to express my support and solidarity. I have no doubt that you will carry through your life those sterling qualities. I hope, when you read my petition, that acute sense of justice will prevail in you, and prompt you to take the necessary action for a crown apology to the Kandyans. [Needless to say, he did not respond such is the arrogance of the British Government on this issue.]

13

The British Owe an Apology to the Kandyans

(The Island 12th Sept.2001)

The final unequal combat for freedom from vassalage under the British Rule began in earnest in Matale in 1848. The Kandyans had been swindled out of their heritage by the colonial British since 1815. Their Buddhist religion had been the state religion enjoying the patronage and daily tangible support of the monarch and his people. Now they found it degraded to demon worship and abandoned by the British so that "the Buddhist would fall before us like dew before the sun" (Rev. Hardy's booklet: Idolatry of Ceylon, 1839). The Kandyans' customs and traditions were trampled on and discarded. Their lands were expropriated for the benefit of the colonial planters, and foreign Indian labourers were planted on those lands to complete the dispossession of the lands of the Kandyans. On almost all issues of political, social and economic nature, the Kandyans and their interests were ignored. Instead, oppression and opprobrium were heaped on them for nearly a century. They have yet to recover from the persecution and exploitation they were subjected to by the colonial British.

Some of them did protest and paid for it with their lives. The first Kandyan bid for freedom in 1817/18 was a gory and bloody affair. The Kandyans were mercilessly massacred and slaughtered by the colonial British government. As I have already referred to those unpardonable colonial pogroms in my previous representations to the British Government and via the press to Sri Lankan public, I shall here confine myself to events after 1817/18.

All protests by the Kandyans were ruthlessly suppressed. Any protest against the British was a treasonable offence. After a nominal court hearing, the protestors were condemned as "Rebels" and executed. In 1823 two were hanged in Matale. In 1833 three were hanged in

Kandy and two in Bintenne. In 1843 an anti-British movement to eject the illegitimate usurpers of power gathered strength in Badulla. Maj. Rogers used all his military resources available to him to brutally suppress this spontaneous revolt. He captured a Buddhist monk named Seelawansa Saranakara, and had him tried in a kangaroo court before Capt. Kelson. True to form, the monk was found guilty of treasonable offences and sentenced to death by hanging. Later the evidence was found to be unreliably porous and circumstantial. He should have been set free, instead the sentence was commuted to imprisonment with hard labour for fourteen years. That was British imperial justice then!! In this brief description of events after 1817/18, I have left out the many Kandyans who were deported and left to rot in jails both in Sri Lanka and abroad. They too were martyrs in the cause of freedom for their country.

The colonial British government doggedly pursued a programme to completely demolish and dismember the former Kingdom of Kandy. This the British did accomplish within a few years. They correctly perceived that the Buddhist religion was the lynchpin binding the Kandyan society together. Therefore, via the British missionaries, a concentrated attack was launched on Buddhism. This was immediately supported by James Stephen, the Permanent Under-Secretary at Colonial Office in London. Steps were taken to demote Buddhism and to degrade the status of Buddhist monks in their society by withdrawing government support and patronage to Buddhism. At the same time the colonial government set upon the Kandyan elites. They were subjected to "show trials" for conspiracy against the British. On the pretext that they were conspirators against the Crown, all the privileges of the Chiefs were abolished, and they were reduced to subordinate paid servants of the Crown, and made dependent on government handouts. British law, British administration and British taxes were vigorously enforced in the Kandyan provinces. Virgin forests were vandalized, and the Kandyan lands were expropriated on a vast scale by colonial planters. British Governors and colonial civil servants were also guilty of this plunder. Finally the geographically defined Kandyan Kingdom was dismembered by apportioning it among the newly created British

Administration Districts. The Kandyans did address a Memorial to the Crown in 1834, pleading to "save their country from dismemberment and from being incorporated with the maritime districts, so that it may continue to subsist in its ancient integrity as Kingdom of Kandy and retain its celebrated name Sinhale" (CO54/137). The colonial government was stone deaf to such pleadings. Today we are paying dearly for this wrong colonial policy, as it has been hoisted on the nation by the separatist terrorists in their bogus claim for exclusive Tamil Homeland.

When Governor Torrington's government imposed a variety of oppressive taxes and surrendered out and out support for Buddhism contrary to the pledges given in 1815, the Kandyans rose in rebellion in Matale and Kurunegala in 1848. The massacre of Kandyans among the coffee bushes of Wariapola coffee estate in Matale was enacted with ruthless efficiency at the very initial stages of this struggle for freedom in July 1848.

Troops under Capt. Lillie marched to Matale from Kandy. He established contact with a group of rebels and parleyed with them "without being molested". When he tried to surround them, they panicked and started to flee. Many a fleeing Kandyan was shot down. There were some still hidden in the nearby coffee bushes and the forest. The Rifles under Capt.Watson was ordered to capture them. He and his Rifles slaughtered every Kandyan they could lay their filthy hands on. Capt. Lillie at first reported on 31st July that only six were killed, several wounded and eight were taken prisoners. This was a blatant lie. Governor Torrington later (14th Aug.1848) admitted to Grey that "it has since been ascertained that the total number killed and wounded amounted to little less than two hundred" (CO54/250). A massacre indeed by any standard even though Torrington did not state the exact number killed!

Lt. Henderson was an eye-witness soldier who took part in this expedition. His version of events, in his book, The History of Rebellion in Ceylon, at Wariapola estate contradicts the official version. According to him the rebels at Wariapola estate were at the point of surrender to their superior force and arms, when they were mowed down by the Rifles, and in the bushes, the surrounded Kandyans were disarmed and slaughtered with daggers, bayonets and bill-hooks. Hence the Governor had to revise upwards the casualty figures. This non-combat butchery was also evidence why there were no casualties, not even a scratch on any of the British soldiers, even though Capt.Watson maintained before the House of Commons Committee that a hand–to-hand fight took place in the bushes and in the forest. This Committee Report abounds with evidence of many atrocities committed both in Matale and Kurunegala under an unnecessarily prolonged Martial Law by the British. For brevity's sake I do not propose to enlarge on them here.

Capt. Watson was a blood-thirsty marauding soldier. He plundered and set fire to Kandyan property. He issued blood-curdling proclamations, shot dead suspected Kandyans on sight and nailed death threatening notices on individuals on the trees of Matale. He was found guilty of all these depredations by two independent judges from the Madras Presidency. He was not punished for his proven monstrous crimes. Governor Torrington's excuse was that "the zeal displayed by Capt. Watson in the active discharge of public duties, induce me to think that his case is deserving of the utmost consideration and indulgence" (CO54/260). That was Torrington's appalling sense of justice! Mr. Hume MP in the Parliament condemned Capt. Watson's behavior towards the Kandyans as "acts of atrocity more suitable for the destruction of mad dogs than becoming proceedings which involve the lives of human beings".

The Kandyans have not given up hope that a proper Crown apology will be issued for all the dastardly crimes committed against them by the colonial British. In a petition to Queen Victoria in 1846 they pleaded that " the infringements of promises and engagements, amicably made and entered into are contrary to British law, are in opposition to British Equity, Justice and Impartiality of the British Government and discreditable to its good faith". The present-day Labour Government of Great Britain has the opportunity to sort out this long-standing grievance, and enhance its reputation by taking the necessary steps to tender the Crown apology much due to the long-suffering Kandyans.

14

A Letter to Mr.Peter Hain MP

(The Island, 10th Jan,2001)

I have herewith attached petition to you. I hope you will seriously consider it. I did also write to your predecessor, late Hon. Mr. Fatchett on the same issue in June 1997. I also sent him my two books on the subject of British rule of the Kandyan Kingdom. The books are shortened version of the long story available in the big volumes of colonial office papers in the archives at Kew. In case you need to look at my books, they are available at the British Library and at SOAS library at the London University with the reference shelf-marked JS954.93. The names of my books are: (a) *Rebels, Outlaws and Enemies* to the British, and (b) *The Kandyans' Last Stand Against the British.* There are many other books on this subject by British colonialists, the two contemporary ones being, Dr.Davy's *An Account of the Interior of Ceylon* and Dr. Henry Marshall's *Ceylon*. No matter what books you look at, you will find that, without exception, all of them validate the case I have made out for an apology from the Crown to the descendants of Sinhala Buddhist Kandyans, who were singled out victims of colonial brutalities.

Your lingering interest in our country is evident from the many statements you have made on the present crisis in our country. I refrain from commenting on those statements as our Minister of Foreign Affairs has already done that. However, the important matter of justice on the part of the HMG still remains to be discharged, despite the fact that the Kandyans did initiate their request as long ago as 1834.

You were one of the staunch supporters of black African majority in South Africa. You were instrumental in exposing the many brutalities committed on them by the minority Africaaners. They even tried to frame you for bank robbery at Putney. I too have occasionally stood with the small protest group outside Traffalgar House on my way home from the British Library. I too took part in the demonstration against your arrest by the police outside Putney police station. I too was imbued with the sense of justice you then preached from the platforms of the Liberal party. I hope that the same sense of justice has not forsaken you, now that you are a Minister of Her Majesty's Government.

The case for an apology to the descendants of the Sinhala Buddhist Kandyans stands out like a sore thumb. I hope you will initiate the necessary steps towards discharging this long ignored obligation towards the descendants of an oppressed and repressed people, who are now threatened with further erosion of their inheritance by the Indians your colonialists planted in their lands.

As a doughty fighter against oppression from any quarter, it is incumbent on you to put right this long saga, and enhance the confidence the Sinhalese have on Her Majesty's Government. I hope you will not be found wanting in this respect. Best wishes.

Yours truly,

Durand Appuhamy.
(A copy of this letter was sent to the British High Commissioner in Colombo) The petition was titled as set out below.

The Madulla Massacre by the British

Many British citizens know that their government very seldom accedes to any demands made by its ordinary citizens, more so, if such a demand emanates from abroad. Therefore, as I have done many times before, let me make this a polite request. This is not a request for a statement of regret full of empty words bereft of any remorse. This is a request for an apology from the Crown, of the same mould and gravity, as was tendered to the Canadian Indian Tribal Chiefs in the mid 1980s and to the Maoris in 1990. The basis for the apology is the same as in the cases of Canadian Indians and New Zealand Maoris, viz. the repudiation of treaty obligations and the atrocities committed by the colonial British. In the case of the Kandyan provinces, the iniquitous and outrageous brutalities lasted from 1816 to 1848. This overdue gesture of atonement would enhance Britain's strident advocacy of Human Rights and democracy throughout the world, and justice would have been done to Sri Lanka's downtrodden Kandyans at the same time.

The Convention of 1815 was signed in Kandy between equals. The Governor represented the British Crown and the Imperial government. This is why a Crown apology is in order. The Kandyan Chiefs represented themselves and their people. The Kandyan Kingdom was ceded (not conquered) to the British by this Convention without any conditions or undertakings on the part of the Kandyan Chiefs. The quid pro quo on the part of the British was the solemn promises and undertakings they enshrined in this treaty document. This was a deliberate deception from the beginning. Thus, it was no surprise that the British subsequently broke their promises and proceeded to demolish the Kandyan Kingdom itself. Leaving aside for the moment the many other colonial depredations, one of which I shall describe below, this international deliberate deception of a trusting nation alone deserves an unreserved apology from the British Crown.

Let me start this exposition with a quote from the Cabinet Papers (Jan.1914) of Sir Winston Churchill. "We are not a young people with innocent record and a scanty inheritance. We have engrossed to ourselves....an altogether disproportionate share of wealth and traffic of the world. We have got all we want in territory, and our claim to be left in the unmolested enjoyment of vast and splendid possessions, mainly acquired by violence, largely maintained by force, often seem less reasonable to others than to us" (Clive Pontting, Churchill p.132). This is a rare and frank admission of the unacceptable and unjustifiable basis of British colonialism by an arch imperialist. This then is the basis for my request for an apology from the Crown.

"Colonialism is not a thinking machine nor a body endowed with reasoning faculties. It is violence in its natural state. It will only yield when confronted with greater violence" (Fanon, The Wretched of the Earth p48). This brute force was employed in Kandy to reduce the inhabitants to slavery and to dehumanize them. Everything was done to wipe out their traditions, customs, culture and religion. Mind you, the Kandyans were promised that this would not happen, and that their customs and traditions would be maintained (cl. 4, 8 of the Convention). However, the Kandyan villages and farms were burnt down. Their paddy-fields were scorched. Their cattle slaughtered and their fruit bearing trees were simply chopped down. Starved and ill, the survivors were finished off with the gun as if they were stray dogs in a stranger's land, so said Mr. Hume MP in the British parliament. British civilians then flocked in to take over their land, clear the virgin forest, and convert them to cash crops for the benefit solely of the settlers and their financiers in Britain. To the Kandyans, the most concrete and foremost in value was the land. This land not only gave them their daily plate of rice but also their dignity. It was to preserve this land that they fought off successfully three European Imperial nations, Britain included. Now having ceded their country to trickery, they remained helpless against planters who insolently trampled over their lands and their rights to that land.

Theravada Buddhism was their state religion, protected and promoted by their kings who ruled the country from 2300BC. It was part and parcel of their ancient civilization of over two millennia. It had come down to the Kandyans in its pristine glory, surviving the vicissitudes of temporary schism and persecution. Therefore it was natural for the Kandyans to seek warranties from the British for its protection and patronage by the colonial government. The British gave an unconditional warranty that Buddhism would remain inviolable (cl.5 of the Convention). The British colonialists knew well what this warranty entailed, because they have, indeed had, nearly twenty years of experience of Buddhist religion and popular Buddhist practices and rituals in the maritime province that had been under their control. However, it was a swindle of the first order; Governor Brownrigg later admitted that he gave this assurance merely to gain control of the Kandyan Kingdom and that if he had not done so, he would not have been able to gain possession of it, let alone maintain its continuing possession of it.

The British Evangelists, who were not party to the Convention of 1815, and therefore had no right to interfere with it, then waded in. They condemned Buddhism as heathenism and its rituals and practices as barbaric idolatry. They easily persuaded the colonial government to violate the inviolability of Buddhism solemnly agreed to in 1815. Deprived of government support, the colonial government expected Buddhism to fade away into oblivion. It was following Sade's advice to the imperialist in De Juliette, "take their gods from the people that you wish to subjugate, then demoralize it; so long as they worship no other god than you, and has no other morals than your morals, you will always be their master" (p324).

The Kandyans did perceive their ineluctable drift to serfdom and servitude. They sought their freedom and their self-respect. It was quite clear that the British interloper had acted fraudulently. He had to be ejected from the lands of their fathers. As justice Harding Gifford suggested at that time, the British should have abandoned Kandy to the Kandyans. This was too galling for the colonial governor Brownrigg. He was determined to maintain his reputation and that of the Crown "unsullied and unimpaired". He decided on using brute force to subjugate the Kandyans. Thus began the first bloody Kandyan struggle for freedom. The colonial intruder misnamed it as a "rebellion against the Crown".

There were some colonial functionaries who suggested the extirpation of the whole Kandyan race, which Hardinge Gifford condemned as "too revolting to humanity to be entertained even for a moment". Nevertheless, Browringg was determined to rely solely on the exercise of force and the effects of terror to subjugate the Kandyans. He threatened the refractory and the disaffected with extermination.

The colonial army officers carried out governor's determination with ruthless efficiency. A few examples will suffice to prove my case. Maj. MacDonald was the first to resort to arson in the Badulla district. In revenge for Govt. Agent Wilson's death, he burnt down to the ground all the peaceful villages near Hausanvella. It was their fault that those villages happened to be located near the place where Wilson died! He plundered and destroyed their cattle, grain and other property. He then informed his governor, "this act of severity, I trust, will not be disapproved of" (CO54/ 56, dated 7.11.1817). It was, in fact, approved and praised by the governor and was held out as an example for others to imitate. The scorching of the earth and villages soon became the main method of oppression and punishment.

Lt. J. Maclaine of the 73rd Regiment was a notorious sadist. Before the House of Commons Committee on Ceylon 1849/50, Col. Braybrooke reported that Maclaine hung Kandyan prisoners without any trial, and particularly relished having them hung up outside his quarters, while he ate his breakfast.

Capt. Fraser, Brownrigg's aide-de-camp, one night killed nineteen and took ten prisoners. Seven of the latter were executed without any trial, and the other three were forced into service as his guides to catch other Kandyans. His men hung up the bodies in the roadside ambalama (a wayfarers' rest) at Godamunne. The blood from the corpses polluted the nearby stream and made it unusable by them the next morning.

Col. Hook was another monster. In May 1818, he burnt down all the villages between Kadulova, where his garrison was posted, and Yatavatta Pass in the Matale district. In his frenzy he also executed Mawatagama Nileme (a Kandyan Chief), the brother of High Priest at Asgiriya Temple in Kandy. In this instance, the governor apologized for the outrage, and made restitution to the family.

This terror and wanton manslaughter visited every nook and corner of the Kandyan Kingdom with monstrous regularity. Wherever any sign of hostility was reported, troops were let loose to impose extreme measures of repression; houses were burnt, stores looted, women and children seized, and any captured men were summarily executed. "There was seldom a day passed but we had parties out scouting the country for a distance around burning all they came across and shooting they could not take prisoners" wrote sergeant Calladine. Small detachments were authorized to put to death anyone who opposed the British, reported Dr. Davy. The pillage, plunder and cold-blooded murder were so common that Dr.Davy was moved to write, "such system of warfare as this, of which I have partially sketched in outline, had better not be given in detail". Even London Times on the 7th of Oct. 1818 declared Brownrigg's brutal "method of conflagration" (a term used by his Gazette) as "dreadful measures".

The barbarous brutality committed by the colonial British on the Kandyans , can, of necessity, be only brief here. Anyone just perusing through the colonial documents of this period will find plenty of additional material on this matter to fill volumes.

So what happened at Madulla? On the 9th of Dec. 1817, a few Kandyans armed with bows and arrows waylaid a convoy of provisions escorted by Malay soldiers in the forest near Tibbottugoda. In the ensuing melee the British lost both their provisions and the soldiers. Andawala Mohotala who lived nearby, was the chief suspect for this raid. His property was destroyed, other buildings in the neighbourhood were all burnt, fruit trees were cut down, all stores were also plundered. Madulla was the next adjoining village. The people there feared the worst when five men were executed, and houses of six headmen were also burnt down. Driven by fear, the remaining villagers scales the nearby rock and hid themselves in the cave there. What then happened was described by Brownrigg himself. "Having got information of the hiding place of the villagers, it was decided to surprise and seize them the same night. The rebels, as is supposed, to the number of fifty men were in the cave....which being silently approached by our detachment, small divisions under Lt. Lillie and sergeant Murray of 73rd regiment were posted in the pathways at each end of the cave, while Capt. C. proceeded with the remainder of his brave soldiers, for the front. The alarm being given within, the inhabitants set up a hideous yell and rushed from the cavern. Twenty of them were killed by our troops and the remainder precipitated themselves down the deep declivity of the mountain, (ie. they jumped to death than be killed by the British) by which they must have severely suffered. In the darkness that prevailed, one woman and child were also killed" (General Report issued on 6th Jan. 1818).

The original intention was to seize the villagers. Instead, the trigger-happy soldiers simply shot them on sight as they came out of the cave shouting ("hideous yell" above) in Sinhala not to shoot. It was for a similar shoot-to-kill policy that Prime Minister Blair tendered his apology to the Irish not long ago. The villagers in the cave did not attack the soldiers, and the British did not sustain any injury or casualty. To salvage their conscience, a bogus excuse was then issued to the effect, that because the army acted with due care to protect the women and children in the cave, many of the rebels were able to escape. No credibility can be attached to this statement as they had already killed twenty Kandyans in cold blood. Further, as Brownrigg had admitted above, all escape routes were closed by Lt.Lillie and Sergeant Murray. Further it was this same army that had earlier seized and raped many women all over the Kandyan province.

In 1848, under governor Torrington, the colonial government staged a repeat performance of this manslaughter of Kandyans. The House of Commons Committee Report gives a comprehensive report of them. I draw HMG's attention to them also here.

Let me conclude my request in Fanon's words. "Colonialism and imperialism have not paid their score when they withdrew their flags and their police forces from our territories....The wealth of imperial countries is our wealth too....For in a very concrete way Europe has stuffed herself inordinately with the gold and raw materials of the colonial countries" *(Wretched of the Earth, p81)*. Reparation has got to be made not only for this daylight robbery, but also, for the numerous massacres committed on their way to their opulence. The Kandyans did articulate my request in 1846 in their petition to Queen Victoria in the following words: "the infringements of the promises and engagements, amicably made and entered into.... Is contrary to British Law, is in opposition to Equity, Justice and Impartiality of the British Government and discreditable to its good faith".

The case for a British Crown apology is overwhelming. Until such an apology is delivered, the present-day descendants of Sinhala Buddhist Kandyans will carry the scars of victimization by British colonial pillage, plunder and wanton manslaughter. They shall not cease to press the British government for an apology from the Crown.

15

HISTORYLESS CITIZENS

(The Island, 4th Nov.2002)

[This letter was prompted by the few articles in the press at around this time which denigrated our history and urged the newspaper readers to forget our history and come to terms with the LTTE]

"It is a pity that still many people in the country lack knowledge of history. Some of them do not know much about Sigiriya or about King Kasssapa who built the place" said the Prime Minister at the launch of the book on Sigiri Graffiti by W.J.M. Lokubandara. (Daily News. 4th Oct.).

My question to the Prime Minister would be what he has done about this and what does he proposes to do to remedy this appalling ignorance of history. Prince Charles in England is also worried by the utilitarian type of education imparted in schools. He seeks the revival of history and literature in schools' curriculum. He summoned 16 luminaries for a four-day conference so that they could point the way to incorporating English literature and history in education with the objective of enhancing pupils' cultural, moral, political and social values. The historian Dr. David Starkey and the play-writer Sir Tom Stoppard have been singled out to spearhead and expound on ideas for teaching cultural heritage coherently.

History has fallen by the wayside in today's technological and commercial world. Yet those countries with hardly any history going beyond 200 years are very proud of their heritage, and jealously guard historical monuments and documents with the full might of the state. Our history is over 2500 years old. We have given up studying it. We now blandly accept the mutilated and deconstructed versions of it by some west-oriented crackpot professors in foreign as well as our universities, who probably are in the pay of parties interested in dividing this country based on false and fabricated history.

History is a form of inquiry or research about things we do not know. We seek to find out res gestae, or actions of human beings that have been done in the past. History proceeds by interpreting archaeological, epigraphical numismatic and other documentary evidence. It is through history man knows himself. "Knowing yourself means knowing, first, what it is to be man; secondly, knowing what it is to be the kind of man you are; and thirdly, knowing what it is to be the man you are and nobody else is. Knowing yourself means knowing what you can do; and since nobody knows what he can do until he tries, the only clue to what man can do is what man has done. The value of history, then, is that it teaches us what man has done and thus what man is" (R.G.Collingwood, *The Idea of History*).

Our deplorable political predicament today is very much due to lack of appreciation of what we have received from our ancestors and what we should pass on to posterity. As Edmund Burke would aver, we are only life-renters and not masters of our world. There is an implicit partnership between those who are living, those who are dead, and those who are to be born. We have no right, therefore, to cut off the entail or lay waste our inheritance by destroying the whole fabric of our society so that our progenitors would be left dilapidated, truncated and a ruined bifurcated country.

We are all bearers of tradition. I am born into a family. From the family I inherit my city, my nation, a variety of debts, inheritances, rightful expectations and obligations. I am born with a past. National consciousness springs from sharing values, traditions, and memories of the past and plans for the future contained within a culture and communicated by its specific language. We have primordial bonds. They are authenticated by the history of the country. The formation of our nation, the unity of the Sinhala people, language, religion, territory and government is part of our historical memory of spectacular achievements. A comprehensive knowledge of history is, therefore, indispensable to evaluate the present crisis realistically, and also to plan the future with foresight and confidence.

For centuries Sri Lanka was the Buddhist religious metropolis of other Asian nations. Indelible epigraphical records and ancient literary works moulded our social and our political expressions. Not many nations are privileged to possess a record of an identifiable national entity preserving its language and religion for more than two millennia. This is an exceptional cultural heritage that should inspire present-day citizens. Alas, to the bureaucrats in our education department, history is the dead past deserving only to be interred for good. Their folly has given birth to rootless citizens prepared to sell their birthright and their country to anyone with a fabricated and forged Oppuwa (Testamant). Long on words and short on actions is not what we expect from Prime Minister who has bewailed this inadequacy in our people. We need action to impart historical knowledge to the young in an interesting and endearing way.

16

DO WE WANT TO BE GOVERNED BY FOREIGNERS AGAIN?

(The Island, 1st Nov. 2007)

Many people would answer the above question in the affirmative without any hesitation and without much thinking. This is because all the governments of our people and by our people have failed the people who elected them. The huge contingent of scoundrels among our elected representatives, both at national and local levels, have subverted the sacred position of power based on trust to shamelessly enrich themselves and have perpetuated corruption and self-aggrandizement. The people and their welfare have become mere empty rhetorical cloaks to plunder the peoples' treasury even to the extent of publicly parading their ill-gotten wealth with profligate extravagance. This is the reason for their conspicuous failure. We the voters are partly guilty. We do ardently worship these morons as if they were demigods, and elect them to their political offices, election after election.

The political parties also connive to force our hands by including these individuals in their electoral lists. This should change. Like in many other countries, the politician should submit himself/herself for selection to the local constituency in competition with other candidates, and convince those selectors that he/she is the best candidate for that area. This power to select the candidate must be combined with the power to recall the candidate if he/she fails to live up to expectations. In short, the remedy for our political malaise is in our hands. The many arrests of politicians in Bangladesh for corruption have shown us the way to rid ourselves of parasites in our political system.

We need to look at our recent past to provide a thoughtful answer to the above question. We had the Portuguese and the Dutch as our governors for nearly three hundred years. None of us living now lived under their regimes to qualify for judging those foreigners at first hand. But many scholars, both Sri Lankan and foreign, have left us vivid descriptions of the lives of indigenous people under those foreign imperialist powers. Those who have read these works and pondered on the messages in those volumes, will unanimously agree that, it was by and large enslavement of the people, and exploitation of the country's resources for the benefit of the foreigners. Therefore, the history of this period clearly tells us that foreigners should not be allowed to govern this country again. I do agree.

Except for few octogenarians and nonagenarians still alive, most of us were not alive or of mature age under the British rule from 1796 to 1948. Therefore, most of us cannot really speak from experience about British rule in Sri Lanka. The British did leave behind many records of their administration of our country, and many books written by contemporaries have been available to those interested to study them. We do glean some "good things" they did in our country. To mention a few: they resurrected some of our ruined archaeological sites, they ushered in modern education, they brought in rapacious capitalism, they built roads and they left behind a relatively honest and hard-working bureaucracy. The 'catch' in all those beneficial works was that they were aimed at serving the imperialists first and then only by accident the people thereafter. The people did pay intolerable prices for those good things the British did. Let me illustrate with a couple of examples.

The education was aimed at training a class of people to serve as clerks in the British administration. It was confined to a very restricted few in Colombo and Jaffna. Elsewhere it was badly neglected. Thus the Colonial Secretary Tennent admitted in 1848, that there were only "five government schools in the whole of Kandyan Kingdom and two of these are within the town of Kandy itself, and out of pounds 12,354 voted for general education, only pounds 793 expended on the entire of central province and pounds 252 on the north-western including the Seven Korales and Kurunegala" (CO54/250). Later improvements in education had to be fought for until Mr. C.W.W. arrived on the scene.

The Road Ordinance of 13th April 1848 was as good an extortion at that time as that of LTTE's levy on all goods and persons at their Omanthai checkpoint today! The ex-government Agent, J. Forbes' observation on the commutation tax of 3 shillings levied in lieu of labour on road construction was scathing enough to force the government to reduce the levy. Mr. Forbes wrote that "every male, from 18 to 55 years of age, is now by Road Ordinance, to work 6 days or pay three shillings, if I take the population at a million and a half, and that of Europeans, not exempted at half a thousand, we shall at once see that it was removing a moderate indirect taxation from European capitalist, to inflict a large direct taxation on the native" (My book: The Kandyans' Last Stand Against the British p391). Such was the price paid by the locals for the set of roads built by the British. In addition to this, both private and temple lands were commandeered for road construction some of which were directed at new coffee plantations. The transportation of coffee (later tea) to the harbour and subjugating the rebellious Kandyans were the two main motives for the road construction.

The fact remains that the British got control of the entire country by duping the Kandyans. The infamous Kandyan Convention was signed merely to take control of the country. The British reneged on the conditions solemnly undertaken in that document. The Kandyans rebelled in 1817, "rebellion" is the pejorative incorrect word invented by the British to describe that fight for freedom. The Kandyans merely wanted to eject the illegal usurpers of their lands, therefore they were truly freedom fighters. The insurrection was put down by the British with utmost severity. By their own count more than 10,000 were murdered. Scorched earth policy coupled with shoot to kill policy was enforced. Entire villages, fruit trees and paddy fields were set on fire, domestic animals were mercilessly slaughtered just as much as their owners.

Here is one massacre that demands an apology even today. Nearly 60 Kandyans hid themselves in a cave to escape the marauding British soldiers led by Col. Hardy. He managed to find them and frightened them to come out of the cave. As they came out they were shot at point blank range, a few, unwilling to die at the hands of the British jumped to death into the ravine below. H.E. Mr.Chilcott, your government has lot to answer for what it did to our people. (H.E.Mr. Chilcott was the High Commissioner in Colombo at this time). First an apology please, before you preach to us about Human Rights. (A fuller description of the atrocities committed by the British is found in my book: Rebels, Outlaws and Enemies to the British. There are also many other excellent sources for those interested).

There was also another major rebellion in 1848. Then too beastly and sadistic atrocities were committed by the British army. Public notices threatening death on individuals were nailed on trees in Matale and Kurunegala. Many Kandyans were shot on sight and numerous houses were burnt by Capt. Watson and his soldiers. He was found guilty by two judges from Madras Presidency, but was not punished. Do Human Rights not apply to imperialist running dog-soldiers Mr. Chilcott?

Here is an eyewitness British soldier's account of a massacre that took place in the vicinity of the Wariapola estate bungalow in Matale. "The men (Kandyans) stood under the Jack tree panic-struck. There they stood with guns in their hands without attempting to fire on us or fly….had they been called, they would have at once surrendered. This was not done. They were shot ….the Malay British soldiers now used their bayonets and krises plunging the whole blade into the chests of the Kandyans till the hands rested on the chests of the men" (my Book: The Kandyans Last Stand Against the British, p 428). The governor later admitted that more than 250 were dead and fatally injured with no scratch on any British soldier (CO54/250).

Perhaps the reader can now understand why I keep demanding an apology from the British Crown and why we cannot allow ever any foreigner to govern our country again. These western foreigners have now adopted the new strategy of proxy government by using Human Rights (HR) violations to plant UN institutions in our country. It is true that we have had unacceptable series of HR violations in our country in the recent past. The remedy for this is in our hands and we should take the necessary robust measures with enforcement powers to stop this in-bleeding. A mere planting of foreign institutions in our soil would not cure this malady. Such a solution is aimed at controlling the activities of the government in power, including our efforts to eliminate LTTE terrorism. Therefore the government was right to refuse Ms Arbour's request for an UHHR office in Sri Lanka. Her long arm, if established in our country, would simply throttle us, unless we did obey her orders. Remember Mr. Soldheim? He came as a facilitator, later promoted himself to the position of a mediator and then an enforcer and arbiter in the Chairman's Chair at Geneva!

In a statement released by Ms.Arbour to the press, in addition to abductions and extra-judicial killings, she included "issues of discrimination and exclusions, gender inequalities, low participation of women in public and political life, the rights of migrant workers and press freedom". Clearly as HR impinges on all aspects of government activities, she has flagged that she wants to control the government and the way we are governed. Given that she is acting unilaterally flouting the set procedure of the UN as pointed out by Mr. Ladduwahetty in *The Island* of 17th Oct. 2007, it is open to suspicion that she is acting as per a secret agenda for the benefit of western powers. Once appointed, she will certainly seek to extend her power and influence in every aspect of the government. The defeat of the LTTE would diminish the influence of the West in the affairs of the country. It is likely then that we would be able to achieve international independence of the same order as Malaysia today, and be in the same position to tell the West to "do or depart". In the context of an emergent China in the Indian Ocean, both via Myanmar and Pakistan, this would be an unpalatable predicament for the West. Herein inherent is the reason for this sudden attention of the West dominated UN on Sri Lanka. Their sanctimonious pronouncements on elimination of terrorism is pure rhetoric as far as Sri Lanka is concerned, therefore we should do what is right for our country our way. [After the defeat of LTTE on 18th May 2009, we now see more clearly the machinations of the West to control us.]

17

A Critique of the Constitutional Proposal

(The Island, 18th Aug.1995)

This is a commonsense contribution to the discussion on the recent Constitutional Proposal (CP) seeking amendments before it passes beyond the Parliament to the people. Among the many topics, I have singled out just five main areas which need urgent attention by the many constitutional pundits in our country.

In this exercise it is very important to keep in mind that though the government talks of "devolution of power" yet in substance, many of the proposals are an abdication or surrender of power by the Central Government (CG) in the very fundamental framework of the Constitution. Once various powers are vested in the Regions, they cannot be revoked or retrieved. They will be vested in the Regions irreversibly in law and in fact forever and a day. Later on, in the light of experience, should there be dissatisfaction with the settlement, then we might have on our hands the very repudiation of the Constitution itself, with no means or power to restore the status quo ante. This is why safeguards are necessary like those found in all Federal Constitutions such as India, Malaysia, Nigeria, Switzerland, Canada and Australia. So, why do we have this glaring omission in the CP?

This is the other important point to keep in mind. The changes introduced now will affect generations to come. Their full impact will become apparent only in the distant future. They will also be operative into the indefinite future. Therefore the CP should be assessed and evaluated from long term perspective, not merely from the point of view, whether it solves the immediate problem on hand. Of course one cannot forecast the future turn of events, other than make valid inferences from current experiences. As the Romans would say, *ab esse ad posse vallet illatio* (from reality to possibility an inference is valid). This very uncertainty of future itself commands caution and consideration.

The other imperative consideration is that all citizens in the country should be afforded equal rights to, and equal access to all the resources and facilities in the country and there should be an equitable distribution of the social product among the citizens. This is already pledged by Art. 27 (2) of the present Constitution. Would not the CP violate this by making the Central Region a landlocked country? What happens if some Kandyans want to set up a fishing industry? Would they not be denied access to the resources of the sea, which properly belongs to all citizens in the country? Having highlighted some general relevant issues, I list below the five points I initially selected for this article.

First: there are no anti-secession provisions in the CP. Our neighbor India provides a good example here. It was Mr. Ramasamy Naickar of Tamil Nadu who set in motion a virulent campaign under the banner of 'Hindi language imperialism' demanding an independent and separate Dravidistan. Mr. Nehru was prompt in his reply. He amended the Indian Constitution in 1963 making it a criminal offence to demand secession of any territory from the Indian Union. All plans and actions aimed at making the Constitution unworkable should be outlawed expressly under this provision, and the powers and actions the CG can take to preserve the integrity of the country, should be specified, together with the legal argument of inference from omission of any topics or powers in any list be anchored in favour of the CG. At the moment there are no checks and balances against abuse of vested interest and surrendered powers to the Regions in the CP.

Second: the vesting of land and its use in the Region need to be circumscribed so that the Region cannot vitiate or remove the basic Human Rights of all citizens of Sri Lanka—ie., the liberty of movement and the freedom to choose his or her residence anywhere within the country as guaranteed by Art.12 of the International Convention of Civil and Political Rights. There are many surreptitious subterfuges a Region can adopt to deprive a section of its own population land they are entitled to. In such an event can the CG interfere? No, the CP is silent on this issue. Allied to this is the question of immigration into a Region. If a Region legislates to stop immigration and settlements in its Region, what can the CG do? Nothing is the answer. Finally there is the reality of interstate migration both temporary and permanent. Who really has the power to regulate this? The CP is ominously silent on this too, even though this is a very important aspect of everyday life of all of us. In this respect, the handing over of so much land to a mere 800,000 to 1,000,000 people begs the cannon of distributive justice, and is likely to generate a further succession of intractable problems as the population increases in the years to come in other Regions. It is, in fact, Tamil chauvinism to demand so much for so few.

Third: the independent Police in the Region together with the High Courts with Appellate and Writ jurisdictions are an open invitation to defy the central Constitution at the earliest opportunity. In a situation of conflict between the CG and the Region, can Supreme Court issue a Prerogative Writ against the judge of the first instance in the Region? How will such a Writ be implemented? If the Writ of the Supreme Court becomes non-implementable in a powerful Region, the whole Constitutional set-up will disintegrate into anarchy.

In the land of democracy, USA, we have a CIA and the FBI who do not need initially the permission or the cooperation of the police in the component States, to investigate and prosecute a criminal or maintain surveillance over individuals and organizations so as to protect national security. Why such powers for National Police not specifically stated in the CP? This is all the more important given that at least in one Region, many of the police officers might be men and women who failed in their murderous fight for separatism, and pursued a policy of slaughter of non-Tamil civilians in order to drive them away from those areas. Could the CP prevent such atrocities in the future? If not, why give them such powers?

In this context it is also important to realize that the internal security of the Region is also a matter of internal security of the nation. In times of emergency, if a powerful Region resists the centre when it sends its security forces to that Region on grounds of internal security, then the constitution will become null and void and the country will disintegrate into civil war. What safeguards are there against this eventuality in the CP? None.

Fourth: the Region's ability to have direct access to foreign financial markets is fraught with many pitfalls. It is likely that the most economically developed Region will attract more of the foreign investment and aid, and thereby accentuate the economic inequality further. This will lead to unequal development of the country and a host of problems, the most dangerous one being interstate migration of people to those prosperous Regions. Has the CP anticipated this? Apparently not.

Does the power to obtain foreign funds tantamount to concluding a Treaty with a foreign state or organization? If so, who takes up the tab, should there be default or cancellation half-way through the deal? If it is the CG, then, is it not grossly unfair that the rest of the country be made to pay for the folly of one Region? Does this power enable a Region to maintain their Envoys in foreign capitals of the world? Can there be a Kandy Kade in London and an Eelam house in Washington to negotiate foreign loans and foreign aid? Pursuing this logic to the extreme, it is apparent that Regions should also be allowed to obtain their own seats in international organizations. If this happens the recognition of Sri Lanka as a sovereign nation will vanish into thin air in the eyes of the international community. Is this what the CP wants?

The power to establish foreign multi-national companies, whether banks or other international concerns needs close scrutiny. These industrial and commercial giants of today have the ability to milk-dry the economic resources and wealth of the country and a small Region will be a mere pawn in their hands. They can also impose conditions on a Region, which might be detrimental to the Region as well as the country as a whole. In this respect what might be the repercussion on the Region and the country, should a huge financial institution to which a Region was attached collapses? Well, we already have the example of a BCCI and other banks in USA, UK and Japan. Foreign finance is the irresistible song of Sirens bewitching everybody approaching it.

Fifth: the imposition of a division of a country into autonomous Regions is also a division of an otherwise undivided people, who have over the years moved towards unity and a national identity. Germaine to this CP is the possible emergence of further division, distinction and alienation among people on class, religion and caste bases. Thus the Kandyans in the Central Region can, if they wish, pursue a narrow Kandyan identity based on the historical factuality, just as much as the Tamils in Jaffna can pursue their own identity. So where is the unifying principle which will bind everybody together as one nation in one land?

From a purely Sinhala point of view, this appears as an emasculation of their majority position, so that, should there be another UDI in any Region, they will not have the will, nor the heart and debilitated by this division, they will also not have the means to fight to save the nation from disintegration. Is this not a possible scenario in 10, 15 years hence? It is division rather than unity that is emphasized by the CP. This is why strong anti-secessionist provisions are imperative and necessary. Why fight shy of such provisions which are enshrined as sacrosanct in other federal states?

In general the CP is bestowing a plenitude of powers more than is available in the already existing federal governments of the world. Canada, Australia and Switzerland are countries where strong and already independent units came together to form one nation. They all vested overriding powers with the CG. In Canada Art.95 of its constitution forbids the provincial states to enact laws that are repugnant to any Act of Parliament in Ottawa. In Australia, Art. 51 lays down 39 areas of power for the CG. But its interpretation has become a minefield even for the lawyers as illustrated by the celebrated case of Tasmanian dam, which the CG sought to forbid from being built in order to preserve the national wildlife heritage. Australia had to appoint a Constitutional Commission's Committee on Distribution of Powers to sort out this tangled knot. In Switzerland numerous exclusive powers are given to the CG, Banking is one of them (Art.31, [4]).

In Malaysia, where incidentally there are nearly two million Tamils of Indian origin, there are three lists of powers, the first is the Federal list, the second is the state list and the third is the concurrent list. Our government's new CP has abolished the concurrent list already in the 13th amendment to our constitution. Further in Malaysia, Art 91 creates a National Land Commission to formulate a national policy for the promotion and control of land utilization throughout the Federation for mining, agriculture, forestry or other purposes.

Further the federal list includes the audit of State Accounts, and Art. 128 gives express powers to Federal Court to decide whether the laws of any State are invalid on grounds of lack of power of the State to make such laws.

Nigeria bears the closest resemblance in circumstance to Sri Lanka. It has a minority population of Ibo people in the east. Yet like the Jaffna-man of today, about 50% of the Ibos lived outside their alleged homeland of Biafra. There was also a secessionist civil war in the mid 60s. Yet its present constitution has only two lists, the Exclusive list and the Concurrent list. There is no State list. This means the CG has not abdicated any of its powers, but permits the component State to exercise concurrent powers with the centre on matters specified in that list.

Among the Exclusive list, the borrowing of monies for purposes of Nigeria or any State (item 7) is reserved for the CG. Only our PA government knows why it is compelled to mark out a constitutional path in stark contrast to those available in Federal nations like Australia, Canada, Switzerland, Malaysia and Nigeria. In my book, the CP, as it stands, is a lethal constitutional concoction which will eventually kill off the patient as one land and one nation, notwithstanding the many platitudinous assurances now given by its makers.

They will surely not be there to pick up the pieces or to save the nation when the vultures gather to feast over the disintegrated carcass of the nation. Legislators of today, you have an onerous task, cast away your narrow party loyalties, just keep in mind one simple question.... Will there be one sovereign Sri Lanka in 10, 15 years' time? That is the paramount objective towards which you should direct your efforts when you come to consider the CP

18

Land is a Core Issue

(The Sunday Times, 29th Oct. 95)

The government has employed its cohorts to daily intone the raucous ear-splitting chorus that the PA Proposals (PAP) are not intended to divide the country; they only devolve and distribute power to the Regions. One might designate this PAP as *suppressio veri, suggestio falsi* (suppressing the truth while suggesting the false). Many powers are simply surrendered and abdicated to the Regions without any provision for any recall by the central government (CG). Such an abdication cannot be devolution as described by the Shorter Oxford Dictionary as "to delegate to deputies duties for which the responsibility belongs to the principal". In the PAP there are many areas where the CG has no say whatever, once PAP becomes the law of the land.

Perhaps the government has seen the error, that it is now reported, that an overall amendment will be in place, giving the President the power to abolish a Regional Council acting contrary to the interests of the nation. Precisely what actions would constitute detrimental to the interests of the nation have yet to be spelled out. By itself, this new amendment is an admission of the gaping hole in the PAP. If a division of the country is not intended why not change the title of the PAP to 'United Sri Lanka of Regions, or United Regions of Sri Lanka'? As the PA government considers the name as a matter of semantics, it would be of no great concern to them to change from 'Union' to 'United'. This might satisfy the country at large, to whom, the name of their country does matter and is of serious concern.

Powers abdicated by the CG will inevitably engender a whole gamut of laws which need to be enforced. This requires specified land and people within marked boundaries. This demarcation process of land

and territory reinforced by surrendered powers to be exercised within such a specified area, constitute in the minds of many as the division of the country. This fear and suspicion is further enhanced when one considers the power of the Regional Chief. His supremacy and sway over the Regional Police, the law enforcers, and the Judiciary, the dispensers of justice in the Region, alone is sufficient to make him the dictator par excellence, to steer his Region to a Unilateral Declaration of Independence. The many verbal assurances now given by politicians that this will not happen are simply not acceptable. Prevention is better than cure. Therefore such preventive measures should be incorporated in the PAP. Besides, is there anyone in the country today, who will accept promises made by politicians of any variety?

It is foolish to presume that the question of land, its extent and its boundary are matters of insignificance, which can be confined to be resolved by mere demarcation. The demarcation of boundary to create a mono-ethnic Region in one part of the country, while the other Regions should remain multi-ethnic, is unacceptable by any standards of social morality. It is also dangerous to the minority ethnic population in other Regions. At least to the LTTE, if not to PA, land is of central issue. This is why they have deployed their men to fight for it all the way from Puttalam to Potuvil. This is why they have proclaimed in all international fora that they want this land for their exclusive use. This is why they fabricated history and created the myth of 'Homeland' to prove that this extent of land is their Eelam. It is therefore silly and idiotic to make a Region out of such land and hand it over to a Regional Supremo with sovereign powers, and expect him to abide by the legal niceties and conventions.

Further the politicians seem to have forgotten that we have a burgeoning multi-ethnic population within a very small island, which will require further land for houses, schools, recreation, hospitals, food cultivation and other industries. This limited resource of land cannot be simply partitioned away as if it were the private property of the PA government. Every new baby that is born everyday will require land as it grows up. Every one of them, a true citizen of Sri Lanka, should have the freedom to live and earn a living in whatever part of the country. He would expect some land for this purpose.

Demarcation and exclusive use of some part of land and its resources by a minority is contrary to the Human Rights of the rest of the population. A constitution erecting such an edifice has its foundations on the fault lines of a volcano. The architects of such a monolith should be required to live and work there permanently until their handiwork collapses on them.

A possible solution to the land problem is a National Land Commission a la Malaysia. With a 33% Chinese minority, nearly two million Tamils, and many other ethnic minority communities, the majority community of Malays seemed to have solved their land problem via their National Land Commission. We do not hear anymore of ethnic conflicts there. Nor has this institution prevented the rapid economic development of Malaysia, and the ensuing prosperity of that country. The government should seriously consider this model for incorporation into its PAP. The many daily harassment, intimidation and slaughter of Muslims and Sinhalese border villagers in the North and East of the country, are clear indications of what will happen to them in the future. A Constitutional Proposal that fails to make provisions to prevent such pogroms in the future for all times, deserves to be voted out and discarded as rubbish.

18 - B

The myth and Reality of Devolution

(The Island, 17th Feb. 97)

Professor Peiris' reply to Maverik on the above topic was based on the hypothesis of good governance by the Regions. We have a constitution not because the governors of our country are all good men and women, but because they are all wolves to other men ***(homo homini lupus)***, when they come to exercise power over other citizens. Thus a constitution should ensure protection from the protectors too.

Leaving aside the many debatable points in your article, I like to concentrate on Prof. Peris' paragraphs on "Plantations, State Land, and Mahavelli". According to Sec.24 (1,2) land and land settlement is vested in the Region. This is an out and out alienation of land. The Central government (CG) has first got to consult (24.3) with the Region, if it requires any land in the Region. Such land could easily be sold to private individuals by the Region, and there is no power in the CG to obtain that piece of land it needs from private individuals. Is this not contrary to what is prevailing at this moment in terms of the Land Acquisition Act? What happens if the process of consultation with the Region is deliberately stymied?

Already it is alleged that Tamils are being exclusively settled by one Eelam political party in Linganagar in Trincomalee, in state land adjoining an army complex. The Land Officer who inquired into this illegal action was brutally murdered not long ago. Who, I pray, will monitor such settlement of persons which you envisage?

I do agree that major agricultural development projects should be in the hands of CG. The vast funds necessary for such projects should come from the CG. Yet I do not see any provisions as to how the benefits of such schemes would be distributed among the Regions. According to the proposal the CG will only shoulder the vast expenditure. The CG should also have the major input as to how benefits of such schemes are distributed. Such provisions should be part of the new constitution.

Indeed "the country has reached the limits of deforestation and new land settlement". According to the Central Bank's projection, it will not be long before we have twenty million people in this small country of ours. All of them will need land to live, land for education, land for hospitals, land for recreation, land for water, land for industries and land to grow food. Are these not good enough reasons why we cannot allow one Region to have exclusive control over land which can be developed? Or is it the professor's case that the Regions will make available such land of their own goodwill?

As it is possible that even learned constitution makers can be sometimes naïve and ignorant of reality, so let me list below the names of the villages in the Yan Oya basin which are today deserted by the Sinhala farmers, who managed to survive the slaughter of kinsmen: Ralapanawa, Kelepuliankulama,Kunchuttuwa, Vihara Halmillewa, Halmillewatiya,Dutuwewa, Yakawewa, Indigollewa, Kanugahawewa, Kele Nikawewa, Morakewa, Thalgaswewa, and Maha Nikawewa. There are many other villages in other areas too. The fact is that to all Tamil parties, the Sinhalese farmers in the North and the East are illegal immigrants. They will be subject to various harassments and pogroms in the future as they are today. What safeguards have been built in the NC? I can see none. It appears to me, that at least in this respect, as Ovid had said, Prof. G.L.Piris has thoughtlessly devised an unjust law which argues against ourselves, *quam temere in nosmet legem sancimus iniquam.* Suitable amendments to cover the points made above are still possible. Over to you Professor!

19

Ecce the Devolution Chief

(An Unpublished limerick, composed 2nd Oct.95)

In the silence of pensive legal Bhavana, amidst tomes of erudition,
Dreamed a learned professor with utmost yearning, by a Proposal
To bring to life a Chief of Region, that potent creature most unique.
With fake mythical claims to land and sea from Putalam to Potuvil and beyond
Whose tumultuous lust for power and sway, a thundering torrent,
Flowing through all Region's veins, aspiring ever higher, ever further.
A superman is he, wrapped in intricate legal knot, beyond vulgar ken,
He appoints, he promotes, he dismisses his Region's cop, mighty IGP,
Thus a pansy quisling he makes of his law enforcer, that he conforms,
A fervent devoted fanatic soul in loyalty bound and in prostration,
Before this deus ex machina, a monstrosity per defectum.
Born of a legal brain, latifundia of powers he handsomely inherits,
That the dispensers of justice, the Judges of courts deemed so High,
Are his puppets, balancing and trembling under his flashing eye.
Clutching the scepter of faded ravaged blossoms of impartial justice,
United they proclaim, all his law is legal, but ones by him unbegotten,
Which as alien claptrap they discard as babel of words of irrelevance.
Thus enabling their Chief the entry to enchanted portals of Eelam.
This is the fantastically silly dalliance, a professor's untidy task,
A prophylactic remedy down the throat of fair Lanka in dire distress,
To end her days no more one country, one land, beloved of the Buddha.
What under the lens of honest scrutiny is the meaning of devolution?
Aye, a sophism for abdication and surrender of powers sans retrieval?
In sophisticated dialect they whet and hone this ignoble counterfeit,

As only a sharing of power to resolve a murderous conflict unending,
But answer professor Sir, how can this power and the laws it begets
Be applied and enforced sans land and territory marked out for such?
Unusquisque tantum juris habet, quantum potentia valet said Spinoza+,
A drivel isn't it, power and right in vacuo to apply, sans peopled land?
Ave et hosanna my people sing from London to Frisco, Jaffna to Toronto
Your pleasure and sway we serve and obey in our silken haven of Eelam.
While here I sit a Supremo moulding men and land in my fascistic image,
A society leavened from top to bottom by the racist cult of apartheid.
Muzzling all freedoms, forcing all spirits to loyally serve his Ego,
The cultic Chief they exalt, else perish without a nay, whim or whisper.
Tragedy sits in sublime rapture in this traumdenken of a professor,
Should it alight on land so fair, crumble it will to pieces, I espy.
So my friends grasp the moment to bid your MPs to take careful note,
That Tigers don't lie down fawning at their feet, sold on a Proposal.
To quench their thirst for Eelam, they kill and maim at his behest,
The Regional Chief, the Superman, the Hero they worship sine die.
(+ Each man has as much right as he has power).

[The professor referred to above was the person mainly responsible for the drafting PA's Constitutional Proposal known as the Union of Regions]

20

Eelam: Nurtured over the last seventy-five years

(The Sunday Times, 21st July 98)

It is usually a deliberate ploy of most Tamil politicians and commentators to accuse the Sinhalese of majoritarian mindset discriminatory and detrimental to their interests. They conveniently ignore their mindset of ethnic communalism, nurtured over the last seventy-five years, since the Tamil Mahajana Sabha (TMS) was formed in 1921. At its first meeting Sir A. Kanagasbai passed a Resolution demanding "Tamil seats in the Legislative Council equal in number to two-thirds of Sinhalese seats". Communal and confrontational ethnicity in politics was born then. A.Ramanathan, the Secretary of TMS, nurtured this ethnic baby on a historically fatuous and dubious declaration that, "the Tamils are the original inhabitants of the island and have been here for millennia, and the researches of Sir John Marshall, Dr. Sayce and others have proved that Tamil land was the cradle of the human race". It was from this time onwards that the Tamil leaders used the separate Tamil identity and interest as their calling card with the then British rulers of the country.

Governor Manning, the father of communal politics, soon rewarded the Tamils in the 1923 Reforms with 8 seats for 11%, while giving 16 seats to Sinhalese for their 67% of the population. The Donoughmore Commissioners (DC) claimed that this introduction of communal representation had been unfortunate, and had hindered the development of a true national identity. However, this ethnic monster has been, to this day, continuously fed on a diet of anti Singhalese prejudice by the Tamil politicians and their propagandists.

In 1923, before the DC, A. Canakaratnam of All Ceylon Tamil Conference (ACTC) demanded the ratio of two Tamils to three Sinhalese. The DC, in its Report, condemned communal politics "as the canker on the body politic eating deeper and deeper into the vital energies of the people, breeding self-interest, suspicion and animosity, poisoning the new growth of political consciousness and effectively the development of national or corporate spirit". Today those words need no verification. In four constituencies in Jaffna, a boycott of the first elections to the State Council of 1931 was enforced by the Jaffna Youth Congress. This was indeed the partie honteuse (shameful part) played by the Tamil politicians in the springtime of Sri Lankan politics.

When the Sinhalese Board of Ministers with three Jaffna Tamil Deputy Ministers was formed in 1936, there were vociferous protests from Jaffna, and G.G. Ponnambalam (GGP), who in 1937 was the Acting Minister of Communication and Works, demanded a Commission to inquire into the working of the Donoughmore Constitution; the protests by the Tamils were so unreasonably vehement, that Governor Caldecott had to remind them, in his address to the State Council in 1937 that the " strength of the minorities must be commensurate with the reasonableness of their demands". The Reform debate, however, continued unabated on ethnic lines.

Rev. Dr. T.I. Tambyah, the President of ACTC, was the first to enunciate in 1937, the formula of equating the minority votes with that of the total Sinhala votes. It was this formula, which in the hands of GGP became the notorious "fifty-fifty" slogan. In his presidential address at the Tamil Congress in 1944, his warped arithmetic was clearly stated thus, "We merely want that 65% of the Sinhala population should receive 50% of the seats". The same address opened a can of worms of Tamil racism. He stated "I may with pardonable pride recall that our race.... One would call it a nation that the Tamil community remains indivisible and elementary rights are not denied to any section of our race." He backed this up by ethnic rhetoric against the Sinhalese. Sane voice as of C. Sivasubramaniam, Secretary of the Tamil Congress till Aug.1947, that a communal Tamil party was a "fatal anachronism and blunder under the Soulbury Constitution" was totally ignored.

In more recent times, the Federal Party incorporated this communal and separatist ideal as part of its constitution by demanding that they be permitted "to have their own autonomous state guaranteeing self-government and self-determination for the Tamil nation in the country; and to work for indefatigably to the attainment of this objective". It was Prof. C. Sunderalingam who used the discredited Cleghorne's Minutes to claim a Tamil homeland "from Chilaw, northwards and eastwards…to comprise the present Trincomalee District, Batticaloa District, right down to the mouth of Walawe Ganga". The TULF's Vaddukkodai Resolution of May 1976 formally asserted the right of Tamil nation to form a "sovereign, secular socialist State of Tamil Eelam". This was further refined in 1977 election manifesto of TULF to suit the fabricated history that "even before the Christian era the entire island was ruled by the Tamil kings", and that the claim for the "traditional homeland of the Tamils" was simply the continuation of that pristine kingdom of Jaffna. Reputable historians have already discredited this much trumpeted historical basis of this spurious Tamil claim.

After the election of 1977, A. Amirthalingam, the leader of TULF, was able to claim that the people of Tamil Eelam had given TULF the mandate to restore and reconstitute the free sovereign socialist State of Tamil Eelam. The separatist slogan nurtured and fostered by Tamil politicians, had now matured in the LTTE, with devastating consequences both for the nation and the Tamil people themselves. The separatist ideology had lost the Tamils everything, their wealth, their jobs, their homes, their self-respect and even their children. Thousands of them are reduced to living under duress in hovels in the wilds of Wanni. The other Tamil parties have not given up this genie either. They still have Eelam in their party names. This is the mindset of the Tamils, which refuses to accept, that we come to exist not in or on our own terms, but in reference to, and in respect of others. So long as this mindset persists, the Tamil politicians have ruled themselves out of any compromises with the rest of the country. Non-negotiable conditions and unreasonable demands will be part of the bargaining strategy. The mindset of the Tamils, therefore, needs as much change as the mindset of anyone else. But can they? Will they? One has only to look at their recent entrenched and intransigent stance before the

Parliamentary Select Committee for an answer. It was very much in line with their Eelamist objective.

It was Hobbes who pointed out that everyone originally had a right to everything, but an exclusive right to nothing; but one could obtain an exclusive right to individual things by renouncing his right to all the rest, while others did the same with regard to what was chosen by him. The same applies to Tamil separatists. Have they convinced us, the rest of the population, that they have exclusive rights in respect of 30% of land and 60% of the coastline and the exercise of absolute power therein? No. It is exclusive privilege at the expense of rest of population that they demand. Any country that gives into such outrageous demands does not deserve to, nor will it remain as one indivisible country. The country has the right to demand the complete dismantling of all vestiges of separatist ideology before any political settlement.

21

The Packaged Finance Commissioner

(The Sunday Times, 10th Nov.96)

There are three Finance Commissioners (FC) under the new Constitutional Proposal (CP), mistakenly called the Devolution Package. One Commissioner for the 74% Sinhalese, one for the 12% or less Tamils, and one for the 6% Muslims and none for the other communities as they have no legal recognition under the CP. The discerning reader will note the warped arithmetic trying to equate 74% with 12% and 6% via just one FC for each community.

This letter is, in fact, a public declaration of my candidature for the Sinhala FC. Usually, for political appointments, qualifications are glossed over, though distinction in one of the fields mentioned in the package is required here. In my case, I can assure the government that I do have more than one paper qualification and plenty of experience too tedious to mention here. My experience does include a bit of amateur acting as well in case this is relevant given the predilection for actors by the President. I fancy this job so much, that I do also volunteer to do the job on expenses only basis, and have my monthly expenses claim studiously exposed for public scrutiny. I am sure I can do a better job than the mélange of mediocrities in top positions in many government institutions today. Read on and judge for yourself!!

While you might rightly wonder why I am so fond of this job, I am aware some readers of this letter may also readily become my competitor candidates for this job, once they reach the end of this letter. Believe me, this is the best job you can ever have in this paradise of ours. It, in fact, is an appointment by the CP itself via the Constitutional Council and the President. Being charitably disposed let me expose to all my potential competitors some of the enormous attractions, not to mention, the bountiful perks of the job.

It is only a three year stint. You can be removed before then, but by whom, for what reasons are not specified. This really means that unless you are run over by a usually suicidal private bus, you can be sure of staying the course to the last day. So job security is assured. Further the highly developed Fundamental Rights legal industry in this country will also provide the additional job security. In any case, at the end of your tenure, you are bound to be head-hunted for other equally remunerative positions elsewhere, if not dispatched as ambassador to somewhere.

The powers this CP bestows on the FC are what the Roman lawyers would term as monstra per excessum (monstrous to excess). The job is basically a pleasant one, similar to cutting the cake at some festive celebration. It is the annual division of the national cake or the national revenue among the new Regions and what remains of the Central government (CG) under the CP. It is at this point that the CP is really over-generous to bestow monstrous powers to FC. For, by Art. 20(8) of CP, "no Court or Tribunal shall inquire into, or pronounce on, or in any manner entertain, determine or rule upon, any questions relating to the adequacy of such funds , or any recommendation made or principle formulated by the Commission".

This then is the first attraction of the job. It is a pleasant job with absolute independence and without any accountability to anyone. The FCs will have at their disposal billions of Rupees to do with it as it pleases the FCs. The guidelines are so broad and subject to a wide variety of interpretations, that the FCs could, without any difficulty, follow their own whims and fancies in the allocation of national revenue. Not only is the rationale of any decision by the FCs not questionable, but also the size of the national cake allocated to any Region cannot be a subject of dispute. Given this immunity, as a FC, I certainly will unceremoniously bounce out of my door, all politicians who will try to influence me to comply with their vested interests. If this does not tempt you to apply for this job, there is more.

By Art.20(6), the FCs are required to determine their own procedure. The same article also says that Parliament too will confer powers to the FCs. If these powers are additional to the powers already stated in the CP, so much the better. My first demand as the Sinhala FC would be that my vote carries the 74% weight. It is likely that this demand could lead to a deadlock. I had my education before the PA system of arithmetic came into existence, when 74% was not equal to either 12% or 6%. It is also likely that the cohorts of foreign-funded mercenary ink-slingers would attack me as a Sinhala chauvinist with a majoritarian mindset. Do I care? As far as I am concerned my claim will be based on statistical fact and therefore fair. The Tamils act exclusively for the Tamils, the Muslims for the Muslims, but I shall try to abide by the dictum, Lakam nactus est, orna (Lanka is your birthplace, be a credit to it). It is likely that my demand will be acceded to. Otherwise there will be no funds for anyone and the government of the country will come to a grinding halt. Thus whether I win or lose, my power will be enormous by any standard. Once I win my demand, the FC will be basically a one man band, with my other colleagues acting as my rubber stamp. Surely, this is a super position to be in by any account? Still not interested in the job?

In actually allocating the funds, I can, for instance, take a large chunk from the Western Region and pass it on to Oluvil, Pottuvil and Kokkavil. Given that my reasons for such a decision cannot be challenged, nor can the reduced size of the allocation to Western Region be subject to question, the consequences of such a step would be the burden of Western Region politicians. Or as the Sorborne educated will say, it will be *un petit cours de sensecommunologie* (a short course in common sense) to our Western Region politicians, who are just now determined to pass this topsy-turvy CP into law. Such a step will starve the Western Region of funds, politicians' pet projects will have to be closed down, many will lose their jobs, other developments and much of the recurring expenditure will have to be drastically curtailed. In short there will be no relief until my term of office ends! What is illustrated above as applicable to the Western Region is also applicable to other Regions. Western Region politicians, are you listening?

There are many more juicy plums in this jobs, too numerous for a letter in a newspaper. Yet let expose what the Paris educated might say is the piece de resistance of this job. It is that it will give me the opportunity to close down the talking shop by the Diyawanna Oya for at least three years! How can I do this? It is Tom Paine who said *du sublime au ridicule il n'y a qu'un pas* (from the sublime to the ridicule is but one step). I can allocate the National Revenue in such a manner that there is nothing left for the Central government. Without funds it will have to shut down.

If I have kindled your interest, do rush in your applications for the job. On the other hand, I hope, you will agree, that I deserve at least the first rejection. Do put in a word to the powers that be on my behalf, if you have such influence.

22 - A

The Packaged Sovereignty

(The Island, 28th Aug.97)

The Devolution proposal (DP) wrapped up in the sovereignty of our nation in so porous a package, that any unbiased reader will find, that it has all leaked out even before the reader got to the Regional List in the last pages of the DP. In Ch.3sec.3 the DP boldly asserts that "in the Republic of Sri Lanka, sovereignty is in the people and is inalienable. Sovereignty includes the powers of the government, fundamental rights and the franchise". It then proceeds to list five ways in which sovereignty shall be exercised and enjoyed. The sovereignty of a nation is the crux of its constitution, and as such, it should be anchored on solid foundations. Sadly this is not the case in the DP. Indeed some provisions of the DP are detrimental to the generally accepted norms of sovereignty intrinsic to and abiding in an independent nation like ours.

Some terms used here need clarification before proceeding further. ***Society*** cannot be defined easily with precision. Here it means "a group of people held together by actual or potential common interests". By ***state*** is meant "a society organized to make law possible". And by ***government*** is meant "an organization within society, whose function is to make, administer and enforce the laws". By ***nation*** is meant "a distinct race or people, characterized by common descent, language or history, organized as a separate political state and occupying a definite territory".

The sovereignty of a nation has essentially two perspectives, external and internal. Both are inextricably bound together. From an external point of view, sovereignty is the recognition by other nations of the world that a given state is a competent authority for concluding international treaty obligations of economic, political, social and cultural affairs. Usually such a state will occupy a seat at the UN as an equal among other nations of the world. This crucial current status and position of Sri Lanka is put into jeopardy by this crazy DP.

However, the internal perspective is subject to various interpretations by political philosophers. Two men whose thoughts are echoed in the published DP need to be briefly cited here as benchmarks for the critique that follows.

Hobbes in his Leviathan (1651) argued that sovereignty was entrusted to the Commonwealth by consent of each individual "giving up his right to govern himself". He then listed nine "rights which makes the essence of sovereignty". Among them were the non-transferability of sovereignty, the power of prescribing laws and the right to make war and peace. He further emphasized that those rights were "incommunicable and inseparable".

Rousseau in his Social Contract (1762) based his theory on common need, common confrontation with conditions, which no individual could handle if left to himself. The social compact was created when "each of us puts his person and his power in common under the supreme direction of the general will; and, in our corporate capacity, we receive each member as part of the whole. This act of association created a collective body, received its unity, its common identity, its life and its will. The public person so formed was called body politic, it was a state when passive and sovereign when active. The individuals collectively become known as a people, severally citizens and subjects as being under the laws of the state". Law was merely the declaration by the whole people for the whole people. The sovereignty so created by social contract was unitary, inalienable and indivisible.

The crucial constituents of political sovereignty therefore are a unitary regime however organized, representing legitimacy through law, established from an impartial standpoint above particular conflicts, and enforced through discontinuous interventions which aim to suppress illegitimacy. Does the DP satisfy the above criteria of sovereignty? Sadly not. The newly concocted phrase "Union of Regions" clearly goes against the grain of unitary and individual nature of sovereignty.

As per ch3 s15.2 the Regional Council has exclusive power over forty-six items in the Regional List. Four of them can easily be manipulated to destroy the external aspect of our sovereignty. They are the control over (1) Broadcasting and media including TV, (2) Domestic and international borrowing, (3) Regulation and Promotion of foreign direct investment, International grants and Developmental assistance to the Region and (4) Regional Financial and Credit Institutions.

The caveat that international monetary transactions be subject to the "criteria and limitations specified by, and would require concurrence of the Centre" is merely a baneful prosaic mantra which cannot be effectively enforced. Today, we live in a world where trillions of dollars move electronically round the world each day. They effortlessly flow from one terminal to another leaving behind in its wake, currencies reduced to confetti, and governments reduced to beggars knocking on the doors of World Bank for help and succour. The DP provides access to such facilities to a Region. This could easily be manipulated to completely destabilize the entire country and ruin our financial system. To a Regional Chief, hell-bent on separatism, this will be a very small price to pay to attain his objective.

The modern Molochs of the world economy---The World Bank, The IMF and WTO---today descend on countries with their blueprints demanding privatization and the relinquishment of national control over exploitable resources. Their cohorts are the multi-national companies, to whose melodies of tax holidays, concessions, subventions and subsidies, poor nations are expected to dance, while they milk the country dry, and then migrate elsewhere to greener pastures. They easily seduce the politicians, elected as well as unelected by making them trustees of the chimera of wealth generation. A Regional Chief with exclusive control of the Region, his people and land could easily succumb to inducement and bribes, and compromise the economic plans of the Centre, and plunge the country into turmoil. The control over the media will provide him all the cover he wants, while the dance of destruction is played out remorselessly, in accordance with his strategy of separatism.

At this point it is appropriate to remind the readers of Jacques Parizeau. He was the Premier of autonomous Quebec State in Canada. He wanted more than mere autonomy. All separatists do. In Oct. 1995, he engineered the Quebec Separatist Referendum. He lost by a mere 27,000 votes. In order to lure the voters to a 'yes' vote, he made many promises. In substance, he promised, that if he won the Referendum, he would undertake a long-drawn-out orderly negotiation with the Central government in Ottawa before declaring independence, so that it would be a cost-free and relatively painless process. In the meanwhile, the Quebecers could keep their Canadian passports and use their Canadian dollars. Yet in his book---For a Sovereign Quebec---published recently, he admits that all those solemn promises were deliberate lies just to win votes. His intention was to declare unilateral independence within ten days of winning the Referendum. Such an indecent hasty action would have caused social panic and would have plunged the whole of Canada into political chaos and economic turmoil. Such is the stuff separatist politicians are made of. This is axiomatically true of all separatists all over the world including Sri Lanka. It was probably the unscrupulous actions of these men Nietzsche had in mind when he wrote, "everywhere in all beginnings we find only the crude, the empty and the ugly…. Everywhere the way to beginning leads to barbarism".

From an internal perspective, the sovereignty of a country is endangered not only by the fact that each region will have its own bureaucracy, own High Courts, its own police and control over demarcated state land, its disposal and its alienation, but more importantly , by the fact, that all these will effectively be under the control of the Regional Chief.

These really give him a handle to beat the sovereignty out of the country. A Sri Lankan Parizeau has got all he needs to blaze the trail of separatism and reduce the country to anarchy. One way of preventing such a course is to follow the example of the 16th Amendment of the Indian Constitution where such actions are made criminal offences. Ch1 s2.2 of DP merely prohibits such initiatives and is too feeble to deter a determined separatist. Further I would advocate an FBI type

Security Force with powers of investigation, surveillance, monitoring and the power to arrest anyone promoting separatism or secession. If a FBI is good enough for USA, the home of democracy, why is it not good enough for Sri Lanka?

In any case, the inalienable and indivisible sovereignty of our nation cannot be reconciled with the oft-repeated four cardinal principles of Tamil politicians. They are that the Tamils of Sri Lanka are a distinct nationality, they occupy a an identifiable homeland, they have a right to self-determination and all Tamils who look upon Sri Lanka as their country, do have the right to full citizenship and other fundamental rights. All these demands go to the very heart of sovereignty of the nation, and if ceded, would lead to the vivisection of the country. This is the end-point of all Tamil politicians who openly aver that the DP is only a 'starting point'. It is perhaps time to tell them plainly that these impossible demands cannot be delivered without breaking up this country into pieces, and that the country is not available for partitioning now or in the future.

In a properly run democracy, one does not need a DP for power sharing. As Michel Foucault has pointed out "power is everywhere not because it embraces everything, but it comes from everywhere". Power is dispersed across complicated and heterogeneous social networks marked by on-going struggle. Power is not something present at specific locations within those networks, but is instead always at issue in ongoing attempts to produce effective social alignments, and conversely to avoid or erode their effects, often by producing various counter alignments. In short, even when a person exercises power over another, that power very much depends upon other person or groups acting in concert with what the first person does. The democratic institutions are expected to discharge these functions. Unfortunately in Sri Lanka, most of our institutions have been perverted by our politicians to serve their narrow vested interests. They, therefore, fail to function properly. What we urgently need is not a DP, but a thorough de-politicization of our institutions, starting with our police force and our bureaucracy. If this is done then common man's interests will come to predominate, and that would be genuine power sharing.

The DP, as it stands, is a document dangerous to the sovereignty of our nation. The Kalutara Tangerine man and women, who apparently accepted it wholesale, were mistaken in their belief, that this DP will one day usher in the peace we all need and seek. To those perplexed politicians, I commend the advice of philosopher Descartes "omnia semel in vita evertenda atque a primis fundamentis denuo inchoandum" (once in a lifetime we must demolish everything completely and start again right from the foundations). I hope they do take note. [At this time there was a conference attended by politicians and others at Tangerine Hotel in Kalutara to put the seal of approval on the DP].

22 - B

An Aussie Lesson on Sovereignty

(The Island, 3rd April 97)

Many pro-package protagonists did use Australia's constitutional set-up in support of their arguments in favour of the package. I hope they will also adopt the exemplary practical exercise of sovereignty by the government of Australia, given below. This refers to the law concerning the termination of life of the terminally ill patients.

The State of the Northern Territories (SNT) passed this law and four patients legally ended their lives under this law. The doctor who advocated this law wanted it extended throughout Australia. The Central/Federal government thought otherwise, and has made this SNT law invalid. Thus it has overruled a law passed by one of the State in the Australian Federation.

What concerns us and is relevant to our package, is this power in the hands of the central government to overrule a law passed by a Region, as it would be in our case. Australia has demonstrated the usefulness and the expediency of having such a reserve power in the hands of the central government. It provides a second chance to look closely at a particular law passed by a Region. Such a scrutiny would be conducted by another body not directly or parochially involved with the issue at hand.

In Australia this cancellation has not resulted in rebellion, nor any movement for secession by the SNT, nor any secession or protests by the Tamils living in SNT and Australia. So why cannot we have such powers in the hands of the central government over here? The separate States of Australia came together to form the Commonwealth of Australia in 1901. They voluntarily surrendered their own sovereignty by transferring such a paramount power to the hands of the federal government. The case for such a reserve power in the hands of the central government becomes a compelling necessity where an existing unitary country like Sri Lanka, is set to fragment itself into autonomous pieces with potential for separation constitutionally or otherwise.

Given the chaotic nature of local government now prevailing, the caliber of persons seeking power in such institutions, and the potentially damaging legislation such individuals could engender, it is paramount that such reserve powers be enshrined in the hands of the central government.

Prof. Peiris, you were one of those who waxed lyrical on Australian Constitution as an example for us to follow. On this particular point, I am in full agreement with you. So please introduce the appropriate amendments in the package to strengthen the hands of the central government, so that it will have the same powers as in Australia to invalidate a law passed by the Region, where it is considered necessary. Over to you, Professor.

23

The Scottish and PA Packages

(The Island, 16th Oct.97)

The British government published the White Paper (WP) on Scotland's Parliament in July 97. On the basis of this WP, a Referendum was held on the 11th of Sept.97. The Scottish people overwhelmingly voted in favour of the proposals for devolution in the WP. Some (CAT's EYE in Sunday Island, AGOTIC in Sunday Leader, both of 5th Oct), have rushed to use this WP as a basis for support for PA's Package (PAP) for devolution in our country, while choosing to ignore the crucial differences in the two documents. To start with the openness and candour in the WP, is in stark contrast to the PAP, where only a favoured few actually know the geographical/ethnic/linguistic units to which powers will be devolved.

In the PAP we have the country divided into a Union of Regions where the sovereignty is in the people and is inalienable. It includes "the powers of government, fundamental rights and the franchise"(S.3). Then by S.15.2, as if to countermand the above, "exclusive power" is ceded to the Region to make laws concerning 46 items enumerated in the Regional List. Some of these items could easily be manipulated by a shrewd Regional Chief to convert the Region into a separate state. The safeguards in S.1.2 and 26 (1to4) are too feeble and not pre-emptive. These provisions enjoin actions when it is already too late. There are no government agencies like National Criminal Intelligence Service of UK or the FBI of the USA to maintain a continuous monitoring and surveillance function, so that preventive action could be taken before, and not after, sedition has taken place.

In the WP, Scotland is firmly anchored "within the United Kingdom". This phrase is used twice by PM Tony Blair in his short Preface in the WP and once by D.Dewar, the Scottish Secretary, and is proliferate throughout the document. Ch.3 is titled "Scotland within the United Kingdom". Notice it is not a "Union of Kingdoms"!! But for Wales the rest of England remains an integral unit, and the majority English population has not been enmasculated or divided into smaller units of this United Kingdom as had been done in the case of Sinhalese and others in living in Sri Lanka.

In the Summary of the WP, it is clearly stated that "Scotland will remain an integral part of the United Kingdom, and the Queen will continue to be the Head of State of the United Kingdom. The UK Parliament is and will remain Sovereign". This is repeated in Ch.4. "The UK Parliament is and will remain sovereign in all matters: but as part of the government's resolve to modernize the British Constitution, Westminister will be choosing to exercise that sovereignty by devolving legislative responsibilities to a Scottish Parliament without in any way diminishing its own powers". There is no compromise or any equivocation here. The fundamental difference between the PAP and the WP is quite clear here in that the Scottish Parliament remains a subordinate body. This is further reinforced by the fact that by Ch3.3 of the WP, the Constitution of UK is a reserved matter, and by Ch8.7 the "responsibility for Scottish Parliamentary electoral arrangements and constituencies will be reserved matters". The implication is that the Scottish Parliament could, if the need arises, be abolished by a simple majority in the UK parliament. Only the actual legal draft will specify the precise terms.

There are 47 devolved matters in the WP. Ch2.3 merely states that the "role of the Scottish Parliament will be to make laws in relation to devolved matters in Scotland". The PAP's phrase "exclusive power" is nowhere to be seen in the WP.

The WP envisages future disputes between the UK and Scottish Parliaments. Such unresolved disputes would be referred to the Privy Council before the Royal Assent is given. The Privy Council will also adjudicate in matters where the dispute arises after the Royal Assent.

In the case of PAP, the Regional Government Agent can "invoke the jurisdiction of the Supreme Court to determine the constitutionality of such statue or any part thereof" after it has been passed against his advice by the Regional Council. By this time one would have a grave constitutional crisis on hand.

There are many other occasions where there could be disputes between the Regional Chief Minister (RCM) and the Central Government and its functionaries, especially on the appointments of important Regional Officials. No procedure for resolving such disputes have been provided in the PAP. The RCM therefore will be able to impose his will on all such matters, and have his men appointed by mere force of his authority. No such individualized power exists in the WP vis-à-vis the First Minister of the Scottish Parliament.

In the PAP, "the Board of Ministers shall be collectively responsible and answerable to the Regional Council" (14.5). No further elaboration of this is given, other than the usual requirement that if a statement of policy or an Appropriation Bill is rejected or a no confidence motion is passed, the RCM is deemed to have resigned.

In WP the accountability is more elaborate and far reaching and seeks to enforce effectiveness and efficiency in the Scottish Parliament. In 4.7 "the Scottish Parliament will hold the Executive to account for its actions. Ministers of the Scottish Executive will be answerable to Scottish Parliament, and the Parliament's Committees will be able to scrutinize and report on the effectiveness of the Executive's administrative action and its use of public monies voted to it by Parliament". Further by (9.10), "it is envisaged that these Committees might for example initiate legislation, scrutinize and amend the Scottish Executive's proposals as well as having wide-ranging investigative functions. Such a role for Scottish Parliament Committees means that the proposals of the Executive will be appropriately scrutinized". This is indeed a case of in-built checks and balances to prevent abuses as well as misuse of power. Why no such ckecks and balances in the PAP?

In the PAP, by 18.1 the RCM has to be consulted for the appointment to the Regional Judicial Service Commission. This Commission has power over the appointment, transfer, dismissal and disciplinary control of judicial officers of the Region.

In the PAP by 25.3a the Head of the Regional Police Service is the Regional Police Commissioner. "who shall be appointed by the RCM in consultation with the Governor of the Province"; and by 25.7 this "Regional Police Commissioner shall be responsible to, and be under the control of the RCM, in respect of the maintenance of public order in the Region". Given the prevalent abuse of power by our politicians, this concentration of power in the hands of the Chief Minister is inexcusable and needs to be drastically amended.

In the WP judicial appointment and police service are devolved matters "over which the Scottish Parliament will have legislative power". These are not exclusively in the hands of the First Minister. The Lord Advocate's traditional independence in carrying out his responsibilities of prosecution and the investigation of crimes and offences in Scotland is expected to be maintained (4.8).

The appointments to the Highest Judicial Office such as Lord President of the Court of Session and the Lord Justice Clerk, are made by the Queen on the advice of the Prime Minister on the basis of the nominations of the Scottish Executive.

In the whole of UK the police are a fiercely independent lot. They are not subject to the whims of politicians nor will they allow themselves to be easily influenced by politicians. Their conditions of employment are beyond the interference of any one politician. Proper and transparent procedures exist for their appointment, promotion, transfer and dismissal. Thus a devolved police service is desired under these conditions, and this police will be more attuned to the needs of the population of Scotland, and, will no doubt, serve them well.

Under S27 of the PAP billions of Rupees will enter the coffers of the Regional Council. "No money shall be appropriated except in accordance with law or statue and for purposes and in the manner provided in this Constitution" The PAP is ominously silent on how this will be enforced. In short there is no provision made for audit of accounts of the Regional Councils. This is an unpardonable omission, unworthy of any constitution maker.

Even with a Public Auditor in place, the present government is constantly telling us that the Treasury has been plundered by the previous regime, and has appointed a Presidential Commission in pursuit of the culprits. The fate of the Regional Treasury without an independent auditor, could therefore be a desperate one. It will be at the mercy of greedy politicians who will misappropriate public funds at every opportunity. An era of Sri Lankan Mobutus owning apple orchards and chateaus in foreign lands will be upon us for sure.

The WP is very clear on this matter. By 7.27 the "Scotland Bill will lay a general obligation on the Scottish Parliament to establish effective scrutiny and audit arrangements....In common with other central government expenditure grant to Scottish Parliament will fall to be audited by the UK Comptroller and Auditor General".

Under S24 of the PAP all state land is vested in the Region. It will have exclusive power over such land "including land tenure, transfer or alienation of land, land use, land settlement and land improvement". The central government can obtain land in the Region only after consultation with Regional Authority, which could easily subject this process of consultation to undue delay by bureaucratic prevarication. In any case, in a country where there are millions of landless peasants, living in hovels in areas of intolerable population density, for the central government to have abdicated its duty to settle such peasants on developable land, can be construed as dire dereliction of its duty to its poor citizens.

In the WP, land use planning and area regeneration are devolved matters to the Scottish Parliament. There is no problem of land hungry peasants in the UK. Therefore the question of ethnic cleansing does not arise. Given the checks and balances already pointed out, one can expect that any dealing in this respect by the Scottish Parliament would be above board. There are also EU regulations in this respect.

Given the obvious prevalence of rule of law, the existence of strongly independent democratic institutions and political culture, a vigilant and investigative press and electronic media, the British government yet thought it necessary to build into its devolution package limitations, and checks and balances. In contrast in the PAP, we see the abdication of power with gay abandon in favour of Regional Chief Minister, who will be in realty not accountable to anyone, even though in 14.5, we have the usual manthra that the Board of Ministers shall be collectively responsible and answerable to the Regional Council. Given the powers vested on him, he will be the petty dictator in the Region, who can, if he so desires, surreptitiously obtain all the SAM missiles and the submarines he needs to convert his Region to an independent state. This is the vital difference between the effete PAP and the robust WP.

24

WHO IS AGAINST PEACE?

(The Island, 13th Oct.99)

The armed conflict in the North and East of Sri Lanka has engendered two main strands of opinions. One, including this writer, considers it a terrorist problem. The other, including the numerous Tamil political parties, a section of Catholic/Christian clergy, and some NGOs, project it as an ethnic problem. It is often said that the proper understanding of the problem is half the solution. It is because of this confusion in understanding this seemingly intractable problem in Sri Lanka, that the many efforts made to establish peace had ended in failure. That would be the bleak future too, so long as this confusion remains.

The recent slaughter of civilians in Gonagala was a calculated and deliberately planned execution. Such pre-meditated murder of civilians is the indelible signature of a terrorist. Over the years the LTTE has committed many such cruel and bloodthirsty actions intended to infuse terror among the civilian population. The prevailing bus-bombing is another act of terrorism intended to kill and maim civilians. It is inexcusable that there are people, who are prepared to project these cowardly perpetrators of terror as freedom fighters. It is because they have so much freedom that the LTTE are able to infiltrate into the heart of civilian population and bomb them out of existence. On top of this the LTTE Supremo has averred, inter alia, that he would not allow "the footprint of the Sinhala aggressors to remain embedded in our sacred soil". He had also ordered his acolytes to kill him if he did agree to anything less than an independent Eelam.

This is mad fanaticism. The naïve idea that one could parley with such a man, and arrive at a reasonable solution, is an illusion entertained by all those who are against peace. Negotiation implies compromises. A compromise to the fanatical adamantine mind of Pirapakaran would indeed be the proverbial change of leopard's lovely spots. What he stands for is appeasement and the establishment of Tamil Eelam. This is also what the many peaceniks want under the cover of their "peace-walks" and "peace-meditations". The viperine tooth of the demagogic idea of a racist Tamil homeland is projected, as if it were quod simper, quod ubique, quod ab omnibus (has been always, everywhere and believed by all). One cannot forget the many words written by these peaceniks, when LTTE was in tyrannical control of Jaffna peninsula. They then wrote and lectured to others that Eelam was a fait accompli, and therefore it was opportune to recognize its existence. They sought a peace a la Pirapakaran. They wanted to reward him for his terrorism. This was what our Minister of Foreign Affairs recently denounced at a UN forum. Appeasement always leads to oppression and further aggrandizement. In my books, therefore, these vociferous peace-beggars, as they are now called, are in fact, closeted cohorts of LTTE. They are doing everything necessary to obstruct the attainment of a true and durable peace.

To the LTTE there is no ethnic problem. In fact they have resorted to many intolerable and atrocious acts of provocation against the Sinhalese and Muslims just to create this ethnic problem in our country, but without any success. To them there is only a separatist cause. This is why they have rejected the PA Package in toto, and have also started butchering prominent pro-Package Tamils. This is also the reason for their on-going unrelenting pogrom against the non-Tamils in the areas marginal to the conflict. They simply want a racist separate country with a pure Tamil population. How the pro-LTTE Catholic clergymen could explain this to their Sinhala Catholic flock, and to the many Tamils living among the Sinhalese and Muslims, would need all the casuistry of the Middle-Ages. In Marxian terms, "the phantoms of their brains have got out of their hands. They, the creators have bowed down before their creations" ***(German Ideology)***. No wonder that even J.N. Dixit admitted that "what was fascinating was that Tamil Catholic clergy kept arguing in favour of LTTE throughout my tenure in Sri Lanka" ***(Assignment Colombo, p228)***. Those clergymen do have a case to answer.

To all those who consider it a terrorist problem, the solution is quite clear. Terrorism has to be eliminated using all the powers at the disposal of the government no matter the cost. It is true, that to-date, this policy has not yielded the desired solution. This is not the fault of the policy itself, but rather, the way the policy has been implemented. Many obstacles have been put in the way of pursuing a planned and determined course to eliminate terrorism in the country. We have had India itself intervening to stop our army in its track. We have had political objectives imposed on military campaigns. We have had NGOs and other vested interests pressuring three Presidents of this country to talk peace with the LTTE, thereby giving the LTTE the time and opportunity to launch fresh onslaughts on a temporarily unprepared army. Today we have peace-marchers, peace-meditators and Lord Haw Haws of the present Cabinet calling for appeasement from Lipton Roundabout. At Least, the real Lord Haw Haw had the courage of his conviction to reside among the Nazis and broadcast his appeasement appeals to the beleaguered British over the radio. Our Sinhala Lord Haw Haws have no such convictions nor the gumption to reside among the LTTE in the Wanni, where they really belong. They are bent on destroying the morale of the army and preventing further recruitment to the army. In any other country, such despicable men would be locked up for spreading disaffection both within as well as against the army.

More than anyone, it is the soldier at the warfront who wants peace. This much maligned patriot had been invested with all sorts of motives for joining the army, except his love for his country, by peaceniks. All such theoreticians of peace brigade have forgotten the elementary fact that these soldiers are physically at the warfront quite ready to die for the country. The peace they want is not appeasement and a new prolonged war. They are indeed fighting for a durable peace sans terrorism in the country.

The country expects them to do their duty by supporting them in their arduous task. These soldiers and their supporters are not warmongers. They are fighting a ruthless enemy for lasting peace. The Lipton-Circus army morale busters are certainly making our soldiers pawns in the hands of LTTE terrorists. These fly-by-night Lipton Circus demonstrators are the real enemies of peace.

Any peace settlement, for it to be durable and lasting, should be based on justice. Justice is the first virtue of political life. Notwithstanding the many and varied conception of justice, I would like to contextualize three of them to our proposed peace settlement. The first notion of justice comes down from Aristotle via Cicero, St. Augustine and St. Thomas Aquinas. "Justice is what is rightly owed to another either in accordance to natural law or positive law. Distributive justice requires that each person receives his due in respect of his status, office and function and how well he fills it and so contributes to the good of all. Commutative justice is satisfied when restitution is made, so far as is possible, for wrong done, and when penalties for wrongdoing proportional to offences are administered" (Alasdaire Macintyre). The other two notions spring from the current liberal philosophy of egalitarianism, where the modern society is, at least in surface appearance, a collection of strangers each pursuing his/her own interests under minimal constraints, and where prestige, status, power and money matters. "All social primary goods liberty, opportunity, income and wealth, the bases of self-respect are to be distributed equally unless an unequal distribution of any or all of these goods is to the advantage of the least favoured" (Rawls, A Theory of Justice). This is the principle of equality of needs. The third conception of justice maintains that only if you have justly acquired anything, only then, you are entitled to hold it and appropriate it for your use. "The complete principle of distributive justice would say simply that a distribution is just, if everyone is entitled to the holdings they possess under the distribution" (Nozick, Anarchy State and Utopia). In short, the last is the principle of equality with respect to entitlement.

Leaving aside the details, the two main provisions of the PA Package are contrary to the notions of justice stated above. The Proposal hands over nearly 30% of landmass, and 60% of seacoast with all the food and other resources therein; and then also the exercise of veto power over the sovereign actions of the central government (Package, 3,2ab) to a mere 6% of the people is totally unjust, no matter which conception of justice one applies. Hegel's advice is appropriate here. According to him "the guarantee of a constitution lies rather in the indwelling spirit and history of the nation by which constitutions have been made and are made" (Constitution of Germany, Preface). Thus all those who project the Package as a panacea for peace are sadly mistaken. They are the advocates of greater cataclysms to come. They are the true enemies of peace.

[The LTTE have on various occasions admitted that half of Tamil population has left the areas of conflict. This has been indirectly corroborated by the ICRC in the number of persons to whom their aid has been projected and provided. This is how the 6% figure has been arrived at. This is probably an over estimate.]

The many compromises the country has made yet need acknowledgment by the minority Tamil community as well as by its leaders. The Tamil language has parity of status with the Sinhala language. The practical difficulties of implementation would not be solved by the division of the country. It needs more recruits with knowledge of both Sinhala and Tamil. In any case, do we have Sinhala throughout the country's administration, commerce and industry? The method of admission to universities has been changed. For this purpose, Jaffna is today a disadvantaged district with added weights for its students. Not long ago the Jaffna-man cried foul at this disadvantaged district system. The allocation of land on major irrigation schemes are today based on the population profile as agreed by the Tamil political parties. Yet, on all the above, the Tamil politicians keep vilifying the majority community with the shrill cry of discrimination. There is no respite here for the majority community. Justice is the beacon they should rigorously follow, so that we and everyone else would be able to pursue our ends, whatever they are, within a framework which provides peace, order and stability in the transactions and exchanges of social reciprocity.

25

The Oppressed Sinhala Majority

(The Island, 21st July 99)

It is lamentable that the Sri Lankan polity is badly divided on racial lines. Recognizing the regrettable reality does not tantamount to acceptance. Nevertheless, it is also a reality that the Sinhala people are a majority in this country, and today subject to many vicissitudes, to the amelioration of which, I expect to submit my suggestions below.

The systemic oppression of the Sinhala people started with the British after 1815. The British expropriated Kandyan Sinhala lands and laid waste many acres of farmland and burnt down numerous homesteads. They literally starved the Kandyan Sinhalese into submission both in 1817/18 and 1848. They planted foreign labourers in Kandyan lands. They demonized the Buddhist religion. They reduced the Kandyan hierarchy to paid servants of the British. They looked down on the Kandyan Sinhalese as primitive savages and degenerate demon worshippers and executed many Kandyans for opposing British oppression. They insulted the Buddhist clergy as "artful dissemblers and conspirators". The Kandyans did demand justice for all those depravities committed on them. The colonial British government rejected their petitions with contempt. Today I still do demand an apology as well as compensation, and will continue to do so, no matter the shameful conspiracy of silence on this issue by the Kandyan Sinhala politicians.

After independence the oppression of the Sinhala majority started with the bifurcation of the Sinhala electorate by the United National Party (UNP) and the Sri Lanka Freedom Party (SLFP). Today this Sinhala majority is further fractionalized among numerous political parties. The PA Package has proposed fractionalization on a territorial and ethnic basis. This is, in fact, an oppression of the majority by emasculating it and by making it vulnerable. In the process the Sinhala community has been deprived of its authority of its majority status. Many are the consequences of this impotent imbecility.

In order to win and maintain themselves in power, the main political parties have, in recent times, more or less abandoned national interests and concentrated on partisan interests. The national interests loudly proclaimed at the hustings remained a rhetorical exercise in public propaganda. The government of the day is more concerned about pandering exclusively to the greed of its supporters, by providing them with opportunities to enrich themselves. Thus we have the culture of plunder of Treasury and other valuable assets of the state. As the country suffered due to this spoliation, so did the majority to a greater extent. Yet the majority Sinhalese is usually blamed as pursuing majoritarianism and chauvinism. This is a lie uttered frequently to harass and deplete further the morale of the Sinhalese.

Seeds of division among the Sinhalese are also sown both by Christian Sinhalese and Buddhist Sinhalese zealots. Conversion to Christianity by proffering economic inducements by some fringe Christian Organizations is unacceptable by the very tenets of Christianity. This odious practice stands condemned and should be stopped. Even though some Catholics and Christians have fallen prey to these inducements, yet this unholy method of conversion to "born-again-Christianity" is destructively divisive, and has led to suspicion and uneasy relationship between the Christian and Buddhist Sinhalese. It is also alleged, that many poverty-stricken rural Sinhala women are promised a better life by marriage partners of the Muslim community. After marriage, the women are compelled to accept the religion of the partner, the dress code and other social practices of that religion. In this case, the women as well as their children lose their Sinhala identity. This allegation, if true, is also harassment, and stands condemned.

There are also some Buddhist Sinhalese who still live in the Portuguese era of our country. They are prone to attack and blame the Christians for almost everything that is degenerate in this country. To them globalization and the consequent Westernization are part of the Christian conspiracy. Christians, as a body, are also mistakenly and unfairly perceived to be supporters of separatism in our country. It is true that there are some among the Catholic/Christian clergy and laity who support separatism. Those individuals, whether Christians or Buddhists, should be exposed and pilloried for their treachery. For that matter, there are also a whole lot of Leftist Sinhala Buddhists who also support separatism of some sort. One cannot blame Christianity for this misguided position taken by individuals. At the same time it is opportune to point out that there are thousands of Sinhala Catholic/ Christian servicemen/ women in the frontline enduring deprivation, losing their limbs and their lives while fighting for their country. They stand side by side with their brother Buddhist soldiers ready for the supreme sacrifice. Their service to the country is incomparable; gratitude, homage and appreciation are due to them. Their unison in the battlefield is a magnificent example for us to follow in civil society to wield together a united, coherent and articulate Sinhala society.

Recently there has emerged a mix bag of Western and Sri Lankan academics/journalists. They appear to have concocted an intellectual incestuous and clannish relationship to rubbish Sinhala majority, its history, its traditions and its religious practices. The Heideggerian phenomenological method they have adopted is reduction, construction and contrived construction of our history, customs and traditions. This is what they call "pack journalism" in America. As Kamalika Peiris has pointed out in many of her articles in The Island newspaper, they quote and cite one another forging a uniform point of view as if what they and their companions have written were indisputable facts. This too is oppression of majority, because it is aimed at debilitating the majority by attempting to demonstrate that the Sinhalese are rootless nobodies undeserving of the country they inhabit. Their drapery of such invented concepts so prolifically displayed in their books and monograms only serve as a cloak for the concealed propaganda for separatists in our country.

There is no quarrel with most NGOs in our country engaged in praiseworthy activities trying to improve the living conditions of our people. Among them are a few political NGOs, who appear to work in cahoots with the above mentioned academics and some journalists.

They organize seminars and conferences in this country as well as abroad. The end objective of their parleys invariably leads to passing resolutions dictating to the majority community how it should conduct its affairs. This is usually an exercise to intimidate the majority by propaganda and publicity. While they are allowed to exercise their freedom of expression, the majority should be resolved not to be cajoled by these five-star-hotel resolutions.

There are the minority political parties. They openly pursue partisan racial politics. They even proclaim themselves to be "king makers". They hold the balance of power in the government due to the fractionalization of the majority. They are the main exploiters and extortionists of the Sinhala majority. They assert their strategic position by making unreasonable economic and political demands. These are often granted by the main political parties in order to remain in power. Some of the members of these parties are more equal than the rest in the community at large. Their diktats prevail in their fiefdoms. Any police officer not complying with them would be soon bundled out of their domain. Such is the power these puny men have arrogated to themselves due to the imbecility of the majority community.

From 1983 onwards the Sinhala majority has substantially lost its status and freedom. It has been subject to terrorist attacks all over the country, the latest in May this year in Kokilai and Padaviya. Even its sacred precincts have been desecrated. Colombo alone was subjected to 21 bomb attacks so far killing over 600 and maiming thousands. The infra structure instruments of economic progress, such as fuel, electricity, telephone and transport have been under siege since 1983. The North of the country is forbidden area for any Sinhalese to settle down. Going by recent events in the hill country, a creeping "no-go" area in Nuwara Eliya is being imposed on the Sinhalese by a partisan minority political party. They even had the gumption to dictate to the government, that it take action to deny to the Sinhalese equality before law, by preventing the Sinhalese from carrying out propaganda activities against LTTE. This is notwithstanding the fact that the government had declared the LTTE a murderous terrorist outfit.

It would be a long haul to restore the Sinhala majority to its rightful place in this country. The main obstacles are the two main political parties. My suggestion would bypass both these parties by including members from both parties. I suggest that we the Sinhala majority form a grass root Solidarity Movement (SM) with no immediate political ambition. It should be open to all Sinhalese no matter their religious faiths or their political creed. It should be established in every town to act as a pressure group to challenge as well as to take legal action against any act or omission by anyone, detrimental to the majority community. The SM should affirm solidarity with our security forces fighting the LTTE so that a terrorist free peace is established in this country.

Ideally an ex-security service officer, with no political hang-ups would fit the bill as the leader of this movement. He would have had the experience of working under very difficult circumstances, and moulding together men of varied faiths and attitudes to fight as one unit for this country. This is the dedication and leadership one would require for this worthy task. There certainly would be monumental organizational problems along the way. Many political ego trippers would also pose problems.

However, certain fundamentals need to be restated and re-contextualised not only for the guidance of the majority but also for allaying any fears in the minds of the minorities. This is the firm commitment of the SM to democracy and rule of law. Political equality, equality of opportunity for those similarly endowed and motivated, together with constitutional guarantees of other fundamental freedoms do legitimize majority rule without victimizing anyone. In the present context of the Package and the intransigence on Thimpu aspirations, it is also important to state clearly that there is only one border in this country and that is the sea surrounding this country. As Rousseau has pointed out the sovereignty of the people is inalienable and therefore indivisible. Like in the post devolution Britain, sovereignty should remain solidly and firmly in the hands of the elected parliament, and not divided as in the Package, among the Parliament, the Regional Councils and the People at a Referendum (Ch3.a). The SM should also take the lead in agitating for a completely independent judiciary, police force, bureaucracy and freedom of the press and electronic media.

As the SM gathers momentum, it is bound to be listened to by the powers that be, because by then, it would have encompassed within it the vast majority of the Sinhala people. It will then be the opportune moment to enter the political arena. The SM will have the opportunity to put into practice, at least in this small country of ours, the Fifth Proposition of Emmanuel Kant , namely, "the highest problem of human species, to the solution of which it is irresistibly urged by natural impulses, is the establishment of a universal civil society founded on political justice" (Idea of Universal History).

Majority rule is the best available way of ensuring just and effective legislation. It is true that the majority will not always be right nor the majority will always enact just laws. This is why one assents to effective constitutional constraints of independent judiciary (balance of power), on top of political equality before law of every citizen. So long as the liberal democratic principles are in place, the majority rule would lead to a contented majority without victimizing the minority. It is also true that a contented majority will be good news for the minority which depends on that majority. Then, perhaps, we shall have every reason to join Stanley Senior to sing:

"But most shall he sing of Lanka
In the brave new days that come,
When the races all have blended
And the voice of strife is dumb;
When we leap to a single bugle,
March to a single drum".

26

The Aspirations of Sinhala Society

(The Island, 12th Jan. 2000)

On examination of general pattern of votes cast in the recent election, it is quite plausible to assume, that a second term in office for the President, was given her mainly by Sinhala voters. It is indeed odious to classify people of a country on a divisive basis. The present real politick in Sri Lanka is, however embedded in racial divisions, and racial terrorism stalks the country. The intransigent objective pursued by a minority is the establishment of a racially homogenous separatist Eelam within Sri Lanka. Given this tragic situation, it is imperative for the majority Sinhala community to take the predominant role to unify our people, and persuade them to accept the fact that we are all Sri Lankans, and that alone is our one and only identity that matters above all else.

Over two millennia of existence, the Sinhala society has been tied to just one place, Sri Lanka. The individuals in this society had been assigned to them various institutionalized roles to play in this society. No matter the deconstructionist/ reductionist historians, it remains a fact that the Sinhala society did have for over two millennia, a territorial organization, institutional structures and an unbroken continuity until the arrival of the colonialist British, whose imperialism imposed the discontinuity in our serendipitous existence. The British colonialist William Knighton captured the enormous significance of the Kandyan Convention of 1815 in poignant words thus, "from this day we date the extinction of Sinhalese independence, an independence which had continued without material interruption for 2357 years". It is this rudely interrupted independence, we now have to carry forward into this new millennium, while taking into account that the world, and Sri Lanka within it, had changed beyond recognition since 1815.

A society is said to "consist of individuals living in an organized community that controls a particular territory; the organization of such a community is provided by institutions political and religious that serve to define the status occupied by different individuals and ascribe to them the roles they are expected to play in perpetuating the continuing existence of that community" (Mandelbaum). This modern definition fits well the Sinhala society, such as, territorial occupation, political, social and religious organizations and their durability over a long period of time.

The culture of this society covers "all of the achievements stemming from social creations and implicated in individual use that are transmitted by a tradition: language, techniques, arts, philosophical or religious attitudes and beliefs, in so far as these diverse functions are included in the social heritage of the various individuals living within a particular society" (Ricoeur). Generation after generation, in varying degrees of consciousness, and at times, at enormous sacrifices of lives, limbs and possessions, the Sinhala society had exhibited its participatory belonging on numerous historical occasions. The sedimentation of all these over the ages had bestowed on us the claim to an identifiable Sinhala civilization. As Braudel had pointed out "a civilization exists fundamentally in a geographical area which had been structured by men and history. That is why there are cultural frontiers and cultural zones of amazing permanence: all the cross fertilization in the world will not alter them, their foundations remain. They are not indestructible, but they are many times more solid than one might imagine. They have withstood a thousand supposed deaths, their massive bulks unmoved by the monotonous pounding of the centuries". Thus the Sinhala society and the Sinhala civilization were born of the soil and grown on the soil of Sri Lanka. Therefore it is natural, factual and logical to consider Sri Lanka as the country of the Sinhala society.

The first aspiration of the Sinhala society is, therefore, the perpetuation of itself in the land of their forefathers, in a manner attuned to the exigencies of the modern age. As Burke had pointed out, "people will not look forward to posterity who never looked backward to their ancestors". As a society one ignores one's roots at great peril to future generations.

This does not prevent the non-Sinhalese from claiming Sri Lanka as their country too. In fact this is what they should do. After all, the minority populace does accept this to be their country and home in their daily life, and in their jobs and professions. All the people born and bred in this country should be just Sri Lankans, no less, no more. We do have problems only because some minorities do want racial, and some others religion based exclusive "compartments" of their own, in addition to the claim to live as equals among the Sinhala population everywhere else in the country. So long as this mindset remains unaltered, the problem will remain unresolved.

The second aspiration is the purification of our society in line with the ethical norms widely accepted the world over. This cleansing should start with our politicians, because those who make laws for others should also keep and obey the laws. The calibre of our politicians has sunk to very low levels. Most of them are not even mediocrities. Their main concern is their salaries, perks, commissions and their slavish attachments to law-breakers and thugs. They have also encroached on the public sector, and have driven it into near paralysis, where the dictum appears to be; obey the politician or have your career ruined. How else could one explain the list of police officers for punitive transfers, allegedly compiled by a Cabinet Minister, on the ground, that those officers did not support the government in the recent election? If this allegation is true, that particular politician has openly displayed his sub-mediocre understanding of democracy, because even a mediocre politician would have realized that the policeman's duty is to impartially enforce the law as it stands, and not support this or that political party. The politicians' effrontery to legal processes and their deluded assumption that they are above the law, need to be yanked out of their system. Perhaps it is time that their oath consisting exclusively of their duties should be made to be taken, in all solemnity, in public before the electorate. The politicians have rights and perks only because they have duties to perform. It is also opportune that we have a fast-track Accountability Court fully equipped by a cadre of untouchable (by politicians) officers with investigative as well as enforcement powers as in Pakistan today.

When the present democracy, as administered by current politicians, fails to command the respect of the majority Sinhala society, is it any wonder that some minority communities have decided to opt out of this decaying, decadent and downgraded system of government? So the white-hot reformation needs to begin with our politicians.

The third aspiration is that the Sinhala progeny does have an up-to-date education with the relevant cultural and religious baggage enhancing human dignity and freedom. One does not want them to be, as Spengler has noted, the new nomads of cosmopolis, recognizing no past and possessing no future. "The new sort of nomads, cohering unstably in fluid masses, the parasitical city dweller, traditionless, utterly matter-of–fact, without religion, clever, unfruitful contemptuous of countrymen". Or in modern parlance, the custom-built morons one frequently comes across in the lobbies of Colombo hotels.

One expects an education that would equip the young minds to acquire the knowledge and skills necessary to earn their keep, pay their way in this highly competitive world, which is still tilted towards the rich and developed nations of the globe. The alleviation of poverty of the majority of our people, and the protection of the vulnerable old and the young are objectives nurtured over centuries in our land. The progress of these programmes is part of this aspiration.

The continued existence of this country as an undivided (unitary) nation is the fourth aspiration of this Sinhala society. Devolution of power does not necessarily stop the drift to separatism as is evident in the cases of few well-known examples. In Britain the Scottish Nationals did not want devolution and did campaign for independence during the May elections in 1999. The Basque separatists are not satisfied with their asymmetrical devolution of power in Spain. They did recently announce that they have espoused violent means to attain their independence. In Canada, the Quebecers are not satisfied with their enhanced statehood of the Quebec state and the Official Language status of the French language. They too want independence from the rest of Canada and have resolved to conduct another Referendum this year. In Chittagong the devolved powers are far from comprehensive, and in no way compromise the sovereignty and unitary character of Bangladesh. The troubles there too have not abated. In Ireland, the achievements of the peace process have been remarkable. The progress here is not towards separatism, but towards a united Ireland. The present Irish Prime Minister has voiced his optimism on a united Ireland in tune with the poll results to the same effect (The Island, 4th Jan. 2000). Thus devolution might appear as an attractive expedient, nevertheless, it also has the potential to usher in more problems than one bargained for in the long run. Therefore utmost care and thought are needed. In addition, it should also be tested to breaking-point with "what if" suppositions, situations and scenarios. After all, there will always be persons who will want to test any new system to breaking-point.

The final aspiration is lasting peace in our country. This peace, in Marxian lingo, "must nestle everywhere, settle everywhere, establish connections everywhere". This peace cannot be attained by appeasement of terrorism. It cannot be attained by the division of the country. Nor will peace prevail when exclusive racial enclaves become a reality. This peace should be built on the solid foundations of democratic values of supremacy of law, equality and freedom of its citizens. It should be preserved and protected by accountable and transparent institutions manned by men of proven probity, who would enforce the law without fear or favour.

The many years of armed conflict had not been successful because our military campaigns had also become political campaigns. On numerous occasions, the leading military personnel had been those judged incompetent by their peers, and able and willing military leaders have been sidelined and shunted away from the frontlines. Further, the governments in power had not sincerely pursued the military option with an unflagging zest, well-thought plans and resolute determination to win. Today, this is evident from the many Cabinet Ministers who parade about the streets of Colombo, calling for peace through appeasement of LTTE terrorists. Like leeches, they suck dry the already flagging morale of our men in the frontlines.

However, on the 24th of Dec 1999, the President enunciated the most relevant, requisite and appropriate path to peace when she said that "those who inflict such wounds can no longer be allowed to go unchecked or unpunished. The days of terror in this land are numbered, and that number is small". The Daily News had it in blazing banner headlines "The President vows to crush terror, achieve peace". (Alas this did not happen under her presidency). There is no doubt in my mind that the Sinhala society which voted her to power, as against her opponent who wanted peace-talks with LTTE, would support her all the way to achieve this objective, which by itself, is the consummate solution to the terrorist problem and the restoration of lasting peace in the country.

27

The Rule of the Majority

(The Island, 2nd Mar. 2000)

Government by the majority is the prevailing rule wherever democracy prevails. All true democrats accept it. This hallowed practice is otiose in Sri Lanka. It is condemned as majoritarian chauvinism. Yet, its detractors, in their own organizations and committees, do accept majority verdict on their policies and plans and act on such verdicts. Their hypocrisy pursues an insidious plan to emasculate the already fractured and fragmented Sinhala majority. Their end-objective is to shackle it with various manacles in the form of redundant and expensive government structures. Once the majority is thus chained to the Procrustian bed of oppressive suppression, the vivisection of Sri Lanka could proceed piecemeal, and the vultures could then feast over the carcass of the erstwhile undivided and sovereign Sri Lanka. As pointed out by Mr. S.L. Gunasekera, (The Sunday Island, 30th Jan. 2000) once this happens, there will not be any going back. We would have lost our country for good.

One Guru in the constitution-writing industry has already pronounced that a "constitution is essentially a counter-majoritarian document. Protection of the majority is unnecessary and superfluous". Such befuddled wiseacres do ceaselessly labour to produce oftentimes an absurd little mouse (parturient montes, nascetur ridiculus mus). It is in this hostile milieu, that the Sinhala people have to fight for their country, if not, "well then they have to disappear" (dann sol les verschwinden). A necrophilous minority is today already engaged in this demolition work.

The pristine Sinhala Buddhist civilization did contain many salutary ways of good governance and social organization, even though it was caste-bound, full of intrigues at court, and had to fight off many invaders from India and Europe. Our forefathers had technical knowledge and skill to undertake and complete vast projects. They did not go cap-in-hand looking for foreign aid. It was an integrated and inclusive society where ethnicity mattered little. Whenever ethnicity became the catalyst, as pursued by some invaders, then we had misery, suffering and destructive conflicts. Some kings were ethnically different from the Sinhala population, but they made it their primary duty to integrate fully with the society, its norms, customs, traditions and religion. Our ancient civilization was not one based on death and tombs as in Egypt and China. It was a society, though based on Status (not yet on social contract of Descartes and Lock), yet it gave first place to the prosperity of the people by the protection and promotion of irrigation works. The predominantly prevailing Buddhist attitude "to nature was not the conquest of nature by the mastery of her secrets, but the conquest of nature through mastery of self" (Dr.Ariyapala, Society in Mediaeval Ceylon). Who prevented the development and progress of this integrated society? Long before our independence, there were many Tamil politicians who insisted on special consideration for their ethnicity. They were the modern equivalents of the invader Magha of Kalinga (1214-1235 AD), and those Tamil politicians were responsible for the current deaths and destruction of the people, and the ethnic division of the country. The power-hungry Sinhala politicians are also responsible, to the extent, that they ignored lessons of our history, and created the ambience for the racist Tamil politicians to thrive and pursue their outlandish adventure.

It is true that there are no rules or fundamental principles for establishing the rule of the majority. It is based on sheer expediency, practicality and the absence of any other effective way of arranging our affairs in a democracy. It does involve a subtle form of coercion where the minority submits to, as well as voluntary accepts majority rule. The very fact of contesting elections already presupposes the acceptance of majority verdict. Therefore all minorities, whether they be the political parties that lost the election, an ethnic or religious minority, need to accept majority rule. Otherwise democracy is impracticable, law and freedom will vanish and anarchy will prevail.

This does not give the majority the license to do anything and everything ignoring the minorities in their midst. The ideology of justice should pervade all social and political institutions, acting as the glue binding all the people to the country. All political institutions, the judiciary, the police and the bureaucracy should be permeated with sincerity of purpose, transparent in their actions and be imbued with the ideals of the primacy of the law of the land. This requires the freedom of the individual, of associations and of the press and of the electronic media. Any one, or all of these institutions should be able to project the searchlight of transparency on corruption and inequitable practices, and bring to book the plunderers of state treasury and the saboteurs of democracy.

Unfortunately, what we have in Sri Lanka are questionable election procedures and a sham democracy. Since our independence, our country has been ruled by a minority of political elites. Most politicians have become, in the words of Machiavelli, "ungrateful, wanton, false and dissimulating, cowardly and greedy, arrogant and mean, their natural impulse is to be insolent when affairs are prospering and abjectly servile when adversity hits them". Such men care little for liberty, which is placed well below their security, their prosperity and even their desire for revenge. These political bandits are formidable obstacles to equitable economic development, and consensus on solutions to vital issues affecting the country. The sham democracy they practice has become unacceptable to both the majority and the minority people of this country. No amount of elegant constitutional provisions will solve this problem.

A thorough political clearing is urgently required. This must emanate from the political parties. Otherwise, our society will not go anywhere. For long our Sinhala society has been dragged along the cartwheel of scandalous politicking. This has eroded our traditions, our common values and genuine social ties with others. On a social level, the Sinhalaya is isolated and lonely, even though part of the crowd. He is led by empty promises of politicians and slogans from the media. He is held together by cash nexus. Emile Durkheim's phenomenon of anomie (the destruction of traditional social bonds and subjugation to the state), is evident everywhere. This anomie is at the root of our degradation and accounts for much of the socially disruptive evils, such as suicides and murders.

This sad state of affairs is further enhanced by the market economy. "To exist in a market economy is to live out a double tragedy, beginning in inadequacy and ending in depression" (M.D.Sahlins). Acquisitiveness, competitiveness and selfishness are the norms in a market oriented society. This modern man today has become a routinized, stereotyped and an unspontaneous moron under the sway of political demagogues. This ready-made pattern only pretends to give meaning to man's life. The deep existential needs of man, such as need for relatedness, the need for unity, the need for effectiveness, and the need for stimulation remains unsatisfied. Instead he turns to hero-worshipping the politician, drunkenness, drug-addiction, masochistic destructiveness and the greedy pursuit of ever changing pleasures. This state of affairs cannot be simply changed by a new constitution, nor can it be changed by legislating for morality in society. It requires exemplary behavior by the leaders and their constancy to live by the law of the land, and to enforce the law of the land without fear or favour.

Racism, cunningly camouflaged as grievances, was first hoisted on the nation by the minority Tamil politicians. When this was exposed, they graduated to aspirations and confederation. The impatient Tamils youth formed the LTTE. They took up the gun and resorted to terrorism and separatism. Now the LTTE has escalated it to sado-masochism and group necrophilia.

Erich Fromm in his book (The Anatomy of Human Destructiveness) defined necrophilia as "the passionate attraction to all that is dead, decayed, putrid, sickly; it is the passion to transform that which is alive into something unalive, to destroy for the sake of destruction. It is the passion to tear apart living structures". Necrohpliacs that they are, the LTTE is now engaged in an attempt to transform all that is alive to dead matter, they want to destroy everything and everybody, often themselves. Their enemy is life itself. Such men have lost their sense of humanness and their reasoning powers. They believe only in their leader, his thoughts, his plans, and his wishes. The world is real only as far as it is the object of the leader's schemes and desires. For every step towards the satisfaction of their narcissism many hecatombs had to die. This malignant aggression is moribund from within itself. Yet the suffering, fear and wanton destruction they perpetrate on the civilian population is ruthless. This cancer in our society needs sturdy surgical procedures. Elegant constitutional provisions concocted by politicians matter little to these men. They will continue their depredations until they are defeated on their own terms. Peaceniks and appeasement will not stop their murdering and butchering the ordinary civilians all over the country.

Those constitution-making medicine men should remember that when they enforce their fantastic ideas on the whole body-politic, they may succeed for a short time, but this triumph remains ephemeral, unless they took into account the logic of the social world. Montesquieu epitomized this logic. He pointed out that the laws "should be adapted to the people, to the way of life of the people, to the religion of the inhabitants, to their dispositions, to their habits and manners". Any Constitution that ignores the paramount interests of the majority population of the country would not promote harmony within the nation. It is not necessary to abandon the unity of our nation, and the salutary lessons of our history to march forward to progress in the present-day global economy, and in our fight against centrifugal forces in our country.

28 - A

SELF-DETERMINATION IS SEPARATISM

(The Island, 24th Apr.2000)

Foreign scholars seem to be fond of prescribing ready-made solutions for the terrorist problem in this country. However, they do not conceive it a terrorist problem, even when gun battles rage before their very eyes in the heart of the civilian city of Colombo and many are being killed. Earlier there was one Dr. Spencer, preaching to us that what the Tamils seek is simply recognition. Then we had Dr.Ignatieff. He asserted that "this is an elementary point, but it needs to be said again and again: self-determination for minorities does not have to mean separation or separatism. It means recognition of that community as a political actor. It does not mean giving them some enormous portion of your real estate, [it does mean] giving them power to educate their children and teach their languages and reproduce what is fundamental to their collective existence" (Daily News, 20th Mar.2000). The Daily News in the editorial of the 23rd Mar. sheepishly parroted the same message. This provocative statement was one among the many jewels of doubtful wisdom pronounced at the BMICH on the 19th of Mar. It invites investigation and comment by others, equally liberal in outlook, but do not agree with the Canadian scholar and consider his stance untenable.

What exactly does self-determination in politics mean? Equally important, what does it mean in the context of Thimpu aspirations of Tamils, narco-terrorism, ubiquitous suicide terrorism, virulent ethno-nationalism based on fabricated 'homeland' history, and intensive armed conflict in the north and east of our country between the legitimate armed forces of the country and the terrorist LTTE?

In this presently prevailing context, self-determination is simply a proclamation that the Sri Lankan Tamils are a sovereign nation living in a separate territory of their own, having their own independent government and possessing the power to designate its citizens. Simultaneously such a nation would seek recognition from other nations of the world. All it needs is recognition by one other nation, and we would have a stalemate like in Cyprus, where the northern Cyprus is recognized as an independent nation by Turkey. If this not separatism, what is? Is this the recognition the two speakers above advocated with respect to the Tamils in Sri Lanka? The other Thimpu conditions already embrace what I have spelt out above.

Dr.Ignatieff distinguishes between individual and collective self-determination, and favours individual self-determination, which he equates with liberty of individuals; "the freedom of individuals to speak and act, not the collective freedom of some community, manipulated and directed by a single tyrannous leader".

I would like to suggest, that the individual freedom he opted for, already exists in ample measure in Sri Lanka, even under the dire conditions of suicide terrorism. The Tamil language has equal constitutional recognition with Sinhala language. Today Sinhala children are forced to study Tamil in the futile hope that it will appease the terrorist LTTE. The LTTE on the other hand simply do not allow Sinhala in the territory under their control. I do admit that successive governments have failed to implement the provisions of the Act making Tamil an official language of this country.

What is certainly lacking here is the practical application of a Tamil language policy. One does not need to divide the country for this. Recruitment of sufficient translators will solve this problem. Another avenue would be to require proficiency in the three languages from all those who seek higher positions in government service, and from those public servants who come in contact with the public on a daily basis.

As for the rest, we do have Tamil schools in plenty in this country. We do have universities where Tamils and their Tamil language predominate. We do have Tamil streams in other universities too. We do have numerous Hindu festivals celebrated as public events, almost one a month in my town Negombo. We do have Tamil socials and literary events and popular Tamil musical events. We do have Tamil radio, Tamil TV, theatrical and popular dances such as Arrangethrams. If one looks at any leading commercial/industrial entity in this country, one will find at least two Tamil executive directors on the Board of that company. Take any profession, law to medicine, accountancy to engineering, one will find plenty of Tamils recognized as leaders and specialists peacefully and profitably pursuing their professions among the Sinhalese and others. Thus we do have individual freedom, and as advocated by Dr.Ignatieff, the "power [to the Tamils] to educate their children, teach their language, and reproduce what is fundamental to their collective existence". Thus it is completely incorrect to maintain that the Sinhalaya has failed to give due recognition to the Tamils. On the contrary, the Tamils as well the visiting foreign scholars, have woefully failed to recognize as well as acknowledge the prevailing reality in this country. In fact Tamils in this country enjoy more rights than as minorities than in many other parts of the world they have emigrated to. In this area of freedom can anything more be done? Please specify.

It is also untrue to maintain that the Sri Lankan state is "owned by a particular community", that is, the Sinhala community. The fact is that the Sinhala community is badly divided and fragmented. It has no sole representative or spokesperson. There are many in the Sinhala society, who lament, that their interests are totally ignored by the state today, except at times of elections as a rhetorical exercise. The needs of the original Sinhala community of the hill country are one among the many Sinhala grievances neglected by the state. Above all the present government is an amalgam of several minority political parties. It therefore is properly "owned by all communities" as Dr. Ignatieff would like to see. Further under the present constitution, in the past as well as at present, the major Sinhala parties have depended on minority parties to get control of government. Majoritarian chauvinism is a canard perpetrated by LTTE propagandists and sympathizers. If the state had been owned by the Sinhala community, then there would not have arisen the need for a Sinhala Commission, nor the current disagreements between the government and the Buddhist clergy on the terrorist problem in our country.

What is at stake is indeed collective self-determination for separatism and the forced acquisition of vast real estate at gunpoint by the LTTE. This as Dr. Ignatieff asserted is a "recipe for a single-party dictatorship. The means they (LTTE) employ have betrayed the ends". This indeed is the reason why Eelam cannot be allowed.

Constitution making and constitution revising as in Canada would not solve the problem either. The Quebecers there have opted for separatism and sovereignty of the state of Quebec. They do want to get there by Referendum rather than by the bullet. The fact in this instance is that a collective self-determination will be used to effect a political separation. Constitution making and its revision also took place in Spain. A section of the Basque people remains not satisfied. They have taken to terrorism to effect a separation and obtain sovereignty for Basque territory. In the Phillipines too some constitutional settlement was effected to solve the separatist demand of the Mindanoans. Today they still have terrorism and the demand for separatism via a Referendum. Metrivica in former Yugoslavia is what we shall have in Padawiya in Sri Lanka, if a constitutional settlement is made with LTTE. There the Serbs are daily butchered by the Kosovars in an effort to chase away all the Serbs and claim more real estate for Kosovo. The same butchering of Sinhalese is already taking place and will intensify in and around Pdawiya and Trincomalee.

Thus one comes to the inevitable conclusion that we do have a virulent terrorist problem and it needs to be fought on its terms and defeated wholesale militarily first. This military victory cannot "turn to ashes" as the majority of the Tamil community already live in the south among the Sinhalese, and do have the right to live the way they want, wherever they want and pursue whatever avocations they fancy. The military victory would entail only the defeat of the LTTE and their murderous policies, which spared neither Tamils nor Sinhalese, nor even Dr. Tiruchelvam. It is the Sinhalese and the Muslims who do not have the freedom to live where they want in this country. They will be shot like stray dogs if they ventured anywhere beyond Vavunia.

It is probably true to claim that given the way the military campaign has been so far prosecuted a "military unification of the island is not possible". When we have Cabinet Ministers at street corners advocating appeasement, when we have daily TV propaganda frightening prospective recruits for the army, when we have politicians meddling with army campaigns, when we have failed yesterday's men at the top echelons of the security forces, when we have side-lined soldiers of proven ability, and removed them away from the frontline, how can we win against a ferociously Kamikazi enemy? We do need a real overhaul among the forces. We do need a single-minded determinism to finish the job, and a war council of professional men (both military and lay) to guide the forces to this end. Only then this military campaign would lead to success, and with it, the demand for self-determination by the Tamils will wither away. The last Presidential election demonstrated that the people are willing to finish this terrorism, yet the political leadership in the country has been found wanting.

We do have to welcome foreign scholars turning their high octane mind-power towards our problems. At the same time, we have to remind them, that we do expect them to be impartial, if they expect serious consideration of their views by the Sri Lankans. They also need to be reminded that there is also the point of view of the majority, no matter how badly fragmented the majority is. Finally, let me remind the readers of what Isaiah Berlin, the acknowledged academic Guru of Dr. Ignatieff had to say of minorities: "the tendency to idealization is most frequently found among those who belong to minorities.......They are liable to develop either exaggerated resentment of, or contempt for, the dominant majority, or else over-intense admiration or indeed worship for it, or, at times , a combination of the two, which leads both to unusual insights and---born of overwrought sensibilities---a neurotic distortion of facts" (Against the Current,p258). Amen.

28 - B

Self-Determination is Separatism

(The Island, 20th April 2000),

As the article on Minority Rights and Self-Determination by Mr.R.M.B. Senanayake (The Island, 19th Apr.) was a critical commentary on my article on the above subject, it warrants a short reply.

I am aware that some minions of the LTTE have floated the idea of Confederation. This pales into insignificant casuistry, because Pirapakaran himself has commanded his cohorts to shoot him, if he obtained any settlement less than separatist Eelam. Is this not self-determination for separatism?

There is no confusion in me as regards minority rights and self-determination. It was Dr.Ignatieff who equated the two. My endeavour was to point out that individual freedom, and now RMBS's rights extracted from Mr.Lawson's writings, exist in this country in ample measure.

Just look around at the census defying array of businesses ranging from jewelry-marts to Thosai boutiques run by Tamils. They speak volumes for the prevalence and actual exercise of minority rights and individual freedom. Look more sharply at the many customers who patronize those places of business. Most of them are Sinhalese. It therefore is a figment of your imagination that conjure up a Sinhala Majority "who continue to assert that they [the Tamils] must be subject to the cultural hegemony of the Sinhalese". Indeed could the Poosaris of the Sri Muthu Vinayagar temple, have recently held their magnificent Ther festival at Sea Street, Colombo, if they had no freedom, and if they were "subjected to the cultural hegemony of the Sinhalese?" I deplore this readiness to ignore the factual existence of minority rights and individual freedom in this country, even in the dire circumstances of omnipresent suicide terrorism.

Mr.RMBS is entitled to his opinion that what we have is a minority problem and not a terrorist problem. I do hope he will not be unfortunate enough to be caught up in one of those ubiquitous terrorist attacks in Colombo. No victims of such attacks have pronounced them to be fascinating, and splendid exercises of minority rights and individual freedom!

It is wrong to maintain that LTTE is invincible. Late Maj. Gen. Algama evicted them from the East. They were also chased out of Jaffna peninsula. They have assumed the aura of invincibility because, as pointed out, of the failure on the part of the government to pursue a properly conceived pure military strategy and because of the myths created by the LTTE's apologists.

I wonder which country in the world accepts "the validity of the Tamils taking to arms". How come then that the armed LTTE are banned by many nations that matter? If Norway is the world you have in mind, then the answer is that Norway is not equal to the world and that Norway is a partisan supporter of LTTE.

Finally no Sinhalese, in my view, denies minority rights nor acts to prevent the exercise of minority rights. This is patently evident from the many examples I cited in my article. What most Sinhalese are against is a racially homogenous exclusive Eelam in this country of ours. The self-determination the Tamil politicians are clamouring for is this separate country of their own. It would be a grand delusion to consider it otherwise.

29

The Sovereignty of Yakkos and Politicos

(The Island, 22nd Sept.2000)

The present and proposed (by PA) Constitutions do solemnly proclaim that the people are sovereign and that sovereignty resides in the people of Sri Lanka. This is a grand fiction as far as Sri Lanka is concerned. In reality, what we have is the sovereignty of the politicians and their Yakkos. The forthcoming election is a good opportunity to break-asunder this usurped strangle-hold on power by the politicians.

The sovereignty of the politicians starts with the election campaign. They flout almost all election laws with impunity. These laws were enacted by them and for them---for their benefit and lawful conduct of elections. Yet they completely disregard these laws. They pursue their felonious ways with immunity from any punishment. In short, they set themselves up as above law from the very start of their mercurial career in politics.

The motorcades, the processions, the life-size cut-outs and posters are simply political virility symbols. Their objective is the projection of the power (sovereignty) of one candidate upon other candidates and upon the public, and thereby to intimidate the voter to cast his/her vote for the politician concerned. Sometimes they are simply meant to intimidate the voter. This is patently clear when posters are plastered on private walls, which carry "no stickers" notices. In these instances, it would be quite clear to the politician, that the desecration of those walls would forfeit the votes of the owners of those walls. Yet he and his Yakkos carry on their despicable deeds regardless---just to project their arrogance on the public. There will be threats to person and property, if the owners of those walls dare to remove those posters.

The Yakkos are the retinue of goons and thugs in toe, and the financiers of those politicians. They too assume themselves to be above the law.

They are the foot soldiers prepared to indulge in any activity both legal and illegal, at the bidding of their political master. Thus in the recent murders of a JVP youth in Kirulapone and another youth in Kegalle, it was alleged, that the identities of the criminals were notified to the police, yet their apprehension has not yet taken place. Those alleged criminals are a protected species. They have the protection of their sovereign political masters. It is therefore in their prime interest to ensure the success of their masters by hook or by crook.

The Yakko financiers are subtle and cunning in their ways. There are those who ply their illegal trades, such as smuggling, piracy, drug-dealing, running kassipu dens, prostitution and sex video parlours. These underworld denizens would primarily seek protection from various law-enforcing agencies, and the freedom to carry-on their proscribed trades. Other up-market "corporate" financiers would be after the plunder of the treasury by tax evasions and the resources of the country. They will be looking for state contracts at inflated prices. They will seek to manage, at exorbitant cost to the country, the means of distribution and supply of many state-sector goods and services. They will also seek to plant their minions---almost all of them unqualified, incompetent, inefficient and corrupt----at the top of almost every state as well as semi-state corporation. They will also seek control over the natural resources of the country at nominal cost to them, and then proceed to exploit those resources to the detriment of the country and leave behind misery for the locals and man-made environmental disasters. Recently we have also witnessed a spate of land grabbing by the Yakkos. In all these abuses, they remain protected by the sovereignty of their political masters.

Once elected to power these sovereign politicians subvert every law that hinders their pursuit towards bloated foreign bank accounts and conspicuous new mansions on prominent places. In the process they corrupt everyone connected with their enterprise along the way. What can the voter do to stop this degradation of democracy?

First we need to take into account the true meaning of the concept of "sovereignty of the people". A democratic society is a social union of social unions. The ultimate social union is arrived at by an implicit contract among citizens. "This act of association creates a collective body, receiving from this act its unity, its life and its will. This public person, so formed by the union of all other persons, takes the name of body politic. It is called a state when passive, sovereign when active, and power when compared with others like itself. Those who are associated in it take collectively the name of the people, and severally called citizens as sharing in the sovereign power, and subjects as being under the laws of the state" (The Social Contract by Rousseau). A society organized to define and enforce its laws is the sovereign. As a corporate body, it alone has the supreme political and coercive power. The MPs are only delegates. They are not demi-gods. They are accountable for their omissions and commissions to the society via the many institutions set up for that purpose.

A forceful parliamentary opposition, fearless judiciary an independent police force, a devoted and independent bureaucracy and a free and vigilant press and electronic media, are among the foremost of those democratic institutions that will make the MPs accountable for their actions, and constantly remind them that they are merely delegates appointed to carry out the wishes of the people.

The Courts of Law are the last bastions of defence against errant and arrogant politicians. Though many improvements can be made in the way judges are appointed, yet they have served the public well. Character assassination of judges, and challenges to their probity, sincerity and independence should be cast aside as malicious, especially when such unfounded accusations emanate from politicians. Such politicians should be in the blacklist of all voters. Further, all those politicians who have been found guilty of breaking the law of the land by the courts should be included in this blacklist. One should not vote for such individuals.

The Police are the first port of call of a citizen in trouble. It is their duty to enforce the law fairly and squarely on all citizens. Today, any brave police officer upholding the law has become the target of politicians. The politicians are attempting to make the Police Force their vassals, beholden to them, and doing their bidding. It is this power over the police that has made many a politico, a sovereign in his district. One should not vote for such politician.

Our educated Bureaucracy was once an admirable lot. Today the politicians have made them men of straw, and carriers of politician's portmanteaus and their umbrellas, and mere "yes-men" in their departments. Such abusive politicians should be voted out.

In a democracy the primary aim of the Constitution should be to bring about political and economic equality among its citizens. Sadly the two main political parties ignominiously failed in this overarching objective when they concocted the new Constitution. I am referring to Art.22 (6) of the proposed new Constitution by the PA. It says "Every child between the ages of five and fourteen years shall have access to free education provided by the State". Art.22 (7) does not tell us what then happens after age fourteen. From that age free education is not a fundamental right. The way is opened to do away with the current Sec.47 of the Education Ordinance which ensures free education in our schools. Free education is likely to stop at age fourteen. The child will then be condemned to the scrap-heap of uneducated and unskilled labour force. Or, the parents will have to pay for the education of their children. This enormous and unfair change will perpetuate inequality in society, and deny to nearly ninety percent of our children the benefits of free education. This odious aspect of intended legislation remains unexplained by its advocates.

Except for few exceptional prodigies, most children do not pass their GCE (O/L) by age fourteen. All parents therefore will have to pay to get their children over this first hurdle in their educational career. How many of them would be able to afford the going rate for such education to GCE (O/L), A/L and the University? This is a deliberate attempt to relegate a large section of our society to further degradation, and promote elitism among the rich. It denies the basic right of the child to education and opportunity to further his/her career, and become a useful and contributing member of the society. This attempted abolition of free education by the present beneficiaries of such free education would be an unmitigated disaster affecting generations to come. Such hypocrites do not deserve our votes. They want to keep a large section of the population ignorant, while their siblings grace the lofty portals of prestigious universities in the US and UK, mostly financed by ill-gotten booty obtained while ensconced in power.

How many pro-Package MPs have explained this sinister aspect of this new Constitutional Proposal? How many parents are really aware of this likely vast, adverse change in the education of their children? Well, take heed, they have aimed the hatchet at your Paramparawa. Do not vote for them. There are many more such hidden traps spread all over this document. Most of them have been exposed by other commentators. It is time for you the voter to study this infamous document carefully, and discover for yourself, that it is not the panacea that it is made out to be by those who have vested interest in it.

Finally, the three main issues affecting our country at the moment are terrorism in the North and the East of our country, the new Constitutional Proposal and the cost of living. On the first, we are kept in ignorance and are expected to believe and accept the pronouncements of the government. In the past many such disclosures were proved to be incorrect. Therefore one cannot attach any credibility to such claptraps. One has to vote in ignorance of a vital issue affecting the country, its sons and daughters in the war-front. The censorship of the press is not part of a sincere democratic process. I leave it to you to decide whether you should vote for anyone who subjects you to this humiliating condition. Remember your sovereignty is at stake. You have the right to know.

I have already touched on just one horror embedded in the small print of the Constitutional Proposal. There are many more. Once this Constitution is passed, there will be no going back. The situation will be irretrievable for good. Should we vote to be caught in such deathtrap? Certainly not. Do not surrender your sovereignty to the opportunistic Chief Minister of the Region!

So far the candidates of the main parties are seen to be hurling insults and innuendos at one another. They have no time to discuss the economy, its strengths and weaknesses and how best it can be managed to benefit the society at large. Therefore this is the opportune moment to abandon one's slavish loyalty to one political party. It is time to look at other political parties, the men and women who manage them and the proposals they have made. Perhaps, among them, you will find the one that sincerely tells the unvarnished truth, one that has not abandoned our historical roots, and our chiliastic heritage; and one that endeavours to create a society where certain fundamental rights, liberties and opportunities are specified and prioritized. One that lays out the measures, assuring all citizens, whatever their social positions, adequate all-purpose means to make intelligent and effective use of their liberties and opportunities. You owe your vote to such a party and its candidates. They will surely end the suzerainty of present Politicos and Yakkos.

30

Negotiation with LTTE Nationalism

(The Island, 27th Dec.2000)

It is quite apparent that the government of Sri Lanka has been bumped into negotiation with LTTE by a couple of partisan Western nations. We do not know their agenda, but it is safe to assume that they do have an agenda of their own, which serves their interests, rather than that of Sri Lanka. Any constitutional negotiation, if it is genuine, has its own inherent dynamic, which would open up otherwise unavailable opportunities to nationalist desperado entrepreneurs. It is in this context that the country, as well as our negotiators, needs to be reminded of the virulent nature of LTTE's rabid nationalism.

Nationalism is simply the belief in the primacy of the particular nation, real or constructed. Or, as Miroslow Hroch has pointed out, "nationalism is that state of mind which gives an absolute priority to the value of one's own nation over and above all other values and group interests" (Nations and Nationalism). It is in fact harder to define a nation than nationalism. Leaving aside many classical definitions, Prof. Michael Mann's (of UCLA) working definition that "a nation is a community affirming a distinct ethnic identity, history and destiny, and claiming its own state" appears to be a neat fit for the 2500 years-old nation of ours. Yet other political thinkers and researchers do tell us that there is "no sociological moorings whatever to a nation, not in language, not in religion, and not in ethnicity" (Gellner). This same Cambridge political theorist asserted that "nationalism is not awakening of nations to self- consciousness, it invents nations where they do not exist" (Thought and Change). Precisely this is what the Godfather of Tamil separatism, Mr. Chelvanayagam did long ago (long before Sinhala only Bill) by claiming that the Tamils were a "separate people" and that they constituted a "separate nation" entitled to self-determination. He invented Tamil nationalism.

Over the years, LTTE nationalism has become an upwardly mobile power-hungry and blood-thirsty ideology making false universal claims. It started off with "grievances" of minority Tamils and then graduated to "aspirations" and "self-determination" backed by terrorism. Today it stands for separatism and sovereign Eelam with fully equipped army, navy and a subversive Fifth Column among the civilian population. That it will then propel itself to further territorial aggrandizement and a "Greater Eelam" of the Indian Ocean cannot be in doubt. Even India has now come to realize this threat to its integrity. Other nations in the Indian Ocean rim--- Myanmar, Thailand,Malaysia, Maldives and Kenya ---please take note.

LTTE nationalism has scavenged on our democratic institutions. It had exploited our corrupt, chaotic democracy of competing parties and patron-client corruption at the bottom of our political system. It has made use of them to spread its pathological form of identity. It roams all over the world and in cyber space condemning and denigrating Sinhala culture and history and vilifying the Sinhalaya as an ogre deserving death and damnation. It maintains boldly that the Sinhalaya does not deserve this beautiful country. It ought to be in the hands of Tamils!

LTTE nationalism is fanatical to the core. It demands unquestionable belief in itself and in the LTTE's belief that they are a separate nation on the road to immortality. A bovine will, backed by cyanide pill, drives them on to this paradise beyond time and space. In this venture, it is prepared to crush and throttle everything and everyone (including Tamils) who cross its path. It feels no shame for its acts of terrorism and atrocities against civilians, women and children. It revels in macho glory and fills its devotees' memories with fabricated stories of noble ancestors, fallen heroes and their bravery in defeat. It seeks to create an aura of invincibility hoisting its flag even at peace-talks, and further bloodying its hands on all those who disagree with its fanaticism. Even Mr.Hain, a junior Minister in the British Government, did swallow this propaganda, and insulted our brave security forces by declaring on our soil that the war against the LTTE was unwinnable. Translated, this meant that our security forces were no match for the LTTE. [We do today in 2010 know how wrong he was].

LTTE nationalism is all inclusive. Everything for Eelam, nothing against Eelam, nothing outside Eelam. Either you belong to LTTE or else you are a foe to be eliminated. They believe in the survival of the fittest and the powerfully armed. They are imbued with a judgment disorder of single-minded arrogance. Their rampant racism condemns others as inferior rubbish having no entitlements. Thus the Sinhalese in the marginal villages are shot at, herded at gun-point from their burning homes and executed under cover of darkness in the shrub jungles nearby. A few lucky escapees, the next day, with bulging eyes and lamenting faces, would appeal to the deaf and dumb world, all to no avail. Their pleas remained unheard. In fact they are lectured to by European nations, "go talk to your erstwhile executioners and accept the crumbs, if any, those butchers are prepared to give you". The ICRC, the NGOs, the Bishops, and those partisan embassies see nothing, hear nothing and say nothing when the Sinhalese are the victims.

LTTE nationalism is a serious dirty business based on demonic cult worship of one man. Their motto is that of ancient regime, "Un rod, une foi, une loi" (one king, one faith, one law). In this set-up there is no place for "La Nation, la loi, la roi" (the nation, the law, the king, if any). Pirapakaran is a convinced practicing acolyte of Saint Just who proclaimed that "terror was purity, compromise was corruption". That he would therefore compromise in peace-talks is delusion. I humbly submit to be proved wrong.

This incubus needs to be urgently excised, however, as Hegel had observed, gangrene cannot be cured with lavender water. This monster of terrorism will surely gobble up the entire body politic and destroy our nation. Political scientists have suggested many ways of neutralizing minority nationalism. One sure-fire way is elimination by brute force, as this is, in fact, the language the nationalists utilize and therefore understand well.

The elimination of LTTE nationalistic terrorism from our country would require a rigorously sensitivity-tested military plan, to be executed with a single-minded determination by proven professional personnel, with full support of the country and its leader and its representatives in Parliament. It should have a military objective to be achieved within a set time scale. Such a military campaign should be complemented with a propaganda campaign to galvanize the nation and to inform the world at large. Unfortunately, what we have is a blanket censorship, and ad hoc campaigns with political objectives, where the chief occupation of the Security Forces is projected to be score-keepers of dead bodies, and surveyors of square meters of devastated real estate gained or lost. So long as this happens, it is true to maintain that this visceral struggle is unwinnable. It has only engendered the exclusive politically influential clique, who does swear by the Spanish saying that the war is both quicker and more honourable way to wealth than commerce. Tom Paine, (the author of Rights of Man, 1791) did warn us against this tribe of parasites in the following terms, "there are men in all countries who get their living by war and by keeping up the quarrels". If only we could have a single fixed point during the duration of a well planned military campaign----the salvation of the nation from terrorism---- then victory will surely be ours. Evidently this will entail sacrifices, and those sacrifices should be shared by the nation at large.

Institutional pluralism is another attempted solution. This usually takes the form of federalism and/or consociation. The PA government's proposed constitution is seeking a federal solution to our national crisis. It is a formal description of a type of territorial division of power by devolution. It is a dispersing of the institutions of our unitary nation-state downwards and sideways in order to develop regional power with autonomy in all spheres of day-to-day government of that region. It is the pious hope of PA government that this constitution, once implemented, will lead to the end of terrorism and usher in peace. Many others, self included, have plenty of reservations about this document, its content, as well as its short and long term objectives.

Arend Lijphart (of Berkley) studied consociation in his book, The Politics of Accommodation. He noted that two conditions were essential for consociational democracy. They were, a prior tradition of compromise, and an overarching loyalty to the state among the subcultures. Based on this, the political institutions are scattered to preserve and nurture the cultural cleavage prevalent in society. It therefore is a "difference-preserving form of political regime and strategy of ethnic conflict regulation". In the dire circumstances of Sri Lanka, consociation would be a non-starter.

The LTTE on the other hand has suggested the idea of Confederation or dual sovereign states for the country. The downside here is the same as in the case of federation. Both arrangements could be easily manipulated as launching pads for out and out separatism.

Prof. Amersfoort (of Amsterdam), a specialist on Eastern Europe, acknowledges that only in the context of long periods of gradual political economic development does institutional plurality contribute to the solution of ethnic antagonism in the state population. He came to the conclusion that "it is too optimistic to state that institutional plurality offers the solution to problem of multi-ethnic state, but too pessimistic to deny that it may form part of the solution" (Institutional Plurality, Problem or Solution?, in his book, Notions of Nationalism).

After a careful study of the plurality of institutions and consociation of Quebec with the rest of Canada, Prof. Hudson Meadwell (of McGill, Canada), came to the conclusion that Quebec is today at the verge of secession from the rest of Canada because of the combined effects of federation and consociation, which were originally designed as solution to the ethnic problem. He warns us thus "Quebec has come as far as it has down the road to independence because of the politicizing effects of constitutional negotiation" (Quebec : Independence and Secession in the Developed World).

It is paramount that we seek a solution to our problem. There are no easy answers other than simple surrender to all LTTE demands and the vivisection of the country. All other avenues are expensive. Such expenses have to be borne and shared to preserve the nation intact by eliminating the LTTE. In the meanwhile, we should explore in depth the intertwined problems of nationalism, national identity and democracy. It may be that we have to stretch democracy to its limits or invent new democratic ways to neutralize rabid racist nationalism of the LTTE variety.

31

Manufacturing Consent for Eelam

(The Island,30th May 2001)

The LTTE has always been engaged in the subtle art of manufacturing consent for Eelam. They have suffered internationally by the proscriptions imposed on them by various countries. This is only a temporary set-back to them. They will continue their relentless highly effective propaganda backed up by intensive lobbying of foreign politicians to restore their status as "liberation fighters" of Eelam. Even now with a banning order hanging over them, they are functioning as normal in UK. This is evident from the many consultations Mr. Soldheim (ES) has had with Mr. Balasingham in London as the accredited representative of the LTTE in UK. Instead, Mr. Balasingham should be tried as a war criminal in UK.

The statement released by LTTE after ES's latest visit to the Wanni quite recently is quite blunt. To quote: "the international community should understand that we cannot participate in peace-talks as an illegal, criminal entity with a distorted false label as 'terrorists'. We have fought a liberation war for more than two decades. It is the collective aspiration of our people that a ban on our liberation organization should be lifted" (The Island, May 19). The lifting of the ban would amount to recognition of legitimacy, and that would be their initial positioning of themselves on the high road to Eelam. Therefore the Sri Lankan government should not yield on this point.

What should be of concern to everyone are the efforts made to manufacture consent within our country and among the Sinhala electorate. This takes many forms. First among them is the 'engineering of our history", or rather the pure fabrication, to create ex nihilo the concept of homeland and self-determination. Though many a learned person has exposed this hoax, the fact remains that these concepts are still at play as crucial items for negotiated settlement. The Sinhala politicians opposed to Tamil homeland are in fact afraid to voice their opinions in public. Those few commentators, who have opposed this racially homogenous enclave within Sri Lanka, have been condemned as rabid racists and Sinhala chauvinists. The rest tacitly accept them as matters for negotiation. Thus willy-nilly the Sinhala constituency has come to accept the LTTE concocted geographical area known as Eelam. In this respect the LTTE have won their case to the extent that both the government in power and the opposition are prepared to consider this issue as matter for formal negotiation. In fact both parties should have taken a stand against it from the very beginning, on the ground, among others, that it was a fictitious apartheid entity divisive of the country. The government in power over the period never took the offensive to expose and dispose this phony fiction in any convincing manner, even though, they had all the arguments on their side.

The NGOs and their allied peace brigade are the foot-soldiers engaged in untiring effort to manufacture consent for Eelam. Their anti-war advertisements are calculated to discourage recruitment to the Security Forces. One wonders why the government has not arraigned them for disseminating sedition and defection among the Security Forces, and sowing disaffection among the populace for the war effort of the government. Such saboteurs should not be allowed to ply their outrageous pro-LTTE propaganda. Yet the government is fleet-footed to pounce on the independent newspapers when they expose corruption and the many inexcusable shenanigans among the hierarchy of the armed forces. These exposures are regarded as inimical to the morale of our fighting men and as acts of treachery. In fact, cleaning up the army of corrupt officials would do wonders to the men in the frontline. In fact when the culprits in the forces are promoted, one can only expect the army to degenerate. Is it any wonder that the hapless citizens, deprived of any balanced report from the war-front, due to the draconian press censorship in operation, are wont to swallow wholesale the partisan propaganda of these peace-peddlers? This is, in effect, a cunning strategy of the NGOs to break down the resistance of the public to the prospective creation of Eelam.

The written propaganda of these peaceniks is silent on the villainy of the LTTE. The numerous acts of terrorism, murder and pillage committed by the LTTE are not subjects for any comment, let alone condemnation. Elimination of all opponents of the LTTE by brute force is practised to perfection. The essentially evil nature of the LTTE and its leader should be the core theme of the peace brigade, the NGOs and the Christian Churches. What we have instead is the promotion of LTTE as a suitable organization to be given the control and power over people and territory. They are all apologists trying to manufacture consent for Eelam.

One NGO dug deep into published data to exhume the monetary cost of this anti terrorist conflict. They then made proclamations about the impossibility of the nation to bear such costs without economic chaos, and the very disintegration of democracy in the country. The objective of this exercise was to wean the public from supporting the struggle against terrorism. They carefully omitted to tell us the cost incurred by the LTTE and imposed on the nation by the LTTE. They knew of one item of enormous cost imposed on the nation by the LTTE, and this is the thousands of child soldiers sent to the frontline as sacrificial lambs to satiate the overweening ambition of just one man---- the fascist dictator of prospective Eelam. This wily suppression of relevant factors pertaining to the LTTE is another tactic to manufacture consent for Eelam.

Recently the Chinese Prime Minister Zhu Rongji reminded our moronic politicians and other dollar guzzling pro-LTTE NGOs that "Sri Lanka is a country with time-honoured history and brilliant culture" (Daily News, May 18th). If we do not defend this country against the evil centrifugal forces of LTTE, there will not be a Sri Lanka the next time the Chinese Prime Minister visits our country. "People define themselves in terms of ancestry, religion, language, history, values, customs and institutions" wrote Samuel P. Huntington (The Clash of Civilization). This has happened in Sri Lanka over the last two millennia, and is worth defending at any cost.

The peace overtures made recently by the LTTE had been further enlarged and projected by the peace brigade as a lifeline thrown towards a drowning man. Those spokespersons for LTTE did not tell us what their Master Velu had been clandestinely doing in the meanwhile. It became evident at the battle for Pallai. Also via the Eelam nation website (8th May), he informed the world that, "the goal of the liberation of Eelam Tamils would not be complete until Sri Lankan state recognizes their fundamental aspirations". Translated, this means that he would not stop short of his racist Eelam. Then what would happen to the Sinhalese and Muslims in Eelam and the Tamils in the rest of the country bears comparison to the holocaust that took place when Pakistan and Bangladesh came into existence. Just last week, LTTE cohorts attacked and killed Sinhala paddy farmers north of Polonnaruwa. What sort of existence will they have in Eelam under LTTE? Further, there is no guarantee that a new border war will not be engendered and a new water war will not ensue in the vivisected country. In short the total disintegration of the country is what Velu wants. The patrons of this evil genius in Colombo deliberately choose to ignore all those so that the Sinhala population could be hoodwinked into accepting their manufactured consent for Eelam.

Mr.Soldheim is actually a busybody midwife who peddles about the world trying to sell our country for the Nobel Peace Prize. What he will help to give birth will be nothing short of a separatist Eelam for the simple reason that this is what Velu wants. ES is not prepared to tell Velu that all troubles would end if he gives up his clamour for Eelam and surrenders his deadly armoury. Es is not prepared to tell Velu that he is an illegitimate brigand who has taken by force the charge of a territory and its people, and that it is time to let them go. What all the peace NGOs and ES should be doing is to put pressure on Velu and firmly point out, as did the US envoy recently, that aspiration for Eelam is the expiration of the Tamil community, and that there is no support for it whatever in Sri Lanka and internationally. Velu may ignore such advice, but some of his cadres might start thinking otherwise and set in motion the downfall of Velu himself within his deadly organization.

Finally, it is astonishing that the world community has to-date ignored the war crimes committed by Velu. There is a better documented case against Velu than against Millosevic. I urge this government and the interested NGOs to press the UN for a War Tribunal to try Velu even in absentia. So long as Velu is at large, there will not be peace in this country.

32

To the Sinhala Sri Lankan Nation

(The Island, 28th Nov.2001)

Sometime ago, Dr.Nalin de Silva raised the question in The Island newspaper whether the Sinhalese were the only Sri Lankans. He had before him, the unseemly haggling that took place among the minority communities, over the appointment of one of their kind to the Constitutional Council, under the newly passed 17th Amendment to the Constitution of the country. So long as the minority leaders---- the Tamils and the Muslims----continue to pursue the exclusive interests of, and seek to enhance their sectarian interests at the expense of others, they project themselves as communalists first, and invite others to treat them as such. They have today succeeded to enthrone discrimination in the Constitution itself by obtaining recognition for Tamil and Muslim minority communities and ignoring the likes of Sinhala Christians (equal in numbers to Muslims?), Burghers and Malays. Those belonging to the latter minority communities are reduced to second class citizens of Sri Lanka. Ideally, the 17th Amendment should have recognized only Sri Lankans, or alternatively, recognized all the racial and religious communities in the island.

These communalist forces in conjunction with peace-NGOs, some academics, business leaders and some LTTE-front organizations are engaged in destroying the Sinhala Sri Lankan nation. It is therefore primarily to the Sinhalese Sri Lankan nation that I direct this address at this crucial hour of another General Election. Taking on board Edmund Burke's advice that "people will not look forward to posterity, who never looked backward to their ancestors"; I need to delve a bit into our history to substantiate as well as to remind our fellowmen, the fact, that the Sinhalese are the endangered Sri Lankan nation at the moment. The six generally accepted attributes of an ethnic nation would be found perfectly fitting when applied to the Sinhalese Sri

Lankan nation, thus establishing the fact that the Sinhalese are the Sri Lankan nation. (The following points are based on Anthony D. Smith's book: The Ethnic Origins of Nations).

1) We have had a common name ---Sinhalese---- from the days of cave inscriptions predating the Christian era. This is why our kings assumed the title of "Sinhala Adhisvara". This name (Sinhalese) was applied by foreigners to an identifiable set of people living in Sri Lanka and has survived to the present day.

2) Like most great nations of the world, the Sinhalese have a myth of common origin and descent from august founders of the nation. The myth of Sinhabahu and the legend of Prince Vijaya need no repetition here. These were (and are living in poetry, art, music, dance and drama) symbols that inculcated and attached new generations to the mores of their ancestors and signposted the common way of life and the institutions of the community.

3) The Sinhalese have maintained common historical memories of their experiences over the last twenty-five centuries of their existence. The Sinhala Athakathas, the Mahavamsa, the many amazing art, architecture, and even our pristine ruins with their many slab inscriptions speak eloquently of our glorious past. They perpetuate our collective historical memories.

Ernst Renan, in his book "What is a Nation?" thought of a nation as a living soul, a spiritual principle consisting of a past and a present. "one is the common possession of a rich heritage of memories, the other is the actual consent, the desire to live together, and the will to preserve worthily the undivided inheritance which had been handed down. A heroic past, great men and glory form the social capital, upon which a national idea may be founded. We love in proportion to the sacrifices we have consented to make, to the sufferings we have endured. We love the house we have built, and will hand down to our descendants. A nation is a great solidarity, and the nation's existence is a daily plebiscite, as the individual's existence is a perpetual affirmation of life". The disturbing question at this juncture is whether we shall have a "house" to hand down to our descendants!

4) From the time of the founding of the Sinhala nation, its kings and queens had considered the whole island as their "homeland". There was a deeply felt symbiosis between the territory that was Sri Lanka and its community. This was why the kings resisted foreign invasions, defeated the invaders and united the country under a sole ruler. At times of crisis, the floundering nation was rescued by Sinhala heroes. The efforts of one such hero, Vijayabahu, impressed a modern day south Indian scholar so much that he boldly pronounced, "had it not been for Vijayabahu, there would perhaps have been no Sinhalese today. But beyond a shadow of doubt, he was the author of Sinhalese freedom and one of the chief architects of Sinhalese nationality" (Nilakantha Sastri in RAS Journal Vol.iv).

   Paraphrasing Hegel, the natural features of Sri Lanka, its mountains, air and waters form the outward material property of the Sinhalese, their fatherland. The history of this state is their deeds. What their ancestors have produced, belong to them and lives in their memory. All is their possession, just as they are possessed by it; for it constitutes their existence, their being (The Philosophy of History). Today, the whole of Sri Lanka belongs to everyone born in this country. The LTTE and other communalists have made untenable claims to parts of this common property. There are Sinhalese politicians who want to appease those illegitimate claimants. Do not vote them into power.

   Notwithstanding this fact of historical possession of the country, the Sinhalese of today accept the rights of non-Sinhalese to live as equal citizens anywhere in this country, even though, they themselves have virtually lost their right to live in some parts of this country. The communalist forces are seeking to legitimize this discrimination against the Sinhalese by partitioning the country on ethnic and religious lines. This betrayal of our heritage should be resisted at all costs. The Sinhala voters and politicians who pander to sectarian demands would be guilty of treachery on the present and future generations . They should be hounded out of office.

5) The elements of common culture ----language, customs, traditions and religion----were the integrating forces of the Sinhala nation. The Sinhala Buddhist civilization began at Mihintale in the third century BC. The Buddhist monks have made a very significant contribution to it. They did, not only communicate, record and transmit our legends and beliefs, but were also the chief guardians and conduits linking the peasant masses with the elites of the country. They stamped their religious outlooks and life-styles, myths and symbols, music, festivals and rituals on the state and traditions of the whole population. They were responsible in creating the Dharmista society, in search of which, many foreigners came to our shores in ancient times. Buddhism was the state religion until 1815 and our language and customs grew with it. Today the communalist forces are not prepared even to give it the foremost place in society.

6) There has persisted from time immemorial a sense of solidarity among most members of the Sinhala community. This is a strong sense of belonging that overrides factional or regional divisions within the community. "All the elements of tradition and culture---- the myths, symbols, values and memories encoded in laws and customs, institutions, religion, art, music, dance, architecture, family practices and language---- help to bind families together in a community of ancestry, a totality of expressions and representations, a totality that gains with every generation and evokes veneration and respect for ancestors and the past" (Anthony D Smith, The Ethnic Origins of Nations).

This sense of solidarity is spectacularly absent among the present-day politicians. This is due to their self-aggrandizement, their drive to obtain and wield political power, and their all-consuming Tanha to acquire conspicuous icons of grotesque wealth. These men totally lack any sense of responsibility to the present voters as well as the generations to come. They would easily betray the country for the proverbial thirty pieces of silver. The voters' duty with regard to these men is quite clear----do not vote for them.

The solidarity of the people is vital for the nation to survive the terrorist crisis in our country. We see this clearly illustrated in the case of USA, where politicians, businessmen, religious leaders and ordinary folks are all united in fighting terrorism both within and outside the country. In the case of Sinhalese Sri Lankan nation, a motley crowd of LTTE sympathizers have launched a massive propaganda assault to break this solidarity and the will of the nation to fight the fascistic terrorism of the LTTE. The day this tragedy becomes a reality, that day will mark the beginning of the end of the Sinhalese Sri Lankan nation. It is not difficult to see the ominous signs of this degeneracy. Could you allow this to happen?

33

A Reflection on Terrorism

(The Island, 21st Feb. 2002)

It is patently obvious to anyone, but the terrorist, that terrorism is an evil that employs terror as its primary weapon. It affects the public at large. It creates uncertainty combined with the probability that persons unknown could shower upon us palpable danger to our lives and limbs without our being able to anticipate them. Violence targeted at ordinary people makes ordinary people everywhere feel uneasy and fearful.

Terrorism renders the citizen utterly powerless. The terrorist could attack anytime, anywhere while on our routine business, or even while peacefully asleep. The citizen could do nothing to alleviate this insecurity. As a victim, the citizen is being used, and is at the mercy of the terrorists. There are no innocent victims for terrorists.

From an ordinary citizen's point of view, the methods of terrorism are absurd in that they totally fail to advance the cause of the terrorists. Terrorism only steels the resolve of the victimized nations to fight it to the finish (except probably in Sri Lanka of President Mrs. Kumaratunghe and PM Wickramasinghe and the war-fattened businessmen). People are pointlessly sacrificed, treated as jetsam to be cast away and as fodder for indiscriminate and unconstrained violence.

Terrorism, therefore, is a random use of violence on non-combatants for social/political ends with deliberate intention of infusing fear and panic in the population. Paul Wilkinson defines political terrorism as "coercive intimidation. It is the systemic use of murder and destruction in order to terrorize individuals, groups, communities or governments into conceding to the terrorists' demands" His conclusion is that terrorism is "a moral crime, a crime against humanity" (Terrorism and the Liberal State).

The terrorists are also shrewd publicity seekers. They always seek a conspicuous canvas to express their "grievances". They put on a spectacular show of self-righteous violence. They want to command the attention of the powerful in the land to display the seriousness of their purpose and the ruthlessness of their will. In this process they would consider it a success to litter an airport with dead bodies and turn a Central Bank and its environment to an abattoir. This coercive violence is directed at gaining a hearing for a view and/or exacting concessions from the opponents, to obtain maximum publicity for their cause, to destroy the morale of the nation and to undercut its solidarity, to provoke repression and backlash, to break down the social order and to build morale in their movement and enforce obedience to it.

For a society to function normally there should be order, rules and regulations, and laws governing the conduct of its citizens. By and large, the citizen would have consented implicitly or explicitly to such laws, as otherwise, "there can be no security to any man" (Hobbes). It is the expectation of all citizens in society that each will be better off by participating in and by living according the laws in the country. It follows that a citizen cannot pursue his routine life purposes by resorting to violence against others. The terrorists' violence without warning, without mercy and without recourse to help is an assault on this very fundamental structure of society. A terrorist attack plunges society to the Hobbesian state of nature where "every man has a right to everything; even to one another's body". It is in this light that Paul Johnson wrote that "terrorism is the cancer of the modern world. No state is immune to it. It is a dynamic organism which attacks the healthy flesh of the surrounding society. It has the essential hallmark of malignant cancer: unless treated drastically, its growth is inexorable, until it poisons and engulfs the society on which it feeds and drags it down to destruction" (in Terrorism, How the West can Win, ed. B. Netanyahu).

To the citizens the society is a co-operative venture for mutual advantage. Therefore any terrorist attack would thrust the entire society back to nature where no rules of behaviour exist. A terrorist has actually forsworn the rules of justice thereby he also looses the protection of those rules. When this situation obtains, Hume advised that those "who observed no rules of war, [the affected state] must also suspend their observance of them: and must render every action or encounter as bloody and pernicious as possible to the first aggressor" (An Enquiry). Hume would consider the modern terrorist as a deadly threat to civil order as his indiscriminate targeting of civilians is an explicit rejection of familiar political arrangements and the limitation of violence those arrangements impose on citizens.

John Locke too believed that by "unjust violence and slaughter he (the terrorist) has declared war against mankind, and therefore (he should) be destroyed as a wild savage beast" (Second Treatise on Government).

Emmanuel Kant propounded the maxim that human beings should always be treated as an end not merely as a means to an end. This implies that humans are rational agents with autonomy and dignity, and these are unconditional and are of incomparable worth. On this basis we are endowed with certain fundamental human rights, the right to life, the right to personal security, the right to liberty, the right to property and the right to respect from fellow citizens. The terrorist violates these rights. Therefore it is always wrong to kill or risk killing innocent human beings. This is an indefeasible prohibition. Terrorists stand condemned in Kantian ethics.

The terrorists themselves and their acolytes usually argue that the end justifies the means. In evaluating the "means", we need to establish first whether they were efficient, effective in bringing about the attainment of the proclaimed end, and whether alternative less costly means were available. The immediate objective of crippling the tourist industry was achieved with thorough efficiency by attacking our airport. So was the demolition of WTC in New York. Yet the proclaimed goals were Eelam in Sri Lanka; and in the latter, the withdrawal of US troops from Saudi Arabia and the dismantling of the state of Israel. These ultimate ends remain unachieved and unlikely to be achieved even in the distant future. Therefore, just like other terrorist carnage and destructions, (and in the case of Sri Lanka, over the last eighteen years), they remain spectacular failures causing misery, death and destruction and inviting retaliation and retribution.

The intended ultimate goal too needs to be a desirable objective not only to the terrorists but also to others affected by terrorism. In the case of Eelam, we know that it would be an apartheid enclave governed by a bloodthirsty dictator who would not tolerate dissent. The Tamil population would have to live in servility under his unbounded supremacy and tyranny. The rest of Sri Lankan population would also be worse off as they would have lost part of their country and the right to live anywhere in their country. On top of this they would have to face wars of aggression in the future both over territory and natural resources like water, minerals, timber and fish. The goal of Eelam fails to match up to be a desirable end for the Tamils as well as others, except of course, to the LTTE. Therefore on utilitarian and consequential grounds terrorism to achieve this dubious state of Eelam cannot be justified.

The conclusion is that if we want to preserve our society and improve it piecemeal for the benefit of all its citizens, we cannot allow terrorism to flourish in the same society. It has got to be eliminated. The sure-fire way to root out terrorism was laid down by Mr. Colin Powell on Sept. 12, 2001. He said that the terrorists "have to be destroyed. It requires a worldwide response. And that response has to be diplomatic. It has to be political. It has to be going after their means of support. It has to be going after nations and states and other organizations that give them harbour and haven and support. And it has to be military as well, if targets can be found that are actionable. And it has to be justice too if that is possible to bring somebody to justice. But it has to be a complete comprehensive response". In endorsing this master-class action plan, I would also suggest that all funds belonging to terrorists should be confiscated and be made available to be paid out as compensation to the victims and for the destruction caused by the terrorists.

Buses, trains, ships, aircrafts and buildings have been blown up with no concern for people in them. Down this road we could envisage chemical, biological and crude atomic weapons coming into play in the future. Already such panic appears to have caught hold of the British public as there is a panic buying of gas masks over there in anticipation of terrorist threat. The terrorists are outlaws, to them all fields are battlefields and there are no non-combatants. The terrorist has to be fought on his own terms and destroyed root and branch (as our Security Forces did among the mangroves at Nandhikadal on the 18th of May 2009). There is no room for chicken-hearted negotiations. As Hobbes enjoins we can seek peace and lay down "our rights of nature" when the terrorist does the same, and has been defeated into accepting that covenants do matter, and that covenants have to be observed without recourse to mindless violence. According to William Borman even Mahatma Gandhi preferred violence to cowardice. He had written that Gandhi admitted that "my non-violence does not admit of running away from danger and leaving dear ones unprotected. Between violence and cowardly flight I can only prefer violence to cowardice" (Gandhi and Non-Violence).

34 - A

Internal Self-Determination

(The Island, 22nd June 2002)

Internal self-determination (ISD) came into our vocabulary via Wanni. Many have accepted it as a way out of the terrorist conflict in the north without any examination of what it really means in de facto political terms.

Long ago, comrade V.I. Lenin (in his Right of Nations to Self-Determination) came to the "conclusion that self-determination of nations means the political separation of these nations from alien national bodies and the formation of an independent national state". He further emphasized that " it would be wrong to interpret the right to self-determination as meaning anything but the right to existence as a separate state". Any other interpretation of self-determination by various "spin-doctors" would be mere meaningless semantics, and an attempt at deception of the people. As pointed out by many commentators in The Island newspaper, many provisions in the UN Charter do not admit the right to self-determination by minorities that will fragment and/or bifurcate an already existing member nation of the UN.

External self-determination is usually applied to a situation where a group of people who considering themselves to be a duly constituted nation had won their independence by military means. The LTTE has over the last twenty years sought external self-determination by fighting a terrorist war. It has failed. Why fight, if the same objective could be attained by deceiving our moronic Sinhala politicians by a mere substitution of words---- INTERNAL to external?

If the whole of Canada were to decide at a Referendum to allow the State of Quebec to secede from the Canadian Federation, then it might also be termed an external self-determination. The same might be said if the whole of United Kingdom voted to allow Scotland to exist as a separate country. In these cases external self-determination can be construed as the endowment of the right to exist as a separate nation to the minority by the majority of the citizens of the nation concerned prior to the countrywide Referendum and confirmed by the Referendum. The LTTE knows that such a situation has not arisen anywhere in the world and is unlikely to happen in Sri Lanka. This perhaps is the reason for inventing ISD. So what does INTERNAL self-determination means?

Mr.Balasingam (LTTE's deputy leader) did provide a sort of explanation. "By self-determination, we mean the right of our people to decide their own political destiny. It can also mean/apply to autonomy and self-government. If autonomy and self-government is given to our people, then also we can say that internal self-determination is to some extent met. So self-determination entails autonomy and self-government. In the extreme case, in the last resort, it means secession" (April 10th Wanni News Conference).

On the face of it, an independent Eelam would be an extreme case, it appears that the LTTE, via Mr. Balasingam would be happy to settle for an autonomous state. It was probably on this basis that the British/Sri Lankan Euro MP Mr. Nerj Deva recommended for consideration the current devolution of powers to Scotland. If the LTTE is genuine then there is scope for adoption of that model with suitable modifications. Nevertheless, there are certain facts about the British devolution that are conspicuously significant. There is only one Prime Minister in Britain. There is only one Royal Air Force, one Royal Navy and one British army. The Scottish Police Force is under the control of the Scottish Assembly Minister of Home Affairs. Yet the Police Force itself owes allegiance to the Crown. It is politically accountable to the Scottish Assembly through the Minister and civilly accountable to the Courts of Law. This is not the case with the LTTE police force. It is appointed by LTTE boss. It owes allegiance to one man, it enforces the law promulgated by him, it also a fighting force of Eelam. It is not subject to any democratic control. It is not accountable to the citizens. Above all, in Britain, the Parliament at Westminster is the supreme body, the embodiment of sovereignty of the people. Some local constitutional pundits might consider this to be obsolete, but the British did not think so. They deliberately did not create a Federal system when devolved powers were given to Scotland. The current Westminster Parliament has the power to undo everything the previous parliaments have done with a simple majority. If the LTTE is willing to accept devolution under these conditions, then it is possible that they have changed their minds on separatist Eelam. But have they?

Another important aspect of the Scottish Assembly is that democratic, open and fair election is held to select its members. They represent various political parties. It is not a case of one man rule and one party appointment as in the case of LTTE in the North and East. The Scottish National Party is at the moment a minority in the Assembly. They have sworn to hold a Referendum for secession if and when they control the Assembly. This is another version of INTERNAL self-determination that can lead to separatism. It is my opinion that Mr. Balasingam is pursuing this easy path to Eelam.

In an interview to the Tamil Guardian (The Island, 6th June), Mr. Balasingam explained at length what was meant by core issues to the LTTE. There he changed his tunes from internal self-determination to "Tamil homeland and right to national self-determination". The Tamil homeland for him "was an objectively existential reality grounded on the material history of Tamil speaking people who have lived and toiled for centuries in a district, contiguous territory of the northeast over which they have an inalienable right to ownership". He asserted the right to both internal and external aspects of self-determination. Again he reiterated the determination to realize Eelam "by struggling for secession, political independence and statehood", if the LTTE is denied the conditions necessary in the forthcoming devolution package for it to attain Eelam without such a struggle. He is boldly telling us to provide the LTTE the political ambience, to give it all the prerequisites and all the opportunities to one day declare Eelam as a separate state. No Eelam now, but do give us the power over the territory we have specified as our homeland, and all other wherewithal that would constitute a separate state, and the LTTE shall, one day, declare it a separate and independent country at the discretion of the LTTE!! How is it that our clever constitutional experts are so stupid not to see through this cunning strategy?

Mr. Balasingam delivered the knock-out blow in crisp language too plain not to be understood even by our local political clowns. He said "we do not think that Mr. Ranil Wickramasinghe has the necessary political authority to deal with the core issues as perceived by the Tamils underlying the Tamil national question".

"His theory of one nation, one country and one people is the very negation of the core demands of the Tamils for a homeland, national identity, and the right to self-determination". Is this not clear enough that what he wants is two nations, two governments and two centres of sovereignty? If the LTTE is unwilling to be part of one nation, one country and one people, then there is no possibility of devolving powers preserving the integrity of the nation and its national boundary. The deception underlying INTERNAL self-determination remains exposed by Mr. Balasingam himself. The business magnates and the clerics who crowd our TV programmes with "one Sri Lanka" slogans are surely braying at the wrong target population. They should turn their attention towards Mr. Balasingam and his LTTE cohorts. It is they who need to be converted to one nation, one country and one people.

34 - B

The Self-Determination of Sri Lankans

(The Island, 16th nov.2002)

We have all had a good dose of headlines dominating pronouncements by Mr. Balasingam on self-determination, autonomy and homelands for Tamils. At times contradictory, at other times confusing, those statements were cunningly contrived circumlocution to keep the nation guessing as to the true meanings and intentions of the LTTE. We are so immersed in the debate on self-determination of the minority Tamils in our country, that we have forgotten and ignored (deliberately by politicians?) the self-determination of the Sri Lankan nation itself.

Given that Sri Lanka is hic et nunc a state, a self-governing political unit, with a democratically elected government, it has its own right to self-determination. What this means is that this state of Sri Lanka has the right to acquire or continue to possess the status of a state without it being abrogated or abridged by anyone. It has the right to form its own government and enforce its legal system over its territory. Outsiders have no right to interfere with the government of this territory. The state can protect its rights by use of force where and when necessary.

Exactitude in my explanation of the above right requires that I resort to elements of Wesley Hohfeld's matrix of legal relations. Anyone endowed with a legal right or claim is legally protected against someone else's interference with that right. The persons required to abstain from interference are under a duty to behave so. It is a genuine right, therefore an enforceable right. It does not matter who precisely holds the power to enforce the right. (Fundamental Legal Concepts by W.N. Hohfeld). It is this right that Sri Lanka possesses.

A legally constituted state like Sri Lanka already possesses the right against other states not to interfere with the formation of a government. It has the right to expect the other states to deal with its government in the normal way business is conducted between states. It has the right to immunity from the power of another state to extinguish its right to government. It has, however, the right to conduct a plebiscite to abandon its status as a state by unification with another state or by bifurcation. The right to self-determination of an existing state is the power it has to carry on its right to government without interference with the freedom to conduct a plebiscite to determine its future status.

A plebiscite, however, should be unequivocal. It should not be befuddled with jargon and verbiage. The citizens should be asked whether they wish to abandon their current status of an integral state or not. Once they vote "yes", then an appropriate constitution should be devised to give effect to that decision.

The Sinhalese have been an identifiable group throughout the history of this country. They identify themselves with a set of traditions and express appropriate feelings of pride, shame and resentment with respect to events both current and historical. They have been moulded into a coherent whole by their language and religion. But this was not a mere ethnic cultural group. It was a political group from time immemorial. The formation of a state and government took place at the very beginning of our history. This state did occupy the geographical territory, we call Sri Lanka. When it lost temporarily its power over the territory, it fought the enemy, and won back its suzerainty over its territory. The above characteristics single out the Sinhalese on their own truly as a nation. Yet this nation intermingles with others in its territory on an equal footing. We have today a multi-national society forming our nation. The non-Sinhalese citizens are recognized as fully participating members of this society.

We are governed in accordance with a constitution. Authority over political decisions are divided equally among its citizens, even though, some by virtue of being elected to Political Office of authority, do exercise special authority and even abuse that authority. The whole underlying process of government of our society is democratic, even though due to corruption of our politicians, it is defective in its applications. The right of self-determination is possessed by such a society. It is this right that the LTTE have challenged. It is this right, the government of the day, is duty bound to protect with all its might. Unfortunately for the country, the present politicians seem to have abandoned this sacred duty to protect the right to self-determination of our state. They are and will be judged as guilty of grave dereliction of their duty by future generations.

According to Prof. Allen Buchanan there are three primary justifying grounds for secession of a group from an existing state. First, the prevalence of persistent and serious violations of individual human rights of a group within the border s of a state. Second, past un-redressed unjust seizure of territory. It is a legitimate rectification of justice to claim annexed territory. Third, discriminatory redistribution. This occurs when the state implements taxation schemes, property rights systems, regulatory policies, economic development programmes that systematically work to the disadvantage of a targeted group while benefitting others. Quite simply there is no justification for this inequality. (The Morality of Political Divorce by Allen Buchanan). The reader can judge for himself that these conditions do not apply to the Tamils as a group. There is therefore, no morally justifiable grounds for self-determination to the Tamils. This is why the LTTE have resorted to bullets, bombs, rockets and terrorism to force the government to yield to their demands.

The people who form our society, the Sinhalese, Tamils, Muslims, Burghers and Malays have the right to self-determination. Given the fact that they form the nation and have a democratically elected government, they have the prior right to continue to govern themselves without any hindrance. Self-determination to them is self-government without interference. This right ought to be protected by the use of force when necessary. This is why the UN Resolution 1514 (of 14th Dec. 1960) ended with the proviso; "any attempt aimed at the partial or total disruption of the national unity and the territorial integrity of a country is incompatible with the purposes and principles of the Charter of the United Nations".

35

Fascism of the LTTE

(The Island, 29th Aug. 2002)

It is a relief to everyone that "Peace Talks' are due to take place in the near future. The country hopes that it would be successful. If one has to judge by what has so far happened under the present MOU, then, I suspect, it would be a one-sided unfair peace. Such an appeasement would lead to untold misery and suffering for the non-Tamils in the North-East and the lakhs of Tamils (626,304, Census 2001) now living elsewhere in the country. This is the reason why the government negotiators should take account of a few elementary factors regarding the LTTE, especially, when the euphoria of peace is likely to lead to mass amnesia. An important one among them is the blatant fascism of the LTTE that brooks no opposition to their ideology.

Fascism was defined by the EEC's Committee of Inquiry on the Rise of Fascism in Europe as "a nationalistic attitude essentially hostile to the principles of democracy, to the rule of law and to the fundamental rights and freedoms, as well as the irrational exaltation of a particular community, in relation to which people outside it are systematically excluded" (Quoted by R.Griffim in The Nature of Fascism). The EEC men did not think of the LTTE in formulating this definition, but that it fits the LTTE is all too plain to see. For a complete portrait of LTTE fascism one needs also to include the cult of the elite, of youth, of force and violence and the advocacy of authoritarianism. It has become an all-consuming attitude towards life that involves all aspects of the individual life of LTTE cadres.

The cult of the leader is at the centre of LTTE's ideology and charisma is crucial to the success of the LTTE in arousing the masses. He is the embodiment of the myth of Eelam, the final destiny of his people. In order to achieve coherence and internal harmony within his organization, he needs to claim infallibility in all matters of LTTE's fascist faith, morality and politics. This leader (Fuhrer, Duce, Thalyvar) always projects the claim that his power is based on the belief that he intuitively understands and articulates the real will of the people. This quasi-religious relationship is supported by its own rituals. It reached its culmination via a carefully cultivated strategy to the deification of the leader---- the deity Sooriya Dhevan----the venerated and worshipped deity of the LTTE. The Tamil Catholic high priests have yet to anoint him as the "Appointed Deliverer" of the Tamil nation!

The use of symbols, ceremonials and rituals become the new style in LTTE politics. The LTTE flag, the expansionist map and Pongu Thamil parades are prominent and distinctive features of their fascism. Their public parades, banners, zealotry and iconoclastic worship are efficiently organized to infuse fear in the minds of their opponents, and admiration in the minds of their supporters. The participating marchers, dancers, road-rollers and singers are made to merge their identity with that of the group. This emotional participation and public demonstration in the cause of a mythically constructed nation acted as potent elixir to even sacrifice one's life according to the wishes of their new deity. This was what Hitler's Minister for Cultural Affairs, Alfred Rosenberg articulated in 1934, "a weltanschauung could not be expressed properly in only principles or needs and had to 'take on the form of a cult'" (quoted by P.Brooker in Faces of Fascism).

The fascism of the LTTEis imbued through and through with biological racism and virulent anti-Sinhala and anti-Muslim propaganda. Its projected end is the sense of uniqueness of and a self-centred Tamil community. Paraphrasing Hitler, "Eelam is only the vessel and Tamil race is what it contains. This vessel can have meaning only if it preserves and safeguards it contents" (Quoted by N. O'Sullivan in Fascism). This is why the LTTE identify the Tamil society with the nation, the nation with Tamil Eelam state and their economic activity with their political activity.

The fascism of the LTTE has already drawn the boundaries between insiders and outsiders. These boundaries are not merely territorial, but also cultural and biological. The existence of the outsiders is perceived as a threat to their distinctive existence and therefore the elimination and eradication of all those that are different, whatever their attitude and ideas, are just a matter of logic of the intolerant fascism. The brotherhood of blood cannot be allowed to be jeopardized in any way.

In this context it behoves the government negotiators to take into account the Tamil population in the areas of conflict in the country. It is estimated (together with actual census of 2001) that the Tamil population is in the region of 1,347,386. This is only 7.3% of total 18 million in the country. When this tiny population is projected as a contrast with the vast areas of territory claimed by the LTTE map recently on display, it does make the whole Eelam claim untenable. The map concerned stretches from just north of Negombo to just north-east of Hambantota. How could any negotiator ignore such an unjustifiable claim detrimental to the country and endangers the lives and livelihood of all the millions of non-Tamils living in those areas in the LTTE map? This then is the lovely dream of LTTE fascism, you ignore it at your peril.

36

The Lethal Debris from Sattahip

(The Island, 28th sept.2002)

The megaton propaganda bomb exploded by Mr. Balasingam spewed a lot of debris, some lethal to the existence of this country as one nation. This propaganda ***gundu*** was the statement that LTTE was not asking for a separate state outside Sri Lanka's national integrity. It had an initially blinding effect on even the usually skeptic scribes of reputed newspapers of the world. Their editors splashed it as headline that Tigers had renounced Eelam as a separate state.

It was only later that some realized that the LTTE had only invented a new epistemology; "we operate according to concepts and categories that are entirely different. We operate according to the concept of a homeland and self-determination. Homeland does not mean a separate state as such saying that LTTE is fighting for a state has no relevance" (Mr.Balasingam at Sattahip Press Conference on 18th Sept.).

Yes folks Eelam is not relevant to the current peace talks just yet. It has merely been postponed for the moment. Because the solution sought is an alternative incorporating the LTTE's core issues of self-determination, homeland and nation-hood. It came with a blackmailer's explicit injunction, "if this is not granted, we will have to pursue a separate state as a last resort". This is what is usually known as squaring the circle with pure semantics. The LTTE, however, have scored a conspicuous victory in the international arena. They are now the good guys sans their separatism, a bogus stance though it is. We are indeed a desperate gullible lot.

If the LTTE have really and truly given up separatism, why cannot they elucidate in constitutional and institutional terms, the meaning they attach to self-determination, homeland and nation-hood? Man does not live by concepts and categories alone, nor are we linguistic philosophers. Two different governments have openly laid out their plans for the settlement of the dispute. One is the District/Provincial Council system already on the Statute Book, and the other is the Package of Proposal for Regional Government by the former PA government. Having rejected them both, it is now time for the LTTE to detail their plan for the restructuring of the state and government of the country; only then we would know whether separatism has been abandoned for good. Until then, forget the empty words, judge by the actions of the LTTE in the northeast. Those terrorist actions do not lend credence to the "no Eelam" claim.

The lethal debris branded the north east as the homeland of the Tamils and Muslims. The merged Tamil population could not justify the grabbing of so much land as well as miles of the coastline. The Muslims were inveigled into the equation. The addition of 461,382 Muslims of the Ampara, Batticaloa, Trincomalee and Vavunia (Census 2001) make the case for a homeland respectable. In this linguistic homeland what would be the fate of the Sinhalese? In the four districts mentioned above, there are 323,681 Sinhalese living now. Are they not living in the homes and lands of their birth? Why should they not have a stake in the peace process?

The Muslims appear to have forgotten that it was the Kandyan King Senerat (1609-1636) who saved them from the persecution of the Portuguese, and settled them in 1625 in the Kandyan homelands in the east among his Sinhala subjects. If those lands could now become the homelands of the Muslims, what about the descendants of the Kandyans who already lived there before the arrival of the Muslims? The LTTE, the Muslims and the United Front government have obligations towards those Sinhalese. The fate awaiting them, in this newly designated real estate of Tamil-speaking people could be tragically traumatic. They are at risk of being demoted to second class citizens, and probably aliens and massacred. This lethal debris has the potential to engulf them as well as the rest of the nation in an orgy of killing!

Hitherto the LTTE did not utilize any of the funds they raised to improve the conditions of the people economically or educationally. The health of the people under their control was not a matter for their concern. To the LTTE, the Tamils under their control were merely resources to be exploited unto destitution. A large proportion of food and medicine sent to the people by the government was appropriated by the LTTE for their use. Such was the rapacity of the LTTE. Under the agreed Joint Task Force, the LTTE have been undeservingly elevated to the status of Joint Fund Raisers with the government.

It would indeed be a matter for celebration, if true, that such extortionists have become born-again developers of the land and its people. Yet the lingering doubt remains as to where the foreign funds would be diverted. Given the existence of Eelamist bank, the need for hard currency to finance the purchase of the latest military hardware, the myopic and indulgent attitude of United Front government to the shenanigans of the LTTE, a large amount of the funds is likely to end up elsewhere, other than for development and rebuilding.

This particular spark from Sattahip has given the LTTE access to international sources of finance. It is the exclusive prerogative of a sovereign government to conduct negotiation for foreign finance, whether it is a loan, donation or just foreign aid. This sovereign privilege has been abandoned by the UF government by including the LTTE as a partner "to raise funds jointly". The government appears to have forgotten that LTTE still remains a proscribed unit in the international arena. By including the LTTE in their fund-raising activities, the government is, in fact, advocating either the de-proscription of the LTTE or naively embarrassing those foreign governments and jeopardizing the favourable outcome to their financial negotiations. The LTTE as well as other private organizations should have been involved in the rebuilding effort at the ground level only after the government had obtained the necessary funds by its own efforts.

Jaw- jaw is better than war- war, they say. But the jaw-jaw at Sattahip seems to be a one-way traffic in the direction of giving into all the demands of the LTTE as well as the Muslims. The fact that to-date, the country has not been informed of what happened at Sattahip is an indication of the many concessions yet to be handed over to the LTTE. The government appears to be urgently concerned to appease western foreign governments, than inform its own citizens. Is it because they have set the agenda and want the negotiations to conclude the way they want? Well the Sinhala population of 74% in this country appears not to matter to any one, they have been reduced to mere pawns in the hands of politicians. Peace yes, surrender no!

37

Up the Creek in a Peace-Boat

(The island, 7th Dec. 2002)

A creek is a small tributary of a river with many bends and inlets branching off in various directions. One usually needs a good knowledge of the area to explore such creeks without getting lost. The government's peace endeavour appears to be an exploration of a creek without even an improvised map in a boat full of holes. However, Pirapakaran and his men in this boat do know the way and are acting as guides to reach the destination mapped out by them.

The failure to recognize the consistency of the demands of the LTTE had led Sri Lankan governments to embark on a porous boat of peace journeying towards the fulfillment of those demands. Let me substantiate what I have asserted above with Pirapakaran's words. On Nov.27 in his hero's day message he said that "we have always been consistent with our policy with regard to our struggle for self-determination, Tamil homeland, Tamil nationality and Tamils' right to self-determination. They are the fundamentals underlying our political struggle. We have been insisting on these fundamentals from Thimpu to Thailand" (The Island, Nov.28).

If Eelam is not the destination why go back to Thimpu principles? True he refrained from using that five letter word----Eelam----, but his Eelam bank, his Eelam police, his Eelam courts, his Eelam kachcheri, and the larger than life map of Eelam, conspicuously projected at every photo opportunity, speak volumes instead. The operative word is Eelam. If Eelam is not on the cards, why these Eelam institutions? The fanatical Eelamists have been ordered to shoot him on the day he abandons Eelam. Therefore, the fact that Pirapakaran is still alive amidst his fanatical Eelamists, is the solid proof that he has not given up Eelam, his devotees know that.

"My government is determined to ensure that people in all parts of the country enjoy the same security, the same quality of life, the democratic forms of government and the rule of law and the human rights, which as citizens, is their birthright. The political aspirations and rights of all communities, Sinhalese, Tamil and Muslim, who live in our multi-ethnic society have to be safeguarded. The right to equality for each and every member of our nation must be maintained in a democratic and pluralistic polity", said our Prime Minister in Oslo (The Island, Nov.26). Those were noble words directed at the West. It is the pantomime season in the Western world, they do understand such panegyrics to democracy. But those words do not carry any conviction or persuasive impetus in the LTTE territory, for those terrorized people, badly affected by LTTE's non-pluralistic, undemocratic rule of a self-appointed outlaw. It is a bandit country there, and no rule of law prevails there.

"The reality on the ground situation" a phrase fondly used by the UNF ministers, is that democratic dissent in LTTE controlled territory will result in death. Thus we find two political parties---- EPDP and SEP (Socialist Equality Party) ---have been under severe attack for challenging the LTTE's fascism in Jaffna. They have been denied work permits. Their offices have been fire-bombed, their men kidnapped and murdered. The Jaffna Municipal Councilor Jayachandran (of EPDP) was assaulted brutally, and Kodeswaran (of SEP) was subject to knife attack on his head, neck and body. They have death sentences hanging over their heads should they continue their audacious dissent against the LTTE. Their assailants have been identified and reported to the police, but no action has been taken. The equality and the rule of law advocated by the Premier did not help those two men. The Prime Minister was well aware of those above incidents, and probably many others too, where people have been subject to terror and wholesale intimidation. Therefore it would have been a convincing stand, had he alluded to at least some of those incidents, and requested international help to change this reign of terror. Such a message would not have been lost on LTTE, the perpetrators of totalitarianism. Perhaps he can take his cue from the British Prime Minister in this case.

Prime Minister Blair too looked kindly on many infringements of the ceasefire by IRA for nearly four years since the Good Friday Agreement. But the day of reckoning came when the IRA was caught red-handed having infiltrated the Northern Ireland Office itself. Yet he had the gumption to tell the IRA that "another inch-by-inch negotiation won't work. Symbolic gestures, important in their time, no longer build trust. It is time for acts of completion. Republicans must make the commitment to exclusively peaceful means, real, total and permanent. There can't be two police forces. The crunch is the crunch. There is no parallel track left. The fork in the road has finally come. We cannot carry on with the IRA half in, half out of this process. Not just because it isn't right any more. It won't work any more" (The Sunday Times 20th Oct). Those were powerful and hard hitting words backing his suspension of the power-sharing government of Northern Ireland. Why, in contrast, do our politicians bend over backwards to ignore not only the human rights violations of the LTTE, but also rush to defend them and appease them, while preaching democracy from international platforms?

The government has failed to support our Security Forces when they were subject to ridicule and humiliation by rabble-rousers of the LTTE. The organized "peoples' protest" at Hartley College camp and Kanjirankuda camp were patently aimed at eviction of the army from their secure position. There were no words of comfort for the army from the government. They were left to fend for themselves, while the government rushed in to compensate the stone-throwers and the arsonists who invaded those army camps.

The government, having reduced our Security Forces to the level of an escort agency for the erstwhile terrorists, is now in the process of negotiating away its sovereign right to station the army in the areas that threaten the very sovereignty of the nation. Yet the right to operate and maintain High Security Zones (HSZ) has been accorded to the LTTE without even a whimper of protest. What is the necessity for these LTTE's HSZ if Eelam has been abandoned? Should not those LTTE's HSZ be also opened up, cleared of land mines and be freed for occupancy by the people? That would be true equality advocated by the PM. The secrets they hide are too sensitive and would totally expose the duplicity and bellicose nature of LTTE. Yet the government and the Opposition in Parliament appear to be frightened to broach this subject. Cowards they indeed are!

There are decisive pointers to the desired destination mapped out by the LTTE. The prolific use of the phrase "united Sri Lanka" by the Prime Minister (Mr. Wickramasinghe) and other UNF Ministers is indication that a division of some sort of the country is being prepared to be foisted on the people, with the carrot of many millions of foreign aid. Autonomy and internal self-determination are other coded words used by both the government and the LTTE. The gestation that is taking place in various parts of the world is simply the pretended labour pains to deliver Eelam in the guise of Confederation of United Sri Lanka. That would be the never never land, where Sri Lnaka would never be the same as it is now. When you are called upon to choose, remember what happened to the Kingdom of Knady after the Convention of 1815. The Kingdom of Kandy simply disappeared for good.

38

The Rickety side of Federation

(The Island, 23rd Jan. 2003)

The few MPs on their junket in western capitals to study federalism are likely to see and hear only the sunshine stories about federalism. However, there are many hidden and open pitfalls not fully apparent to the students of federalism. I explore below three main corollaries that inevitably result from federalism. I hope our MPs will, at least, take on board Montesquieu's celebrated dictum that laws must be adapted to the circumstances in which a nation lives. Federation is clearly not the answer to the pluralist circumstances of the Eastern Province. It needs the immediate and undivided attention of our MPs. This is because the Eastern Province has been forcibly merged with a mono-ethnic North without the consent of the people living in the East. Is this not a denial of the fundamental rights of those people?

The language of nationhood advocated by the LTTE is aimed at equalizing the bargaining power between the majority Sinhalese plus the rest of the country (roc) and the minority Tamils. This language deliberately converts superiority/inferiority into co-equal partnership. Thus the concept of Sri Lanka as the home of two nations necessarily engenders three propositions. The first is that the Tamils should, as far as possible, determine their own future without interference from outsiders. The second is that the majority Sinhalese plus (roc) should also likewise be able to determine their own future without outside interference. The third is that common issues, such as foreign policy, currency and macro-economic management should not be decided in a common forum as the Tamils could be outvoted there. It would have to be settled by negotiation between leaders representing the two nations.

It is likely that the LTTE would demand asymmetric federalism as this satisfies the first proposition and their agenda of self-determination.

Asymmetry means more than equal to or disproportionate powers. Therefore, asymmetric federalism, by its very nature, may satisfy the LTTE, but miserably fail on the second and the third proposition. This is because due to the favouritism shown to LTTE's Eelam in the new constitution giving effect to the above arrangement, the Tamils will have more rights than the others, they will be more than equal, and will make the rest of the country second-class citizens. They will be the chosen few in Sri Lanka.

The third proposition is anti-democratic as the vital common issues of the country would become the subjects of secret intrigues between the leaders, one of whom is (World Bank please note) at the moment, an un-elected dictator, whose power base is not democratic votes, but multi-barrel rockets and lethal designer suited suicide squads! All Sri Lankans should take a special interest in the way the three propositions above are tackled by the negotiators. It could be another give-away leading to catastrophe. Asymmetric federalism given to a fanatical unit that has relentlessly constructed all other infra-structure of a nation state, is simply another separate state, no matter, all the assurances to the contrary given by our spineless and unreliable politicians. A federation is simply a formal description of a type of territorial division of power. It is Janus-faced, as it is both a solution to and a cause of ethnic conflict leading to separatism.

Asymmetrical federalism as well as devolution to a minority usually undercut the rights of other minorities within that minority. They are likely to lose their rights. This is of vital importance to the Sinhalese and Muslims population in the Eastern province. They will then be reduced to second class peoples, a powerless minority within a minority. They will lose what is due to them from the state, if not by design, but likely by deliberate default and prevarication. Their Sinhala language might become the first casualty, followed by denial of, or obstruction to access to other facilities and amenities generously provided to the Tamil community by the new state Tamil government. In Canada, the Quebec Language Charter (Bill 101) does permit education in English to the children of parents only if they themselves had received education in English in Quebec itself. An Anglophone educated in English in (say Alberta) cannot educate his children in English in Quebec (Attorney-General v Quebec Association of Protestant School Boards, 1982). This is despite The Canadian Charter of Rights and Freedoms (sec.23), giving the parents the right to have their children educated in the minority language of the province they reside, provided the parent was educated in that language in Canada. Such is the power of asymmetrical devolution!

In the Canadian Federation, Prime Minister Trudeau made significant changes to the Canadian Constitution giving explicit recognition of Canada as a bilingual and bicultural society. Yet the provincial government of Quebec refused to ratify the Constitution Act of 1982. The Quebecois then demanded the right to be recognized as a "distinct society" within Canada's Federal system. The Meech Lake Accord of 1987 acceded to this demand, but failed to get into the Statute Books. The Charlottetown Agreement of 1992 further enhanced the position of Quebec and other indigenous minority communities. This was agreed to by the ten provincial premiers, but was rejected at a vital referendum held in Oct. 1992. This rejection was a clear example of peoples' power over that of politicians. This is a good example for us to follow.

In the eyes of the Canadians at large, this asymmetric federation gave Quebecois more rights than they themselves had, and therefore, was against the liberal values of democratic equality of all Canadians before the law. No matter what the foreign lecturers and local pundits on Canadian Constitution have to say about the salutary effects of federalism on a pluralist society, it remains a fact that the Canadian federation has not managed to halt the pro-independence movement in Quebec. We are likely to wake up one day with another new sovereign independent state there. How can this be a model for us to emulate? Is it any wonder why the LTTE went to Canada to scrutinize this constitution?

Resorting to federal structure means, accepting in principle to recast the structure of government, and also acceding that the LTTE's Eelam is either sovereign, or at a minimum, quasi-sovereign. For, a federation exists only if formed by equal partners as free to withdraw, as to enter into, such an association. This is the fundamental raison d'etre of a federation. Would our MPs have learnt this elementary lesson of freedom of exit and entry underpinning a federal association?

Belgium was formed as a unitary state in 1831 by uniting the southern French speaking part (Wallonia) with the northern Dutch speaking part of Flanders (Flemish). It became a federal state in 1988 divided on linguistic lines, with Brussels having the special status of a bilingual state. It has three----Dutch, French and German---- cultural councils representing the three cultural communities. Each has its own region. Within each region language regulations prevail. If tax support is required and the Diplomas awarded to students are to be recognized, the language of instruction in the school must be the language of that region. The constitution also prescribes that the Cabinet be composed of equal number of Dutch speakers and French speakers. In Belgium we have near full autonomy for two national groups plus bargaining power over state-wide policies.

What our peripatetic MPs need to look at is the constant and endless process of haggling taking place in Belgian politics. This has resulted in undue delays in the legislative process. The rigid language rules have continued to hamper mobility of labour. Many independent observers would tell you that it is almost a certainty that the country would have broken up but for the problems posed by the wealthy Brussels which is also the HQ of the European Union. Brussels is a rich Francophone enclave in Flemish territory. It is too big a prize for either side to relinquish. However, this federal decentralization has not satisfied the Flemish fully. They have not given up separation and independence.

In Spain the Basque province was given asymmetrical autonomy with wide powers over many aspects of government. There too we still have terrorism almost on a daily basis to force the central government to yield to the demands of the separatists.

Finally, I hope, the most important lesson our MPs should learn from their expedition in Europe is that the country is not their estate. It does not belong to them. It cannot simply be parceled out to others they fancy. The words of Abraham Lincoln are most appropriate to our present situation where partition has been on the cards of some politicians; "this country, with its institutions belongs to the people who inhabit it. Whenever they shall grow weary of existing government, they can exercise their constitutional rights of amending it, or their revolutionary right to dismember or overthrow it" (First Inaugural Address 1861). Will our politicians respect this right of the people of Sri Lanka? In political terms, we have arrived at the brink of hell, throwing wet towels will not help.

39

My Eelam, Right or Wrong

(The Island, 10th Jan. 2003)

The thirst for Eelam or my Eelam, right or wrong can never be satisfied until it becomes a reality with the help of Norwegian midwifery. This is the ultimate of arrogant chauvinism pursued by the LTTE, by confusing everybody with ambiguous, dubious and contradictory verbiage. The government and the peaceniks are blinded by the artful circumlocution and equivocation, no matter, the obvious drift of events towards that LTTE objective. It is quite clear that they are in the driving seat of the peace boat.

To the government, federalism has become a leitmotif of peace. Yet it is obvious that it means different things to different people. So long as politicians and people deeply respect and abide by the Rule of Law, and the Provisions of the Constitution as regards not only the Institutions of the Polity, but also the Human Rights of fellow citizens, then it is just possible that a federal constitution could be a solution to a minority problem. But do we have such men and women as our political leaders? Have we not seen them trying to bend, amend and even jettison the Constitution in pursuit of personal power over others? Can we expect respect for the Constitution from such ambitious persons?

Oh yes, what of the LTTE? Its leader is and has been an absolute dictator with self-assumed powers over lives of others. In his bandit country, what he proclaims is the law and he is infallible. Would he voluntarily subject himself to a Constitution and abide by its rules? What evidence do we have of his commitment to obey democratically promulgated Rule of Law? While such unpleasant questions are unwelcome, they are also vital parts of the peace process. Such questions need to be satisfactorily answered.

To most Sri Lankans, the federalism prevailing in most parts of the world appear as an attractive proposition. Indeed we could replicate one or a mixture of those models to suit our conditions. This is the nub of the question. What exactly is our condition? Let me explain from the point of view of "my Eelam, right or wrong".

In a previous article (The Island, 29th Aug. 2002), I have quoted from the Census 2001 that the Tamil population in the areas of conflict was (in my view generously) estimated to be no more than 7.3% of the total population. This then is our first condition. A mere 7.3% of the population wants to take possession of nearly 30% of landmass and 60% of the coastline. This patently unjust demand is further compounded by the fact, that in the eastern province, the Tamils are a minority, the Sinhalese and the Muslims constitute about 65% of the population of the province. In short it is a pluralist province ethnically and in terms of religion. Therefore it is quite clear that what is suitable for the mono-ethnic Jaffna cannot, by any stretch of imagination, be considered suitable to the eastern province. Besides how many of these citizens would want to live under the dictatorial suzerainty of the LTTE? Therefore the first condition based on ground reality, requires that the east be de-merged and made to stand on its own. {I am happy that the Supreme Court did effect this separation}.

The second condition is the very apparent fascist nature of the LTTE. Though the LTTE has recently expended many words to hide this fact, their actions have not matched their words. Democratic dissent is anathema in their badlands. Regressive and rapacious taxes are vigorously enforced. Kangaroo courts deal out punishments designed by Pirapakaran himself. Designer suicide squads are still being trained and paraded in public. Little boys and girls are still being abducted on their way to school to be trained as killers of the future. Shiploads of arms are still being clandestinely imported and set up ready to blast everyone in the vicinity to smithereens. Tamil Gulags or slave camps in the jungles of Mankulam are in operation to service the needs of the LTTE hierarchy. Has the LTTE over this one year of ceasefire given up any of the activities listed above? No. A federal state under these conditions would be a ready-made separatist dictatorship with its own army, navy, police, courts, kachcheries, banks, and gulags. Such a state will, even without any provocation, manufacture a casus belli to break away from the federal set-up on any flimsy ground. This unfortunately will be the outcome and the present Sri Lanka is now living on borrowed time. Some LTTE Sinhala sympathizers have already started to talk about a new "united Sri Lanka".

In this context the controversial radio equipment supplied to LTTE by courtesy of Norway, was a well-planned strategic move by the LTTE. The LTTE has always excelled in black propaganda throughout the world. Their virulent and unabated vilification of the Sinhala Buddhists has been a success story until recently. It was audaciously repeated in Oslo by Mr. Balasingam in the presence of 40 other nations, and shamelessly acquiesced in by the leaders of our government. Sooner than later the LTTE are bound to embark on this black propaganda trail again. Now this new powerful toy would give them ample opportunity to insult ad libitum the Sinhalese, our security forces and even our neighbor, India. Mere paper cancellation of license would have no effect unless we have powerful signaling mechanism to jam such disparaging broadcasts. We should then dispatch to the Vanni the bunch of stupid VVIPs who granted permission for these gadgets. They should be under orders to physically dismantle and impound the equipment, with the injunction, not to come back without the equipment! They deserve this picnic in the paradise of Eelam!.

The third condition was enunciated by Pirapakaran in his hero's day message. "We want to protect our national identity, pursuing the development of our language, culture and economy". The fact is that there is no hindrance whatever in Sri Lanka to a Tamil person to maintain his Tamilness, whether in terms of his religion, language or culture. Even on the very mundane levels of practicing a profession and engaging in economic activities, the Tamils fare well and most of their clients and customers are non-Tamils. It is no cause to wonder that a large number of Tamils live among the Sinhalese and Muslims. Their cultural efflorescence is evident everywhere. There are nearly a quarter of million Sri Lankan Tamils in Colombo alone. They are unlikely to uproot their present connections and restart their lives under

LTTE. The unpleasant question, therefore, is how a made-to-measure federation given to placate and appease the LTTE in one corner of our country could be of any help or enhance the lives of those Tamils now living outside LTTE controlled territory?

A negotiation is a matter of give and take. There cannot be a concession without a consideration, a quid pro quo. Major General Fonseka has (with regard to the question of vacating High Security Zones in Jaffana) taught our negotiators the way negotiation should be conducted. So far we have seen only concessions from the government in it's over eagerness to maintain the peace process: Could we now expect the LTTE to display the genuine desire for peace by actually allowing a plural political culture, and reinstating Human rights and Rule of Law in their territory? On these matters the LTTE is intransigent as ever. This is why a federation with them would be fatal for the country. They are not federalists. They are separatists masquerading as federalists.

40

Tyranny and Tragedy in the North-East

(The Island, 27th Feb.2003)

No freedom of expression, no freedom of movement and no freedom of association, this is the ground reality in the LTTE controlled part of the north-east of the country. This situation anywhere in the world, would be condemned as intolerable tyranny. In our country this tyranny is not only tolerated, it is, in fact, encouraged by those who stride about in political arena, as stalwarts of democracy, peace and decency. They are the collaborators and apologists of the tyranny imposed on the people by the LTTE. I have listed only three, yet many are the freedoms denied by the LTTE to these people living in bondage.

Included among these partners in crime are those heads of religious establishments (Catholic, Christian and Hindu), who have failed to alert the world to the oppression the people suffer under the tyranny of the LTTE. Then there are the NGOs and some Emissaries of foreign governments who shamelessly fund this terrorist outfit without any quid pro quo, not even a request to eschew terrorism. Yet in their own countries they hunt down terrorists to the point of complete elimination and even invade other countries in pursuit of terrorists. Imagine how the Government of Japan and the Japanese people would react, if we were to donate funds to the Sarin gas terrorists who killed innocent commuters in Tokyo underground railway!

Included as accomplices are also those Sri Lankan politicians and fellow travelers in the "conflict resolution" circuit, whose jobs these days is to trot out wishy-washy explanations, specious and lame excuses on behalf of LTTE, whenever the wounds caused by the LTTE are exposed. These Sri Lankans stand condemned as traitors to our nation. They are guilty of surrendering the Tamils to the clutches of the LTTE for unalleviated servitude, and endangering the lives and livelihood of the Tamils and non-Tamils living even in government controlled areas.

The government and its servile media-wallahs too are fast running out of excuses. They have now adopted the strategy of speaking on behalf of terrorists and pretending that they neither see nor hear anything, least of all, the many naked infringements by LTTE of the heavily pro-LTTE loaded MOU. They do not report the belligerent speeches emanating from LTTE. They (the media) are guilty of gross deception of the people. Their incompetence and pusillanimity is so apparent that they have become the butt-end of jokes by their counterpart LTTE negotiators. The dire warning is in the results of the recently held elections in Cyprus. The incumbent President Clerides lost because the majority Greek Cypriots believed that he was making too many concessions to the minority Turkish Cypriots in the negotiation for the unification of that divided country.

The mantle of "sole representative of the Tamils" is an imposition at the point of the gun. It cannot be acceptable in any democracy on that point alone. True to form, therefore, the LTTE is able to use the gun to silence all dissent and dissenters. Only LTTE's opinion prevails in their bandit country. Any other opinion is silenced ruthlessly, and the authors of such opinions are slaughtered without mercy. The Tamil people are even denied all access to anti-LTTE opinions expressed in the south in Tamil medium. Anyone caught trying to smuggle such printed matter will be summarily executed. This is a Stalinist Soviet in Sri Lanka, ignored by the democratic nations of the world. They are also prepared to fund its renewal and rehabilitation into respectability. Those pro-LTTE nations are in the process of establishing a cruel and murderous totalitarian unit in the north east of Sri Lanka. A robust expose' of this fact is not anti-peace, but a contribution to an endurable democratic peace.

The fates of other Eelam driven political parties (EPDP, PLOTE, EPRLF) in the Jaffna peninsula speak volumes about the tyranny of the LTTE. The members of these parties are hunted down, shot at and their offices are bombed. They cannot carry out their political activities without risking their lives. An estoppel was imposed by the LTTE on the grand opening of the Jaffna Library by the pro-LTTE Tamil National Alliance (TNA) politicians. It was a humiliating fiasco even for the proxy LTTE TNA. These elected politicians had hitherto pledged their full support to the LTTE. They had promised to represent the LTTE interests in the south and assiduously to follow the orders and instructions of the LTTE. This was not enough. Now they have realized that what was required of them was outright vassalage. Now their humiliating submission to LTTE too support my thesis presented herein that there is no democracy possible with the LTTE. The elected Mayor of Jaffna, who together with 23 members resigned on this issue, has alerted the "global community to the situation in Jaffna peninsula, where LTTE is preventing democratically elected representatives of the public from carrying out their functions" (The Island, 17th Feb.). Would anyone listen? Ambassadors, have no ears?

According to the MOU there should be freedom of movement for people on the A9 road. But there is no such freedom. Permission to travel is allowed only to those forced to pay to the LTTE the rapacious toll charges at Muhamaly and Omanthai. This flagrant and continuous breach of MOU is not the concern of the government, the government negotiators, and the government media. Worst of all, no part of this extorted fund is utilized to improve and repair the roads. The foolish government has undertaken to do that and thereby afford more opportunities to the LTTE to levy illegal dues from the people. On top of this, there is a pass system in operation in LTTE controlled areas for those who need to and want to move in and out of those areas. This was what apartheid South Africa did, and was rightly condemned as totally inhuman and unacceptable. Have our Human Rights activists lost their eyes and ears?

The LTTE has not opened its palmyrah- cadjan fences to the outside world. The government and the world should demand that the LTTE too should open its High Security Zones for the settlement of the people. The LTTE too have taken over by force the lands and houses of Tamil, Muslim and Sinhala people. They should be made to surrender such ill-gotten gains or pay market-rate compensation to their rightful owners. Are these actions not part of bringing about normalcy? Normalcy appears to be only about creating conditions for the LTTE to pursue their objective of Eelam behind the privacy of cadjan fence surrounded by opaque veil of secrecy. Cowardice appears to have overwhelmed our negotiators.

The tragedy of the Eastern province is the impending catastrophe facing the non-Tamils in that region. Especially, the Sinhala people have already become non-entities there, though they are nearly one-third of the population and have prescriptive right to live out their lives there based on historical and illegible evidence going back to pre-Christian times. "To address land issues" in the east the negotiators agreed to elect committees manned by LTTE cadres, other Tamils and Muslims only. The Sinhalaya was completely ignored, even given the fact, that they too own land and other properties. This is not only foolish and unpardonable, but also smacks of open hostility to anything Sinhalese by our government negotiators. They have become part of the problem for the Sinhala majority in this country.

The greatest attempt to bribe the nation would occur post Tokyo Conference. Those yellow-belly negotiators would then issue the ultimatum to the nation a la Mr. (not Dr.) Balasingam: accept our solution of a tyrannical totalitarian LTTE state in the North-East or lose all those foreign loans. Sinhalaya your time is up! If we allow this spurious negotiation to proceed any further, the end of Sinhala history will be inevitable.

41

The Gravediggers of Sri Lanka's Sovereignty

(The Island, 30th April 2003)

What do I mean by sovereignty? To answer this question one has to start with the fundamental structure of the world as it exists today. What we see is an international society of independent states. These states function through governments to protect their citizens and enhance the interests of the countries they govern. Domestic political heresy, the practice of particular economic policy and aggressive pursuit of a religion are not actionable in the international set-up. They cannot be challenged by other states. However, Fundamental Human Rights do pose limits on this aspect of sovereignty.

The international system is regulated by the laws that all nations are expected to obey and respect. These international laws recognize specific sea and land boundaries of a state. Within the boundary of a state, the government of the country has the monopoly of power to legislate and enforce obedience to the laws promulgated by the government. This is the principle of territorial integrity and political sovereignty.

A state has no right to cross the boundary of another state without its expressed permission. Such invasions are unwarranted aggressions and the victim state has the right to defend itself by using all means at its disposal. This is also known as "fighting a war against war". Thus the invasion of Iraq is an illegal use of force, no matter the laudable reasons given by the invaders of Iraq. Those reasons do still remain unproven. This is the principle of the criminality of foreign aggression and self-defence against aggressors.

In domestic society we punish crime to prevent violence. Similarly, among the nations international law provides for punishing aggression to prevent war. This principle usually results, more often, in punishing individuals of the brigand state, though war reparations might also be imposed. This principle accepts the fact that just as much as states are subjects of rights, they are also objects of punishments.

Thus the doctrine of sovereignty has embedded within it the corollaries of territorial integrity, exclusive jurisdiction and non-intervention by other states in the internal affairs of any one state. In the words of J. Breuilly "a state cannot become sovereign except within a system of other sovereign states, its sovereignty being acknowledged by them; in this there is a strong pressure towards mutual recognition as equals, whatever the factual situation in respect of differential power" (Reflections on Nationalism).

As far as Sri Lanka is concerned, it is a sovereign country recognized as such by the club of nations (UN). This has been the case until the explosive Tamil ethnic claim to self-determination in a homeland was ignited by the terrorist and separatist LTTE.

In response to this strident and irrational claim our politicians have sought refuge in craven retreat to compromise the sovereignty of the country. The gravediggers have begun the gruesome task. Funeral orations are being compiled. Funds are being canvassed and collected for the grand funeral and internment of the sovereignty of our state. Even as the funeral pyre is being prepared, soon it will be the turn of the citizens to assent to this betrayal via a referendum or forsake the bribe of billions of dollars they will inherit. Mark you, most of it will be loans which will have to be repaid with interest sometime in the future, even by the generations yet unborn!

The first among the gravediggers was the J.R.Jayawardene's UNP administration. It created the North-East Province by fiat. Some claim that this was done under duress with the Indians breathing down the neck. All the more the reason why this amalgamation of two very unlike provinces should have been annulled after the Indians left our shores. There are many cogent reasons why this mixture of North and Eastern provinces will not work. In short, the majority population (Muslims + the Sinhalese) are made disenchanted and disoriented citizens by the merger of the two provinces. Once the LTTE establishes legal control over them, they will be reduced to a segregated underclass (untermenchen) without any rights. Our politicians are aware of this situation from the reports they get on many bellicose statements made by the leaders of the LTTE in the East, and yet they will not do anything to dismantle this merger. Thus the territorial integrity of Sri Lanka has been jeopardized by labeling a part of the country as a spurious homeland territory.

The Norwegians with their one-sided MOU are literally pushing us to the grave itself. They have flouted the principle of non-intervention. A good example of that was the importation of radio transmitting equipment for LTTE under cover of diplomatic immunity. Often we have had the utterly one-sided Norwegian reports on the MOU infringements by the LTTE, trying to exculpate them. If we are to believe the reports in the media, the Norwegians are now on the verge of designating an "Eelam sea". This will be the bolting of the nails in the coffin, and the Norwegians would have by then graduated from gravediggers to undertakers for the sordid exercise of the internment of Sri Lanka's sovereignty. The creation of "Eelam sea" would be in gross violation of both the territorial integrity, for, our territory extends 200 miles at present into the sea, and exclusive jurisdiction of the sovereign state of Sri Lanka. Are we prepared to acquiesce in this process of disintegration of our country? If we are, let us be done with it, and stop all the pantomime in different parts of the world. A patriotism not prepared to defend the country does not deserve it to survive.

Both the previous PA and the present UNF governments have had their respective share of digging the grave. The PA foisted on us the prospect of a federalist constitution by accepting the legitimacy of the claim to a homeland. They remain unburdened for seeking to strengthen the homeland territory, while trying to divide the rest of the country and the Sinhala community into pieces.

The present UNF government appears hell bent on appeasement of the LTTE. They signed the one-sided Ceasefire Agreement (CFA). They find various excuses for the infringements by the LTTE of the same

CFA. They give into even outrageous demands of the LTTE with no reciprocation. They even make concessions gratis and it is possible that they may even assent to the creation of an Eelam sea in the Indian Ocean. The spectacular feebleness of this government is epitomized by its inability or unwillingness to robustly bargain at the negotiating table, let alone act against the infringements of CFA by the LTTE. This engenders confident aggression on the part of the LTTE in taking steps to bury the sovereignty of the country. How true it appears to be, that whom the gods wish to destroy, they first make them complacent!

To defeat European fascism there was astonishing union of opposites----a Roosevelt and Stalin, a conservative Churchill and the British Socialists, a rightist De Gaulle and the French Communists. That is what we need whether we intend fighting the terrorists or devising a peace plan. Unfortunately for the country, unity on such vital issues is beyond the egos of our politicians.

A Constitution can be devised giving the citizens formal recognition of their dual identity. The political identity of every citizen shall be Sri Lankan, while the cultural identity could be Sinhalese, Tamil, and Muslim etc. Thus we shall have Sri Lankan Sinhalese, Sri Lankan Tamils and Sri Lankan Muslims. This would be similar to Irish American, Mexican American and Italian American.

It is also possible to devise a Constitution where power is equally divided at the centre and executive power is distributed in a manner encompassing the minority population. They should be participators in both enacting national policies and the very implementation of those policies. The minority politicians should be able to feed at the same common trough of the state,

Finally the Constitution should create strong and independent institutions to guarantee and preserve the Human Rights of every citizen. Such institutions should be enshrined with immunity from interference by any politician both in its workings and in the appointment of persons to carry-out its functions. They should also be vested with enforcement powers in matters pertaining to their remit.

Once we accept the feasibility of the break-up of a unitary state to form a federal constitution, then there is no retraction possible when ultimate bifurcation is foisted on the nation. A failed federation is an irretrievable situation. There are many with vested interests in the LTTE camp who would deliberately want to wreck a federal set-up, because Eelam then would be an easily achievable goal. Is the UNF government leading us to this inglorious end?

42

Dying for One's Country

(The Island, 23rd April 2003)

The glory of the dead soldiers is inextricably bound with the glory of the state for which they gave their lives. The state therefore should be worthy of the sacrifice. The fact that the citizens of a country are ready to defend it against any aggression is prima facie evidence of the legitimacy of the state. To those citizens the state is part and parcel of their existence. They cherish it and support the government in power. This is especially true of a democratic government as a government is grounded on consent and is accountable to the people. The commitment to defend such a government is really death defying. In risking their lives, the citizens of such a country publicly enunciate their identity, their pride, love and support for their country. Does Sri Lanka's political and social ambience evince a set of values just and worthy of defense?

We have the plundering and blundering politicians whose grotesque wealth ostentatiously displayed, is a mocking expropriation of the daily bread of the vast majority of our poverty ridden population. In addition to this, we have a political system that is milked to full advantage to gain political power at whatever cost. There is no justice, transparency nor fairness in the way politicians get elected to office. Can we honestly expect anyone to risk his life to defend such a systematic exploitation? We have many rapacious businessmen whose greediness to amass wealth and contribute the least to the welfare of the country has been exposed by the press. Yet they go unpunished to stack away their ill-gotten gains in secret foreign bank accounts. They are, after all, the financiers and bankrollers of politicians. Can we expect our youngsters to lay down their lives for these scoundrels?

Nationalism legitimates the need to defend the country. It should be a nationalism that satisfies the urge to seek out roots, the desire for durable stability and connects us to our past, present and the future. It is a continuum in which the personal welfare of the citizens is embedded in the continued existence and prosperity of the national community. Such nationalism would contextualize human action, impart special significance and would endow individual lives with tangible meaning. All social, political and cultural acts become channels for self-fulfillment and therefore rewarding. This membership in a particular national and cultural community would make life meaningful and therefore impart strong motivation to risk one's life to ensure the continuity and growth of the nation. Nationalistic language and symbols enhance the collective mission of the growth and prosperity of the nation. The common endeavour should be as Edmund Burke asserted "to claim and assert our liberties as an ensiled inheritance derived to us from our forefathers, and to be transmitted to our posterity".

The fact remains that we are all afraid of death and our most powerful interest is self-preservation. Some have sought to overcome this fear by glorifying death and by intense mind-bending propaganda that death will help to achieve a nationalistic objective. It is worth defending a Jewish state argue the Jews. On the other side, the death of a Palestinian at the hands of the Jews is always considered as that of a shahid (martyr). Then there are the public ceremonies, memorial days and veneration of fallen soldiers usually connected with a central place set apart for that purpose. Thus we have Arlington National Cemetery in Virginia, Mount Herzl in Jerusalem and our own Mailapitiya off Kandy. Their symbolic purpose is to remind our soldiers that they shall never be forgotten, that they shall linger in the collective memory for eternity; thus assuring the soldiers that they will attain their immortality by their death in defense of the country.

> "This story shall the good man teach his son
> And Crispin Crispin shall ne'er go by,
> From this day to the end of the world,
> But we in it shall be remembered;

> We few, we happy few, we band of brothers" (Henry V, Shakespeare).

Have we Sri Lankans taken the vow to remember our fallen heroes? Have we not a moral obligation to keep the memory of the soldiers who died for us?

The government of the day and its military establishments has the responsibility as well as the duty to project military life as "exemplifying courage, strength, hardness, control over passions and ability to protect the moral fabric of society by living a manly life". Our soldiers should be so trained that they are seen as the best citizens and the finest people. Glory, respect and public idolization should be their rewards in addition to many material benefits. Dharmadasa of Haslaka, Generals Kobbekaduwa and Wimalaratne were such fine men and there are many others among our fallen men. There are also many still in service in the Security Forces who are prepared to lay down their lives for the country. These men and women do deserve our everlasting gratitude.

There will come a time when the country will need such young men/women infused with patriotism. When the peace in the country becomes a matter of pieces for territorial vultures, we shall need men of steely determination to restore the sovereignty of the country. Their lot today is that of derision by the traitorous peaceniks.

A pacifist Prime Minister in the process of appeasing the warlord land grabber in the north of the country was right in saying that he was not willing to sacrifice young lives in fighting this wrecker of peace (Daily News. 13th Mar.). This appalling sentiment of supine surrender is in full accord with his actions and measured steps towards appeasement. He perhaps wants to make our army redundant and this will becomes apparent when one considers that the division of the country is the trajectory and the thrust of his policies.

It is imperative that we become a just society embodying fairness in the way we conduct our affairs and treat the minority population in the country. The 17th Amendment to the Constitution was aimed at directing us in this direction. Alas, silly politicians have stymied this thrust towards justice and fairness. So long as we have self-seeking politicians behaving in this manner, our society will remain corrupt and unworthy of being defended at the risk of one's life. Pro patria mori (to die for the country) would become a distant call evoking no response. Could this be the end envisaged by the deranged script-writers of the inglorious and pusillanimous peace process? They surely have forgotten that this country did produce its saviours when needed. They dare not acknowledge that lasting peace cannot be established by pandering to the outrageously unjust demands of a murderous child-snatcher.

43

Fatal Strategies of Failed Negotiators

(The Island, 24th June 2003)

The government and the LTTE have had six expensive sessions of negotiations all over the world. What really happened at those sessions was not revealed to the people. At the end of each session, the world at large was told that the negotiations had been successful and many 'breakthroughs' on various issues had been achieved. The rhetoric and the sunshine stories emanating from both sides were too good to be true. Alas, the truth had to come out sometime, and it did, from the mouth of one of the negotiators. He (Mr. Balasingam) said that the negotiations were a "waste of time". Now we know that those sessions of negotiations had all been fatuous non-events. They have not even been comic opera staged for our amusement. Therefore the verdict on the work of government negotiators is that they have failed miserably in their task. If they have any sense of dignity and self-respect, they should resign and abstain from taking any further part in this onerous task. But will they? No. Nevertheless, it is right that we should remind them of their duty.

The nation had all along been misinformed and misled by the negotiators in their paeans of praises after each session of negotiation, when in fact all was not well and crumbling around them. We were all suckered. Is this not a matter for resignation? Observe how Blair and Bush have been hauled over the coal by their respective representative bodies for fomenting the dodgy doctrine of Weapons of Mass Destruction to go to war and kill thousands of Iraq's population. An alert opposition in parliament should be baying for the resignation of those ineffective and incompetent government negotiators. The Prime Minister behind this debacle should also be called to account. At Tokyo he acknowledged that it was a high risk strategy. His strategy has failed therefore he must also accept the reprimand and the penalty due.

The government's overall strategy had all along been one of appeasement. The most important question of Rule of Law in LTTE controlled areas, was ignored to the extent that the LTTE could set itself up as the Rule of Law, and do as they please in any part of the land. This was fatal impudence. The terrifying consequence was the impudence of the LTTE to dispense with the law of the land and implement their own brand of tyranny on the people. Now every effort to exorcise them only serves to precipitate them. Any contumacy of the LTTE confirms and legitimates the one that preceded it.

In any case the government should on its own bring in new minds and new mindset into its team. Clearly its strategy of appeasement had failed. Every concession to the LTTE has had the effect of ratcheting up the ever escalating demands to the current position of Interim Administration (IA) outside the present Constitution. That is outside the pale of law and order, here and now applicable to every citizen in the country, notwithstanding the roguish regime in the ganglands under the LTTE. We have now the triumph of LTTE's blackmail as a strategy. Blackmail is the worst kind of relationship, and the acceptance of blackmail is the worst kind of dishonour. We have now no war, no peace, only a weak kind of deterrence. Peripeteias of an anorexic negotiation without a vigorous strategy can no longer deliver peace. The Oslo declaration by the LTTE (on the federal set-up), should have been pursued to the end and the LTTE should have been called upon to deliver on their democratic pretences. Their defunct ideologies, bygone utopias, dead concepts and fossilized ideas cannot be allowed to pollute our mental and political space any longer. The LTTE should be called upon to practice what they preach. In this respect, whatever the hidden agenda of USA, their recent call on the LTTE to prove their democratic credentials by their actions requires commendation.

Immediately following Oslo, the government should have embarked on restating the Rule of Law and democratic Human Rights in LTTE areas and then set about devising institutions to settle the conflict with the LTTE. Without first establishing the supremacy of the Rule of Law, a Constitution, however well formulated, will be subject to subversion and eventual disintegration. The same goes for the

Interim Administration. Though the PM announced that the Interim Administration "should not be in conflict with the laws of Sri Lanka", this in fact was only be a pious presumption. This is why we have today Eelam courts, Eelam Police, Eelam banks, Eelam Kachchery and Eelam army, navy and an emergent air force. They are all in conflict and contrary to the law of the land. Let me repeat, principles come first before institutions, and institutions should be based on firm principles of law and order.

The PM has accepted at Tokyo that he would "seek to involve the Opposition in the decision making process wherever possible". This is the right approach, and the IA he has proposed is a golden opportunity to involve the Opposition in decision making. He should seek inputs from the PA on this venture. Mere consultation, where the Opposition's views are promptly ignored after consultation, is not enough. Without this input and involvement their cooperation could not be assured and should not be expected.

In Sri Lanka anything interim eventually becomes permanent or semi-permanent. The merger of the North and the East was at first an interim measure. Today it is more or less permanent despite the many protestations by all sections of the people. Therefore any future IA should have attached to it an unmistakable timetable when it would cease to be interim and degrade to invisibility and illegality.

It has to be acknowledged that the Tokyo conference was a success for the UNF. It was also a success for the "International Community" in that they have now got a substantial handle on Sri Lankan affairs. In future it would be legitimate for them to dabble in our internal affairs under various excuses. Could they now force us to compromise on the sovereignty of the country? Has anyone thought of the debt burden on our community? These are cogent reasons why the Opposition should get completely involved so that those funds would be utilized to enhance economic growth of the country, which in turn, would help to pay off the debts. Could it be the case that the only growth would be the foreign bank balances of politicians, their cronies and that of the LTTE?

The need of the hour is a new strategy. It should start with a plan of at least the basic outline of a solution acceptable to both the UNF and the PA. A new negotiating team should be chosen from both the UNF and the PA. This unity in purpose would deny the opportunity for the LTTE to exploit the political division in the country and trot out excuses in order to drag on the peace process so that they can import all the arms they can buy in the arms markets of the world. This unity would also signal parliamentary support for the outcome. It would also be consonant with what the PM expressed in Tokyo. There should also be a think-tank supporting the negotiators. They should be given the active task of sifting through the events and arguments and eliciting whatever that would contribute to a durable peace. Where necessary this think-tank should rifle through the dustbins of recent negotiations and look for resumption of peace talks in the rubbish itself. If the terminator in the Vanni has already decided on another course of action disastrous to all, then we expect the international community to send us the bunker-busting smart bombs, missiles and the delivery systems to put a permanent end to destruction of the country by the LTTE.

44

The Chaos Theory of Peace Process

(The Island, 23rd May 2003)

The government made the peace process sacrosanct by making unnecessary and gratuitous concessions to the LTTE just to keep the peace process on tract. The government even made our army an unpaid escort agency for the terrorists. Yet, who screwed up the works and caused panic in the government's ranks? Mr. Balasingam himself. In the eyes of the government, what he does and says is not Tamil chauvinism, nor is it war mongering by the LTTE, even though, they hold public parades of their armed might in the Vanni with artillery in toe, and are caught with boat-loads of mines and other explosives!

Only Mr.Balasingam can play monkey tricks with the peace process. Only he can make the diplomats rush to Vanni to present their pleadings for compliance to the LTTE. The peace process is not sacrosanct to him. It is merely a process for manipulation to achieve his end-objective of Eelam, come what may. No, history does not repeat itself, the stupidity of men does repeat itself. Such moronic men have lost the capacity to learn from their mistakes. Until tangibly proved otherwise, we can only expect the worse from them.

It is jokingly said that a butterfly stirring the air today in Tokyo can transform storm system next month in New York. Seriously though, in the theory of chaos, the "butterfly effect" is sensitive dependence of outcome on initial conditions. In layman's terms "tiny differences in input could quickly become overwhelming differences in output". Edward Lorenz at MIT was engaged in predicting weather conditions. He came up with the observation that as small pieces of weather concatenated, any prediction became impossible. Errors and uncertainties multiplied cascading upward through a chain of turbulent features. Events do have a nasty habit of tending towards a point of crisis that could magnify small changes. This turbulence itself was found to be an orderly disorder, sometimes stable, sometimes unstable; randomness had its own underlying order, a pattern inside a pattern. Chaos scientists also discovered strange attractors even in turbulence eventually bringing everything to a steady state of relative stability. A wide range of initial conditions will lead to an equilibrium attractor---- and not necessarily a static equilibrium. These elementary ideas from Chaos Theory are sufficient for us (laymen) to have a fresh look at our peace process.

The initial conditions of peace process were the de-proscription and the CFA between the government and the LTTE. Further concessions were added to them over the period of the peace talks. All those concessions were one-way tugs to expedite the peace process towards the strange attractor----Eelam. Then there were also the numerous deliberate infringements of the conditions of the CFA in the north and east of the country. The "Butterfly Effect" of all those forces has pushed the peace process into turbulence. This turbulence has affected only the government. It is the government that has ended up in blue funk. It is the government that is scrambling to save the peace process without taking the necessary steps to stop the one-way tugs the LTTE is infusing into the peace process. The trajectory of the peace process is all one way and the tentative equilibrium it will reach would be catastrophe to the country. The LTTE would, of course, welcome such an end.

Have you seen or heard anything the government has done to halt the ever cascading demands of the LTTE? Has our government done anything to stop the violations of the CFA? Has our government done anything to stop the murder of opponents of the LTTE? Has the government raised the issue of LTTE's High Security Zones in Killinochchi and Mullaitivu? Has the government ever queried why the LTTE needs armed parades and live-fire practicing at sea if they are for a peaceful solution? Has the government ever demanded from the LTTE that it stopped ethnic cleansing and harassment of people in the government controlled marginal areas? Has the government ever subjected any LTTE men to the full force of law even when caught while committing a criminal act? Did we see any of these issues raised by the PM in his letter to Mr. Balasingam? What we have seen and experienced is that the LTTE has the freedom of the country to do what they want anywhere in the country, even commit murder in daylight in the streets of Colombo. The LTTE have not given up an iota of their fascism, their belligerence nor their war preparations.

One expected the peace process to be one of give and take and hard bargaining on issues that will restore dignity and rights of all people and so bring about the permanent cessation of conflict. This is not the case. Most objectives have been ignored in the talks and this has given the room and space for LTTE to strengthen their strangle hold and impose its tyranny on people even in government controlled areas. What we see is certainly not bargaining, rather a knocked down sale of the country to the LTTE.

The loans from our newly acquired foreign friends would not lead to lasting peace, so long as those countries avoid taking issue with the totalitarian thrust, the oppression and the complete disregard shown to Human Rights by the LTTE. It is the government of the country, and not LTTE, that will be called upon to pay the interest and repay the loans. Therefore should we not have a condition that no interest and no loan repayment, if LTTE does not renounce violence, respect political pluralism and permit democratic institutions to function in their gangland and also abide by the law of the land?

The apparent chaos had been a deterministic contrivance by the LTTE. At the start as well as during the progress of the talks, the LTTE built various conditions into the peace process that were not countermanded by the ever-ready-to-appease government. They (the LTTE) knew and still do know the pattern within the pattern. They know their destiny. They know that the sensitive initial conditions they have built into this process would not destroy but create their beloved Eelam. As for the government, it is sliding into entropy, decadence and randomness. As folklore would have it:

> "For want of a nail, the shoe was lost;
> For want of a shoe, the horse was lost;

For want of a horse, the rider was lost;
For want of a rider, the battle was lost;
For want of a battle, the kingdom was lost"!

And I might as well add that for want of courage and love for our country by our present politicians, the country would certainly be lost.

[All quotations are from: Chaos, Making a New Science by James Gleick]

45

Is it a USD 4.5 Billion Bribe?

(The Island, 12th July 2003)

The political culture in our country is predominantly prone to bribery and corruption. To most politicians bribery has become a way of life to finance their ostentatious life of grotesque wealth and luxury. That this corrupt mindset would be projected on society to maintain the politicians in power does not require far-fetched imagination. Just as much as politicians do buy votes, they do know that if they try, they might also succeed in bribing the populace to sell the sovereignty of the country.

It is true that the fifty-one nations and twenty-two finance organizations in Tokyo could have pledged their funds to another nation and not to Sri Lanka. That they were persuaded to help Sri Lanka is creditable to the UNF government. Yet one cannot help pointing out that recently, the President of Pakistan was able to obtain a package of three billion dollars in aid from just one country! He also expects a number of F15 Fighter planes in the near future!

In the international realm there is no free lunch. We need to delve into the motives of those apparently altruistic countries to make ourselves aware of the destination we are being shoved towards by those countries. What do they want from us? Why are they helping us? Are they seeking proxy control of our country?

It is true that we have immense economic problems. We do need lots of money to repair, restore, rehabilitate and develop the terrorist affected areas. We also need lots of money to do the same in many other areas in the rest of the country. Due to terrorism these areas also suffered indirectly as funds were diverted away from them to fight terrorism. It is also true that we cannot generate the necessary funds by ourselves for this purpose without imposing many stringent and austere economic regulations on our consumption expenditure. Borrowing from abroad is therefore a necessity. But this is no ordinary borrowing to tide over hard times. It is a borrowing under duress.

The difference is that we are forced to borrow with artillery and Sam missiles aimed at us by a very hostile army, navy, submarine force and a crude air force. Can one conjecture that there could also be WMDs (weapons of mass destruction) in this arsenal? Under such coercive conditions it is easy for the lenders to impose conditions detrimental to the very stability of the country. The UNF government has simply capitulated to the demands of the lenders. The country is now assailed on three fronts. There is the abject appeasement of the LTTE by the UNF; there is the servile submission to foreigners and the crafty projection of bribe in the guise of aid that the people dare not reject.

Would the people benefit to the tune of 4.5 billion dollars? That would only be a dream. This is because there is an enormous gap between available foreign aid and utilized foreign aid. Over the last many years the utilization of foreign aid has not been more than 21% and according to one commentator (in the Daily News of July 10th), it is the earnest wish of current Finance Minister to raise this to 45% by 2004. This then is one big plughole that immediately devalues our sovereignty to less than half the amount pledged by foreigners. There is also a vast distance between the amounts pledged and the actual amount of funds released. The donors have left it vague the precise event or action that will trigger the release of funds. Like in the case of large building in progress, perhaps Mr.Akashi will act as the architect who will evaluate the progress in the peace talks and the issue a certificate for interim payment! I wonder the basis on which he will determine the quantum of payment due.

The LTTE eschewed all obligations embodied in the Tokyo Declaration. They will therefore press for what they want, Eelam by any other name, plus their hands in the till to make it a reality. The UNF has actually offered to allow them to poke their trowel into the foreign aid trough. As the LTTE has renounced all responsibility, transparency and accountability, how would anyone know that the funds diverted to them would be spent according to projected plans? To-date the LTTE has not shown any interest in ameliorating the living conditions of the people under their control other than to tax them to near starvation. It would be naïve to expect them to become benevolent developers of land and people. Given their contempt for accountability to anyone on anything, those dollars in their hands will most certainly be disbursed to strengthen their outfit with the most modern weapon systems available in the marketplace. That is their virility symbol. This would be a veritable dollar guzzling black hole.

The transfer of technology is a concomitant of all aid projects. Technology covers materials, machinery, methods and techniques of management. Most of this will invade the country from abroad. They will have inflated price-tags attached to them. Thus a sizeable proportion of aid will go back to those exporters of technology. This type of imported technology is usually non sustainable without a continuing dependency on foreign expertise. This is why we do have a proliferation of abandoned projects and machinery all over the country. Those politicians who salivate at the mere sight of a dollar note would opt for this dependent technology, because it is sure fire way to accumulate dollars in their foreign bank accounts. This then is another plug-hole that will not benefit the country, but will reduce the amount of funds flowing into the country.

Ultimately with the paltry sum left we might get a few roads repaired, a few buildings rebuilt and might give subsidies to the politically favoured few to have their houses too rebuilt and decorated with marble walls and wall to wall carpeting even though this is foolish extravagance in our tropical climate. This kind of expenditure has a nil effect on the economy. Any direct enhanced effect on production of goods and services is unlikely to ensue. Therefore this kind of expenditure will not generate the growth necessary to pay off the loan and the interest. This spells looming disaster of a debt trap. Unable to pay the interest and the loan from our own resources, the country will be forced to continuously borrow to service the previous debts. It will be like the multiple credit card holder who keeps transferring his debts from one credit card to another until the whole fantasy world collapses around him. Argentina is a case in point. That country has yet to recover from the total financial collapse a couple years ago. Needless to say this predicament will drastically reduce government funds available even to pay the salaries of its employees. Thus even if I have to starve, I would not accept this loan/bribe. Our moronic politicians are, of course, prepare to mortgage this country and in the process divide it too by giving parts of it to LTTE.

If the peace process fail to comply with the script of those donors, it is possible they might resolve on direct intervention and impose a solution on us. They did this in the bitterly ethnically split Croatia in 1995. Now that we have given a big handle to the international community to interfere in our affairs, we would also be prevented from reclaiming our lost independence and sovereignty. Sad to say we are in a nasty situation. The USD 4.5 billion is likely to remain only as a pledge, while for a paltry sum of loans we might be made to abandon our claim to this country. In the light of what is happening at the moment, it would be foolish to be optimistic. Only the UNF politicians can indulge in this luxury.

The Three fatal Conditions

(The Island, 31st July 2003)

As reported by the Hindustan Times (20th may 2003), Mr. Tamilselvam, political head of the LTTE, had demanded an Interim Administration for the North and the East which "would be (a) fully autonomous, (b) completely controlled by the LTTE and (c) entirely outside the constitution of Sri Lanka". If this is the expected nature of an interim or temporary administration, what would be the true nature, character and powers of the Final Administration? Those conditions are fatal to Sri Lanka. They also flatly contradict the various statements issued by the LTTE that they would welcome a political settlement of a federal nature within a united Sri Lanka.

When those deceitful statements were made by the LTTE, many commentators did point out the ambiguity inherent in the camouflage of verbiage used to hide the true intentions of the LTTE. The UNF government simply ignored such comments. Even now given the penchant of the PM (Mr. Wickramasinghe) for appeasement of the LTTE, we see the government personnel desperately jetting over oceans to find expedient measures to placate the LTTE. Given this attitude, is it any wonder that the LTTE do make outrageous demands? In short, what they want is to kill off Sri Lanka and carve out the cadaver. It looks as if we do have many politicians prepared to take on the role of butchers and carvers of Sri Lankan polity.

Let us look at the flip side of the three conditions. There is no "interim fully autonomous" administration anywhere in the world. If at all, such bodies do have some autonomy, both legislative and executive, over some affairs under their jurisdiction and no autonomy in many other subject matters. In any case all of them follow the laws, rules and regulations passed by a democratically elected assembly. Partial autonomy subject to Rule of Law is the prevalent state of affairs all over the world. This power structure has, in many cases, satisfied the aspirations of many ethnic/religious minorities all over the world and prevented the vivisection of those countries.

The Scottish Assembly has autonomy over many subject areas including the power to tax the people up to the maximum of three pence in the pound. Yet it is not fully autonomous. It is under the control of Parliament, to the extent, that the Parliament can abolish the Scottish Assembly on a motion to that effect, on any day anytime by a simple majority of the votes.

It is true that the Scottish National Party is very vociferous for separatism, but has failed to obtain the support of the people at the polls as the Scottish people appear to be content with the present set-up. Mind you, unlike the LTTE, the Scottish Assembly is democratically elected, and has no control of a separate fully equipped army, navy and air force. The Police force owes allegiance to the Crown, is politically answerable through a Minister to the Scottish Assembly, and is liable civilly in the Scottish Courts. This partial autonomy has strengthened the unity of the United Kingdom and has also enhanced the emotional and political aspirations of the Scottish people.

Quebec State does have autonomy too in many areas of government. It too has a very strong separatist political party opting for an independent Quebec at any cost. In the recent general state elections this party was soundly defeated and was replaced in government by a pro-federalist state government. The Quebecers unequivocally rejected full autonomy amounting to full independence. Separatism is a dirty word now in Quebec. According to the prestigious Economist magazine, this is one reason why Canada is considered today as the most favourable country for inward investment, production and growth.

Full autonomy is possible only if we kill off the present system of government. Consent for such surgical procedure will not be forthcoming. Therefore it remains as an impossible objective. But partial autonomy is achievable, is conducive to peace, and can be designed to enhance the aspirations of the minority. Such an eminently suitable system should be the driving theme of all democrats. Many peaceniks and some Tamil Catholic clergy have hitherto blindly supported the LTTE, now they have the duty to persuade the intransigent LTTE that it is time to settle for real peace under the Rule of Law.

The second condition is for the full control of the provinces of the LTTE. China, North Korea and Cuba are fully controlled by the local communist parties to deliver to their people the workers' economic and social paradise. Even after many years of sacrifices, blood and sweat, the reality is still economic and social misery with no political freedom even to question the atrocious economic system in operation. The military Junta in Myanmar is a close clone of the LTTE. Complete control there means complete suppression of all dissent, political freedom and Human Rights. There is freedom and economic prosperity only for the cadres of the Junta. Given the many political assassinations of political opponents by the LTTE here and now, while not having full control over the Eastern province, what tyranny awaits the hapless people once full control is obtained can be easily imagined. The end objective is quite clearly a fascistic administration where the LTTE cadres will reign supreme over the people. Power to anyone through the ballet and not the bullet should be the clarion call of democratic Tamils, Sinhalese and Muslims.

The alternative is a pluralistic administration acknowledging the very mix of people of different races living especially in the Eastern province. To start with, the Eastern province should be demerged from the North, as the three communities live there in almost equal proportion. It can be a truly multi-racial, multi-religious province living under the Rule of Law respectful of the rights of others and promoting one another's welfare. If we allow LTTE's obstinacy and its bullets to stand in the way of this desirable political, social and economic goal, we shall remain a nation condemned to endemic racial and religious confrontations without end.

The third condition demanded an administration outside the present Constitution of Sri Lanka. All constitutions are man-made, therefore imperfect. This is why they get amended with progress of time. Our Constitution is not perfect and we do need many amendments or alternatively a new Constitution. There are legal procedures to effect such changes in the normal course of events. It is not within the powers of the President or the Prime Minister to bypass such legal requirements. One cannot act outside the Constitution as it will be struck down as ultra vires by the Supreme Court. Therefore this is an impossible condition and ought to be rejected without reservation.

However imperfect our Constitution might be, we do have our Fundamental Rights enshrined in it. Many citizens have obtained relief against the government and/or its functionaries for infringement of their fundamental rights. If an administration was created outside the Constitution, then the people of that province will be deprived of their fundamental rights and the power of impartial courts to enforce such rights. The supreme law of that bastardized administration will be the decrees of Pirapakaran. It will be administered by his kangaroo courts and enforced by his Gestapo police. We would have created an abominable and tyrannical state where political freedom will be the first casualty and oppression will be the order of the day. Those nations who pledged millions of dollars surely would not permit such a monstrosity outside their own constitutions in their own countries. How could they in good conscience bankroll it in our country?

47

The International Safety-Net

(The Island, 20th Aug. 2003)

In the wake of Tokyo loans ballyhoo, the government promoted the idea of international safety-net (ISN), but it has yet to explain to the people what it means and its implications. Could it be another concoction of empty words without substance and meaning?

In the context of the dire predicament into which Sri Lanka has been thrust by the so far sham/failed peace process, it would be reasonable to expect that the international safety net was devised to safeguard the sovereignty and the territorial integrity of the country from the depredations of the LTTE. At least that is the way the government has promoted and presented it to the people without a full explanation. There is somewhere in some form an agreement between the government and the international community that embodies the following principles. First, both the government and the LTTE are expected to accept democratic laws and behave according to the norms and laws commonly accepted by the international community. Second, anyone violating such laws would be prevailed upon to desist, failing this, sanctions of some sort would be applied until normality returned. Third, economic aid will flow in to develop the country even if the LTTE is stalling the peace process by making outrageous demands that cannot be met without vivisecting the country. Fourth, if terrorism breaks out again, the international community would physically help Sri Lanka to eradicate terrorism in our country. If the government has anything more to add to this list the citizens would surely like to know.

On the other hand, if such an agreement does not exist, then it is a fiction invented by the PM (Mr. Wickramasinghe) and his failed negotiators to hoodwink the people yet again, is plain to see.

As regards the first point, the LTTE has totally rejected the Tokyo declaration, on the excuse, that they were not a party to the formulation of that declaration. The aid donors wanted a settlement "based upon respect for human rights, democracy and rule of law". This declaration linked donor support to, among others, "full compliance with the ceasefire agreement by both parties, and effective promotion and protection of human rights of people" (The Island, 11th June 2003). In words and by actions, the LTTE has made it quite clear that they will not abide by any democratic rule of law. The only law they recognize and enforce is that promulgated by Pirapakaran their fascist leader. This law is based only on the unbounded rights of the leader that brooks no dissent. His laws do not recognize the rights of others to live as they wish. Like Stalin before him, Pirapakaran eliminates all opponents to his scheme of Eelam by murdering them almost every week, if not every day, the latest being Ratheeskaran (EPDP) of Batticaloa, and two Muslims Fareed and Riyaaz of Uppuveli (SLMC) on the 14th of Aug. 2003.

Rather late in the day, even Amnesty International (AI) too has just woken up from their slumber to announce to the world that LTTE has been guilty of gruesome murders of opponents to their oppressive regime. For once AI has been brutally frank. "The use of political assassinations, abductions and other human rights abuses threatens to seriously undermine the moves made towards establishing a representative system of government grounded in human rights principles", thundered the Interim Director of AI (The Island, 14th Aug. 2003). To this must be added the catalogue of violations of private as well as public rights of people attested to by the SLMM.

The critical flashpoint at the moment is the invasion of government territory by the LTTE at Manirasakulam. After due investigation, the SLMM's decision was that this LTTE camp should be removed. The LTTE however did not budge. They instead claimed that it was part of their territory. This saga is likely to be repeated many times over in many other marginal villages currently held and controlled by the government. This new LTTE camp has amply demonstrated the strength of the LTTE and the cowardly weakness of the government.

It has also established the hidden agenda of the LTTE to surround the government positions with heavily armed combat units so that a military putsch could be imposed relatively easily at a time of their choosing. It will not surprise the readers of The Island newspaper that the latest sojourn of Thamilselvan in the east in government helicopter was to ensure the readiness of the LTTE for such a blitzkrieg. It is also a bold declaration to the people of the area that LTTE's regime has arrived, and it would be in their interest to comply with LTTE's various demands on the people.

It is also an unmistakable manifestation of the plan for territorial expansion harboured by the LTTE. They will never be content with the present area of land under their control.

According to the ISN some sort of sanctions should have been imposed on the LTTE given the blatant violations they have committed so far. All we have had so far was the statement made by the US State Dept. Deputy Spokesperson Mr. Reeker. He only reiterated that the LTTE's camp at Manirasakulam violated the Ceasefire Agreement and called upon the LTTE "to renounce terrorism and cease terrorist acts, including political assassinations, and to comply with CFA". Such words are water on duck's back to the LTTE. They have heard them before and have brazenly made their own retorts even when Mr. Armitage himself called upon them to renounce terrorism. These inane words also demonstrate my thesis that ISN is hollow figment and has no teeth to enforce any sanctions on LTTE.

Clearly mere words are insufficient and inappropriate to deal with LTTE. If ISN means anything there ought to be some sanctions by the international community on the LTTE on their activities abroad, especially in the UK and the other countries in Europe. France could have denied the LTTE the opportunity to assemble in Paris until such time that the LTTE camp at Manirasakulam was dismantled. That would be tangible evidence of a forceful ISN to both the LTTE and the Sri Lankans. No such action was taken. Instead the Japanese and the Norwegians were ushered into the Tiger den in the Vanni, on bended knees, to implore the LTTE for the resumption of the sham peace talks. Can we therefore place any trust in this ISN?

That 4.5 billion dollars loan will be long time in coming. According to the Tokyo Declaration, "assistance by the donor community must be closely linked to substantial and parallel progress in the peace talks" (cl.18 of the Declaration). This is a veritable trap. If we give into all the demands of the LTTE, the country will simply be dismantled, the talks will be deemed a success, the aid will be released and LTTE will be the sole beneficiary as there will not be a Sri Lanka left then to gain anything from the loan. If we do not comply with all the demands of the LTTE, there will not be any peace process, therefore no loans and no gains. Either way, Sri Lanka stands to lose and the power to turn on the loan tap on and off is in the hands of the LTTE. If an ISN is really in existence then the country should be given the loans no matter the stand taken by the LTTE. The sad conclusion is that we have been taken for suckers even on this point of economic assistance by both the government and the international community.

At the moment the easiest help western nations could provide is satellite information on LTTE activities in the relatively treeless areas of Elephant Pass and the wide open seas in the north east. They could also inform our security forces on the international communication between the LTTE in the Vanni and its cells in the Western countries, as well as the rogue LTTE's ships plying the oceans. Given that no such help has been forthcoming, how can we expect marines landing on the northern and eastern shores, and US combat ships loaded with missiles in the seas off Mullaitivu? No Western nation will commit itself to such a safety-net. Anyone who expects such help to deal with LTTE is naïve, if not a fool. In any case we would be foolish to invite foreign intervention on such a scale. Interventionists very rarely leave without devastating the invaded country.

The answer to my question at the start is quite clear. There is no ISN. It is just a ploy by the PM to allay the fear of the people arising from the failure of his appeasement policy. This device will be further used as an excuse whenever appeasement has to be made on the many LTTE's Shylockian demands yet to come.

48

Thus Speaks an Appuhamy from the South

(The Island, 7th Nov.2003)

The political head of the LTTE, Mr. S.P. Thamilselvan (SPT) was reported to have said at the news briefing on Sat. 1st Nov. that "mutual relationship and brotherhood between Appuhamy of the south and Rasiah of the North-East as fellow Sri Lankans would eventually be accomplished with the advent of time following confidence build-up by the ISGA" (The Island, 3rd Nov.).

Clearly SPT deliberately ignored the fact that many Appuhamys, Rasiahs and Kandiahs are living quite amicably, sometimes as next-door neighbours, and have mutually flourishing businesses and social dealings with one another all over the south. They do not need an Interim Self-Government Authority (ISGA). The ISGA concocted by SPT will only destroy this life of tranquility and conviviality now prevailing all over the country, bar the exclusive Tamil enclave controlled by the LTTE in the North and East.

How can the ISGA destroy this prevailing savoir vivre in the south? By the very failure to recognize this fact of life of intermingling racial mix, and the failure to accept that a large contingent of Tamils, nearly half the entire Jaffna Tamil population, live and thrive among the Sinhala and Muslim people all over the south. If this was accepted a reconciliatory preamble to the ISGA would have stated that "whereas the Sinhalese, Tamils, Muslims and others have lived together in Sri Lanka for a long time and continue to live together and will have to live together in the future; recognizing the same, peaceful resolution is a real possibility etc. etc" . Alas that was not the case.

The rambling preamble mentions Sinhala people only twice. This is to assign blame on them, to justify the emergence of the LTTE and the continuation of its terrorism. The Sinhala people are identified with the various Sri Lankan governments that held power. This is patently incorrect. The Sinhala society is a divided one, mainly between two political parties. Thus all Sri Lankan governments had an opposition in Parliament voted and supported by a large section of Sinhala people. Even when the Tamil MPs constituted the Opposition in parliament, there were Sinhala MPs elected by Sinhala people who were in the Opposition to the government of the day. In any case, assigning all blame to just one section of the people and thereby suggesting that Tamils were completely blameless smacks of moral turpitude. This is not the way to embark on a process of reconciliation especially when the hands of the LTTE are heavily soiled with the blood of Tamils, Sinhalese and Muslims.

The proposal seeks an absolute majority for the LTTE appointees in the ISGA. From the view point of the Muslims and the Sinhalese in the East, they now have the right to the complaint in the preamble that they also would be "denied effective role in the decision making process" and that "agreement between the parties to the conflict [should be brought about] on terms of equality". What the LTTE loudly complains of in the preamble, they now impose on the minorities in the north and the east. Would any right thinking Muslim or Sinhala community bother appointing any token members to the ISGA? There is discrimination in the very heart of this ISGA. This will convert the majority population of non-Tamils in the east to a voiceless and helpless minority. Sections 6 and 8 of the ISGA stand violated by the LTTE from the start. What hypocrisy!

The ISGA consisting of appointed (and mind you, not elected) members demands plenary powers over the quantum of activities pertaining to a sovereign government of a country. With the absolute LTTE majority in the ISGA, they will appoint the Chairperson, The Election Commission, the Human Rights Commission, the Executive, the Judicial Institutions and personnel, the Finance Commission, control the funds, negotiate foreign loans, create District Committees, appoint Land Commission, make unchallengeable decision on resettlement, rehabilitation, reconstruction and development and hire and fire anyone at its discretion. It demands exclusive powers over marine and offshore resources and powers to issue/deny permits for those who want to enter the adjacent seas. It wants to assume control over all natural resources in the north and the east.

As one can see there is no question of sharing anything with anyone, the absolute majority in the ISGA will see to that. So how can one even begin to build confidence in the ISGA? Long before the end of its five-year term, this ISGA would have converted the whole area to a fully fledged fascist state. No elections will be necessary thereafter. Plenary political and executive powers combined with an army, navy, an air force, pistol gangs, suicide squads and a paramilitary Stassi police, have all the makings of a Pol Pot regime beyond the control of anyone, let alone the rule of law, piously intoned at the very beginning of the preamble to the ISGA.

The sop sections 4 to 8 on Human Rights and non-discrimination are merely for the benefit of the foreign Godfathers of the LTTE, so that those foreigners will close their eyes to all brazen infringements that are taking place now and will undoubtedly take place in the future. A Human Rights Commission appointed by the LTTE dominated ISGA will no doubt paint the LTTE in innocent lily-white colour. If they failed to deliver for the LTTE, the pistol gangs will be at their doorsteps. Will anyone dare to act against their behest? There surely cannot be Human Rights where suicide squads and pistol gangs operate!

The LTTE operate outside accepted and democratically legislated laws. This is the example they want us to follow. They want the UNF government to flout the laws of the country, disregard the provisions of the Constitution and grant them plenary powers. The fact is that such renegade actions are not consistent with the rule of law, the human rights and the equality of persons as asserted by the first paragraph of their preamble.

There are proper procedures for amending the Constitution or for casting a brand new Constitution. No elected government can bypass those provisions. The LTTE are fully aware of this situation. Therefore their demand for the impossible is a slap in the face of India, Norway, Canada and the USA. Those countries wanted "reasonable proposals" from LTTE for negotiation. Perhaps the ulterior motive is simply to assign blame on the UNF government for not delivering on the proposal, and an excuse to go to war and achieve Eelam by conquest.

While the LTTE has enunciated the doctrine of exclusive right to everything in the north and the east, they do want us to share with them our resources in the south. This applies not only to tax revenues of the country, but also to water resources in the country. They demand an international type of agreement to share this precious water with Jaffna. They expect the vile Sinhalaya to have a soft heart! Even if this was made possible the problem would be free access to the Vanni fascist gangland by employees of the Water Authority.

The piece de resistance that militates against building any confidence in the ISGA is the requirement that any dispute shall be resolved by taking into account the parity of the LTTE with that of the Government and the final resolution should be "by reference only to the provisions of this Agreement". This means that the absolute power of the LTTE cannot be compromised in any way. Further, there is also provision to go for international arbitration in case of dispute over the appointment of the Chairperson of this conflict-resolution tribunal. Given that International Court of Justices adjudicates on disputes between sovereign states, is this not a sly attempt at international recognition of sovereignty of the LTTE?

Sorry Mr. Tamilselvam, this Appuhamy is not fooled and far from being convinced. Your ISGA proposal as it stands stinks to high heavens. If acceded to by our spineless government, it is bound to wreak havoc among Appuhamys and Rasiahs now living quite amicably in the south. Unfortunately the Rasiahs from the north and east would remain alienated forever.

49

Some Questions for Foreign Experts

(The Island, 17th Nov. 2003)

Many foreign experts were engaged by the LTTE to enable them to produce their proposal for an ISGA (Interim Self-government Authority). It was alleged that a former Tamil Attorney General of Sri Lanka, now resident in Australia, too had contributed to this effort. Most of the experts were from the academia while some were seasoned politicians of repute. Besides obtaining advice from these worthies, the LTTE also expected authoritative legitimacy for their deliberations and international approval for their final proposal.

A secondary payoff was the impression created on all concerned that great efforts were being made to comply with the pursuit of peace and push forward the peace negotiations the LTTE themselves had unilaterally stopped. After all the mountainous labour, the LTTE and the experts ended up producing a booby trap for Sri Lanka. You lose Sri Lanka if you accept the ISGA as demanded, and you also lose, if you reject the same, not only the $4.5 billion, but also the good reputation of our bona fides to end the conflict in the country. It is in respect of the latter, that I have some serious questions for foreign experts.

The opening paragraph of the preamble needs to be deciphered first. It states that "consistent with the principles of the rule of law, the human rights and equality of all persons and the rights to self-determination of peoples". Consistent with whose rule of law is the first question? There is no model set of universally accepted rules of law laid down by someone and followed by everyone. What we have are laws promulgated by democratically elected legislatures, enforced by independent judiciary via the police forces. Those police forces are not only politically accountable, but are also accountable for their actions before the courts of law. When countries do formally adopt international covenants, then such covenants also become part of the law of the country.

At the moment the Constitution of Sri Lanka is the relevant fundamental law of the country. It embodies the fundamental rights of the citizens, and guarantees the equality of all before the law, (except of course, the President of the country). If the LTTE and its advisors wished to be consistent with the rule of law, then the applicable rule of law in Sri Lanka at the moment is the Constitution of Sri Lanka.

Why then was the ISGA framed and pitched outside the Constitution of Sri Lanka? The intention is quite apparent. The experts have ignored the very existence of Sri Lanka as a country! Yet they want to negotiate with Sri Lanka, a non-entity in their books!

From the point of view of government, the ISGA is inconsistent with the applicable rule of law of Sri Lanka. Is it therefore legally valid to even consider the ISGA as a basis for negotiation? It thus appears to be a nonsensical donkey-work in sophistry to trap the unwary and to demolish the sovereignty of Sri Lanka. Do the experts have an answer?

The assertion that the Tamils did not participate in the making of the 1972 and 1978 constitutions is a patent lie. There were Tamils in parliament who did take part in the debates on the constitution. They might have opposed some sections of the constitution, just as much there were other Sinhala members who were also opposed to some sections too. Can those Sinhala MPs too claim that they did not participate in the making of the constitution? However, eventually the constitution was passed and all and sundry did abide by the constitutional provisions. It is now the law of the land. One cannot flout it to suit the one's convenience. The current political crisis is a case in point.

It is true that our Constitution is not perfect in every respect. It is violated often by power hungry politicians. Such loutish politicians are eventually hauled before the courts and are made to make amends and pay the penalties due for their culpabilities. Yet it is far more eminently suitable and a workable one than any rules of law promulgated by a non-elected tyrannical dictator who rules by the gun.

If this Constitution needs to be changed then the laid down procedure should be followed so that the end result would be acceptable to all.

The rule of law envisaged in the ISGA is what it will enact once given all the powers demanded in the ISGA. First of all the absolute majority of the members of the ISGA will all be appointed (not elected by the people) by the LTTE. Therefore the laws they promulgate will be LTTE laws as determined by the supreme leader Velupillai Pirapakaran. His wishes, whims and fancies will be the fountain of law in the eight districts usurped by him. This will necessary be the case, notwithstanding sec. 4, where lip service is paid to international human rights law. The fact is that there is no independent judiciary to apply and interpret the law and enforce sanctions if and when violations occur. Both the Human Rights Commission and the judicial system together with the personnel to man them will all be LTTE appointees. The LTTE police will be a paramilitary junta of its cadres. Therefore, that the very opening words of the preamble to the ISGA harbour uncompromising contradiction is apparent. The impersonal rule of law has been perversely invoked to cunningly convert it to a personal rule of law as promulgated by an individual whose trade-mark is murder incorporated. How come that the experts agreed to such a monstrosity?

Sec. 4 pays lip service to human rights and proclaims that "every law, regulation, rule order or decision of the ISGA shall conform to internationally accepted standards of human rights protection". Noble sentiments indeed probably influenced by the experts. But those experts miserably failed in setting up the independent institution with enforcement powers, manned by personnel endowed with immunity from personal attacks, not only to simply monitor, but also to impose sanctions, if and when rights are violated. What we have is a LTTE appointed Human Rights Commission. It really is a mirage held out to the gullible western sympathizers of the LTTE. It will no doubt report according to the directions of the LTTE leader. How could it fearlessly function when there are the invisible suicide squads, and the stalking pistol gangs prowling all over the tribal land?

Terror is the name of the game in the LTTE regime. Ample evidence has been unearthed of the appalling conditions of humans in the Eelam paradise. Just now, even in the government controlled marginal villages, the children and parents are in a state of absolute terror not knowing when the ogre will pay them a call to abduct the children to be trained as killing machines. When the ogre has taken his share from the family, the parents are paralyzed by fear to report the criminal act of abduction. How will they have the courage to report such atrocious deeds to the LTTE appointed Commission? Reputed independent reporters of international organizations have visited those areas and have alerted the world to the inhuman conditions prevailing there. Given such evidence, it is inexcusable that the liberal minded experts simply accepted the Human Rights Commission of LTTE appointees.

Let me confine myself to just one more point. What is the source of authority for the LTTE to self-government of a pluralist society in the north and east? The rambling preamble proclaims "that the majority of the Tamil people in the north east, by their actions in the general elections held in the year 2000, gave their mandate acknowledging the LTTE as their authentic representative". This is another specious assertion for the consumption of the foreign Godfathers of the LTTE. We all know that at no time has the LTTE stood for elections. We all know that a few Tamil parties, for reasons known only to them, assigned the title of "sole representative" on the LTTE only after they had been elected to parliament and not before. Even among them, there are dissenting voices that publicly declare that this "sole representative" status is only a pro tem arrangement only for negotiation with the government. In any case when did the Sinhalese and the Muslims in the east give the LTTE mandate to be their "sole representative" and impose the rule of law of Pirapakaran? My conclusion is that there is no democratic basis for the claims and demands made by the LTTE.

The LTTE are still, even after all the whitewash by the western nations by hosting their junkets in plush western hotels, is a through and through a terrorist organization. They have no functioning democratic institutions, they have no claims to votes by the people, they have no rule of law, they are all self-appointed by the power of the guns.

Therefore I agree with Nick Hesam (Legal Advisor to former President Mandela), that there are no legal foundations for the LTTE proposals in the ISGA. The foreign experts who participated probably in good faith, in producing this inoperative junk of an ISGA, have a case to answer, lest they all be condemned as fellow conspirators in a plot to dismantle the sovereignty and demolish Sri Lanka as a unitary country.

50

Wanted Sinhala Secessionists

(The Island, 10th Feb. 2004)

In a country where 75% of the population is Sinhalese, it is ridiculous for me to broach the subject of Sinhala secession. Unfortunately the deplorable plight of the Sinhalese in the Eastern province requires the urgent marshalling of all forces to save them from the jaws of the Tigers! Our self-seeking politicians are responsible for this humiliating situation because they have willy-nilly agreed to include the eastern province in a new unit of settlement with the LTTE. The Sinhalese form 26.5% of the population of the eastern province as against the Muslims 40.1% and the Tamils 32.3% and others 1.1% (The Island, 17th Jan 2004). Nobody in authority appears to care or be concerned about the fate of the Sinhalese in the future LTTE controlled ISGA. Sometime ago we did see some Sinhala politicians making a razzmatazz of a pilgrimage to the sacred shrines of Anuradhapura, and making solemn pledges to safeguard the interests of the Sinhalese. It probably was only a political gimmick calculated to enhance their egos. To-date they have not done anything to save these Sinhalese from enslavement by the LTTE. In the words of the eminent lawyer H.L.de Silva, now there is an "ominous conspiracy of silence" about the fate of the Sinhalese in the eastern province, even when everybody knows of the iniquitous villainy about to befall them in the lands of their forefathers.

My arguments for Sinhala secession from the ISGA are simply based on the same arguments adduced by the LTTE demanding an ISGA for the north and the eastern provinces. The preamble in the ISGA claimed that "the people mandated the elected representatives to establish an independent sovereign, secular state for Tamil people in the election subsequent to the Vaddukoddai Resolution of 1976" This is a blatant lie. Here are the figures for the 1977 election. In the northern province (consisting of Jaffna, Killinochchi, Mullaitivu and Mannar), the TULF obtained 278,393 votes and the votes against TULF were 125,504. Here the TULF won the day 2 to 1. In the eastern province (consisting of Trincomalee, Batticaloa and Ampare), TULF got 117,482 votes and the votes against TULF were 316,247. Here TULF lost nearly 3 to 1!! Taking both provinces together, TULF polled 395,775 votes and against TULF there were 441, 751 votes. Thus the verdict of the people was against separatist claims now made by the LTTE and supinely accepted by the UNF and the peaceniks. In the eastern province it was nearly two to one against TULF and its Vaddukodai Resolution! LTTE's shameless lie remains exposed.

The LTTE based their claim on the 1977 election. The results of the election made it a false claim and in no way gave a mandate for TULF to establish an independent sovereign state in the north and the east. Taking both provinces together, the people were against such a venture, and singularly so in the eastern province. Therefore on the same premise of invoking the validity of the verdict in that election, the people of the eastern province has the right to secede from any ISGA controlled by the LTTE, who were not the contestants at that election. They have not given their consent to such a monstrosity of a fascist administration anywhere any time. This is an unassailable argument for breaking away from the LTTE set-up. By the same token, those people did not give the UNF or the PA/JVP or anyone else, the mandate to dump them under the dictatorial control of a fascist regime. No one has the right to decide the future of those people except themselves. Their informed consent is imperative for a decision on their future.

According to the President of the Council of Muslims of Sri Lanka, Mr. A.H.G. Ameen, 100% of Muslims in the east they contacted for an opinion poll wanted the north-east de-merged (The Sunday Times, 1st Feb.). Further 100% of those polled affirmed that their problems have increased since the signing of the MOU, they lived in constant physical fear and were insecure socially and economically. This is the pathetic situation now where the government is supposed to be in control, and the much touted ceasefire is in operation. What would be the plight of these Muslims once plenary power over them is handed over to the LTTE?

Over the last two years, the Muslims of the east have unmistakably demonstrated their unwillingness to live as the slave labourers of the LTTE. They are murdered and harassed for this recalcitrance. They have in various media expressed their desire for a democratic existence. These Muslims have all the right to secede from any arrangement made by feeble Colombo politicians over and above their wishes and political choices. Their consent too is imperative for a decision on their future, given that they have robustly refused to accept an LTTE regime over them.

The eastern Sinhalese and their brotherhood everywhere need to bestir themselves, and initiate measures to demonstrate their rejection of the despotic over lordship of the LTTE. There are also other powerful arguments for secession from ISGA. The destruction of Sinhala culture by the LTTE started a long time ago. The most conspicuous were the slaughter of the Arantalawa Buddhidt monks, the cold-blooded murder of pilgrims at the sacred Bo Tree and the despicable bombing of Maligawa in Kandy. Even now we know that pristine ancient Buddhist ruins in the North and East are being systematically dismantled and converted to Hindu places of worship. Rahatgala and Pulukunawa are two good examples of this wanton vandalism and desecration. Thus sec. 6 to 8 of the ISGA are just empty words inserted to impress the western dollar barons.

Given that the administration of the ISGA would be conducted in Tamil with little or no regard for Sinhala language, the preservation of the culture of the eastern Sinhalese is a powerful and compelling case for secession from the ISGA. This ISGA is irrelevant and irreconcilable with the way of life of the Sinhalese in the east.

Self-defense is another obvious cause for secession. The Sinhala villages in the east have been subjected to beastly massacres by the LTTE over the years. Neonates and babes in arms have been slaughtered by the bloodthirsty LTTE cadres. This lethal threat has not been abandoned by the LTTE in this MOU period. They still have their pistol gangs roaming and stalking their prey all over the land. Thus the claim by the LTTE to Sinhala territory is dissolved in the acid of their own iniquities. This therefore is another cogent basis for building the protective wall against LTTE depredations. Self-defense and survival compel that the Sinhalese exist independent of the LTTE in the lands of their forefathers bequeathed to them with a unique Sinhala civilization. This right of self-defense grounds a right to secede from this inherently faulty ISGA.

If one looks carefully at the machinery of the ISGA, then it is obvious that it is totally imbued with discriminatory redistribution. What I mean is that the machinery of this administration is totally tilted in favour of LTTE Tamils. Absolute and plenary powers will be vested in them. Therefore it unmistakably follows that political, social and economic benefits too will benefit the Tamils at the expense of both the Muslims and the Sinhalese. Notwithstanding sec.6, there is discrimination inherent in the heart (Sec.2) of the ISGA. This is supplemented by the coercive military apparatus for persecution and exploitation of all non-LTTE citizens. In short, there is neither democracy nor accountability to the citizens living under the ISGA. Therefore all the palliative encomiums to 'Rule of Law' and 'Human Rights" in the ISGA, are just empty rhetoric, without any real meaning and intention to put them into practice. In these circumstances the option for secession is totally justifiable and necessary. The Sinhala people have the right to continue their democratic way of life as at present under the nationally prevailing Rule of Law.

So where does one go from here? In my books the UNF negotiators have all failed the test. Their services should be terminated forthwith. A new team of committed men/women should be appointed and be supported by an able team of experts. This entire body should first evolve a common negotiable position having subjected it to critical problem and potential problem analysis. This new team should have the confidence of not only politicians but also of the wider section of the population and also of the Sinhalese and the Muslims in the east. Like the current review of the Irish Good Friday Agreement, they should start at the beginning, renegotiate the MOU and the CFA and hand over its implementation to an independent body (not SLMM). The de-commissioning of arms should precede all other items. Then will arise the hard-core issues starting with the basic unit of the new political set-up and the powers that such units should have. It is at this crucial point that one would know whether the LTTE are genuine for a settlement without the bifurcation of the country and are really "determined to bring lasting peace to all persons of the island of Sri Lanka" (Preamble ISGA). I am afraid we are engaged in a wild goose chase with the LTTE trying to lead us on to their Eelam!

51

Negotiate Eelam or else.....!

(The Island, 4th June 2004)

The country ejected the UNF government for unashamedly appeasing the LTTE and brought in the new UPFA government with the expectation of non groveling negotiations towards a durable peace based on justice, human rights and rule of law. At the very beginning the negotiations were declared to be without any conditions by the LTTE. Soon the LTTE piled one condition upon another. Under this pressure the UNF negotiators simply wilted and gave into the LTTE, and for that they got booted out of government by the people. Today the new government seems to be following the same booby-trapped path to negotiation with the LTTE, no matter the country had just rejected that strategy overwhelmingly. Bolstered by the stupidity of the UNF government, the arrogant self-confidence of the LTTE is at bursting point, so much so that today the LTTE is able to issue an ultimatum even before the start of the peace talks. That ultimatum comes in the form of exclusive conditions, while in public media Mr.Thamilselvam maintains that talks with the government are not subject to any conditions! One of those conditions is that the government should first establish the ISGA as a functioning institution with the $4.5 billion budget. Note, the LTTE is no more concerned with using the ISGA as a basis for talks. This is blackmail and amounts to "negotiate Eelam or else...."!

The government negotiators have powerful ammunition in their favour against this unacceptable demand. This demand is beyond and contrary to the Oslo "Agreement" with the LTTE and contrary to the Tokyo Declaration made by the prospective international lenders of $4.5 billion. The USA had already made it clear that the ISGA is much more than, and is contrary to what was agreed to in Oslo. But mere words are insufficient to make LTTE comply. The US should go one step further and persuade its EU colleagues to do likewise. The government in the meanwhile should summon the aid of all those who attended and attested the two events and firmly affirm that an agreement is sought within the parameters of those two documents and in conformity with the territorial integrity of the country. Messrs Akashi, Patten and Cushnahan of the EU, should be called upon to stand by their public statements on the peace settlement based on Human Rights, Rule of Law and Pluralism in politics. Thus with apologies to Lewis Carroll, let me rhyme:

> "The time has come Appuhamy said,
> To talk of many things,
> Of Human rights, of Rule of Law and democracy,
> Of pistol gangs, suicide squads and lethal armaments,
> Of why the northern sea is boiling hot,
> And dissenters have no space and life."

Clearly if powers as well money are to be handed over, then it is paramount that the suitability of the recipient ought to be established first. In this case the international lenders have established the criteria for suitability. The first among them is Human Rights. This starts with the right to life itself. Many in the north and east of the country cannot assert this right as against the shenanigans of the LTTE. Most atrocious is the fact that children have no right to their lives. They are born to serve and nourish the LTTE. Murder stalks every step of the folks of north and east. Even as I write these words, it is alleged that Pottu Aman and his gang of assassins are trawling the east to murder anyone opposing the LTTE, and supporting any others. They are also in the hunt for any army intelligence operatives. Even the ordinary folks in the district have no right to life if they refuse to accede to demands of the LTTE cadres. How could anyone have peace, if one's right to life is denied by the pistol-totting gangs of the LTTE? The silence of the peaceniks on this most fundamental issue is explainable by the fact that these propagandists are all apologists for the depredations of the LTTE. Simply put the killings ought to stop. It is part of the infamous CFA. Mere words of assurance are insufficient. The killers should be handed over for prosecution according to the law of the land and suitably punished. Failing that the LTTE should be disqualified for any aid. There should be sanctions for not abiding by the provisions of the ill-conceived CFA. Assurances to establish Human Rights Units in LTTE held areas are simply attempts at deception. Human Rights are simply incompatible with the tyrannical LTTE and their gangs of executioners.

No man is above and beyond the provisions of law democratically enacted by the representatives of the people in the open forum of their parliament, unless so provided by the Constitution itself. This is the normal meaning of the Rule of Law. The citizens of the country are expected to obey such laws. Disobedience is punishable, and only democratically elected state has the legitimate authority to use force to punish as well as enforce compliance to the laws of the land. In the LTTE territory the law emanates from a single source, the Tiger leader, Pirapakaran. He is above his own laws. He rules by force. He lives in a bunker surrounded by heavily armed retinue of men and women. He dares not openly associate with people or canvass their support for his world-view and vision of Eelam. His minions do that work for him by intimidation rather than by persuasion. His laws are impositions on the people at the point of a gun. Without the guns and his butchers, it is most unlikely that he will have the support of the people he claims he has. He denied the people this opportunity to freely express their support for him in the recent flawed elections hijacked by his bootlicking TNA. Therefore one can claim most emphatically that there is no rule of law in the LTTE gangland. So once again one has to ask Mr.Akashi and others who advocated a peace based on Rule of Law, why they are ignoring this blatant absence of any rule of law in the fascist jungle of the LTTE? Should this not be part of the agenda for talks prior to any other topic?

Perhaps Mr.Patten of the EU and Mr. O'Neill of UK could embark on a voyage of discovery in the realms of the Tigers to tell us that vibrant democracy prevails there. Would they dare? All democracies need a robust Opposition and a free press. They will find the dissenting opposition to the LTTE in the unmarked graves, and the free press in the ashes left by the LTTE arsonists who set fire to any newspapers filtering into Tiger-land. After all, we have been told that their loans could only be handed over to establishments only if they are democratically accountable. To whom is Pirapakaran accountable? To whom are the institutions established by him accountable? Those international lenders do know the answers to those questions. They are accountable to no one. We should therefore call upon those lenders to first negotiate the tenets of accountability with LTTE before everything else. They have this responsibility because they have rudely intruded into our affairs.

What is the real basis of the ISGA? It is one man and his gang of heavily armed fanatics. It is this might that propels them to claim the "sole representative" status. Only in a dictatorship one can have a "sole representative". In all other forms of democratic government, there will be an opposition to the government of the day. The LTTE brought in the consultants and the experts to concoct the words of the ISGA to suit the fascist ideas and ideals of Pirapakaran. Those experts were probably inebriated with the exuberance of their own verbosity. As an after thought they probably realized that the monstrosity they fashioned, as instructed by Pirapakaran, was unacceptable to the liberal ideals of the present-day world. Hence they proceeded to garnish it with statements of Rule of Law, Human Rights and International Law. All these remain empty rhetoric because the end-objective of ISGA is a fascist state with oppression of the people, brutal suppression of opposition and exploitation of children and citizens alike. Would Mr. Akashi tolerate such an entity if the Ainu people in Hokkaido demanded it? What would Patten's reaction be if the Basques demanded the same covering a good part of northern Spain?

As the LTTE is after donors' funds, the donors should activate clause 18 of the Tokyo Declaration. Among many things, this clause set out the objectives to be achieved. The protection of human rights of ALL people, a balanced and verifiable de-escalation, de-militarization and normalization were among those prominent tasks. These indeed are the topics the two sides should sort out first. The donor community has a task here on their hands.

Incidentally the north-eastern sea is boiling hot because (metaphorically speaking) it has been singed by the many Sam Missiles, Multi-barreled rockets and other sophisticated weapons and equipment that came floating by to reach the Mullaitivu coast. According to one news paper the latest shipments came a few weeks ago. That is how faithfully the LTTE is observing the CFA. That is also their virility that dares to order us to establish ISGA or else....!

52

Will Suriya Thevan Eat Southern Bibikkan?

(The Island, 18th Nov.2004)

The Bibbikama under issue here is the proposal the present government has got ready to submit to the LTTE. It has been fashioned and designed by Sri Lankan experts on Constitutions and Constitutional law under the guidance of the President. I am not privy to the contents of this important document therefore it is beyond me to comment on the merits, if any, or the demerits of this proposal.

It is the duty of the government and the President to let the people know what is being done in their name. Will this government forget that all secret deals with the LTTE have been anathema to the people? All such secret affairs with the LTTE by the previous PA and the UNP government led to their discredit and eventual defeat at the general elections. This is all the more important because the very many murders of Tamil dissenters by the LTTE do prove that LTTE is not the "sole representative" of the Tamil people. This is beside the fact that in the eastern province of the claimed homeland, the Tamils are a minority and most of them are anti-Vanni LTTE.

The majority of the eastern province is in the hands of the Muslims plus the Sinhalese, and it is their expressed demand that they should not be degraded to unwilling vassalage under the fascist LTTE. A government that ignores all those anti-LTTE citizens deserves to be booted out of office lock stock and barrel. Alas, our politicians very rarely, if ever, learn from past experience.

Sri Lankans are today subjected to fear and intimidation by local and international peace merchants. Frequently they lecture to us to restart the peace talks on the basis of the explosive demands made in the ISGA by the LTTE. This ISGA is not a proposal anymore, it is a menacing demand backed by threats of war. The international interlopers too on the other hand threaten us to deprive us of the loan facilities they solemnly pledged. A mere repayable loan (as against an outright sale proceeds) is what is offered to irretrievably give up forever nearly one-third of our land and almost three-fifth of our coastline to a dictator whose outfit should more appropriately be known as "LTTE Assassins and Murderers Inc.". Who repays the loan with the interest due on it? Not the LTTE. It will be the rest of Sri Lankans, thereafter reduced to two-third of their country! A fantasy deal indeed. Will Norway, Japan or any country in the EU enter into such a ridiculous arrangement to give up forever part of their country? These threats are glaringly reinforced by devotional and dutiful pilgrimages to Vanni by these peace vendors. There they learn to imbibe the anti-democratic Nazi theory underlying the ISGA, and get brain washed to ignore all depredations of the LTTE. These unseemly activities of conspirators, collaborators and mediators have generated the fear that a secret deal with the LTTE has been in the making. Given the consistent intransigent demands of the LTTE, such a secret deal would envisage the propitiation of the LTTE and connivance with their ultimate goal of separate Eelam.

The Norwegian actors in this conspiracy do not inspire any confidence among the citizens. One primary actor, Eric Soldheim, has been alleged to have been a cheer-leader at LTTE's anti-Sri Lankan public demonstrations in the streets of Oslo. The Norwegian government's efforts at restoring peace between Israel and Palestine, have been reduced to mangled corpses on the streets of Palestine, proving that Norway is not a competent peace-maker. Even the bribe of the Nobel Prize miserably failed. The unabated bloody confrontations between Palestinians and Israelis are a testimony to the incompetency of the peace facilitation of Norway. Many knowledgeable commentators blame the Norwegian peace envoys for this spectacular failure because their peace deal, (the Oslo Accord of 1993) imposed impossible conditions on Mr. Arafat that it led to the second Intifada.

In the case of Sri Lanka, we already know that the Norwegians designed the one-sided CFA. We also know that they met many times the experts who drafted the separatist ISGA. Is it possible that they are now engaged in the process of concocting a secret deal with the LTTE to start the negotiation and then lead it on the pre-scripted path to ISGA and Eelam?

The other actor dictating terms to us has been Mr. Akashi. Unfortunately he represents a government for which most Sri Lankans have the greatest respect. However, as a peace envoy, he has been a splendid failure. Dr. Nalin Swaris has revealed to us in his writings (in The Island newspaper), the gory details of the massacre of over 8000 Muslims in Srebrenica where Mr. Akashi was the UN Representative posted there to prevent such a disaster. He failed in his job. Can we trust such a man to bring about peace in our country? Is he also on a mission to pacify the LTTE and make secret deals to demolish the sovereignty of our country and expose the Muslims and Sinhala citizens of the east to LTTE pogroms?

The above actors have been conspicuously silent on many unacceptable violent activities of the LTTE. When in Colombo, they pay lip service to Human Rights, Rule of Law and democracy. Do they ever take up these issues with the LTTE? It is the LTTE that boycotted the Tokyo Conference, therefore all the nations that regarded it as important and attended it, should be called upon to convey to the LTTE that it was a vital part of peace making. As LTTE broke-off the peace talks, the pressure should be on them and not the government, to resume the peace talks. It is the LTTE that violates Human Rights as if it were a daily ritual; it is the LTTE that flouts all cannons of democracy by murdering all dissenters and others they do not fancy. Today the LTTE has become the only persecutor of and assassins of Tamil people. Why cannot the peace envoys deal with these issues in the same manner they are threatening the government to talk peace and settle with this murderous LTTE?

All the peace talks have been really and truly ego trips for LTTE personnel and a wasteful and futile venture for the government (UNP). Mr. Thamilselvam told us that they were all a waste of time. Mr. Balasingam confirmed it and denied that there was any agreement in Oslo to give up Eelam and settle for a Federal Arrangement. Rather he asserted LTTE's right to seek a separate Eelam in Sri Lanka. Have we not heard this demand many times before? Is this not the predetermined one-way street along which all negotiations have to travel? The UNP government has seriously misled the country by repeatedly asserting that they had achieved a significant breakthrough by getting the LTTE to pursue a federal solution. If I had been one of the government's negotiators, I would ask for forgiveness from the country for this deception and forthwith withdraw from all politics and peace activities. The collective mind of the UNP needs psychiatric treatment for keeping these yesterday's men in their ranks and as leaders.

For peace talks to bear any fruits there are a few necessary antecedent steps to be taken by the government. First, the government should make use of the recent Reports on LTTE compiled by the Human Rights Watch (NY), Amnesty International (UK) The International Commission of Jurists (Geneva) and the UNICEF. Our ambassadors of all the western capitals recently visited by Mr.Thamilsalvam should be required to hold seminars for politicians and opinion makers there to apprise them of the contents of the above reports and the many violations of the CFA here and now by the LTTE. The objective of such seminars should be to obtain their help and support in the fight against LTTE terrorism, their false propaganda and the commitment of those countries to a democratic solution to the current problem as against a totalitarian anti-democratic imposition of arbitrary power of one man and his fanatic gun slingers.

Every effort should be made to erode the base support LTTE has in those countries by the indulgent attitude the governments of those countries have shown to LTTE activities and fund raising there. This is the opportune moment to resort to high decibel caricature of the LTTE's violence against Tamils and other citizens of Sri Lanka. Those few sympathizers of the LTTE should be given the opportunity to make informed decision. The recent seminar by SPUR, (an Australian Organization of Sri Lankans), in Oslo was a success in that the Opposition Norwegian politicians have begun to look closely at what Mr. Soldheim and his partners are doing in Sri Lanka. The neighbouring country Denmark has begun the procedure to ban the LTTE in EU. This should encourage our pusillanimous government. Just as much as Mr. Thamilselvam embarked on an anti-Sri Lankan propaganda mission in those countries, so our government too has the right to do the same and urge those countries to put pressure on LTTE to cease and desist from war and violence.

It is also the opportune moment to bring into play the de-commissioning of LTTE arms on a verifiable basis. The pressure for this should emanate from the donors of the loan. After all, they have more or less prescribed the ambit of a possible settlement. A permanent peace settlement cannot be achieved when a terrorist group retains lethal weapons. It is a terrorist group by virtue of its arms and the readiness to use them to subdue all and sundry. So the weapons have to be abandoned in the same manner as it has happened in Salvador, Myanmar and in India. These arms being the virility symbols of the LTTE, active canvassing on an international scale for this will be necessary.

All the indications are that Suriya Thevan will not eat any Bibbikan from the south. He will probably lead us on another merry international dance to consolidate his position internationally. He has only one objective and that is Eelam under his suzerainty. As the current security advisor to the Indian government, Mr.Dixit wrote in his book (Assigment Colombo, p320) Pirapakaran's "commitment to the creation of Eelam, in my judgment, is unalterable". The economic gains to the LTTE from "no war, no peace" are enormous. So are the strategic gains for importing the latest lethal weapons and positioning LTTE cadres near army camps. Therefore the temptations to continue this situation are in LTTE's favour. Suddenly he will present the secret details which he has fashioned with the help of Norwegians, as an ultimatum. The government may think that by the rules of CFA two weeks' notice is necessary for war. But Pirapakaran has so far not abided by CFA rules, he violates them at will and he is unlikely to give any notice of his intentions to anyone. Given his peak readiness and the incipient danger of disintegration of his temporarily inactive cadres by break-away groups, a blitzkrieg will be more to his advantage. Should we not then round up all our peaceniks and dispatch them to the frontline?

53

Is Terrorism Justifiable?

(The Island, 14th Oct. 2004)

Most ordinary people will immediately and instinctively react by condemning terrorism. All terrorists themselves will attempt to justify their terrorist activities by citing various root causes. Our President too attempted to justify terrorism during the recent visit to the UN. It was alleged that she made the following statement in one of her speeches, "even if the expression of conflict may take the most horrendous terror form, we believe that there are justified reasons for it". This is an unpardonable faux pas on the part of the President of Sri Lanka, on whom, the terrorist let loose their human bomb killing many other bystanders attending her public meeting. A crucial point to note is that those victims did not consent to be blown to bits with or without the President. In any case, terrorists do always invent various reasons and causes for their unacceptable and despicable atrocities. In the case of LTTE, the question of Tamil homeland is a good example of root cause based on pure fabricated history, now disputed and rejected by a significant proportion of Batticaloa Tamils.

However, I want to explain why terrorism can never be justifiable, no matter the causes. Whether our society should be changed in fundamental ways, whether the Tamils have been mistreated and therefore ought to be given a better stake in the government are all matters for discussion, agreement or disagreement. My contention is that terrorism as a means to promote these ends is not justifiable. First a word on terrorism is due.

I am here concerned with terrorism as a sudden violent action perpetrated by a group, coercively causing damage to property, inflicting pain, severe injury, distress and death on persons without distinction. It creates fear and panic among citizens. Its objectives might be "to gain concessions, obtain maximum publicity for their cause, break down social order, build morale in the movement or enforce obedience to it" (Political Terrorism by Grant Wardlow). Or as Paul Wilkinson put it "terrorism is coercive intimidation. It is the systematic use of murder and destruction, and threat of murder and destruction to terrorize individuals, groups, communities or governments into conceding to the terrorists' demands" (Terrorism and the Liberal State). Aircrafts, trains and buses have been bombed to kill and maim the civilians in them. Men, women and children have been butchered while sleeping peacefully in their humble hovels. Neonates have been brutally wrested out of their mothers' wombs. Pilgrims at prayer in their temples and mosques have been slaughtered. People at work at their desks in their offices and hotels have been bombed out of existence. It is this wanton random murder that cannot be justified no matter the root cause. Why is this not justifiable?

Art.3 of the Universal Declaration of Rights specifies that all of us have the right to "life, liberty and security of persons". Terrorism violates these rights and therefore it stands condemned. The suicidal terrorist himself does not accept his right to life. He has no moral or humanitarian considerations. He has become a "killing machine without shame or remorse". The victims of terrorism, however, have not consented in any way to this lunacy. They have been degraded to mere fodder for unrestrained violence. The victims are pointlessly sacrificed to an abhorrent or silly cause. They are treated as jetsam to be cast away into oblivion by a brute with arms. No one has the right to treat or use anyone in this despicable manner and totally ignore the rights of others.

Social stability requires the enforcement of mutually acceptable law and order. We need political, judicial and bureaucratic institutions for the orderly conduct of our affairs in society and to act as restraints on violence in the enforcement of our laws on lawbreakers. A terrorist is essentially a nihilist. He breaks down the barrier between civil society and state of nature of Hobbes' conception. Thus all norms of society are abolished, everyone and everything becomes fair game for those in possession of bombs and guns. The terrorist becomes the predator on the helpless and vulnerable ordinary citizens. No society could exist in this nihilist condition and therefore terrorism cannot be justified.

Most terrorists and their apologists offer the following as justifiable root causes. They are the loss of liberty under current political system, promoting conditions of minimally acceptable life, if not, a better life for the favoured group by way of separatism and liberation. Though all these causes seem to be prima facie acceptable, yet they fail to be justifiable if terrorism becomes the means to achieve them. Is the current regime in Sri Lanka engaged in the enforcement of the alleged deprivations using the same degree of force as the terrorists? This is patently not the case. Therefore terrorism on our citizens remains a barbaric imposition. Is it not the case that the Tamils living outside the LTTE's bandit country enjoy a better life than those within the iron grip of the LTTE?

Even the claim that the terrorists will bring about improvements over the status quo has to pass the criteria that their proposed schemes are coherent, genuine and result in a better social system of justice. Such conditions were conspicuously absent when LTTE resorted to the carnage of murder and butchery of citizens. Only now we have their ISGA. Anyone who studies it, would invariably find that it would lead to a fascist totalitarian Eelam and not to a better system of social justice. In the meanwhile, all those victims of LTTE terrorism had lost their lives in vain. How could this be ever justifiable?

There are also other requirements besides self-defense, for violence to be acceptable as justifiable. One needs also to establish the necessity for using violence. The fact is that in a democratic society, there will always be other non-violent, if not, less violent methods available to attain one's cause. All these methods need to be used first before resorting to terrorism.

Some have argued that terrorism is efficacious to bring about the desired change. On this score the LTTE has spectacularly failed. It has failed to attain Eelam after all their cowardly sensational terrorist activities unleashed on the people over the many years. A public subjected to terrorism is likely to condemn the cause together with the very acts of terrorism as it happened in the case of Beslan, where terrorist took hostage a Russian school full of small children. In this sense terrorism is self-defeating in its effects. Finally, is it morally right to promote one's social and political objectives by deliberately killing innocent citizens?

There are no "innocents" or "non-combatants" for the terrorists. So long as the general citizenry have not joined them and actively supported them, they remain guilty of not complying with the whims of the terrorists. Therefore any citizen would be considered fair game by the terrorists. The fact that the ordinary citizen is unarmed, unsuspecting, trustingly relies on the normal societal arrangements for the daily conduct of life, makes him an eminently suitable target for terrorist victimization. In this respect as Paul Johnson wrote terrorism "is a dynamic organism which attacks the healthy flesh of the surrounding society. It has the essential hallmark of malignant cancer: unless treated, and treated drastically, its growth is inexorable, until it poisons and engulfs the society on which it feeds and drags it down to destruction" (Terrorism: How the West can win).

The victims of terrorism are always guilty in the eyes of the gun-toting terrorist. The victims are never preferred any charge sheets nor are they given any opportunity to rebut or defend themselves against the unwritten and undeclared specific charges against them. There never is a trial before a duly constituted authority. These are the very basic requirements of natural justice which are denied to the victims. In short the terrorists treat the victims in their captivity in wickedly depraved ways. No principle of morality can condone, let alone justify such vicious inhumanity practiced by the terrorists. Those in responsible positions in society who even proffer excuses for terrorism stand condemned together with the terrorists.

The principles I have outlined apply also to any government that impose terrorism on its population. Mutatis mutandis they also apply to anyone who takes to terrorism to bring down such a government. Simply put, blowing to bits the citizens of the country cannot be justifiable under any moral order except that of the terrorists themselves. Such a society does not and cannot exist.

54

ISGA Worshippers and Converts

(The Island, 14th Sept.2004)

Given the ear-splitting chorus of "talk to LTTE on the basis of ISGA", it is apparent that there is a very vocal lobby of worshippers of ISGA in Colombo. They appear to be convinced that this Suriya Devan's given document is the infallible way out of our present pathetic predicament of no war, no peace and no foreign aid.

Besides reminding these loquacious acolytes of the LTTE that this very same crafty plan to create Eelam had been rejected by the people in two very recent elections, let me also challenge them to demonstrate how democratic principles of justice, equality and rule of law would be preserved under this ruthless dictatorial supremacy of one man. It is easy to include a few clauses on democratic principles in a document, but it is quite an arduous task to practice democracy. Further as stated by Mr. Thamilselvam many times, it is not any more a question of talking or discussing about the ISGA, it simply is the very institutionalization and legitimization of the ISGA as documented by the LTTE. Accept the ISGA or else war! Is this not blackmail? Where is the room for talks?

Where is the democracy when opposition candidates at election are brutally murdered by the LTTE's pistol gangs? Where is democracy when the election itself is so patently rigged, that the otherwise sympathetic (to LTTE) EU monitors condemned it as totally fraudulent? Where is democracy when pistol gangs roam the streets and dragoon the people to vote for their handpicked candidates? Where is democracy when opposition candidates are not allowed to canvass for votes prior to election? Even with all the violent compulsion imposed on the people, only 40% of the registered voters in the mono-ethnic Tamil Jaffna turned out to vote for the LTTE nominated TNA candidates. The others, a majority of 60% had other ideas and spurned the LTTE by not casting their votes for TNA candidates. The LTTE's claim therefore to be the "sole representative" of the Tamils is at a minimum spurious, and at best a contemptible arrogation of power over a hapless people. Such insolence is to be expected from a fascist leader. Every time the TNA MPs claim that they are the "sole representatives" of the Tamils, they should be challenged to prove this from the results of the last general election. In the whole of North and East, out of 1,778,162 registered voters, only 633,654 voted for TNA. This is 36%. It does not bestow any credence to their claim.

Where is rule of law when highly regressive and onerous taxes are imposed on all and sundry having no regard for their ability to pay? "No taxation without representation" of the Magna Carta of UK does not carry any weight with the LTTE. Does this matter to the UK Representative in Colombo who often acts as the chief guest at LTTE functions? Where is rule of law when the law enforced and administered is one man's proclamations based on his whims and fancies? Where is rule of law when the dissenters are brutally murdered and not given any opportunity to defend themselves? Where is rule of law when the LTTE and its cadres are above any law in their tribal lands and also in the marginal villages under government control? The assertions in the ISGA as regards rule of law are all spurious propaganda.

Where are human rights, when children are forced marched into camps and trained to kill? What is the difference between the outright beastly murder of innocent children in Beslan (Russia) and the indoctrination and training of Tamil children to fight and be killed? In Beslan and in KIllinochchi, the terrorists (were) and are using children as fodder for their implacable racist ambitions. Mr. Putin was annoyed with the western liberal press for treating those inhuman terrorists as "guerillas and liberation fighters". He told them in no uncertain terms that he was not prepared to talk to "child killers". Why is this logic inapplicable to the LTTE? Where are human rights when dissent is brutally suppressed, freedom of expression is totally denied, and freedom of association and movement are allowed only at the will and pleasure of the supreme ruler? These are some of the many questions remaining unanswered by those vociferous peace mercenaries. These slippery traitors have no time to answer questions. They are the vultures waiting expectantly for their dollar rewards when the carcass of Sri Lanka gets dismembered and the country vanishes from the maps of the world.

There is the lethal arsenal of the LTTE. Why is this not on the agenda of "talks based on ISGA"? De-commissioning of arms of the IRA was central to the Good Friday Agreement in Ireland. It still is also the stumbling block to permanent peace there. Why therefore is it ignored in Sri Lanka? Is it because an Eelam, without its army, navy, air force, a police and sophisticated weapons of death and destruction is an impossibility? The LTTE will not give them up, and to this extent, they are untrustworthy when they maintain that they are for an undivided nation. The virility symbol of Eelam is its death dealing forces armed to their teeth. The US ambassador, Mr. Black has reiterated that the LTTE "has to in good faith renounce terrorism in word and deed". While we commend such forthright statements, we also ought to remind Mr. Black that words alone have been ineffective on LTTE. Sanctions on LTTE are called for not only by the US but also by the other members who co-chaired the Tokyo Conference.

The Co-Chair members should stop their pilgrimages to Vanni. They should get the LTTE to come to the nearest border village if they have business to conduct with the Co-Chair personnel.

The present parliament is completely ignored by the ISGA in order to stake its claim that the ISGA is equal to or rather, greater than the parliament. Similarly the Supreme Court is also ignored. Thus the ISGA monster is both beyond the control of parliament, and beyond the jurisdiction of the Supreme Court. You probably guessed my next few words! Yes there is only one man, Pirapakaran the despot, who is the source of power and the fountain of justice in the ISGA. His appalling track record so far only proves, that far from being a wise legislator and fair dispenser of justice, he is the epitome of racist hatred and murder most foul. Should he be vested with powers greater than the present parliament and the Supreme Court? He may have assumed the mantle of divinity, but for many people he is another human wanted for many murders in this country and abroad. In any case, how can this parliament completely ignored by the ISGA, create the very same ISGA and position it completely outside the present Constitution of the country? Can our over eager SLFP politicians explain this conundrum? From the way the CFA/MOU is flouted now almost five times a day, how can one place any trust on the sanctimonious words on human rights and rule of law scattered about in the ISGA?

There are also a few born again ISGA converts and fellow travelers. While they were in the parliamentary opposition, the ISGA was the red rag to the bullish SLFPers. Now they have started to sing the praises of spurious peace and to exert efforts to cover up the murderous depredations of the LTTE all over our land. JHU please note that these people have been converted by the huge inducement of $4.5 billion and the allurement of staying in power to enjoy all the perks and privileges, and also the opportunity to plunder the treasury at will and accumulate dollars in secret foreign bank accounts. Should this not be covered by JHU's Anti-Conversion Bill, given that the consequences of this conversion will be the demolition of Sri Lanka itself, its millennia old religion, language, culture and a way of life that we lead today?

So what options do we have? We have got to reject the ISGA wholesale and request a redraft for our consideration and not negotiation. As President Putin said "we have shown ourselves to be weak, and the weak get beaten". In the meanwhile, a solution acceptable to all communities and a substantial number of MPs ought to be prepared in the form of a negotiating document to be presented as an alternative to whatever proposals might be submitted by the LTTE. The negotiation itself should be in the hands of professionals in constant touch with political authority for ultimate decisions on vital issues. The end game should be a permanent peace within a democratic Sri Lanka. We cannot simply give into the demands of the LTTE. Let me remind our politicians what President Putin said to his people after the Beslan massacre; "as the President and head of Russian state, as someone who swore on oath to defend this country and its territorial integrity, and simply as a citizen of Russia, I am convinced that we have no choice at all. Because to allow ourselves to be blackmailed and succumb to panic would be to immediately condemn millions of people to endless series of bloody conflicts". We do badly need a President like Putin in our present circumstances. The politician converts to ISGA have a case to answer. They have demonstrated themselves to be reckless idiots unfit to act as leaders of our country.

55

Karuna's Mutiny a Missed Opportunity

(The Island, 6th July 2004)

It is easy to be wise after an event. Nevertheless, our moronic politicians seem to be incapable of acquiring even a modicum of wisdom after most events. It is therefore justifiable to dwell on the missed opportunity offered by Karuna to the citizens of Sri Lanka. When will we ever learn?

First, let me take the General Election held on the 2nd of April. The voice of the electorate was quite clear. The electorate delivered a verdict against the abject appeasement of the LTTE by Ranil and his government. Yet what lessons have the new government learnt? Apparently nothing. It appears to be pursuing the same failed objective of "peace process" and not the end objective of peace with justice for all. The new government too appears to have been mesmerized by the LTTE and its demand for the establishment of the ISGA. The UPFA government appears to ignore the fact that the ISGA treats this country as a barren island in the Indian Ocean. It deliberately avoids any link with the government in existence, and cunningly avoids any commitment to devolution or federalism, agreed to, by the LTTE in Oslo. Why cannot our politicians see these fault-lines?

The EU election monitors have now pronounced that the election in the North and the East of our country was a massive fraud. There were murders of candidates opposed to the LTTE in those provinces. Rival Tamil parties were not allowed to canvass for votes under pain of threats by pistol gangs of the LTTE. There were also multiple voting and impersonation on a massive scale. Thus the claim of the 22 Tamil National Alliance (TNA) MPs as the "sole representatives" of the Tamils in the two provinces is not only ridiculous but also unacceptable. Why have our politicians chosen to ignore this devastating (to LTTE)

EU Report? Why do other officials of the EU ignore this Report and continue to go on pilgrimage to the LTTE den in the Vanni jungle?

If one examines the election results published by the Election Secretariat, one finds the support extended to TNA was far from overwhelming as frequently claimed by the LTTE. TNA's share of the total registered voters (1, 778,162) was 15% in Ampare, 53% in Batticaloa, 31% in Trincomalee, 40% in Jaffna and 40% in Vanni. Only in Batticaloa did they score more than 50%. In total, taking both provinces, only 36% of total registered, voted for TNA. I have taken total registered votes for the simple reason that the claim is "sole representatives" of all the Tamils in the North and the East. There were 71,634 invalid votes, and 567,595 did not turn up to vote. Only 68% of the total registered voters did vote. It was obvious therefore that there was only pusillanimous support for TNA, the acolytes of the LTTE. Those who voted for them were the people who had been frightened and intimidated out of their wits by the LTTE pistol gangs. This bit of election statistics firmly establishes the fact that the LTTE and the TNA are NOT the "sole representatives" of the Tamil people.

The majority of the Tamils (64%) did not vote in support of TNA. They could not even be intimidated to cast their votes. In this respect the, the LTTE's massive fraudulent campaign to establish their sole representative status was a miserable failure. We are foolish not to recognize this fact and use it to rebut the oft repeated claim of both the LTTE and the TNA MPs. Does 36% of votes for TNA make them sole representative of the Tamils?

Like the myth of "Tamil Homeland", the claim of "sole representative" is an imaginative fabrication of the LTTE. These were the myths Karuna exposed and exploded by his mutiny. Karuna effectively demonstrated that there is no Tamil homeland. The results of the election did prove him right. If there was such a chimera of a homeland, at least, his revolt has shown that it did not extend to the east. He and his soldiers did fight to establish this fact and are at this moment continuing their struggle against the LTTE. Thus when Karuna mutinied with about 5000 cadres, Sri Lanka was given the golden opportunity to de-merge the eastern province. Cowardly politicians instead issued directions to our security forces to help the LTTE to land armed cadres in Verugal to defeat Karuna's army. The CFA was shred to tatters by the LTTE twice over by this action; once by transporting their armed forces, secondly by continuing a mini war in the east. The incredulous reaction of our politicians was that it was an internal affair of the LTTE, even as it entailed a vast elimination massacre of Karuna's cadres (mind you, they were former LTTE soldiers) in the eastern province. No wonder the LTTE has extended this "privilege" to other areas to eliminate all intelligence operatives of the army and anyone else they fancied. It will not be long before the LTTE bites the hand (government's) hand that fed them with.

Initially Karuna was amenable to accept the fact that the eastern province was a mosaic of multi-religious and multi-ethnic entity. He was totally against Jaffna Tamil hegemony and a mono-ethnic imposition over the east. He should therefore have been seriously engaged to establish the ground reality of the incongruence of dumping the north and the east together into a fictitious homeland for Tamils. Why are our politicians afraid to exert this reality in the east? Have these politicians already conceded the right of the LTTE to eliminate by a pogrom of ethnic cleansing, all the non-Tamils as well as all the dissident Tamils in the east? This, I am afraid is the ominous conclusion. An ISGA with plenary powers, with its own police, law courts and bloodthirsty pistol gangs, the task of racial holocaust is a strong possibility.

A dictator is the sole representative of the oppressed and suppressed people under him. As Pirapakaran is such a deified tyrannical dictator, it is appropriate that he deigns to impose the status of "sole representative" on his stoolpigeons, the TNA MPs. Why should everyone else accept this claim? All true democrats should treat this claim with utter contempt on the basis of the verdict of the electorate. The western nations, who often preach democracy to us, have now a handle on LTTE. They have now ample evidence to show that LTTE is not the sole representative of the Tamil people, and therefore the LTTE has got to make space available for the vast majority of non-LTTE Tamils and make compromises. Could this ever be possible as long as Norway is involved in the affair of peace making on terms pre-determined by the pro-LTTE Norwegians?

The government has got to talk to the LTTE because they have got the arms and the fighting forces. Yet the fact remains that the LTTE too has failed over the last many years to establish Eelam. So why should our negotiators simply kow-tow to the demands of this failed terrorists? It is time that we should also make our demands known and express our unwillingness to concede the many unacceptable demands made by the LTTE in their ISGA.

Karuna established for us the fact that the Tamils in the east do not accept LTTE as their masters. We do know for a fact that the Muslims and the Sinhalese in the east do not accept the LTTE too. Therefore the LTTE cannot in any way substantiate their claim to rule these people. It therefore is opportune to confront the LTTE on this issue, so that, space can be created for all those non-LTTE people to take active part, via their representatives, in the peace process. How can one have peace if all these people are ignored, and thrust without their consent, into servitude under the LTTE?

If this government was serious, then it should have arrested Karuna for the massacre of over 700 security force personnel who surrendered on the order of the President Premadasa. Karuna should have been charged for this war crime and tried in our courts. If the government was unwilling to do this, then the next best was to tap him for all the military secrets of the LTTE and help him to nullify all the bogus claims the LTTE have made so far. There was the window of opportunity here for the deliverance of the country from the terrorist trap with the help of Karuna and his cadres. Sadly for the country, our politicians are so dumb that they are even now engaged in vilifying our troops in public and pacifying the LTTE. Our present politicians have become the bane of our country.

56

The Cremation of CFA/MOU----An Obituary

(The Island, 23rd April 2004)

A premature obituary is usually the stuff of April Fools' joke. Indeed, the CFA/MOU with LTTE has subjected all of us to such humiliating ridicule that I earnestly wish my augury will become a self-fulfilling prophecy. No elaborate requiem is required. A summary internment of CFA/MOU is the most appropriate for the reasons given below. Will the new government have the spunk to take the necessary steps against this unabated humiliation of the country by the LTTE? Will the JVP in the new government deliver the coup de grace to this shameful charade?

Unlike at most funerals in our country, I refuse to express my ***Balawath shokaya*** (my deepest sorrow). Instead, I announce my obvious glee and urge my compatriots to celebrate this coming event. This cremation is an inevitable process of our democracy that voted out the chief architect Ranil and his government, who were responsible for the CFA/MOU. Of the total votes (9,176,147) more than half (52%) voted against the previous government and its sham peace process platform erected on a totally flawed CFA/MOU. This did not mean that the people voted for war per se. Instead, they voted against condescension and prostration before the LTTE. They voted for dignity and robust negotiation based on justice, rule of law, human rights and a durable peace.

Usually obituaries deal with the kindness and generosity the deceased had dispensed during his life and love he had shown to his loved ones and friends. Likewise let me deal with the meagre measures of goodness that emanated from the CFA/MOU. I accept the fact that there was no armed conflict, death and destruction and bombs did not devastate Colombo. I accept the fact that our economy did improve and tourists started to visit our shores. I accept the fact that Tamils living in the areas of conflict did have a measure of relative peace, normalcy and calmness. I accept the fact that the LTTE did change their rhetoric to a "negotiated peace" while pursuing their objective of a fascist Eelam. All these were permitted only so long as they served LTTE's hidden agenda.

The deleterious effects of this CFA/MOU have been too many to detail them all here. Nevertheless, let me outline a few to support my suggestion that the current CFA/MOU should be confined to the dustbin and a new agreement should be forged, even though, it is possible that the terrorists will flout it at will in the future. Thus such an agreement should clearly spell out both national and international sanctions backed by the sponsors of $4.5 billion loan. Further, there should be reciprocity built into this new agreement. It should be entrusted to an impartial monitor with powers to activate and enforce sanctions.

It is not true that the two notorious documents did stop death and destruction. The pistol gangs of the LTTE were given the freedom to kill many, even within one of our police station. Inspector Thabrew and many other government operatives were hunted down by the LTTE in Colombo, Jaffna and the East. Their blood was considered as necessary sacrifice to the LTTE deity by our callous UNF government and its Ministers.

The CFA/MOU did virtually nothing for the Muslims in the east. Many Muslims in the east were abducted and killed. Their lands have been expropriated and large sums of extortionate taxes have been extracted from them under pain of death. The threat of forced expulsion from their lands is hanging over them like the sword of Democles. They too have been driven to take up arms to defend and protect themselves from the depredations of the LTTE in the east.

The Tamils in the LTTE areas have suffered and continue to endure the onerous burden of living under a fascist dictatorship. The Tamil parents have no right to their children. They have no right to their property. They have no right to what they earn. They have no right to any of the freedoms enjoyed by the rest of the Sri Lankan society. The whole Tamil society is organized to serve the LTTE and satisfy the demands made on them by the voracious LTTE cadres. This is indeed the modern version of a slave society.

A practicing Jaffna Psychiatrist observed "from full scale indoctrination at schools and through the mass media, to the strict restrictions on outward travel of those in the recruitable age group through a pass system, all impel the children and women from deprived sections of society, to become the cannon fodder of the terrible war" (Scarred Minds by Dr. Daya Somasuderam). The Tamil society had been degraded and brutalized by the LTTE.

Even the partisan SLMM has now declared that during this truce period there were 1,873 CFA/MOU violations and 1,122 children were recruited by the LTTE (The Island, 17th April). Mind you, these appalling figures refer only to those reported to the SLMM. Imagine the numbers not reported due to fear and intimidation. In the face of these shocking statistics, can anyone claim that this CFA/MOU has worked for the benefit of the Tamils?

The sole beneficiary of the CFA/MOU was the LTTE. They gained respectability to travel the world as VIPs to lobby for their fascist Eelam and to shop clandestinely for the latest lethal weapons in the arms bazaars of the world. They gained access to many foreign government emissaries and made Killinochchi the focus of attention of those diplomats. They got the opportunity to mollycoddle those foreign visitors to the extent that such foreign visitors forgot, and probably forgave, the blatant flouting of the CFA by the LTTE and the many violations of Human Rights especially of the under-aged children. Only the USA has questioned the motives of the LTTE to-date.

The revelations of Col. Karuna demonstrate the stark duplicity of the LTTE. According to Karuna there had been eleven arms shipments during this bogus truce. One hopes that our security men were able to extract more detailed information about those shipments. An active lobbying of the foreign governments is an urgent necessity for stopping any further arms purchases as well as their shipments to Mullaitivu. It should become part of the international "war against terrorism".

Karuna also confirmed the suspicions of the Sinhala voters in his interview with The Island newspaper. "It was reported that we had agreed to a federal solution in Oslo. But, when we returned, Pirapakaran blasted Thailselvam and me for nothing. He asked 'is it for this that I sent you to Oslo? You have betrayed our cause and our homeland. I cannot accept any solution other than a separate state'. The dispute between Pirapakaran and Balasingam was totally based on this issue. Pirapakaran told us to somehow carry on with the peace talks for five years until he gets enough weapons to fight for a separate state". The above statement may sound incredible to the many peaceniks, but some of us never doubted his consistency to fight for Eelam. If one combines it with what we already know about arms shipments, the unabated recruitment for his army, the total prevention of access to LTTE territory and the suppression of opinion there, then we do have the belligerency and the duplicity of this warlord exposed to the world. This is what the CFA/MOU had enabled the LTTE to achieve.

The latest wholesale violation of CFA took place when Pirapakaran moved his men to Verugal to fight Karuna's mutiny. This was a double blow to CFA. The very movement of troops was one violation while the conflict itself was another violation. Even as I write this article, he is engaged in continued violation of CFA by moving his cadres to Batticaloa to consolidate his acquisitions. This process of continued aggression has also the subtle effect of demoralizing our security forces on the frontline. It is also intended to consolidate his claim to territory and freedom of access to government controlled areas without any hindrance. Pirapakaran is gradually eroding the government's grip in the east and is making inroad into the government's claim to the sovereignty of sea routes. Every infringement is an enforcing precedent for a future challenge to the sovereignty of the country.

Clearly the new government has got a tough job on its hands. It should first tackle the international governments. There is ample evidence to present to them and establish the fact that the CFA/MOU is detrimental to a durable peace in this country that they have advocated and promoted so earnestly. Like in Ireland, a review is called for, and a new agreement based on rule of law, and human rights should be forged. It should carry international enforceable sanctions for flouting the same. Such an agreement should not be an end by itself, it should only be a means to arriving at a substantial agreement for a durable peace. The SL government should studiously abide by this new initial agreement and should openly denounce any infringement by the LTTE and initiate measures necessary to bring down sanctions on LTTE. No more appeasement of the voracious Tiger please. Bury the present CFA/MOU without any ceremony.

57

Treason Stalks My Country

(The Island, 27th May 2004)

Our historians would tell us that there had been many betrayers of this country throughout our recorded past. Today the betrayers of our country striving to arrive at a spurious peace might be rewarded with the prestigious Nobel Gold Medal plus about a million dollars. In Palestine this Nobel Peace Prize reward did not result in permanent peace. In Northern Ireland also the Nobel Peace Prize was ineffective. There permanent peace is as elusive as the mythical unicorn. In both cases the Norwegians were the peace intruders though they called themselves the peace-makers.

It is generally accepted that we inherit the genes of our parents and their ancestors. I do not know whether there are any genes in our physiology directly connected with treason and betrayal of one's country. If this is the case, then it would be true to maintain that some do have it in their blood to betray the country. Perhaps that would explain the maddening rush of some of our political elites to palm off a substantial part of our country and the unwilling people living thereon, to be enslaved by the murderous dictator basking in the air-conditioned luxury in the bunker in the Vanni jungle. The ancestors of some of these elites have been betrayers of our country. This has been recorded in our history.

This country has no system of vetting our top bureaucrats occupying very sensitive positions of power. Nor do we have a CIA or FBI to investigate allegations of treasonable conduct of politicians as well as our civil servants. I do not agree with nor condone everything that the above two organizations do in USA. Their spectacular failure was the nine-eleven attack on USA by the terrorists. Yet the principle that we should have a statutory body especially devoted to the protection of the security and sovereignty of the country is the issue here. The Criminal Investigation Department of the Police is, in my view, totally incapable as well as incompetent to engage in such operations. They do not have the personnel, the expertise and equipment necessary to maintain surveillance, gather hard evidence, apprehend and prosecute the culprits. Worse still, even with a functioning Independent Police Commission, we do have the corrosive political influence guiding the police personnel of this country.

The various other intelligence agencies are creatures of the political regime in power. Therefore they bend like the willows to the dictates of the politicians in power. This lacuna of a vetting system in the administration has made our country the playing field of foreign spies and indigenous saboteurs. They boldly ply their seditious trade of espionage with impunity. Shouldn't someone care?

In the recent past a Treasury Official was allowed to sit in on Cabinet meetings against the protests of some ministers. There were many allegations against him. One such was that he was an LTTE spy and passed on Cabinet secrets to the LTTE. No investigation on him was done, nor any surveillance mounted on his activities. When the government changed he fled the country and returned as expert advisor to the UNF government on many issues including the infamous peace process. An investigation on him should have been conducted at least to clear his name.

Then there was another high-ranked legal personality. His position in the government service would have allowed him access to highly sensitive information vis-à-vis the security of the country. I do not know whether there were any allegations against this person's loyalty to the country and its Constitution while he was in office. The fact is that this person was co-opted by the LTTE to produce the notorious ground-work plan for Eelam----the ISGA.

One cannot rule out the possibility of the existence of many LTTE "plants" "moles" and "sympathizers" in sensitive positions of government bureaucracy, the security establishment and the political hierarchy of the country. A stringent system of vetting should be in place to ferret out such traitors. At a minimum, surveillance on their conduct should be maintained by a statutory body accountable to parliament via the Minister of Justice.

We have just had the Athurugiriya fiasco. The judicial inquiry did not mince words. It condemned the event as rank betrayal of the security forces, betrayal of the individual members of the Secret Service, and betrayal of the country. It also charged that the persons who exposed this secret mission by the army, were indulging in treasonable activities disastrous to the security of the country. Those exposed secret service officers have been hunted down and murdered by the LTTE, but the traitors remain unscathed. When will these rascals be brought to justice? Do we as a nation care to fight for our sovereignty? A nation not prepared to fight to preserve its sovereignty is not worthy of that sovereignty. No wonder the LTTE have denied us that sovereignty.

Illegal telephone tapping is the stuff of dark intrigues by shady characters. They are also the means used by legitimate secret service to lay traps to capture both the terrorists as well as the traitors engaged in treasonable activities. The recent revelations of Indymedia, as exposed in The Island news paper (5th May) by a pro-Lankan activist and followed on by other Sunday newspapers were reverting reading. Even though the "telephone taps" are notoriously unreliable and probably inadmissible as evidence in court of law, yet they give us a glimpse into the secret world of our government officials in authority.

In the case so far surfaced it is quite apparent that people in authority were engaged in subverting the law of the country to provide powerful communication equipment to the LTTE. It did not register with any of them that this equipment could be used for propaganda against the country and might also be used to frustrate the confidential communications within and between our security forces. Probably they did not care for such details in their eagerness to please the LTTE. In my books, they were acting traitorously and should be properly investigated for arraignment before the courts. At a minimum, they were smugglers, and as such, they should be hauled before the courts by the Customs. All foreigners engaged in such activities should face the same consequence as the many incarcerated foreigners for smuggling contraband and drugs into this country. Should they claim diplomatic immunity, they should be chased out of this country as persona non grata.

The politicians taking the oath to preserve the Constitution should be put on notice that they could not willy-nilly change the Constitution, or in any way compromise the Constitution in their negotiations with the LTTE. Nor can they engage in creating institutions outside the scope of the present Constitution without being traitors to the country. Properly laid out procedures need to be followed for any change in our Constitution. My anxiety is that we have no proper mechanism to stop any top politician engaged in traitorous activity to betray the country and the people. Thus we had the admission of one of our past Presidents that she offered the north-east to Pirapkaran to govern for ten years without any election! She did treat this country as if she owned it. This is all the more dangerous as our politicians keep changing their publicly expressed statements on the demands made by LTTE. I warn the readers that treason is stalking this country or as the Bard has put it, "O! what a fall was there, my countrymen; Then I and you, and all fell down, whilst bloody treason flourished over us". This fall, of course, is not inevitable, but preventable.

58

More Than 30,000 Corpses had only one Label: Sri Lankan.

(The Island, 12th Jan. 2005).

The official count (still rising) as at 9th Jan. is 30,721 dead, 4,951 missing, 109,143 displaced families and 545,492 displaced persons. All of them are Sri Lankans. They do not carry any other labels such as Eelamists, Buddhists, Christians or Hindus, nor do they have any political party labels. In the same vein the millions of people responding to appeals for help for these devastated people are also Sri Lankans, almost all of them from the non-LTTE controlled south of the country. This is the immutable lesson of unity that the savage tsunami taught us. In glory and in suffering, in victory and in defeat, in death and in destruction, we are just one people of one mother Sri Lanka. We live together, we enjoy life together, we endure our suffering together and now many of our people have also died together. Surely this monumental tragedy should bring out the humanity in us all to settle our differences amicably and live as one in one undivided country. Alas, there are some whose hearts are made of racist zeal, even floating corpses fail to change their racist and separatist mindset. Their hearts have no humanity left after all these years of oppression and repression of their own kind.

The magnificent spontaneous response of the world to our plight is simply on the human level of helping other fellow men in dire need and unbearable distress. To the world at large, and to other governments of the world, we are all Sri Lankans reduced to destitution and starvation, exposed to hunger and disease, and therefore in urgent need of help. Just as much as tsunami did not discriminate and distinguish the Sinhalese from the Tamils and from the Muslims, the world too does not regard us as separate entities. The people of the world accept us all as Sri Lankans and have magnanimously dispatched help for us. Now it is up to us Sri Lankans and the few foreign helpers, despite broken bridges and washed off roads, to endeavour to have these goods distributed fairly and squarely to the needy, no matter in which part of Sri Lanka they languish. The enormous logistic problems are being sorted out one by one even as I am writing these words, and the indefatigable aid workers appear to have reached the needy, the hungry and the thirsty with all the wherewithal of life. No doubt there might still be pockets of destitute people crying out for help.

First the president and then the leader of the opposition toured the north and east coast of the country visiting displaced people. Both of them not only promised aid but also assured those needy people that they would not be neglected and equal treatment would be meted out to them. What was the LTTE's reaction to this goodwill gesture? They threatened the visiting premier and other ministers with broomsticks and hooted and booed them out of a refugee centre! This visit was followed by lorry loads of various goods via the Peace Secretariat and SLMM. The items sent were published in the newspapers. What happened to all those goods that went past the Vavunia government checkpoint into LTTE controlled area is a mystery. Believe it or not, the LTTE claimed that they have not received any help from the government! This was propaganda to discredit the government internationally and to attract direct aid to them from international sources. In the meanwhile the LTTE cadres also resorted to hijacking lorry loads of goods sent to Trincomalee by a private TV station.

The government should give maximum publicity to all aid sent to the north and the east and have it verified by the SLMM and other available officials of the UN Aid Agencies. Meanwhile it is the heartless LTTE that has created the greatest bottleneck in the distribution of aid to people under their control. The LTTE insists that all aid be sent to their NGO (TRO) first, so that they can undertake the distribution to the people. This is the inexcusable separatist mindset. They want special treatment because they are a special and separate people. The deadly tsunami did not so distinguish the victims! Aid givers the world over do not think so either, nor do they specify and single out the LTTE, nor the people under them. In any case, given the oppression they have so far imposed, and the callous exploitation they had inflicted on those hapless people, only the incorrigibly naïve would believe that the LTTE would distribute all the aid to all the people. As on previous occasions, they would siphon off a substantial amount to cater to the needs of their cadres, if not, to sell for cash subsequently. Faced with this problem, the aid donors and the government should insist that they have a part to play in the distribution of aid. Failing this, the LTTE should be internationally exposed as the heartless villains who drove their people to death by starvation and easily preventable diseases.

In the east of the country the LTTE hierarchy has held meetings with the security forces and has opted to co-operate with them in relief efforts in the areas under their control. This is how it should be done. Accept the helping hand to alleviate the suffering of the penniless people, because they are all Sri Lankans in need of urgent help.

From Jaffna down the eastern coastline all one can see is the disaster and catastrophe left by the tsunami. Some of the worst affected areas along this coastline are under the control of the LTTE and tsunami would have badly affected them too as much as the already impoverished ordinary citizens. However, other than in the newly built up Mullaitivu, damage to property could not be in the same monetary scale as in the south west of the country. Most of the properties on the eastern coast would have been fisher folks' shacks, their boats and nets. Nevertheless, their means of livelihood would have been completely destroyed together with their humble abodes. Therefore their needs would be as great for them as that of the people in the southwest. Yet what has the LTTE done so far to help these people? They tell the world that they have established many refugee camps and have employed their militia to provide help to those refugees. No outsiders can have access to those refugees. Therefore no verification is possible. They also burnt down a refugee centre in Jaffna because those refugees had established contact with non-LTTE aid workers and aid supplying security forces. Behind this secretive wall one can only speculate the number of people who may have died of starvation and disease.

As at Jan.9th the death toll in the north and east was 20,509. The Ampara district largely under the government control accounted for 10,436 of the above total. Via the BBC, the LTTE claimed that the death toll could be about 30,000 in the areas under their control alone. While this could be a possibility given the exposed nature of the occupied coastline, it is also possible that this late revelation could be propaganda ploy to arrogate a greater proportion of aid for their cadres. This is the cruel game played by the LTTE. This is the politics of disaster inexorably pushing the people to the edge of life.

The vulnerable youngsters who have lost the protection of their parents have also become prey to LTTE's "relief workers". Under the pretence of helping these youngsters, the LTTE cadres have been caught abducting them to replenish their depleted military force. This aspect of the cruel game is likely to gather momentum in the days ahead as there could be many orphaned children and therefore no one to plead on their behalf. Will the international community do anything about it? They have a handle on LTTE, they should demand that this recruitment by conscription of under-aged children be stopped.

It behoves the many international aid workers in this country to expose the damage LTTE has suffered on their military front. Their military strength was their virility and the arrogance of claims to invincibility. Remember what Pirapakaran said in his Mahaveerer Day speech? "Here we are all with our armed might, no one can do anything to us". Yet it took only fifteen minutes for the tsunami to reduce this mighty force to bedraggled and walking-wounded army, now doing everything possible to hide its true state of affairs. Exposure of this vulnerability should not only prevent any premature outbreak of conflict enshrined in his words, "we are ready, we are ready for war", but will also force him to sue for a permanent peace settlement acceptable to all communities in the island.

One can only hope that the tsunami has pushed all concerned towards peace table to recognize that this country belongs to all born here. It is also an opportunity for international community to ditch Pirapakaran and his marauders for using the disaster-afflicted people to pursue their separatist agenda. We are all one people and as one people let us rally forth to rebuild our land and reinstate our unfortunate brethren.

59

Tsunami choked LTTE's War-Cry

(The Island, 21st Feb. 2005)

In the pre-tsunami days of November and December 2004, we saw feverish propaganda activities on the part of the LTTE trying to prepare the captive Tamil population for war. This was in combination with ever increasing demands on government Agents in the north and east to comply with their demands; be it in the hoisting of Tiger flag, or closing of schools to send the children marching on the roads on some nebulous pretext. Even confrontation with security forces on flimsy issues was fair game for local LTTE leaders. We were also privy to the revelations of the ex-commander of LTTE east. He went public on the shiploads of arms and ammunition the LTTE had clandestinely imported. We were also told by the UNICEF how LTTE went about conscripting children for training them to be killers and be killed as fodder for LTTE's Eelam. Then came the Mahaveerers' Day when both Pirapakaran and Balasingam went public that LTTE was ready for war and that nobody could do anything against them. TNA was summoned to Mullaitivu and apprised of LTTE's intentions and what was expected of them in the event of a war. These MPs then took up active lobbying of foreign embassies in Colombo to force the government to negotiate with LTTE "on the basis of the ISGA." They dared not to leak any information on orders served on them by the LTTE.

Sworn to secrecy and death threats hanging over their heads, those TNA MPs were also captive inmates of the terror cordon the LTTE had woven around all Tamil dissenters and opponents. Then, there followed the feverish activity on the part of the Norwegians. They sought to calm nerves by assuring that CFA would hold. We would never know whether the Norwegians were privy to LTTE's plans and were co-operating with the LTTE to lull the country into a false sense of security and pave the way for international recognition of LTTE's Eelam after the sudden attack to defeat the security forces.

Many Tiger observers and commentators----Tamils, Sinhalese and Indians----were so impressed by these activities that they voiced their belief that the LTTE was getting ready for something big. Some boldly speculated that on the 14thJan, (Thaipongal Day), the LTTE would announce its withdrawal from CFA and thus activate the fourteen day notice required under CFA. In my view, if the LTTE was really intent on renewing armed conflict, it was most unlikely that they would have sought to comply with the provisions of the CFA. As far as they were concerned, the CFA applied only to the government and the security forces. It did not apply to them. They violate it with impunity and nobody could do anything about it. This they have already done more than 3000 times over the three years. Hence there was the very high probability of a sudden double blitzkrieg in both Jaffna and Trincomalee at a time of their choosing, coupled with a few 9/11 type of Kamikazi raids on Colombo in their newly acquired airplanes. It is not a major problem for the LTTE to manufacture a casus belli where blame could be easily assigned to the government.

The tsunami, however, choked the war cry, drowned the battle drums and engulfed all those destructive plans, and temporarily imposed a moratorium on the LTTE. The President was right when she said that LTTE was not in a position to engage in warfare at the moment.

Given the scale of cataclysmic disaster along the coastline under the LTTE control, the loss of their warfare assets could be substantial. The same applies to Tiger cadres, even though, they claim their loss on both counts to be minimal. Their supporters have hitherto been their mainstay in terms of raising taxes as well as their army supplied with personnel and adequate provisions. Now they are reduced to destitution and starvation. They have no wherewithal or any means to support or sustain a prolonged armed conflict. Their abject degradation by the tsunami would have sapped the belligerency and the jingoist morale out of them. The damages to property, roads and bridges are other factors preventing a sudden military campaign by the LTTE. So the LTTE have embarked on the next best alternative to rebuild, reconstruct, and reorganize their fighting outfit first, and at the same time, position itself as the indispensable conduit for helping the civilians in the north and the east.

The unabated conscription of tsunami affected children will not be relaxed, no matter, the noises made by the UNICEF. It is a paramount need of the LTTE to replace, to train and reorganize their depleted fighting force. The intensity displayed to recruit new cadres is itself an indication of the extent of their losses. Perhaps one way of stopping this abuse of children is to invoke the CFA and deny the LTTE the freedom to do "political work" in the government controlled areas, until such time that they stop this despicable recruitment of children and disbanded their baby brigades. All those international high decibel preachers of human rights should support this move. But would they?

It is inevitable that a large proportion of money directly collected by the LTTE from the diaspora will be channeled for the purchase of arms and ammunition from the arms bazaars of the world. The LTTE's arms buyer, otherwise known as KP, is probably, just now, very busy trawling the nations to purchase arms and have them transported to Mullaitivu. At the same time it would not surprise anyone, if our embassies abroad were totally unconcerned about KP's activities. They should keep track of this man, and exert influence on every government to help to stop his purchases and transportation of weapons. At the same time the navy should expect many rogue ships loaded with deadly weapons on our seas. The navy should not only enlist the help of the Indian navy, but also seek information, including satellite information, from all friendly sources to stop this deadly contraband reaching our shores. Even our Colombo port should be considered vulnerable to container loads of contraband. The LTTE had been very successful smugglers in the past, but this time around they should be halted in their tracks.

It has to be expected that the LTTE would make use of this disaster to project their "sole representative" status and to justify their ISGA demand. Their likely strategy would be to exploit the failures of the government in distributing the foreign aid rushed to the country. In fact their propaganda blitz abroad depicts the government as discriminating in the provision of tsunami relief to the Tamils in the north and the east. The corollary to this is that they alone can satisfactorily deliver aid to the Tamil victims. Therefore all aid should be channeled through them. A couple of the aid donors have already succumbed to this spurious argument in the face of the weak defense of what the government has done and is intending to do to help the victims. Many Sri Lankan governments even during times of hostilities never stopped government funds for food, health, education and salaries of state employees. Foreigners should be not only apprised of this fact, but also be adverted to the many complaints by Tamils themselves as to how the LTTE siphoned off what the government sent to the areas in the north and east.

All local victims of tsunami are Sri Lankans, no matter their race and religion. It is therefore the duty of the Sri Lankan government to help them. We do not have two governments in Sri Lanka as maintained by the LTTE. It is the government in existence that will be called to account for the foreign aid received. Therefore it is the rightful duty of the government to be involved in the provision of aid with or without the co-operation of the LTTE. The separatist rebels in Acceh (Indonesia) are not treated as an entity separate from the government of Indonesia. The same applies to Sri Lanka.

It is in the best interest of the LTTE to co-operate with the government. Thereby they could secure a fair proportion of aid due to the people of the area, obtain access to various facilities and expedite the rebuilding and reconstruction required. The LTTE must not be considered as the legitimate owners of government land. Therefore any allocation of state land made by them would be illegal. Only the government could bestow legality to such land transactions. Therefore the direct involvement of government is essential. It is the duty of aid donors to ensure that accountability and transparency are maintained in the dispensing of and its distribution to the people. The LTTE and its NGO/TRO have never been accountable to anyone, let alone expose their transactions to scrutiny. In fact the TRO is still under investigation by the Charity Commissioner of UK for financial irregularities. It is banned in USA and the Canadian Mounties do not consider it a genuine charitable organization. Given these dubious credentials, how could TRO be entrusted with millions of tsunami relief funds?

In any case, the victims of tsunami, no matter where they reside, have a right to help, and no one, not even the LTTE, has the right to prevent them receiving that help. It is this that the aid donors should drum into the ears of the LTTE and insist that they be allowed access to dispense that aid directly as they do in other places like Matara, Galle and Ampara. If the desperate people are denied aid due to the policy of "access only if TRO is given all the aid first", then the blame should be squarely laid on the internal contradictions of the LTTE and its fascist nature of its administration. It is a sad fact that they cannot open up their territory because they are essentially terrorist organization and control their people through naked terrorism. To this must be added the fact that the tsunami did destroy a substantial amount of the war assets and that this fact cannot be exposed to the world.

If the LTTE wish the world to believe in their rhetoric of peace, then this is an excellent opportunity to give it a chance and work for the advancement of all people in this tsunami ravaged country.

60

Tiger Eelam; A Signature Away

(The Island, 18th June, 2005)

The political wing leader of the LTTE, Mr.Tamilselvam has gone on record saying "we do hold at least 65% of the territory, we administer them and if I may say so, we have a de facto administration. The areas under the control of the LTTE are being administered by us like a government. So this is the reality. Based on this fact, only the Tamil people have given the LTTE the real recognition. We have fought for nearly 25 years to gain this recognition and this recognition is considered even in CFA signed between LTTE and UNF government" (Sunday Leader, 15th May 2005). Leaving aside for the moment the contradictions in the above statement, he is telling us Tiger Eelam is here and it has recognition from the Tamil people as well as the government. But has it any legitimacy? No. That is the vital missing element he was searching for all over Europe, only to realize that the proverbial Sinhala morons in government could be more easily persuaded to hand it over on a platter.

How can a budding nation have political legitimacy? There are three accepted ways of gaining political legitimacy. The most obvious is by being elected by the people in a free and fair democratically contested and conducted election. This is clearly not the case, because the present Tiger Eelam is a dictatorial administration of the LTTE, by the LTTE and for the LTTE. The terrorized citizens under them are only the "hewers of wood and drawers of water" for the LTTE. They are only source materials for the Tiger fascist machinery misnamed a "government" by Mr. Tamilselvam. The people are held under coercion with no space to exercise any freedom as in the south of Sri Lanka.

This is why a recently a manacled conscript had to swim miles in the sea for his freedom, and an LTTE "policeman" had to run for his freedom over no-man's-land at Omanthai checkpoint. The Communist East Germany's Checkpoint Charlie is fully operational in the LTTE's Vanni. Today those western nations that fought to bring down the Berlin Wall are apparently in support of the new Palmyrah Wall destroying the freedom of the people held in bondage at gun point. Where are the well-off Tamils who have volunteered to abandon their freedom in the south or elsewhere in the world and opted to settle down in the Tiger Eelam? Thus the Tiger government of Eelam is far from an attractive proposition even for Tamils!

The second way is to have the new nation formally recognized as a nation by one or more existing foreign nations. One objective of the recent LTTE international peregrinations was the pursuit of this goal. Needless to say they failed as no nation that felicitated them at high official levels was prepared to give it the stamp of legitimacy. However we do not know what assurances they might have given in secrecy. Certainly, like Turkey recognizing North Cyprus, one cannot ignore a stalemate situation of Norway formally recognizing Tiger Eelam.

The third way is for our government to bestow legitimacy on Tiger Eelam. When the LTTE was de-proscribed three years ago, the nation was repeatedly assured by the then PM (Mr. Wicramasinghe) that this was ONLY for the purpose of talking peace with the LTTE. We were told that it was not a legitimization, nor even the recognition of the LTTE to be on equal footing with the government. The LTTE on the other hand, cashed in on it for all its worth and today projects itself as an entity equal to the government. Thus any agreement with them is immediately enmeshed in suspicion, no matter the assurances given by the politicians.

The Joint Mechanism (JM) so far revealed to the press is another suspect agreement for many reasons. The fact that it is not in the public domain to date is itself indicative of at least some unacceptable secrets it might be hiding from the people. The unpalatable fact is that politicians are afraid of the truth, and therefore, prepared to do deals behind the back of the people who elected them to power.

The SLFP politicians as well as the President tried to sell this JM to the people on the assertion that the LTTE has "acknowledged the sovereignty of the government of Sri Lanka". This was similar to the announcement made by minister G.L.Peiris in Oslo that the LTTE had given up Eelam and had agreed to a federal set up. Mr. Tamilselvam's angry retort demolished this government's canard. He was reported to have said that "we reject outright the President's comment that we are willing to accept Sri Lanka as a sovereign country". In his eyes the only sovereign country was his Eelam. That is how close we came to lose our country!

The government told us that all tsunami funds would be received by the government in the first instance and then appropriate amounts would be disbursed for each approved project by the government through its officials in the local areas. This was another JM pillar dislodged by Mr.Tamilsalvam. He claimed that "we also made it clear that funds should be channeled directly through international custodians who will monitor the process and not through the government". He was out to deny any primacy to government in the eyes of the donors in providing aid to people.

In the woodworks of the JM there seem to be lurking a few unacceptable JM worms ready to crawl out on us immediately after President's signature is placed on the JM.

The President, emphasizing the temporary nature of the JM, told us that it was initially for one year with the option for renewal. According to the Daily Mirror (25th May 2005), the UNDP officials in Geneva have outlined a different timescale. They have warned us, "you are very rarely talking about a process of less than five years and usually it is more like ten years". This long term rebuilding work would afford ample opportunity for LTTE to exercise their power in the utilization of tsunami funds to convert the entire area to Tiger Eelam.

The northern and the eastern provinces do not encompass the entire country. The Ampara district of the eastern province is under the control of the government. There are pockets of Tamils living there as in Kalmunai and Thirukovil. Further, the coastline under the control of the LTTE and destroyed by the tsunami is estimated, at most, to consist, only between 10% to 15% of the total destroyed coastline. As Mr.Amerasinghe asserted in Tokyo, 655 Grama Sevaka (GS) divisions in government controlled areas were affected by tsunami compared to only 46 GS divisions in the LTTE areas. Given these facts a national level structure in the JM is redundant as well as highly suspicious. Is this a ploy by the partisan Norwegians to enhance the power of the LTTE in combination with the unwarranted right given to them in the CFA to do "political work" in government controlled areas?

What is "political work?" It is nothing other than murder, assassination, abduction, conscription, extortion and destabilization of areas under government control that have hitherto enjoyed peace. The latest where trouble has erupted after LTTE was allowed to do political work is Trincomalee. The JM will, with the power of the purse, extend as well as consolidate the terror heaped on the people by the LTTE so far. Therefore this National Committee should be scrapped. Its function of examining the projects already examined by the Provincial Committee is superfluous and time consuming. It is an unnecessary handle for the LTTE to display their arrogance and insolent behavior.

It is my suggestion that the international community should demand that LTTE open its Palmyrah curtain and allow access to all who want to help to rebuild that 10% to 15% of the coastline destroyed by the tsunami and help the people living there by restoring their livelihood.

It is the people who need our help and the LTTE who control them should be prevailed upon to allow free access and free flow of aid to those people. It is only in this respect we need a JM to work in those areas. Why is the government so keen to involve the LTTE to work in areas that are fully under its control? If it is the expertise of the LTTE, that is so paramount, then how come the LTTE is left out of other government coastline stretching from Kirinde to Wattala? Thus, for the rest of the coastline in the north and the east, there is no necessity whatsoever for a JM. A District Committee would suffice for each district to get the work done with the Provincial Committee acting as Supervisor. What is paramount in all these is that people affected in each area should be allowed inputs into all plans and projects.

The promoters of JM gloat over the minority safeguards built into it. I would like to suggest that such safeguards are mere toothless bulldog decorations for the LTTE to deceive the gullible public and some foreigners. If and when the LTTE desires to impose its plans and projects, they are likely to resort to nasty strategies they already practice countrywide. They are likely to resort to murder and assassination of objectors to their plans in the JM membership. It is not necessary to murder all JM members. Well published assassination of just one or two would work wonders. Soon others will fall in line. Just as it is happening now neither the government nor the donors will do anything about it. The LTTE will reign supreme in the JM. This in fact is the main objective of the JM.

Ven. Ratna Thera probably foresaw the possibility of the LTTE's resort to the pistol gang to get the JM to totally comply with their schemes. He therefore protested at the meeting held in Kandy to sign the JM. It was opportune to have alerted the assembled donors that forcing the government to sign a JM with terrorists was tantamount to the surrender of our sovereignty. He knew that Tiger Eelam was only a signature away. It is salutary that the New York Human Rights Watch is now calling for an end to killing of civilians by the LTTE. Let us hope that the government will rethink its JM and look for quid pro quo from the LTTE and its international allies.

61

Tigers' Post P-Toms Celebrations

(Daily Mirror, 9th July 2005)

If Pirapakaran had a meeting in the jungle clearing off Therevikulam with the LTTE pistol gang to celebrate the successful execution of the gruesome assassination task allotted to them after the CFA was signed, he would have had, among many goodies on the menu, Reindeer sausages and Norwegian smoked salmon sandwiches. The latter would have come from Oslo with the compliments of peace blundering Vikings.

While the treat was being gobbled up, here is the possible text of the celebratory speech, The Thalaivar Pirapakaran would have made to the exultant cheering of his fanatical cadres.

"I congratulate all of you for the excellent work done for the sake of Eelam. Today we have achieved Tiger Eelam by artfully deceiving the Sinhala politician modayas in the south. The P-Toms is simply an interim surrender document giving us the legitimacy to intervene in the affairs of the government under the guise of tsunami work, anywhere in Illankai. Be patient, I shall explain".

"From now on Kilinochchi is the tsunami-work capital of Illankai. It was in no way affected by tsunami, and our affected coastline is only about 150km long, yet we convinced the shallow headed Sinhalayas that it is the only place suitable for any tsunami recovery work! From Kilinochchi I shall direct the work to be done everywhere else. All international organizations will now come to Kilinochchi, reside there, get tutored by our cadres and so will come to accept our set-up as a legitimate government of Tiger Eelam. They will soon get used to dealing with us directly. The Peter Harrolds, Wilson Wouters and Barmeos of powerful international organizations now have all the reasons they need, to deal with us as a legitimate entity separate from the government in Colombo. With your co-operation and your guns held at the heads of all tsunami officials, I shall show the world, how efficiently I get the work done. The Sinhala Air Force will soon be degraded to an air transport ferry service for our cadres assigned on tsunami work. The Sinhala Army will also be reduced to an escort agency accompanying you to wherever you need to travel. It will be baited and insulted at every turn and debilitated to mere bystanders admiring your work".

"I appreciate the loyal service you render me under very difficult circumstances. This is why I protected you by refusing to have any Human Rights clauses in the P-Toms. The Sinhalayas accepted this without any murmur. Our international friends and local friends in the human rights industry also had no complaints and did not show any disapproval. This is evidence and appreciation of your very valuable service to Tiger Eelam. In the near future you will be called upon to redouble your efforts. I shall do my best to ameliorate your difficult circumstances by appointing you as tsunami work-work officials wherever and whenever needed".

"I do foresee that there will be a few people in the tsunami projects who could be dissenters and objectors to our plans. They will become traitors to Eelam and you know the punishment I have in store for such dissidents. Some of you will be assigned to carry out this noble task of eliminating these traitors without any mercy. This is the reason for not accepting any Human Rights clauses in the P-Toms. Do not worry if the stupid Sinhala ministers keep telling the world that I have changed and soon I shall be a democratized politician. On my behalf, you have more than adequately answered these stupid Sinhalayas by destroying three Sinhala traitors in Urani, in the Batticaloa district on the 30th of June".

"All these years I have been saying that the LTTE is the 'sole representative of the Tamil speaking people'. At last the Sinhalayas have accepted this by having my signature as the only other signature in the P-Toms. I am also happy that now a Muslim deputy Mayor is crying out for such recognition by the Muslims. The Tamil speaking

Muslims are now under our control for tsunami work. I shall do my best to extend this power to other areas of political as well as social life of the Muslims. Even the majority Sinhalese in the country have been, by a sleight of hand, made a minority party in the P-Toms. This shows that they too now accept my supremacy in principle; however, we need to establish this as a fact. The P-Toms gives us this opportunity".

"The High Level Committee (HLC) is simply a decoration to appease the Sinhala and Muslim psyches. It is also in a way made to give me formal recognition at national level. However, it has no real power, nor any control over tsunami funds. It is expected that all decisions in the HLC will be arrived at by consensus. As you know I do not depend on consensus of others to execute my plans. If the other two members of the HLC disagree with my formulation of policies, I shall simply suspend the HLC, so that the other two can twiddle their thumbs in their luxury secretariat in Colombo. I shall carry on my mission regardless from Kilinochchi. I shall not yield on this until my proposals are accepted and persons amenable to LTTE's needs are appointed to the HLC".

"As I said before the P-Toms gives us the power to engage in tsunami work all over the island. This is because I got the Norwegian friends to cleverly define the tsunami disaster zone as 'including all the tsunami affected land area of Sri Lanka, which is adjacent to the sea, lying within a limit of two kilometers landwards from the mean low water line' (P-Toms, 2c). In 2d of the P-Toms, the land area can be extended further inwards. The important point here is that I can, on the pretext of resettling tsunami affected people, encroach on state land to settle legitimately people like you in the heartland of Sinhalayas. I envisage Tiger colonies in the heartlands of both Sinhalayas and the Muslims. No reciprocal rights will be given to others in my realm. I have even now appointed a small committee of your comrades to select a few strategically important places in the tsunami affected areas in Amparai and the south for this purpose".

"There is no limit to the extent of the sea area for our operations. Our navy will take maximum advantage of this and extend its naval activities right into the deep blue sea water. Smuggling weapons will certainly be part of our tsunami work. The Sinhala navy will be required to protect our navy's tsunami work. Our submarine force will have ample work on their hands removing debris from the seabed. They will use this opportunity to perfect our underwater war assets and install underwater defense and offence systems right along the sea lanes used by the Sinhala navy".

"Whatever building we undertake on the coastline will be so designed that they will be convertible to fortresses capable of hiding artillery and housing our cadres in times of need. We shall get paid for all these works of consolidation of our military strength (also known as 'unspecified work') both by the Sinhala government and the world institutions. Can you think of anything as fabulous as this deal? The Muslims will be made to cooperate with us on this by gently reminding them of the fate of Muslims who refused our hegemony in Jaffna".

"The real power in the P-Toms is in the hands of the Regional Committee. As can be expected, I shall hold the majority power in that committee. The prioritization of tsunami work, its approval and management, overall monitoring and the fund management will be in my hands. All international personnel involved will be ensured to be Tiger-friendly individuals. Here too I am expected to work on the basis of consensus. As you know I am allergic to consensus. Anyone who disagrees with my plans and objects to my implementation procedures will be considered as a traitor. Such foolish men will be at your mercy to be eliminated at your convenience".

"I have firmly excluded the Sinhala Treasury from the tsunami fund management. The custodian of those funds will be ensured to be a Tiger-friendly organization. I do have many such persons now in various international monetary bodies and our friends, the Norwegians will do their best to ensure an outcome favourable to us on this vital issue. The recent elucidation of this aspect of the Funding Agent by the Sinhala government is only their interpretation. It is not part of the signed P-Toms document. It is my interpretation of P-Toms that matters in the Regional Committee. In any case as the international

NGOs are with us, together we will be able to ignore the Sinhala government and carry on our task of rebuilding and developing the damaged land of Eelam. The lids of the treasure chests of international charitable agencies will soon be opened to us. With that help, I shall do my utmost first to equip my army, including all of you, with all the latest weapons available in the arms markets of the world".

"My country will also have the best educational and health institutions. All of you will live in a prosperous country. We have now got a Tiger Eelam, we have only a few yards to go for our beloved Tamil Eelam. By the time we finish tsunami work, Tamil Eelam will be in existence whether the Sinhalese and the Muslims like it or not".

"Today we have many friends among the Sinhala Ministers. They praise our work on political platforms. We appreciate their help in trying to convince the Sinhalese of our superiority in many aspects of life. We also have many Sinhala-managed NGOs whose unabated and unflagging propaganda work on our behalf, have won over many international friends to our noble cause of Eelam. I remain thankful to them too".

"Finally no matter whether the south has an election or not, we are on a winning ticket. The two main political parties in the south are on our side. Let us all resolve to use this P-Toms to take the final leap from Tiger Eelam to Tamil Eelam. That is our mutual final destination. We are almost there. The next time when we meet, it will be to celebrate the birth of Tamil Eelam".

{Fortunately P-Toms was struck down by our Supreme Court and the imminent danger to our country was averted}.

62

The Supporters of P-Toms Agreement are all Traitors

(Daily Mirror, 28th July 2005)

While the legal eagles battle over the provisions of the P-Toms, I am here concerned with the enactment of the burlesque accompanying the signing of the P-Toms. On any other matter this would be a trifling episode of engaging amusement to be enjoyed by all. But P-Toms concerned a section of our citizens reduced to destitution by the tsunami, and the way the theatrics were played out, the whole citizenry was made a bunch of fools before international society that had rushed to our aid in our dire necessity. Should we allow our moronic politicians to treat us like fools? Certainly not! Hence this protest! We should all vehemently protest at the contemptuous way the politicians treat us, their masters.

The prologue of this drama/nadagama was set by foreign interlopers in the many Colombo embassies. They went about attending various ceremonies in many parts of the tsunami-damaged country, while preaching to us, the virtues of Joint Management (JM) of tsunami relief with LTTE. They took for granted that the whole of northern and eastern provinces were already under LTTE control. This we know is not factually true. They then issued veiled threats that without JM no funds would be delivered to Sri Lanka for helping the tsunami victims. Some even boldly predicted that without a JM, another war with LTTE was at hand! Some wily foreign meddlers in our affairs covered their backs by making statements contradicting their earlier pronouncements. Forked tongues with double talk were common among those denizens of embassies. One moment "no JM, no funds" was heard loud and clear. At another time and place "JM or no JM, funds will be delivered" was also heard, well enunciated by the same inter meddlers. Thus was the stage set for the drama that is yet to be played out to the finish.

Our politicians, being very poor imitators with little or no intelligence, took up the refrain and extended it to frighten the people. Their theme became "no JM, no funds, bombs in Colombo, war in the country and compulsory conscription of all youngsters over 18 years". The President, many SLFP and UNP politicians indulged in scaremongering of the public with gay abandon. In fact all these were parts of the drama, preparing the people to accept the unacceptable. The NGO peace myrmidons followed suit with seminars and conferences extolling the virtues of the JM, already secretly agreed to by the government, the UNP and the czars of embassies.

The next step was the drafting of the P-Toms. This had to be done in secret, as it contained many issues over which the UNP government was booted out by the President, and then kicked out by the people at the general election. Among many crucial issues, a few need to be highlighted here. Making Kilinochchi the tsunami capital, accepting LTTE as the "sole representatives" of Tamils, accepting the legitimacy of the LTTE's illegal administration, subordination of the sovereign government to a terrorist gang, thrusting the unwilling Muslims and Sinhalese of the eastern province to the thralldom of LTTE's oppressive fascism and the abandonment of the government's duty to manage its funds----these are some of the controversial issues needed to be hidden from the masses, until the nation's suicide note in the form of P-Toms was signed and delivered.

Any Pedris Perera or Punchi Menika in the Pettah market would have told the government, had they been consulted, that the proportion of the LTTE coastline destroyed by the tsunami was tiny compared to that of the rest, and therefore such powers to LTTE were unnecessary and unacceptable. Yet men of superior intelligence in government thought otherwise, because the hidden objective of the JM was to make all the claims of the LTTE legitimate, thereby help them to consolidate their stranglehold on the two provinces and pave the way for their formal recognition by other foreign powers. The validity of this conclusion is apparent from the events following the signing of the P-Toms.

The stage, thus set, and hapless audience (Sri Lankans), suitably pummeled with fear, the play proper began in Kandy. Many foreigners gathered there and solemnly promised dollars galore for tsunami work. No blood sacrifices were offered at this celebration, instead a promise to the effect that no blood sacrifices would be offerred, was considered sufficient. This climax came when the President's shrill voice announced to a dumbfounded audience and the world that she would sign the JM even if it cost her life. This crowning moment lost its splendour when Ven. Ratna Thera took the opportunity to valiantly protest publicly on the stage, at the grotesque damage done to the sovereignty of the country. Given the London bombs his poignant words would be echoing in the minds of those foreign emissaries. Similarly, the President's tantrums at this meeting would have lost its impact, as the final document was signed by a mere civil servant and not by the President. If only the President had thought of 1815 when her ancestors gave away the country to the scheming British and lost the king and country, she perhaps would have had second thoughts about this melodrama in Kandy. That is of course, assuming that she had the interest and security of the country at heart!

The anti-climax to this stage-managed drama is that the country is well skewered like the swan in Carmina Burana;

> 'Once I lived on the lakes,
> Once I looked beautiful, when I was a swan;
> Misery me, now black and roasting fiercely,
> The servant (LTTE) is turning me on the on the spit,
> I am burning fiercely on the pyre,
> The steward now serves me up,
> Now I lie on a plate, and cannot fly anymore,
> I see bared teeth; misery me! misery me!

That the country was hoodwinked by this high drama is quite evident from the events subsequent to the signing of the P-Toms. First, LTTE's Thamilselvan was reported to have admitted that the LTTE signed the document reluctantly. If this was the case, how could they have instigated a war on this issue as was previously claimed? Where are the warmongering SLFP ministers now? Foolish men that they are, is all too plain to see.

For a long time the LTTE has been seeking international legitimacy and access to international dollar funds. The P-Toms did open the gates to this kingdom. Therefore they signed it. Their expectations were temporarily frustrated by the Supreme Court. They do not accept this court, yet, they will have to wait until the final verdict on this issue. The fact of the matter is that LTTE's TRO/NGO is flushed with funds coming from the Tamil diaspora and other foreign embassy secret accounts. No one outside the inner circle of the LTTE knows the amounts received, the amounts expended on tsunami work and what happened to the balance remaining. According to a cabinet minister, many LTTE cadres had built two-storied comfortable houses in Kilinochchi and had bought luxury vehicles. Perhaps, these too were tsunami building works!

The international protagonists, who impelled the government towards the JM, soon revealed their hypocrisy and duplicity. They (US, Japan, and Australia) announced that they would not be scheduling any funds to the P-Toms. The British and the EU are likely to follow suit. This makes the P-Toms an empty shell, utterly ineffective and a laughing stock of the world. Now you see why the whole drama was a burlesque. It was not really intended to provide help for the tsunami victims. It was a structure erected to appease the LTTE and enhance their status and help them on the road to independence and international legitimacy at the expense of Sri Lanka. Thus to me, P-Toms was a suicide note. The President and other advocates who supported it were all traitors. It appears only bombs in the capitals of Europe will convince them that they cannot mollycoddle terrorists, nor can they cohabit with them. Unfortunately the wages of sins of the politicians are paid for by innocent citizens both in London as well as in Trincomalee at the moment.

If any reader is still in doubt about the hidden agenda of the P-Toms, let me submit the final evidence from the horse's mouth itself. Mr. Mano Tittawella is the Chief of the Task Force for Rebuilding of the

Nation (TAFREN). At a luncheon meeting organized by the American Chamber of Commerce in Sri Lanka, he-was alleged to have stated the following by The Island newspaper of 20th July. "Somebody asked me whether the P-Toms was required to do tsunami reconstruction and the answer is, no. We can do tsunami reconstruction work anyway. Lots of things were happening in the north and east even before P-Toms was talked about. Housing is going on, the roads are being started, the relief was done, rescue operation was done, transitional housing was done". Well, the government's cover, that the P-Toms was a mere administrative arrangement has been exposed as lame excuse. It was an unadulterated deception, enforced by frightening the people. I do firmly assert that it is the responsibility of the government to help the tsunami victims no matter where they lived. I also believe that the charade of the P-Tom was not necessary to deliver this help to the people. It was already being done, and a kick in the backsides of the bureaucracy was the required push to expedite the process.

Those who objected to the P-Toms, this writer included, were condemned as chauvinists. It appears to me that heir chauvinism was well-placed as against the supporters of P-Toms, who remain now exposed as traitors betraying their country to a bunch of terrorists.

63

Three years of Humiliation?

(The Island, 19th April 2005)

We have had three years of ceasefire between the government's security forces and the LTTE. It ought to be accepted that the very nature of a ceasefire entails no mass destruction of lives and properties due to military action by the contesting forces. Thus the people in the areas of conflict and in the adjacent areas have been saved from loss of lives, limbs and degradation to utter misery. This ceasefire has ushered in a semblance of normalcy in Jaffna, in Vavunia, in Trincomalee and in Batticaloa. Retail trade is thriving in all those towns. Some infrastructure such as roads, hospitals and other government buildings also have been restored.

The health services are limping back to normalcy. The fisher folk have got on with their daily business. Some farmers and horticulturists have also started to produce food for the locals.

Thousands of mines have been eliminated from thousands of acres of land with the help of foreign aid. The children have gone back to schools, or what is left of them, to pursue their studies. Most important of all, the people who did suffer directly and indirectly from war have now cultivated a strong aversion to war. They are not satisfied with this mere ceasefire. They want permanent peace. This strong desire has been reinforced by the cataclysmic devastation and destitution caused by the tsunami.

A properly instituted ceasefire is indeed a case for celebration by the people in general. But our ceasefire had been flawed from the very start, and has been designed to inflict humiliation on the nation.

It was a deal that ignored a directly elected President, the Cabinet and the Parliament of the day. It was drawn up by a flagrantly partisan foreigner in consultation with Mr. Balasingam of the LTTE. It was overtly tilted towards satisfying the outrageous demands of the LTTE with no sanctions for violation of CFA. From top to bottom the CFA was simply a demand sheet imposed by the LTTE in return for their abstention from engaging in military hostilities and blasting with bombs Colombo and other economic targets in the country. It was a piece of paper demanding abject appeasement of the LTTE and freedom for them to engage in enhancing their military strength for the eventual armed struggle for Eelam.

The gutless UNF Prime Minister simply gave into almost all the demands of the LTTE, while engaging in fruitless talks stage-managed by the partisan Norwegians.

All the while the LTTE took the opportunity to bask in international exposure, project themselves as liberation fighters and ingratiate themselves with western nations. They did not, however, abstain from clandestinely trawling the arms bazaars for the latest lethal weapons, weapons delivery systems and electronic surveillance systems.

They were winners all the way to the battlefield. That was when they unilaterally suspended the peace talks and instead submitted the separatist ISGA. International fanfare accompanying the birth of the ISGA was simply an insurance policy to assign the blame on the government if it failed to entertain the ISGA and utilize this failure on the part of the government to resume the military option. The tsunami put paid to this plan momentarily.

The CFA did not stop murders by the LTTE. First among the victims were the informants of the army. They were all hunted down by the LTTE and some were gunned down in broad daylight on the highways and byways of Colombo.

The top politicians of UNF government were alleged to have revealed the names and whereabouts of those unfortunate victims. I agree with those foreign Sri Lanka friendly commentators that those politicians should be arraigned for treason and betrayal of those brave victims of LTTE.

Too numerous to list here are the many other murders of dissidents, of rival Tamil politicians and innocent civilians. Even the brutal murder of eight former LTTE cadres in Kottawa, Colombo, failed to register a protest squeak form authorities, let alone a demand to stop such brutal slaughters.

The CFA has given freedom of easy access to the LTTE into areas that were highly risky for them to enter prior to the CFA. This opportunity they have used and will continue to use to their full advantage. Massive infiltration has already taken place and "sleeper cells" have been planted and are ready for the call to action.

From this perspective the CFA has been not only a threat but also a humiliation of the nation, because most of the murders have taken place in the government controlled areas with the blame being squarely placed on government security forces. The armed forces are not the culprits, but so long as they remain in the straightjacket of the CFA, while the LTTE are accorded all the freedom, they certainly will be subjected to humiliation.

The benefits accruing to the LTTE from the CFA are many. In short, it has enabled them to fully equip their fighting forces with the latest of weapons and communication systems. Their readiness for war was publicly announced by their leaders. In addition, the LTTE also resorted to all the criminal activities possible in any society and obtain maximum gain from such nefarious activities.

Abductions, extortions, harassments, robbing of private vehicles, forcible conscription of children, provocation of security forces, hoisting of LTTE flags in many places and entering the government controlled areas with weapons are some of the outrageous criminal activities as well as blatant violations of the CFA. Such is the immunity the CFA has bestowed on them!

The other advantages the LTTE obtained include the erection of more than ten military camps, of which. Manirasakulam is the most known one. Some of these camps are strategically situated surrounding the entrance to Trincomalee harbour. The sea Tigers boats equipped with powerful engines and guns, have also had many live-fire naval exercises to test their capability to fight the government navy.

A swathe of coastline extending north from Kokilai to Nargarkovil is today a High Security Zone of the LTTE. While they complain about the government's High Security Zones, theirs are sacred and cannot be questioned. In this light the CFA looks like a ridiculous piece of paper and those responsible for this one-sided agreement should be taken to task and hounded out of politics. Alas, the main Sinhala advocate and signatory is still in politics and posing as a patriot! In Sri Lanka failed yesterday's men continue to hold high political office to the detriment of the national interest.

The LTTE has also resorted to 'eelamizing' the north and the east. This they have done by controlling as well as directing the activities of the government agents and the NGOs. One dissenting government agent was shot dead not long ago. The schools and the Jaffna university are required to abide by the orders issued by the LTTE officials. Thus the school children have become mere rent-a-crowd at numerous LTTE agitations. Any dissenting principal of a school will be visited by the LTTE thugs to impart to him a lesson in obedience. All ceremonies are conducted in Tamil only under the Tiger flag. The Sinhalese and the Muslims of north and east are reduced to mere bystanders. The Muslims are engaged only to the extent that their involvement is economically beneficial to the LTTE.

The greatest benefit the CFA bestowed on the LTTE is the Irranamadu air strip. It was during this CFA period that they were able to build this airstrip, smuggle in equipments and equip it with all the gadgets necessary for an airport including electronic surveillance systems. It is now common knowledge that they now have two small airplanes. Two helicopters allegedly destined for donation to LTTE were recently stopped by our Customs. Another neatly packed airplane in broken parts has also been detected and detained by our Customs. Just as much as the LTTE demanded an exclusive sea zone, it will not surprise me if they tabled a demand for an exclusive air zone as well. Nor will it surprise me if our moronic politicians agreed to talk about it too!

The humiliation the LTTE have managed to impose on our security forces is consummate to the extent that they do insult them at every turn and then get them to provide escort service free of charge. Mr. Balasingam had the audacity to complain in London at his Mahaveerer day speech about the escort service rendered to him. He said "we were kept in a separate room for one hour. It took half an hour for the helicopter to take off and finally we manage to take off the ground. Hereafter, I thought, I will not take a copter, but go by bullock cart" (Sunday Times, 5th Dec.2004). If I had anything to do with his transport during his recent arrival in Sri Lanka, I would have distributed this extract of his speech to the media and had bullock carts as well as copters ready on the runway and allowed the media to observe and report Mr. Balasingam's choice of transport to the Vanni! I wonder whether he says 'Thank you' to the pilot officer and others involved in providing him this transport at the expense of the country. The government has not got the guts to demand payment for these services. Such privileges are unavailable to other citizens. Has the government considered the consequences in the event of a helicopter accident and resulting fatalities? Finally it is time for the security forces to stand up to the accusations of the LTTE. They should point blankly refuse to provide escort services of all types so long as LTTE refuses to withdraw all accusations against them for the murder of LTTE cadres in the east.

The murder of opponents was a war game started by the LTTE and now it is their trained and disillusioned men in the east who return the call. This fact the LTTE is afraid to stomach as it will immediately call into question their fictitious 'sole representative' status. Terror begets terror is the lesson the LTTE yet needs to learn, But will they?

64

Idiocy in the Joint Mechanism: Let there be no Blackmail

(Daily Mirror, 5th May 2005)

It is assumed that the government is on the threshold of putting its signature to another Norwegian concocted document called the Joint Mechanism (JM) for the delivery of tsunami relief to the people in the north and east of the country. This document is expected to contain the structure, the powers (both policy making and executive), and the agreement between the government and the LTTE for the repair, reconstruction and rehabilitation (RRR) of the north and the east. Its contents are still hidden from the people.

Many people have argued in favour of this mechanism. Even the usually highly perceptive Foreign Minister has recently spoken in favour of this mechanism and based his arguments on ground realities in the two provinces. While maintaining that it is the responsibility of the government to help all the victims of tsunami, the government cannot allow itself to be blackmailed by anyone to accede to the outrageous demands. A JM for the WHOLE of north and the east (with only six affected areas), is such a monstrous demand, because it is riddled with stark stupidities. Why are we so eager to surrender our independence and sovereignty?

We do have at the moment a CFA and a MOU, two documents designed and formulated by the same Norwegians. Both have been proved to be highly defective. Both documents helped the LTTE to consolidate their military preparations and their bogus status as "sole representatives" of the Tamils. Both documents are used by the LTTE to humiliate the security forces and are flouted with impunity almost on a daily basis. Thus while Mr. Tamilselvam avers solemnly in South Africa that LTTE observes the CFA and the MOU to the letter, his minions shoot at the navy boats, fire motor rockets at security forces at

Toppur (13th April), and slaughter on a daily basis anyone they pick on anywhere in the country. The foreign dignitaries who entertain these terrorists dare not ask Mr. Thamilselvam how these dastardly deeds amount to abiding by the CFA/MOU!

The issue therefore is that any document drafted by the Norwegians should be considered with utmost suspicion and be subject to a comprehensive critical analysis by patriotic professionals. It should also be exposed to public scrutiny. It would be crass stupidity to have another secret signing of a document authored by the partisan Norwegians. A second blunder on this score is totally unacceptable.

Tsunami also devastated the coastal areas in the south and west of the country. All these areas are heavily populated ones, therefore, destruction of lives and of properties has been incalculable. Nevertheless, many organizations have conducted various assessments of the damage and are in the process of rebuilding. Nobody demanded a JM with LTTE for this work as these areas are under government's control. The Education department and the TAFREN (Task Force for Rebuilding the Nation) recently published the names of schools and the corresponding donor partners for rebuilding those schools. This is a good example of objective-defined assistance. No JM was necessary. The urgent task would be to find contractors, assign the projects with time-frames and supervise the work to completion. The government's procedure for selection of contractors will nevertheless apply for the sake of fairness, probity and transparency. An architect/engineer for all major works (say over one million rupees), should be appointed by the government/donor concerned with the project. He should supervise the work-in-progress, certify the value of the work done and the amount of the funds to be released to the contractor concerned. All contractors should be subject to penalty clauses for delay as well as shoddy work. The actual selection of contractors and assignment of work should be in the hands of the local body appointed for that purpose. They should be in constant touch with the appointed architect/engineer. In the case of schools, a committee consisting of members of Parent Teachers Association of that school plus a person from the local Education Office should be given the task outlined above.

The same newspaper gave names of schools in the north and east and their corresponding confirmed donors. Here too no JM is necessary if the schools concerned are in the government controlled areas. The physical work could be carried out in the same manner as for the schools in Galle or Matara. The problem is with schools in LTTE controlled areas. The LTTE would want to appoint the contractors and handle the connected donor funds. It is here that the donors should play their strong hands, (ie. the ability to withdraw/ withhold funds), and insist on value for money and control over the money they have consented to spend on the project. They should be fully aware, by now, that they are dealing with a ruthless organization that demands Rs.100 from the relief given to each tsunami victim. Thus for instance, the German government is the confirmed donor for the rebuilding of Mullaitivu Mahja Vidyalayam. It therefore has the right to demand that procedures outlined above be followed for the rebuilding of the school and ensure that an embassy official is included in the local school building committee. Surely where is the need for JM in this and many other similar cases?

The idiocy in the JM is patently clear if we take the case of the coastal towns in the Ampara district. It is under government's control like Galle or Matara. This district suffered the highest death toll of 11,257 (dead and missing) from the tsunami. The 2001 census table given below speaks volumes against JM for that district. The coastal towns of Ampara district and their population categories:

	Tamils	Muslims	others	Total
Kalmunai	26,663	42,924	852	70,439
Nintavur	1347	23,420	6	24,773
Addalachchenai	603	33,318	1858	35,779
Akkaraipattu	1043	33,679	239	34,961
Sainthamaruthu	8	23,982	28	24018
Potuvil	5668	21,669	262	27,599
Total	35,332	178,992	3245	217,569

Only in Kalmunai there is a substantial Tamil population. This may warrant the involvement of LTTE in the RRR of that area. Given the figures in the above table, how can anyone justify a JM for this district? What the figures eloquently portray is the absolute necessity for the involvement of the Muslim community in all RRR in Ampara district coastline towns. It would be absolutely idiotic to invite the LTTE to this district and hand over the Muslim victims of tsunami to their care. I rest my case. The government controlled areas do not need a JM to handle the work of RRR. The above table too is the other side of the ground reality (against JM), adduced by the Foreign minister!

Only Mr.Anandasangaree, the veteran TULF politician seems to have grasped the situation outlined above. He is alleged to have told the Ven.Mahanayakka Thera that "out of 43 Divisional Secretariat Divisions in the east, 31 are in government controlled areas and the balance under the LTTE. Out of 31Divisional Secretariat Divisions in the north, 17 are under government and 14 under LTTE. Therefore it is unfair for the LTTE to demand majority powers in the JM" (Daily News, 10th April). He wanted the tsunami aid to be distributed through the government officials in those areas under government control.

One point needs mention here. The donors as well as the government should not blindly accept the damage assessment done solely by the LTTE. They should demand access to those areas for damage assessment by other agencies, as has been done in Galle and Hambantota. We do know that the coastal strip from Nagarkovil in the north to Kuchchaveli near Trincomalee has been a sparsely populated area by the fisher folk. The only town of any significance is Mullaitivu, a High Security town of the LTTE. Therefore the monetary magnitude of the damage to property cannot be on the same scale as that of the many towns on the south-western coast. As could be expected the LTTE is likely to submit highly exaggerated damage assessments, together with grandiose plans for reconstruction.

A dire warning is also due for those who want to sign the JM document drafted by the double-dealing Norwegians. In the CFA the LTTE was given freedom to conduct political work in government controlled areas. What, in fact, did they do? Did they conduct classes on abiding by the democratically enacted Rule of Law? Did they preach political pluralism, freedom of speech and association? Did the respect the Human Rights of citizens? No, they only eliminated their rivals by murder!

The LTTE took the opportunity given in the CFA to invade and infiltrate the government controlled areas to slaughter innocent Tamils and others who had long forsaken violence. They used coercion and duress to extract extortionate taxes and levies from anyone vulnerable to their threats. They waylaid unwilling school children, and carried them away to be trained as killers for Suriya Thevan. They humiliated our security forces throughout the three year period of the CFA. They enhanced and consolidated their fighting forces with clandestinely imported arms and ammunition. Imagine what would happen if they are also given access to vast funds, as well as control over terrain, where they hardly have any presence now, let alone any influence.

In short would the Muslims and the Sinhalese welcome LTTE control over the repair, rebuilding and reconstruction work in their areas? Why are our politicians so short-sighted?

65

WAR HYSTERIA IN THE NORTH AND EAST

(The Island, 31st. Dec.2005)

In the north and the east of our country, the LTTE has successfully propagated war hysteria by resorting to open and brazen attacks and murder of security personnel. Claymore mine attack on the army is an attempt to keep the army shut up in barracks. The attack on the helicopter was intended to ground our air assets. The wolf-pack attack on our navy was yet another attempt to legitimize LTTE's exclusive use of the northern and eastern sea (a Tiger territorial sea) as well as to frighten our navy to confine itself to the safety of the harbour. In short, the LTTE is trying out, under the cover of the treacherous CFA, the ability of its cadres to take on the country's security forces on land, sea and air. So far they have triumphed by default of the government's security forces. They have achieved the tasks of intimidating the government, duping again the international community and, most important of all, creating war hysteria in the north and the east.

War hysteria is a necessary and an essential strategy of the LTTE for its own survival. LTTE was born out of violence, it grew up by resorting to violence and it survives by violence. Violence to induce mortal fear is at the core of the strategy of the LTTE to subjugate the Tamils and coerce them to obedience and obeisance to the LTTE. For over twenty years Pirapakaran has waged his eelam war. To-date it has been a monumental failure in that more than 17,000 Tamils died fighting for his dream. There is no guarantee that he will or can win a future war and deliver eelam as he has promised. The Tamils too are war weary. They too want peace and a normal life like other Tamils living in Colombo and elsewhere in the south of the country. Unfortunately for the Tamils and the country, the LTTE cannot survive in a peaceful environment. Therefore they cannot accept peace and political stability in the country. They want absolute rule over one-third of the country for now and perhaps more later.

The one man tyrannical and fascist rule of the illegally controlled areas of the country will collapse if rule of democratically promulgated law, human rights and democracy are installed in those areas. The Tamils now in servitude there have no valid or cogent reason for evincing loyalty to the LTTE. They are the most oppressed by extortionate taxes that have progressively reduced them to destitution; they are the most fettered by the denial of their freedoms of expression, of movement, of association and the freedom to exercise their democratic right to vote. They are the most frightened as their children are daily subject to abduction for forced conscription to the LTTE's brutal fighting/suicide force. They are the most terrorized because any one or more of them could be singled out for assassination by the LTTE at any time. Given these shocking and macabre conditions of their lives, there is no earthly reason for the Tamils to continue and be steadfast in their loyalty to the LTTE. But the LTTE needs these hapless people and the only way to keep the Tamils is have them trampled and crumpled under their terrorist jackboots. Otherwise, like the Cold War Berlin Wall, the Palmyra Wall in the Vanni will collapse and the people will flee the area in droves.

The single-minded effort to instill fear and war hysteria in the people have now surfaced in imposing compulsory military and fire-arms training on unwilling civilians and university students. This "Makkal Padai" is now readily proffered as being responsible for all the atrocities in the Jaffna peninsula. The devilishly cunning LTTE thus claims that it is "not involved in any activity that breaches the CFA". Thus not only the ordinary people are pinpointed as culprits, but will also be made the sacrificial lambs in a conflict situation, as they will be pushed to the frontline and exposed to fire. The trump card will then be that the government forces are engaged in genocide killing of civilians! The Peace Secretariat in Colombo, if it is endowed with any backbone, should have alerted the world, first to the violation of CFA by this attempted conversion of civilians to a military force, and its inevitable consequence, if actual conflict ensues at any time now or in the future. These enslaved Tamils dare not ask why they should be fighting for one man and his fascist dreams while their Tamil brethren in the South are enjoying normal lives. Perhaps the TNA politicians living comfortable lives of freedom in Colombo have an answer. They will certainly have many excuses for their ostentatious life-styles.

To the politicians and peacenik journalists in the south, the bogy is still the JVP and the JHU. These two political parties are constantly blamed for the events in the north and the east. The LTTE too has found them to be convenient pegs to hang their accusations of atrocities against the Tamils. To my mind, the most dangerous and the most strident war-monger in the country today is Pirapakaran and his executioners. The shrill beat of their war drums is quite loud and clear in the country. Ignoring this deadly siren would lead the country to catastrophe. Pirapakaran will strike at a time and place of his choice. He will not stop to think or be deterred by what the world would say or do. He has not shown any deference to such niceties to-date. His cocksureness of victory may have substantial reason behind it. My speculation is that he may have on his hands banned weapons of mass destruction (WMDs) and their delivery systems. Thus army's High Security Zones could be pulverized within no time. Has the army got any effective safeguards against such weapons? I hope the new man at the top will actively consider this possibility and seek adequate safeguards for the soldiers and the war assets. Under-estimation of the LTTE has been the consistent failure of our security forces in the past.

There are a few simple things the government and the Foreign Office can do against the villainy contemplated by the LTTE. The government must review realistically the location of all army bunkers for their vulnerability for easy attack by the LTTE. Over the period of the CFA, it is likely that the LTTE would have studied every one of them in detail. By now they would have plans on hand to decimate them without much bother in the event of open conflict. Has the army any counter plans? I am just asking as such things are taken for granted until disasters overtake them.

The government should also erect large billboards at all government controlled checkpoints in the north and the east. It should explain in Tamil the new president's vision of peace and his endeavours to bring about peace in the country. It should also explain how the Tamils in the south live quietly and peacefully pursuing their livelihoods. They do not pay extortionate taxes to anybody nor are their children forcefully conscripted to fight to death in any army. The second billboard should explain the reasons for the search carried out at checkpoints and elsewhere. It is to eliminate arms being smuggled in; to single out pistol-gangs, assassins and extortionists. It is ultimately to protect the ordinary civilians and their livelihoods. This long ignored propaganda is today a dire necessity against the relentless war-mongering by the LTTE. I hope the defence Ministry will take this suggestion on board and will improve on it.

The Foreign Office should plan a proper propaganda campaign in all the countries it has representatives. All our High Commissioners and ambassadors should be presented with a timetable of the work to be done in this regard. The President's peace vision for the country and his efforts to achieve that peace should be the subject matter to be presented to (1) the foreign governments, (2) the MPs and Legislators, (3) the bureaucrats, (4) the business fora, (5) the journalists and opinion makers, (6) the interested men/women in the academia and (7) the Sri Lankan expatriates. Knowledgeable and able men/women communicators among our expatriates should be recruited for this job to be carried out within a specified period of three months. Any ambassador failing to do this work should be recalled and replaced with one who will stringently carry out the propaganda. Merely dishing out photocopied papers is not what is intended here. Face to face communication with the intention of establishing an on-going relationship should be the expected outcome. This foreign communication blitz is necessary given the LTTE network in foreign countries, where they are still considered as liberation fighters. It is also necessary given the pusillanimity shown to the national problem by many of our embassies. Will the new Foreign Minister take up my suggestion to project the good image of his new government?

It may be that a major shooting war might not break out and terrorist attack on the soft economic targets in the country will not take place. Let us hope this expectation will be fulfilled in 2006.

66

WILL IT BE BLACKMAIL IN GENEVA?

(Daily Mirror, 16th Feb.2006)

At the risk of being labelled a spoiler of the CFA talks in Geneva, one has got to ask the above question, in the hope that pitfalls will be avoided and acceptable objectives will be pursued and achieved. Given some of the Government negotiators being lawyers not currently in practice, it perhaps would come in handy for them to brush up the criminal law on blackmail!

Why do I use the odious term blackmail? Because, Pirapakaran is a tyrannical dictator. He is accountable to no one. He only makes demands. He makes no concessions. If he is not given what he demands, he is ready to kill anyone and everyone to get what he wants. He is also prepared to continue this mayhem sine die until he is in possession of what he wants. Thus his demands are backed up with murderous threats as well as actual murder of innocent persons including Tamils, therefore his demands are in fact a malignant form of bloodlust blackmail. At the moment what is dangled before the country is the threat of war, no matter such a step would impose untold suffering primarily on the people living in the North and the East of the country. His suicide cadres, now roaming the streets of Colombo and other major towns, would also unleash death and destruction in their chosen locations to maximum effect. This then is the realistic prevailing background to the projected CFA talks in Geneva.

Complementary to this grim scenario is the fear psychosis gripping the legitimate political authorities of the country. Pirapakaran knows this and is fully exploiting it. This fear of war has got the country tied in Gordian knots that most escape routes are blocked to the government. The appeasement policy that Ranil implemented with the support of the international interlopers led to "carrots and more carrots" (Mr. Dhanapala) to the LTTE with no tangible results in terms of a peace settlement. So one has got to ask at what point will Mahinda Rajapakse's government will stop feeding this ferocious Tiger beast?

Asolution to our problems without war is certainly a worthy objective. But from the start ruling out war is really a wrong strategy. It gives the opponent the opportunity to thrust the threat of war every time he is in a situation where he has got to make compromises. In short, as I have argued many times before, we should stop talking about preserving the sovereignty of the country, if we are NOT prepared to defend the same sovereignty with arms and our lives. What shameless descendants we are, compared to our worthy ancestors, who waged war against the imperial powers of the time, (Portuguese, Dutch and the British), in their efforts to preserve the sovereignty of their nation! They fought fearlessly with bows and arrows against cannons and guns.

I am not advocating war as the first solution to our problem. Abandoning war even as a last resort is to yield that space to the enemy. He will use it and drag us all into the inferno. The mutual destruction policy worked well during the cold war, because, both the Soviet Union and the democratic world were not only armed to the teeth but were also prepared to use those arms. Such deterrence is conspicuously absent on the part of our government. Our governments, that have been in power, seemed to have been unethically converted to a policy of abject genuflection before the Suriya Deavan and to appease him at any cost. They did this by holding sacred the "peace process" no matter what the LTTE did to violate it with impunity. This is one lesson the present government should learn; the "peace process" is not sacred, it is only a means to achieve mutually satisfactory end to the problem. If this "peace process" is used to pervert the salutary end-objective of sustainable peace, then it ceases to be a "peace process".

The CFA is blatantly partisan towards the LTTE. There is no reciprocity on the part of the LTTE for all the advantages ceded to them in the CFA. A good example of this is the room given to them to do "political work" in the government controlled areas. There is no such allowance made to do "political work" in the illegally controlled areas of the LTTE by other Tamil, Muslim and Sinhala political parties. Here we have a flagrant and unconstitutional surrender of the sovereignty of the nation by Ranil. Is this not reason enough to arraign him for high treason? The LTTE knows that the proper implementation of the CFA would only help them to strengthen their oppression and their Draconian hold on the Tamil people. So what options do our negotiators have? Not many. Yet there are aspects that need to be sorted out before one starts arguing about each clause of the CFA.

It is almost certain that the experts advising the government's negotiating team would have alerted them to the details of failed and frequently violated clauses of the CFA. Therefore one can expect the government's team to have ready answers to the outrageous demand sheet that Mr. Balasingham would table in Geneva. At the risk of a breakdown in the talks, it is quite necessary not to accept all the accusations that Mr.Balasingham would be directing at the government. He should be firmly told that the government is in Geneva not to trade accusations but to explore ways and means of stopping the present spate of killing and pave the way to substantial talks on peace.

It is paramount for the government to first establish the mutually agreeable meaning and the interpretation of the words "Cease Fire Agreement". It is apparent that there is a chasm here between the LTTE and the rest of the country. To me, and probably to all the readers of this short article, "cease fire" means stopping all use of firearms that kill and maim people whether they be combatants or not. It also means stopping all threats to life and property whether such threats are eventually carried out or not. In short it also means no violations of the human rights of anyone- men, women and children. In case such violations do take place, the culprits should be apprehended and punished appropriately. It also means the discontinuation of all measures that would lead to the destruction of life and property. It further means the parties to the agreement should make the necessary efforts to create the conditions conducive to promote peace and well-being of the citizens. The Report that came out today (10th Feb.) on the Ceasefire violations does confirm the fact that the LTTE does have a different meaning and interpretation attached to the words "cease fire". With 562 murders and 5464 total violations by the LTTE over the four years of ceasefire, it is crucially important to sort out the exact meaning attached to these words and how best such agreed interpretations be put into practice. This to me should be the primary task before the negotiating team.

The word "agreement" too needs elucidation. To most of us, it means a willingness to abide by the terms agreed between the parties. It is a voluntary acceptance of an obligation to put into practice whatever one undertook to do or not to do under the agreement. It is primarily an undertaking to pursue actively the terms of the agreement to its successful conclusion. There is no room here for passivity or violations of the terms. Human as we are, such failures will take place, and to prevent such blunders it is necessary to have sanctions in place. This punishment for the violators of the agreement is totally absent in the CFA. What we have instead is a very effete system of score-keeping. This is not capable of reducing, let alone stopping the escalating violations of the CFA. Penalties are part and parcel of all mundane agreements. It also should be part of thls CFA. Both parties should embark on finding ways and means to reduce as well as stop all violations of whatever agreement they strike at the end. After the exact meaning and interpretation of the words "Cease fire Agreement" have been sorted out, the parties could embark on looking at the various clauses of the CFA. This I leave to the legal advisors of the government. My stand here is that we need a totally new CFA.

It is commendable that the US government has expressed support to the government and have pointed out the heavy cost to the LTTE should they embark on war to achieve their Eelam. Would it not be more effective if the US government expresses its willingness extend some of the war facilities to the Sri Lanka Government to "put the LTTE terrorists out of business"? What I have in mind is satellite information on LTTE cadre movements, fuel and arms storage buildings, a few smart bunker-busting missiles together with their delivery systems. A promise of this hardware and the training of our personnel to use them would no doubt have the desired effect to close this chapter of terrorism in the life of the nation. It will lead to a regime change in the north and force the government to conclude a respectable agreement with the democratic Tamils.

67

CONCEDE OR ELSE "WE WILL WALK OUT" !

(The Island, 5th April 2006)

Some time ago I raised the question whether the GoSL would be blackmailed in Geneva. I have borrowed the title to this article from Mr. Anton Balasingham (AB) as the appropriate answer to that question. The LTTE had realized the Sinhala politicians' desperate need for negotiation as well as their mortal fear of armed conflict. So whatever their inner compulsions to parley with the GoSL, the LTTE knows that threats will work both with the GoSL as well as the Co-Chair (CoC) members of the international community. This is no different to what the underworld blackmailers do to their victims. These threats and actual assaults will not abate so long as the GoSL's response is meek and exculpatory of the LTTE. The recent attack on the navy off Mannar is a case in point. The LTTE denied all responsibility for it, and the GoSL did not directly accuse the LTTE, nor did it demand of the LTTE that they stopped forthwith all such attacks. The CoC is in deep slumber having swallowed the LTTE excuse that it was an attack staged by the irate fishermen. In my books, anyone who attacks the security forces is a combatant and the army has the right to self defence against him. It has also the right to disable such combatants in the first instance. Such combatants cannot plead the innocence of civilians after foul murder of security forces. Why cannot our navy adopt the "shoot first and talk later" policy practised by UK on terrorists?

Prior to the Geneva talks Mr. Eric Soldheim (ES) met AB in London. We know that even before ES landed in Colombo, he blurted out that the only topic for the Geneva talks was the "strengthening of the CFA". Mind you, AB had already publicly proclaimed the same in London. In short, the agenda was already decided between AB and ES, and in all probability, they also discussed the strategy to be adopted, including the threat to walk out, if the GoSL insisted on amending the CFA. This was the perfidy concocted in London. I do, however, blame the GoSL for not taking an active part in setting up the agenda for the talks. The GoSL should have insisted on its inputs being included in the agenda even at the expense of postponing the talks for a later date. Well, the GoSL is so fearful of the LTTE that no such actions will be taken even for the upcoming talks. I shall not be surprised if the agenda for the April talks has been already unilaterally decided between AB and ES and imposed on the GoSL. We probably have zombies in our Peace Secretariate (PS). Have they no gumption to be proactive in setting up the agenda? Are these glorified personnel in the PS only mere note takers?

Ranil's CFA was heavily loaded in favour of the LTTE. It was therefore to be expected that AB and ES would want it to be fully implemented, even though, the LTTE was daily utilizing it to commit crimes of unimaginable proportion. The whole world was aghast at the brazen flouting of the CFA by the LTTE when the talks were mooted. The same is true even now. The GoSL has the social and electoral support to end the carnage by negotiation. The unabated forceful recruitment of child combatants, the military training of civilians, shooting at army posts and the blasting of navy boats with bombs laden trawlers by suicide cadres are the daily tragic drama enacted by the LTTE. The whole world, except Norway, would be on the side of the government if it insisted on plugging the loopholes in the CFA. Therefore this time around the GoSL should take a firm stand on mutually setting up the agenda for talks in April.

The GoSL negotiators should always remember that AB (and probably ES too) are not really interested in bringing about peace. They are probably buying time to build up their air force and obtain more lethal weapons. In this context, what strategy can the GoSL adopt to counter LTTE's resort to bluff, deceit and threats during the talks? The first thing to do is to call a "time off" (as in volleyball matches) whenever AB issues a walkout threat, and get out of the room to a more congenial place. There the GoSL team should thoroughly examine the arguments and words used by AB in arriving at his threat to walk out. They are bound to find many a chink in AB's arguments, as his threat signifies that he has in fact run out of any persuasive reasons to carry forward the discussion. All such fallacies should be subjected to analysis and entrusted to one person in the team to expound on the return to the table. Anything positive that came out of AB's mouth also should be utilized to further the discussion. This action to call "time off" might infuse some sense into the mind of AB too.

The GoSL team also should take a closer look at what they said prior to the impasse. They should seek out different words and a different formulation of their argument to present on their return to the table. As 'saving face' is as important a matter as the threat to walk out in a stalemate situation, the different formulation of GoSL's position should be aimed at emphasizing the gravity of AB's intended action and the conciliatory tenor of the GoSL. The government's team should also prepare a statement for release to the press should the withdrawal by AB does take place. This should be unequivocal, succinct and clear to all who read it.

Before the GoSL team goes to Geneva in April there are a few things the President and the team should sort out. As pointed out above the first is to get involved in setting up the agenda. Once the topics to be considered are known, then it is incumbent on them to subject those topics to brainstorming sessions. This is to determine whether any concessions could be made and how and when such concessions should be made during the discussion. All concessions ought to be reciprocated by the LTTE and the appropriate reciprocal actions by the LTTE should be also determined at these sessions. For instance, the government should have come out with the concession to relax restrictions on fishing not now, but at April talks, with the demand that the navy has the right to examine any fishing boat in the sea at their pleasure without any impediments. If this was in operation then the recent tragic incident off Mannar might not have taken place. We should also have penalties for non compliance and a mechanism to impose as well as enforce those penalties. As any concession once made will become irretrievable, it should be subject to problem and potential problem analysis to fully elicit the downside of such a concession and to put in place the safeguards necessary to prevent exploitation by the LTTE.

The GoSL team should also have on hand alternative reciprocal actions they could demand of the LTTE in case AB refuses the first demand of the GoSL team. AB is likely to take the view that "what is mine is mine, but what is yours is negotiable". In such a situation negotiation becomes impossible. Do we have persons in our team to demonstrate to AB as well as the world outside that "what is his is not his, but Sri Lanka's and belongs to everyone living in this country"?

Any concession made should be a stepping stone to further talks. These further talks should be veered towards the substantive issues of peace. Only the other day, the Spanish terrorist organization ETA announced a permanent ceasefire with the commitment to decommission its arms and to discussion with the government to arrive at a solution to their problems. This is the stuff from which real peace could emerge. Such should be the path the LTTE should also take if they are really interested in peace and a solution to their self perceived problems. So long as the LTTE is preparing for "final war" and refuses to lay down their arms, the sincerity of the LTTE remains questionable and their motives for talks deceitful. They are probably engaged in an exercise to sucker the GoSL into an advantageous position for themselves without giving up anything in return.

At the brainstorming sessions it is incumbent on the President to determine the point at which he will have to refuse to move towards any concession on the topics under consideration. He should make himself as well as the team fully aware why he has come to this point of "last stand against the LTTE". The consequences of such a firm stand should be fully explored. How it should be presented to the Sri Lankans and the people of the world should also be detailed and formulated ready for release should the necessity arises. At this point there could be no "behind the scene" dealings or agreements with the LTTE. This is also the point at which the GoSL team would have to stage their walkout of the discussion. Such action should be based on acceptable principles seen to be reasonable to all. A legitimate democratic country has all the arguments in its favour against a fascistic, dictatorial tyrant. He thrives on murder, oppression and suppression of all democratic freedoms. He has no arguments against democratic exercise of human rights of the people and children.

Finally I come to the point I have repeated in my writings to the press. It is that we Sri Lankans do not deserve the sovereignty of the nation if we are not prepared to defend it with force whenever necessary. The legitimate use of force in any society is in the hands of the legitimately elected government. Any foe threatening the sovereignty of the country by the use of force should in the first place be persuaded to settle the problem by discussion. If he is adamant on using force to endanger the sovereignty of the country, then the last option to use force against him should be exercised to end the problem swiftly. Pirapakaran lives and thrives by the use of force on all and sundry. He would therefore understand better our readiness to use force against him.

68

THE TOTTERING SOVEREIGNTY OF SRI LANKA

(Daily Mirror, 26th May 2006)

Read carefully the following words uttered by Thamilselvan of the LTTE, "nobody has the right to pass judgment on the sovereign rights of our access to the sea and air space adjacent to our homeland" (Daily Mirror 13th May). This arrogant man has been infused with the visions of grandeur of his master. Despite the grand pretensions of King, Kingdom and Sovereignty, his master, a coward that he is, dared not to leave his bunker to meet the Japanese envoy recently! He was not ashamed either to admit that he could not meet Mr.Akashi due to lack of security in his tribal land! Who is responsible for this grand delusion of the LTTE? The weak governments we have had in the recent past, headed by self-seeking individuals, have helped to dig the grave for the internment of the sovereignty of this country. The heads of those governments elevated to legitimacy the LTTE terrorist outfit and began treating it on an equal footing, and also allowed foreigners to treat it as a legitimate entity. In doing this they ignored the fundamental status of our country as an independent sovereign nation. Those politicians were guilty of dealing with the country with gay abandon as if it was their private property, but without the due care and solicitude they would shower on their own private property.

The present government was right to refute immediately the sovereignty claims of Thamilselvan. No amount of self-declaration can bestow sovereignty on oneself. No amount of efforts to legitimize the present perfidy with the many perfidies of the past will bestow on the privileges granted to LTTE, by appeasement prone Ranil's government, the status of "past established practice and accepted modalities". Unfortunately this government has been tied in knots by the CFA and by its predecessors. It is this pernicious CFA that has led to the near fatal erosion of sovereignty of our country. To the extent that Norway was involved in drafting the CFA, one can conclude that this harm to the country was engineered by foreigners with the end objective of making it a "failed state", thus justifying direct international intervention without the consent of the people of this country.

The sovereignty of a country has many distinguishing attributes. The interested reader should look them up in Justice Weeramanthri's latest book on "National Reawakening". I am here concerned with the truncated sovereignty of our country ensuing from the moribund CFA. It was perhaps necessary that there was a CFA to get the talks started with the LTTE in the first instance. It is my contention that the type of CFA signed, the way it was signed, and the manner it was implemented, were severely detrimental to the existence of this country as one whole nation. The recent events have amply demonstrated that the CFA exists only in paper but to the advantage of the LTTE. This was bound to happen as it was a faulty agreement ab initio. Attempting to resuscitate it now would be a monumental folly especially because we do now know from horrible experiences, its defects, loopholes and tragic flaws. It needs a replacement as initially argued by the new President of Sri Lanka. Just as much as the LTTE makes demands of all sorts, it is time for the government also to make the demand for a new CFA and discard the old.

Having signed the CFA, the government of ex PM Ranil Wickramasinghe was grossly guilty in allowing the LTTE to think and act as if it was an alternative government in the country. No protests were lodged when the LTTE started eliminating dissidents and security officers under the guise of "political work". No deprecations were issued when the LTTE arrogated to itself the powers and functions of the government. As illustrations, let me take three simple aspects of a modern sovereign state. (1) The capacity of the state to impose and collect taxes. This is a primary and central feature and affects the day-to-day life of the citizens. (2) The state establishes the rights and duties of the citizens towards itself, among the citizens; it empowers as well as constrains its citizens. (3) The state in various ways controls its citizens by enacting laws. So long as these laws are democratically legislated and enacted, the people do obey them as they perceive them to be for their mutual benefit. The CFA did not bestow these powers to the LTTE. Instead it gave them recognition to the lands they illegally held. This single act, while beheading the country's territorial sovereignty, bequeathed to the LTTE dictatorial powers over the land and its people. Those Tamil people were abandoned to a servility that measures the human worth of the people in terms of their utility to LTTE.

In actual fact the LTTE is doing whatever Pirapakaran dictates in the illegally controlled lands. He levies all kinds of oppressive taxes on everyone, he conscripts children as well as adults to serve him in his army or in his assassination squads, he coerces citizens to attend military training and enrolls them as civilian militia, and he controls them with an iron fist; no freedom of speech, association or movement. His goons are everywhere to strike down anyone who is considered a dissenter. Thus elevated to power over the life and death of the people, it is not surprising that Pirapakaran considers himself to be an absolute monarch exercising sovereign rights over land and people under him. Before outlining the strategy to counter this delusion, let us also examine the other factor that has endangered sovereignty of the country.

Nearly five hundred years of colonial rule over us taught us one indelible lesson. That foreign involvement in the affairs of our country led to our ultimate subjugation by the foreigner and the loss of our sovereignty. This lesson was totally ignored by our political leaders.

The CFA allowed foreign interlopers into our country. Our leaders did not query their motives nor seek to examine if they had any hidden agendas. They were invited to interfere in our affairs. Today they have arrogated to themselves various roles without our consent. They make rules that we need to obey. They pass edicts that we ought to carry out. They make wild accusations to demoralize our army. They behave and act with condescension towards a bunch of terrorists, whom, in their own countries, they would have blown to bits with no questions asked. The western nations allowed the LTTE to act and behave as if it was a sovereign entity, even when clear evidence was available that it flouted human rights openly, that it was an intolerant fascist entity, using despicable suicide bombers to kill people, many of them Tamils. Today if these nations have decided to ban this erstwhile protégé of theirs as terrorists, it is to salvage their consciences. They should have done this a long time ago. Nevertheless, serious harm has been done to the sovereignty of Sri Lanka, in that our freedom to do whatever is necessary to preserve our nation's sovereignty and integrity has been severely compromised. We have to abide by what these foreigners tell us.

In these circumstances what can the President do? First and foremost he must prevail upon everyone that human rights should be preserved in this country and the rule of law applies to everyone without exception. Anyone breaking the law of the land should be hunted down and punished according to law. He clearly cannot accuse the LTTE of human rights abuses if such abuses also take place in the country under his control. Headless bodies and point blank shooting of anyone, other than combatants, cannot be tolerated in any way.

It is also time for the government to put flesh into the political solution to be presented to the country. For this he should start talking to the non-LTTE Tamils because it is vitally important to distinguish as well as recognize the Tamils as a distinct entity from the LTTE. This first tract time constrained talks ought to be aimed at arriving at the outlines of a solution acceptable to them as well as the government.

The second tract talks should be the all party conference presently held by the President. It is at this conference that the outline agreed above, should be fitted with the flesh and bones, and made a coherent substantial whole acceptable to the vast majority of the people and their representatives in parliament. Thus it would be a solution having the approval stamp of non-LTTE Tamils and the majority of the MPs in parliament. They would have all contributed in formulating this solution to the political problem in the country. Such a solution requires strong guidance and clear perception of the end-objective and its merits. The present President has to take the plunge now as the world has openly recognized that the LTTE is not the "sole representative" of the Tamil people. Such a solution cannot be dismissed easily and casually by anyone as one concocted by Sinhala chauvinists.

In the meanwhile the President has got to make a clear distinction between the peace process and terrorism. The peace process is what I have outlined above, seeking a solution to the problem and tabling it at the eventual discussion with the LTTE. Talking about the CFA is not peace talks. Terrorism will continue as long there is no change of regime within the LTTE. It will be aimed at attacking our sovereignty and provoking communal violence. We need to train our forces not to expose themselves unnecessarily and strengthen them with necessary equipment to fight the enemy. What is needed when attacked is not gratuitous retaliation, but measured response aimed at taking out the troublesome LTTE cadres as well as their military assets. The military should get their spies to compile a reliable list of the location of vital military assets such as oil dumps, at arms storage and where the top cadres lived. The measured response should be aimed at destroying these assets.

It was Bernard Shaw who reminded us that "a healthy nation is as unconscious of its nationality as healthy man of his bones. But if you break a nation's nationality, it will think of nothing else but getting it set again". We should resist any attempt by anyone to diminish our sovereignty and perrisons en resistante (die resisting).

69

THE EU BAN ON LTTE TERRORISTS

(Daily Mirror, 13th June 2006)

The long awaited ban on LTTE has been declared and is expected to be enforced in all the twenty-five member countries in Europe. In the words of our President to the Asian Wall Street Journal "words alone are not enough". A purposeful and emphatic implementation of the ban is now required and expected.

The EU Resolution also contained many admonitions to the government. The international interlopers were humiliatingly severe with the democratic sovereign Sri Lanka and its present government. Had they issued such edicts to the UK government during the time of "shoot to kill" policy in Northern Ireland, they would have been told to take a running jump in the Irish Sea! The most they should have done was to urge the government to earnestly pursue to create the conditions necessary for human rights to be practised in the country, and seek a tangible solution to the minority problem in the country. Instead they have issued near dictatorial orders and edicts with dire consequences in case of non-compliance.

At the second Tokyo meeting of the Co-Chairs (CC) last month, it was decreed that "the government must show that it will address the legitimate grievances of the Tamils". Have we not heard this before? The CC should have listed those grievances for the government to sort them out rather than spew out an LTTE propaganda slogan. The non-implementation of the use of Tamil language in government administration is perhaps the only grievance of any consequence. This the government should forthwith remedy. The rest would be all economic deprivations applicable to most Sri Lankans no matter their ethnicity. If those grievances were so unbearable then the CC also should explain to us why lakhs of Jaffna Tamils prefer to live in the south rather than in the putative Eelam. These Tamils too have not detailed their grievances, if any, to the nation at large.

The CC also charges the government that "it must immediately prevent groups based in its territory from carrying out violence and acts of terrorism". Why not reveal to the government the location of those groups so that the government could do the needful? What we see is another LTTE slogan shamelessly adopted by the CC. All we do know is that due entirely to the permission granted to LTTE by the CFA to do "political work" in government controlled areas, we have many assassinations and Claymore mines, abductions of and extortions from the people. The CC should have addressed this imbalance and demanded the opening up of the illegally controlled lands in the hands of the LTTE. What about the groups who carry out terrorist activities while being based in the illegally controlled LTTE areas, and admitted to by the LTTE as civilian militias trained and supplied by the LTTE?

The CC decrees that the Government "must show that it is ready to make the dramatic political changes to bring about a new system of governance which will enhance the rights of all Sri Lankans, including the Muslims". The "dramatic political changes" called for is the change of our present constitution. This in itself is wholesome as the present constitution has many defects. But where in the world do we have a constitution of a country that fully accommodates all the aspirations of minorities living among them?

We have communities without boundaries shading off into the residual mass of Sinhalese. Tamil or Sinhalese, Muslim or Burgher, we are all persons, rights bearing ciphers. We should seek to enhance and strengthen these rights. The constitution of the country should be designed to provide the framework of rights or liberties or duties within which people may pursue their various ends, individually or cooperatively. Such a constitution will be inherently solid as well as just. It will be assertive of the moral primacy of the individual. It will be egalitarian because it will confer on all individuals the same moral status. It will be universalist because "it affirms the moral unity of the human species and accords a secondary importance to specific historic associations and cultural forms" (Kukathas in "Are there any Cultural Rights?"). It is patently true that groups cannot be assigned rights unless they are first assigned members. Thus we need to design a constitution that enshrines heterogeneity, cultural and private; equality, economic and political. The unitary character of a state is not incompatible with the above norms. In Aristotle's language the "primary function of the state and of politics generally, is to do justice to individuals" and "in a pluralist society ethnicity is simply one of the background conditions of this effort. Ethnic identification gives meaning to the lives of many men and women, but it has nothing to do with their standing as citizens" (Walzer in "Pluralism: A Political Perspective"). In short, my contention is that with a raging separatist conflict, it would be foolhardy to loosen the ties that bind us to the one and sovereign country. The case for federalism in Sri Lanka remains unproven, a speculative and a dangerous exercise with no fall back position. Once embarked on this venture we would be entering the political abyss with no retrieval or any return.

Of the many demands made by the EU on LTTE, only three crucial ones are under consideration here. The first is that "the LTTE does not represent all the Tamil people of Sri Lanka and calls on the LTTE to allow for political pluralism and alternate democratic voices in the north and east parts of Sri Lanka which would secure the interests of all peoples and communities". It is factually true that the LTTE does not represent the Tamils. They represent only themselves. The reader knows that the LTTE will totally ignore this call and will carry on regardless. Acceptance of this condition would tantamount to acknowledging that the élan vital driving the LTTE to terrorism has become extinct. It is to be expected that they will resort to any action, no matter its moral depravity, to prove to the world that they are indeed the "sole representatives" of the Tamils.

This vital distinction between the Tamils and the LTTE need to be pursued by the government. It should encourage and actively engage the non-LTTE Tamils in its search for a justifiable solution to the minority problem in the country. This engagement should be parallel to the current APC meetings. This is one way to isolate the LTTE and arrive at a solution acceptable to the greater majority of the country.

The second point is that the LTTE should "be prepared to decommission its weapons and set the stage for a final political settlement of the conflict". The Nicaraguan rebels, the Irish IRA, the Acceh rebels and now the Spanish ETA have all accepted the necessity of laying down their weapons first before entering the peace process. Such unarmed peace marches have led to acceptable peace agreements between the erstwhile combatants. Therefore it was no surprise that the EU, with the experiences in both Ireland and Spain, did lay down this condition.

To the LTTE the weapons are their virility symbols. Without their weapons they would be nobodies in the Sri Lankan political landscape. In view of the many dastardly crimes they have committed against the Tamils alone, they would be highly vulnerable and endangered. Thus we need a roadmap leading to surrender of weapons by the LTTE. Perhaps the US senator Michell who masterminded the IRA's surrender of weapons could be called upon for advice and strategy. There cannot be peace so long as the LTTE is armed and is not afraid to use its weapons on all and sundry without any compunction. This is one demand of the EU which is of utmost importance and requires the urgent consideration of the government.

The third point is that the EU "expresses its condemnation of the appalling abuse of children through the recruitment of child soldiers, which is a war crime, and calls on all rebel groups, and notably the LTTE to stop this practice, to release those it holds and to make a declaration in principle not to recruit any children in the future". This unacceptable abuse has gone on for far too long. The EU should initiate action now to arraign the leaders of the LTTE for this war crime. There is no difference between them and the leaders of the "Lords Salvation Army" of Uganda whose leaders stand charged for the war crime of recruitment of child soldiers. Until and unless such an action is taken, it is unlikely that the LTTE will disband its child brigades. Instead those children will be groomed to commit heinous murders like the one committed in the outskirts of Welikanda recently. At least the bravery of the twelve-year-old Sathyan, who was murdered by the

LTTE for refusing to join them, should goad the EU to embark on actions rather than mere words.

The government should also take a close look at this problem. In the first place, political work in government held areas does not include or condone the kidnapping of children. Therefore the security forces should take whatever appropriate security measures to prevent these abductions. Secondly the children who escape from the LTTE camps should be given all the assurances of safety and the wherewithal for a normal life where necessary away from their places of habitat. There should also be active propaganda to educate these vulnerable children that they have a better life outside the LTTE camps than killing people as ordered by the LTTE. To-date what has the governments done to wean the children from joining the LTTE?

Finally, no matter what any international meddlers in our affairs say, it remains a fact that the LTTE are not really committed to a justifiable peace. They want their separate Eelam come what may. The piece of real estate Pirapakaran now holds has given him the grandeur of absolute monarchy and sovereignty. He will not give this up that easily. Therefore it is the paramount duty of the government to preserve the sovereignty of the nation and pursue the policies approved by the people at national election. Ultimately the people in the country matter and not the international sanctimonious Samaritans who like to play football with our sovereignty and dignity.

69 - B

The Fragile Invincibility of the LTTE

(The Island, 1st Sept.2006)

Ever since the new President was elected to office last November, the LTTE had been brazenly baiting him and his government to engage them in battle to settle the question of separatism in this country. The President's patience only encouraged the LTTE to resort to more and more cowardly attacks on the security forces inflicting severe losses of lives and damage to military assets. The last straw was drawn when the Army Commander was targeted in his home turf HQ in Colombo.

That was the day the new President took the plunge to expose the myths of an unwinnable war, the doctrinaire infallibility of the LTTE and its omnipotent invincibility. As many of us have argued ad nauseam before, all the above attributes----- attributes bestowed by his acolyte NGOs in Colombo and elsewhere---- of Suriya Thevan have been now exposed as a vast confidence trick. Unfortunately there are still many in the secretive and treacherous NGO circuit propagating this rubbish to some gullible captive audiences throughout the country. The twin objectives of the NGOs appear to be to demoralize the security forces and infuse fear in the government of Armageddon, so that it will be reduced to impotent paralysis of inaction, thereby allowing the LTTE to pursue unhindered their objective of Eelam.

Many have issued dire warnings that LTTE was trying to trap the government in a new cycle of war by stage-managing a series of humanitarian crises in the country. These prophets of doom also admonished the government to desist from taking any action, but to start talking to the LTTE. They were appeasers in the garb of peaceniks peddling LTTE's mythical invincibility in public.

Imagine what would have happened now had these appeasers been in charge of government! The Mavilaru Anicut would have been lost to the LTTE, to be used by them, on and off, to blackmail the government as well as to chase the non-LTTE Sri Lankans out of the area by depriving them of life sustainable water. Muttur too would have been lost, ethnically cleansed, and now, would have been prepared as the staging post for military onslaught on Trincomalee.

The readers know what happened to Muslim mosque premises at Kurrukupanchan and other dozen or so new bunkers built by the LTTE during Ranil's and Chandrika's abject appeasement period. This is the creeping Eelamization these perfidious NGO men and women want in this country. These peaceniks also wanted the army to evacuate the High Security Zones (HSZ) in Jaffna and the East, What would have happened had the army acted according to their wishes? Could the army have fought off the recent onslaught of the LTTE without the HSZ?

The LTTE accused the government of failure to construct a water distribution project costing Rs.43 million in the Tamil areas of east Muttur. It is here pertinent to ask why the LTTE could not embark on this projec themselves. The amount involved is perhaps only a couple of weeks' extortion money that they levy on the travelers on the A9 road. Then again, given the fact that they have millions of US dollars available to bribe US officials and buy an assortment of deadly weapons, why is it not possible for the saviours of Tamils to spend a miniscule amount of it in the construction of a water distribution system in their gangland?

The guardians of the Tamils are clearly not interested in the welfare of the Tamils. It is also opportune to ask the Co-Chairs whether the war will not come to a stop if the LTTE is deprived of this hard currency illegally obtained from their citizens in their countries. Is this not an easier way to bring about peace in Sri Lanka?

The government did what it ought to do to preserve the security of the people and the sovereignty of the country and this is allowed under the faulty CFA (1.3). In fact, if the previous governments had acted likewise whenever CFA was violated by the LTTE, then the mantle of LTTE's impunity and the myth of invincibility would have been torn to shreds long time ago and the LTTE's brazen arrogance would have been muted, if not, completely stopped. The LTTE now knows that any violation of CFA involves a very high cost to them in terms of lost cadres and destroyed military assets.

At this point the words of British Foreign Office Minister, Mr. Kim Howells in the Al-Hyat Arabic language newspaper in Britain are quite appropriate. He wrote that, "if we give in to the terrorists, if we do what they want, they will not go away. They will come back stronger. And every man, woman and child in this country, of whatever faith, will face a bleak future" (Quoted in the Sunday Times of 27th Aug. 2006). I hope the British Deputy High Commisssioner who recently visited Tamilsalvam in Kilinochchi will take note of this statement by her political boss. A terrorist is a terrorist. He/she kills white, black, brown and yellow citizens both in rich white man's underground railway in London as well as in the indigent brown man's roads in Colombo.

The strategy of entering the LTTE trap and dismantling it also constitutes a trail blazing way towards peace, as it leads to the destruction of LTTE cadres and their military assets. This strategy has now demolished the myth of LTTE's invincibility and their infallibility in planning and executing campaigns of war and terror. The three pronged attack, from the west via Killali lagoon, in the centre at Muhamali , and in the east via the sea and land in Nargarkovil by the LTTE to capture Jaffna in early August was defeated and completely thwarted by the security forces. Their invincibility was shattered.

A severe defeat was inflicted on the LTTE. They have lost nearly 500 cadres and over 1500 had been badly wounded. They have also lost a vast amount of military assets during the last few weeks. We remain eternally grateful to our soldiers for their selfless sacrifices and devoted commitment to their duty to safeguard our country. No doubt our security forces remain ready anticipating the return of the murderous LTTE when the monsoon came on. The government was only conducting a measured response (and not mere retaliation) to LTTE's provocations otherwise there would have been vast territorial gains to the government. This is presumably because the government still wishes to arrive at a solution by negotiation.

It is quite clear that this war against LTTE fascism is winnable and should be won both militarily and politically. The LTTE only understands and communicates via armed conflicts. Therefore military response is the method to employ in dealing with them. Until the decision is taken to go all out for the kill, the best option would be to adopt their method of hit and run guerilla warfare to demoralize the outfit while reducing their military assets. This should also be followed up with intensive propaganda campaigns in the north and the east exposing the oppressive fascist nature of the LTTE to the people, who probably are living in near slavery. It should also reveal to the people what the government is doing to free them from their oppressive and repressive tyrant Pirapakaran. It does not make sense why the government has, to date, not done anything on the propaganda front and left this vacuum to the LTTE to ply their lies everyday all the year.

An all out military campaign is the best course to take. But for a small accountable democratic country with both internal and external constraints and international obligations, this may not be the prudent course yet, unless the war is thrust on the nation by the LTTE. Wide support from the people, based on correct information on the many difficulties the government would face, should be solicited before an all out military campaign. The LTTE have no constraints, nor any obligations to anyone. Pirapakaran will do what he wants when he wants, no matter what others would say or do against him. He will not cease killing people everywhere in the country even while the government is engaged in peace talks. He will declare a ceasefire for talks when he is badly weakened and badly needs to regroup and rearm and replenish his depleted cadres. To this extent peace talks with him will be futile. Therefore any ceasefire for peace talks should start with the condition of decommissioning of arms and a commitment to discuss the core issues of his problems. An agenda-less and a condition-less talks should be avoided and duplicitous Norway's role, as we are stuck with them, should also be strictly defined.

The political defeat of the LTTE is also achievable. The government should get the Expert Committee to expedite their deliberations and produce the outline of a just solution to our problem. A patently just and transparent offer embodying Human Rights, Rule of Law, Democracy and Equality would have the assent of the majority in Parliament and the two main political parties. Such an offer will have the support of the war weary Tamils and the world outside. The sheer force of the sincerity and genuineness of the peace offer will, one hopes, compel the LTTE to negotiate at a table where all stakeholders will have seats. On the other hand, if the LTTE refuses to consider such a solution, then their days to demise would be numbered. A constitutional settlement with the Tamil people, as against the LTTE, is the paramount and the sure road to permanent peace in our country.

[This article was written when there was intense lobbying in Colombo and abroad both by the NGOs and some foreign governments against war. There was also intense propaganda to the effect the a war was unwinnable and LTTE was invincible]

70

Peace Talks: Road to Somewhere or Nowhere?

(The Island, 25th Oct.2006)

The desire for peace exists among the people and politicians. The Tamils and the Muslims in the north and the east, often the victims of armed conflict, do want peace. Our brave soldiers also want a honourable peace. The international meddlers in our affairs do want us to settle our differences by negotiation. They are supported by our big neighbor India, who has so far pursued a "dog in the manger" policy towards Sri Lanka,

To the LTTE, peace talks at this juncture would certainly be the road to somewhere, where they can have the time to repair the damages done to them both nationally and internationally. Nearly 1000 of their fighting cadres have perished in the recent confrontation with the security forces, and at least an equal number are walking wounded needing time to recover. Thus the LTTE have introduced a 'Green Card' system in their bandit country for students in schools. Only students attending compulsory military training are issued the 'Green Card' to attend schools. On top of this, military training is imposed on their parents too. Peace talks will provide them the time interval they badly need to get them all fighting fit.

The government should actively foment a breakup of the LTTE. A regime change in the LTTE would do wonders to the peace talks.

In the recent military defeats the LTTE have lost a substantial amount of arms and armed boats. These losses have to be replenished by importing the best available in the arms bazaars of the world. From the arrests of illegal arms traders in the USA and the sinking of the ship loaded with arms off the eastern coast, we do know that the LTTE is clandestinely engaged in obtaining as much weapons as they can now, and will strive to do so in the prospective interval provided by peace talks yet to take place. The government was wise enough to put it down as one of the conditions to peace talks, that no arms should be imported by the LTTE. Sure enough, they will probably agree to it on paper, but ignore it thereafter, as they did under the CFA. A better deterrence would be to openly append the right to sink such contraband ships by our navy, without mercy in the high seas.

Peace talks would also give the LTTE the opportunity to dust down their Marks and Spencer suits and shoes to attend tuition classes in Oslo. It is possible that their godfathers in Norway have probably arranged various secret sessions on the negotiation process and the strategies to be adopted at the negotiation table. A coordinated approach between the Norwegians and the LTTE towards the foreign dignitaries and the international press attending the talks, would also have been slotted in to salvage the LTTE from the present pariah status.

There are other payoffs from a trip abroad. There will be the opportunity to meet their fund raisers and fund managers to encourage them to greater effort. Then there are the LTTE drug traffickers, people smugglers and arms buyers. Human as they all are, all these nameless and faceless LTTE acolytes need recognition and acknowledgement of their work by their lord and master Pirapakaran and his immediate subordinates. Mr.Tamilselvam could deliver such encomiums to them personally in the secrecy of his hotel room.

Secret meetings with arms buyers and LTTE fund managers would take priority in view of the recent arrests in USA. LTTE fund managers would want the freedom to shift funds from one country to another at short notice without prior sanction from Vanni. As it is now known that Swiss and Malaysian banks were used in the USA transactions, it would be considered wise to have the hard currency funds spread about in friendly country banks. Interpol and the Sri Lankan CID will do well to keep track of the many visitors meeting the LTTE contingent in their hotel as well as at other group meetings.

In view of what I have stated above, it would be wise to hold the next peace talks in Sri Lanka. Our near neighbour, the Maldives could perhaps be an alternative venue.

Norway too would be going somewhere if peace talks get started. They have revealed their partisan approach to this task. The Norwegians are considered as collaborators with and vile schemers for the LTTE. The resuscitation of peace talks would restore on them some lost prestige and give them the opportunity to pursue their secret agenda and perhaps also their secret agreement with the LTTE. When the PM of Norway disowned the partisan statements of the SLMM in New York before our President, the latter should have requested a new team to handle the peace talks excluding Soldheim and Bauer. Both are guilty of many 'crimes' against the sovereignty of Sri Lanka. The most recent examples of their arrogance were the announcement of "unconditional talks by GoSL" by Soldheim and "equality of status to LTTE with GoSL" by Bauer even before the peace talks. It is a pity that we are burdened with Norway. To my way of thinking, far from being facilitators of peace, they are really part of the problem. At the least their role in peace talks need to be precisely defined.

Given the above, it is doubtful whether the new talks will be about peace. As pointed out above, the LTTE's agenda would not be about peace even if they nominally assent to such a programme. The Norwegians will use it to rescue the LTTE, to resurrect them and to remove the 'terrorist bans' imposed on them by EU. At first glance the expected peace talks too appear to be doomed to go nowhere.

Nevertheless, the GoSL so far has embarked on the right direction for peace. The government has exercised the right to respond to the LTTE's continued violence in contrast to appeasement by Ranil and Chandrika. It has demonstrated to the LTTE and the world, that swift retribution will be extracted from the LTTE, whenever and wherever they terrorized the people and the security forces. The right to strike back is one of the conditions for any future talks. The era of impunity of the LTTE conceded by spineless politicians is no more.

The next right approach is the determination of the agenda for the talks. This task should not be left to Soldheim as was probably done on previous occasions. The GoSL has rightly flagged that core issues should be discussed within a set time-frame. Thus dilly-dallying on peripheral issues and consequent prevarication to deal with vital issues are pre-empted. This surely is the road to somewhere over the rainbow where peace prevails. Allied to this condition is the responsibility of the government to produce its purported solution as fashioned and designed by its appointed experts and sanctioned by the All Party Conference. A peace proposal having the support of two-third of the MPs cannot be ignored and would command respectful consideration by all concerned. This would lead us to durable peace and the LTTE will have to reject it at its peril.

Once such a proposal is tabled for consideration by the LTTE, the government should also initiate parallel peace talks with non-LTTE Tamils and Muslims. This will overcome the LTTE's aversion to having non-LTTE others at the negotiating table. At some point the convergence of both talks should be the aim, even if the talks with the LTTE fail to reach an agreement.

There are numerous armed separatist insurgencies throughout India. Not a day passes without a political murder committed by separatists somewhere in India. To my mind, invoking Indian Constitutional model for Sri Lanka to follow, borders on the naivete of blatantly ignoring the fact that the Indian Constitution, as exemplified by the many virulent insurgencies, has failed to fulfill the aspirations of the variety of its people. In any case, as I have argued before, like so many others, a federal constitution to the north and the east will not solve the perceived and imagined grievances and aspirations of all Tamils, especially of those now living (in Colombo) in the south of the country. Just ask the first Tamil you meet in Kotahena or Wellawatte! He would be fearful of pressure on him, post federation, to decamp from his present relatively comfortable abode in Colombo, abandon his job and migrate to the wilds of arid Vanni.

Those peace talks could take us towards peace if Pirapakaran could be tied down to, if not, persuaded to sue for peace. There is an enormous hell-hole between his ideal of separate Eelam and the internationally guaranteed sovereignty and integrity of the country. This gaping hole needs to be plugged first. A compromise by Pirapakaran is paramount on this issue and without it we surely would be on the road to nowhere where death and destruction would prevail. There is an alternative, if only we could bring about a change of regime in the LTTE with leaders ready for suitable compromise. It is time to ditch Pirapakaran in the interest of everyone.

71

The Grievances of the Tamils

(The Island, 3rd Nov.2006)

Tamils usually talk of the many grievances and the discrimination they suffer in our society without specifying them and labeling such inequities suffered to be due solely to the fact that they happened to be Tamils. If one digs deep enough into any such grievance, it would be soon apparent that such a grievance would be common to all our deprived citizens, no matter whether they are Sinhalese, Muslims, Tamils or any other race living here. Many commentators have pointed out this fact in our newspapers but the Tamil still persist in their accusations. Their real grievances, about which they dare not complain, are the ones imposed on them by the LTTE.

Let me accept the fact that there are bigoted people among all ethnic groups and that such persons could resort to discriminatory actions against other ethnic groups. This is true of the LTTE who recently killed the Sinhala mango traders in Vavunia. It is also true of the Sinhala mobsters who attacked the Tamil shops in Galle.

It is also the fact that while the LTTE's aversion to anything Sinhala remains untamed, the Sinhala mob in Galle was soon brought under control and would have faced the bullets of the police and the army had they continued their pillage. What I mean to underline here is that the Sri Lankan society under the control of the government does not overtly or covertly practice discrimination against any ethnic group in our society. The actions of criminal elements in our society against the Tamils cannot be ascribed to the rest of the population as has been done often by the Tamil writers and commentators.

However, let me list the main grievances of the Tamils because they are Tamils, and suffered by them almost daily, but dare not complain, lest they be murdered before daybreak by the LTTE.

Many Tamil children have their future blighted by being coerced into the LTTE's fighting units. They are waylaid on their way to schools, on their way to temples, on their way to tuition classes. They are dragged out from their homes and they are abducted from the playgrounds. Any protesting parent is simply shot, or, if he is lucky, severely beaten up and left for dead.

Once the children are in the LTTE camps, they do not engage in reading, writing and arithmetic (3Rs) like other Tamil children elsewhere in the country in the south. They are put through a rigorous mind-bending programme of anti-Sinhalese propaganda and forced into military and weapons training. They are simply trained to kill or be killed.

This is the biggest and the most heinous criminal discrimination suffered by Tamils because they are Tamils. The victims dare not and do not have the opportunity to complain. The many Tamils in our society such as the authorities of the Churches, Hindu Kovils, Tamil business leaders and Tamil politicians (except a few), have deliberately selected to remain silent on this heart rending issue of future Tamil generation.

Would the BBC's Ms. Luthra interview the teenage children who recently escaped from the LTTE's military camp and allow them space to tell the world the unforgivable murderous life enforced on them by the LTTE? No, that would probably earn her the sack from the BBC.

Who is responsible for this unacceptable inequity? It is the LTTE and Pirapakaran himself. His crime is all the more wicked given his son has been sent to Ireland to study at a university there. One hopes that at least he will learn there that the dreaded IRA accepted the decommissioning of arms, and are now engaged in negotiation for a solution to their grievances which also included discrimination by Protestant majority because they were Catholics.

Another abominable grievance of the Tamils is that they have to pay extortionate and highly regressive taxes to the LTTE. No matter what a person's level of revenue, he has got to pay the tax arbitrarily imposed on him under pain of death. Take for instance a bicycle repair man in the wilds of Vanni. On a good day, if he is lucky, his maximum earnings would be between three to five hundred rupees. From this meagre earnings he has to pay a 20% levy to the LTTE. With what is left he is unable to buy anything substantial to feed his family. This is because the prices of everything are very high due to the taxes imposed by the LTTE.

Emaciated without proper food, it is a wonder that he and his family survive. He is probably rescued by the food items sent by the government and aid agencies. His survival is certainly not due to the benevolence of the LTTE, but due to the concern of the government which still accepts him as a citizen of this country and therefore entitled to be helped.

Who is responsible for this destitution and near starvation of the Tamils in the north and the east? It is the LTTE. The top echelons of the LTTE live sumptuously in spacious and well kitted out houses as evidenced by the recently captured Mr.Soronam's house in Sampur. They also have larders full of all the good food available in the market, all of them probably commandeered from the trader. In addition they also arrogate a large proportion of food items sent to the Vanni by the government and the aid NGOs. Life is made miserable and wretched by the LTTE for the ordinary Tamils. This is the grievance every articulate Tamil should gripe about. It is time to stop blaming the Sinhala society.

Here is another grievance of the Tamils because they are Tamils. Tamil businessmen and professionals have got to pay Kappan to the LTTE even if they are not resident in the Vanni. If they do not or refuse to pay the imposition, they are abducted and a ransom is extracted or the victim is killed and the body disposed of without trace.

It is now alleged that other Tamil racketeers have got into this lucrative business of ransom money. This appalling situation prevails because of omerta (silence) of the victims themselves. They have chosen to suffer this iniquity in silence and pay up whatever is demanded of them. If all of them came out of their self-imposed closets and announced to the world that they have been victimized hitherto, and now they refused to be intimidated any longer, and that they would cooperate with the

CID, then the perpetrators of this dastardly crime would run for cover and soon face extinction.

The Tamil politicians have cited these abductions as violations of Human Rights. Indeed they are. But who is responsible for this situation? First and foremost it is the LTTE and other Tamil villains. The victims too should shoulder part of the blame for their non cooperation with the police. The police will remain helpless so long as information on extortionists is denied to them.

Another grievance of the Tamils in the LTTE's bandit country is the complete absence of any kind of human freedom available in the rest of the country. They have no freedom of speech. Tamil newspapers are burnt and Tamil journalists are murdered in turn by the LTTE and other Tamil gangsters. Note, the Tamil newspapers are available in plenty in the rest of the country and the Tamil journalists ply their trade without any hindrance from the Sinhalese.

Some of Tamil journalists are subject to intimidation by the LTTE even in the south of the country. This is the payoff emanating from Ranil's CFA giving the LTTE permission to "do political work" in the south of the country! If any Tamil spoke about the appalling conditions of life in the Vanni, he will soon find himself inviting LTTE bullets through his head. In short they have no right to dissent, full uncomplaining compliance with Pirapakaran's dictatorship is enforced without mercy.

The Tamils in the Tigerland have no freedom of association. They cannot form any political party different from that of the LTTE. Those already functioning Tamil political parties are at great risk. Almost every day the members of these parties (EPDP, EPRLF) are cold bloodedly murdered by the LTTE.

Even to form a trade organization, one needs the consent of the LTTE and its members should be contributors to LTTE funds. Thus many Tamil traders from the Vanni have fled the area or shut up shop unable and unwilling to comply with LTTE's demands. Who is responsible for this situation? It is the LTTE, not the Sinhalese or Muslims nor the government of the country.

I have listed the genuine and actual grievances of Tamils arising from the fact that they are Tamils. They are all grievances imposed on them by the LTTE. The Sinhala and the Muslim societies in this country have nothing to do with these grievances. Yet they do not feature among the complaints so often made by the Tamil elites, their NGO and New Leftist friends living in comfort in the salubrious environs of Colombo. To the extent they have ignored these genuine grievances they stand condemned as hypocrites and also remain blacklisted as acolytes of the terrorist LTTE.

Some Tamils now living abroad have now come to realize the ruin wrought on the Tamils by the LTTE. They have started to hold public protests meetings against these grievances and blame the LTTE for the sad predicament of the north- eastern Tamils. They have called for real change in the LTTE. It is opportune moment for Tamil in Sri Lanka to join hands with this brave minority of enlightened foreign Tamils and strive to bring about the requisite change in the LTTE. They should stop blaming the Sinhalese and the government of the country for their wretched condition in life under the LTTE.

72

VAKARAI—LIFE AFTER SWARNAM AND ELILAN

(The Island, 2nd. Feb2007)

Sometime ago I maintained in an article in The Island newspaper (1st Sept.06) that the much flaunted "invincibility" of the LTTE was a very fragile one. Our security forces have proved me right in the eastern theatre of the conflict with the terrorist LTTE. They have been defeated in the east. They now do not occupy any main town in the east. They have been driven in disarray to the Thopiagala jungle without much food to sustain them and without many of their lethal weapons to wage war with the army. Given that they do deploy many suicide cadres, the LTTE would be able to mount many destructive campaigns in the areas under the control of the government. Eternal vigilance is the price we have to pay until the LTTE is substantially disabled and neutralized and peace is restored in the country.

Many LTTE sympathizers have tried to down play this crucial victory as a tactical withdrawal by the LTTE. With over 1000 dead and more than a 1000 badly injured the withdrawal was forced on the LTTE by our security forces. This certainly is a victory in my books and the territory gained is of immense significance, in that, the LTTE cannot now site their capital of Eelam in Trincomalee, the physical and political case for the merger of the east with the north has been demolished and the eastern Tamils, the Muslims and the Sinhalese have been liberated from the ogre of the LTTE oppression and the daily artillery barrages.

In the north the LTTE is still a formidable force. This force will now be reinforced by the eastern cadres who managed to escape to the Wanni. It probably has in its possession technically advanced weapons ready for effective use there when it matters by surprise attacks. More importantly, it has a substratum of northern Tamil society that supports the ideology of Eelam. Therefore a consummate military plan need to be put together and thoroughly tested for all conceivable contingencies before any onslaught is made on the LTTE in the north. Any hotch-potch campaign will result in another humiliating Muhamaly debacle. Given the efficient manner of the eastern campaign, one can be certain that our security forces will not again rush in where angels fear to tread.

Perhaps "little now and more later" policy is called for in the north while "the military assets of the LTTE are destroyed wherever they are found" and exposed. The President and the security forces ought also to be congratulated for the demonstrating to the country the successful alternative to Ranil's abject appeasement policy towards the LTTE. Ghandian patience was endured by the government when the LTTE began their attacks in Dec.2005. This appeasement mode continued till April 2006. The international community did not much care about the deaths and destruction caused by the LTTE, nor did they do anything to rein in the LTTE, and their silence only encouraged the LTTE to greater outrages which ended at Mawil Aru. The new policy is the measured military response for any attack by the LTTE. As these unprovoked artillery attacks took place from their entrenched positions in the east, it became quite apparent that the LTTE ought to be chased out of the east for the attacks to stop and the people to live peacefully. This is what has been accomplished at minimum cost to the army and maximum cost the LTTE. All Sri Lankans should be proud of this achievement. We should evince our full support for our security forces in the frontlines.

In Vakarai and other towns captured from the LTTE, the security of the territory would be the urgent immediate concern. Security in terms of clearing the place of landmines and bombs is just one of the problems. The other is the infiltration by the LTTE as civilian returnees. They would return to dig up the weapons they had buried and start killing people, destroying property, disrupting commercial life and agricultural occupations, and de-stabilizing society. The police therefore have a very difficult task of screening the returnees and keeping an ever watchful eye on those people. This is a thankless yet a necessary job.

The pro-LTTE NGOs and other rabid Tamil nationalists are likely to resort to detraction of the police and accuse them of all sorts of crimes not excluding the manipulation of ethnic proportions in the area! Such treacherous conduct should be publicly treated with contempt. This situation calls for maintenance of adequate security personnel in the area and prevents them from being shifted to other areas of conflict. This redeployment of troops happened under Minister Ratwatte and the east fell like a ripe mango into the lap of the LTTE. Let it never happen again.

Once the security is established, and the returnees have been settled, the government should conduct a full population census of the areas not included in the 2001 census and update the electoral register. A reliable census is the basic information necessary for all other development work. Our security forces should never forget the fact that thousands of Tamil IDPs abandoned the LTTE and sought refuge in government controlled areas. They were confident that they will have not only food and shelter there, but also security of life and limbs and freedom from being used as human shields and slave labourers to construct LTTE bunkers. This is the life after Swarnam and Elilan they would now expect in the east. They cannot be thrust into the arms of other armed groups in the east nor should they be allowed to be exploited by such groups. The confidence of these marginalized people in the government and the security forces should be further reinforced by measures restoring to them what is their due in terms of economic development, social improvements, provision for wider educational opportunities and the enhancement of their health.

The government should stop acting as their nanny at the earliest opportunity. Simply handing out food, clothing and materials to build shacks might be considered as immediate necessities. But there is life beyond these immediate needs. For this the people need to be involved in the tasks of building their roads, bridges, schools, hospitals and communication facilities. They should be made to feel proud of being directly involved in building their towns and villages, and the infra structures necessary to sustain profitable economic life in a peaceful environment conducive to healthy life for themselves and their children. The days of victimization and marginalization should be banished for good. They will recover their dignity when they are enabled to lead a life not dependent on handouts from the government and NGOs. Smiling faces in the midst of hard work to restore their shattered lives to normalcy should be the end-objective of the policy of the government and the security forces. The government simply cannot fail them at this juncture.

In rebuilding these devastated areas there is one policy the government has so far failed to consider let alone implement. I am referring to propaganda to de-eelamize these traumatized people. The government has been very successful in its current propaganda TV campaign in favour of the army. A similar local campaign in the east to wean the people from the LTTE is opportune at the moment. Posters, bill-boards local press and radio should be utilized on a daily basis to drive home the point that the Eelam dream of one man is the cause of their dire destitution, destruction of life and property. Pirapakaran has caused them utter misery and robbed them of their children and the future of their children. It is time to ditch him and win back the lives of misguided children under his jackboots. That these children have a real future to lead normal lives than be living as mindless cannon fodder for the LTTE. There is more satisfaction and joy in a society that cares and shares and lives in peace with the neighbours. Surely it is worth trying to instill the positive aspect of our lives living in one free multi-ethnic country rather than the life in a myopic ethnic and fascistic enclave that Pirapakaran had hitherto propagated in the minds of these unfortunate people.

The lynchpin to the successful re-integration of these abused Tamil people is the expected reasonable offer of a new deal to sort out all their problems both real and perceived. In this endevour, one hopes that the government realizes that there are also alternatives to NGO/ Majority Committee Report and Prof. Vitharna's proposals. Justice and fairness to all both the majority as well as the minority should be the bottom line in any new deal.

73

TALKING TO THE ENEMY

(The Island, 8th Mar.2007)

The enemy to our nation is the LTTE. Many intermeddlers in our affairs keep demanding from our government that it talks to this enemy, yet it this enemy that has walked out of talks many times. These foreigners pretend not to know that LTTE is averse to negotiations for peace, other than on an offer of a separatist Eelam on a plate.

The onetime "axis of evil" member North Korea (NK) is today talking to the USA. This came about because of the intransigent position taken by the USA, Japan and South Korea that NK should dismantle its nuclear programme for it to have any social and economic benefits from the three neighbours. It took some time for NK to realize the futility of pursuing its nuclear ambitions, given the fact that it has a starving population and a decaying economy. The desperate economic circumstances under the prevailing obstinate insistence of its neighbours have more or less forced NK to sue for talks and the dismantling of its nuclear facilities. The uncompromising stand taken by the three countries have paid off.

In Northern Ireland, the IRA was reduced to a pariah state and shut off from all avenues to raise funds to continue its violent activities and propagate its objective of unification of Ireland. IRA too realized, after nearly three decades, the futility of armed insurrection against resolute and unyielding UK and Irish governments. It is now engaged in talks to attain power sharing as against its endgame of unification with Ireland and has surrendered its arms and ammunition. A terrorist IRA wilted unable to face the stubborn policies of both UK and Ireland. Vigorous opposition to terrorism has paid off here too.

In Spain Prime Minister Zappaterro is obstinate in his decision that he will not talk to the terrorist ETA until they have renounced in public all forms of violence. His colleagues in the EU dare not tell him to talk to the ETA terrorists ignoring the terrorist violence—a policy they try to ram down the throat of our President. I have no doubt that PM Zappaterro will be proved right and ETA will soon come to him with the tail between their legs.

Syria and Iran, the other two in the axis of evil too are scheduled to attend a security conference on Iraq on the tenth of March. USA has signaled its willingness to participate in this meeting. Under President Bush, USA's stand on Iraq and Israel is uncompromising. This policy is backed by the mighty US military. Probably Syria and Iran too have come to realize that at some point, if they continue with the current policy of meddling in Iraq, they might have to confront the US military even under a new President. There might not be any winners in such a confrontation, but there will be enormous destruction of lives and property. So talking to the enemy and forestalling an armed confrontation would be considered a better option to pursue. Negotiation with Syria and Iran is unlikely, instead the US is likely to demand that the two countries cease and desist supplying arms and ammunition to the warring factions in Iraq. After all, the US "does not talk to terrorists, it simply puts them out of business". Perhaps ambassador Blake could intervene here and help US to make full use of this rare opportunity to talk to and with Syria and Iran and patch up their quarrels and make Iraq a peaceful place to live. His frequent advice to our government is really relevant in the middle-east.

In the above examples, it is the realization that armed conflict would take the armed insurrectionists nowhere, that changed the perception of the problem and opened space for dialogue and compromises. Have we got to this level of perception of our conflict in Sri Lanka? No, we have a long way to go.

The immediate topics for any negotiation would be the compulsory recruitment of children and adults and the militarization of the Wanni, the clandestine importation of lethal weapons and their de-commissioning, the extortion and illegal taxes levied on Tamils and the suicide killers roaming the country stalking their prey to plant claymore mines on their path. In short a full stop to all forms of violence. It is only then other political issues could be taken up for discussion. No way would LTTE accept such an agenda and as the veteran TULF politician Mr. Anandasangaree has said on several occasions, it would be useless to talk to the LTTE. At the moment they know only the language of claymore mines and artillery fire.

So what strategy has the government to get the peace negotiations on course? The current policy of the government to destroy LTTE's war assets on land and sea should be supported by the people without reservation. The virility of the LTTE is in the weapons they possess. Their destruction therefore will reduce them to impotency and loss of morale among LTTE cadres. We should laud the efforts of both the air force and the navy on their recent successes in striking the enemy at his most vulnerable points. The army and the STF too have done us proud by defeating the LTTE in the east. They will no doubt pursue the LTTE until it is completely ejected from the east. At this point all supplies to the LTTE should be considered as terrorists' assets and should be captured where possible otherwise destroyed.

A strategy the government has failed to adopt so far is to actively encourage disaffection among the LTTE cadres. There should be a loud and clear publicity campaign in the North, the East and the Wanni to wean away from the LTTE, the young, the old and the unwilling cadres among the LTTE. The invitation to them to return to normal civilian lives should carry convincing offers of alternative livelihood or substantial help to establish such alternative lives. As the LTTE is on the run in the East, this is the opportune time to try this well establish method of reducing the manpower of the LTTE.

It is most likely that the LTTE would have enforced news blackout of all their recent defeats among its cadres in the Wanni. It is therefore incumbent on the government to penetrate this news blackout and let the ordinary LTTE foot soldiers aware of the many recent defeats and the capture and destruction of the many boats, trawlers and ships loaded with LTTE weapons. This information will have a shattering effect on their morale and help them to desert the LTTE at the first opportunity. This is the most opportune time to institute the psych-ops on the LTTE.

Another strategy is the speedy rehabilitation of the internally displaced people (IDP) in the East. If this is done properly and humanely then these people would soon realize that their security and destiny are tied up not with the LTTE but with the rest of the population. They would see for themselves the rapacity and oppression visited on them by the LTTE while they were enslaved by them. Their loyalty to the LTTE will wither away to be replaced by the desire to lead lives free from harassment and the distress of loosing their children to war. While the physical rehabilitation of the people in houses and towns with proper infra structure facilities is taking place, the government should also take the necessary steps to instill in these people the desire for living under rule of law and democratic norms. Other armed groups should not be allowed to enforce their might on these hapless people.

Once Thoppigala has been cleared and IDPs have been rehabilitated, a full Census of the East should immediately follow suit. The Electoral Register should be updated and local elections should be held without undue delay. The elected candidates should then be entrusted with the wherewithal to rebuild their towns and villages. Some fear that elections at this stage would bring to power the erstwhile LTTE acolytes. This is unlikely as the people would not have so soon forgotten all the troubles and oppresion they endured under the LTTE regime not so long ago. They certainly would not like to go back to that situation again. The parents who risked their lives and that of their families, by trekking through swamps and thick jungle, to distance themselves from the LTTE to protect their young children from conscription, would not want create that insecure situation again. Nor would they want to be subject to arbitrary taxes and extortions again with forced labour thrown in as per the edicts of the LTTE. In short it is time to trust these people and help them to return to normalcy and freedom.

When the LTTE is sufficiently debilitated, it is possible that there might be regime change within the LTTE itself. That would be the time to talk to the LTTE on the larger issue of a political settlement.

Until then, we need to persuade our international friends, some of them covert supporters of the LTTE, to either actually support us to fight terrorism or leave us alone to fight LTTE's terrorism in the same manner as they fight their terrorists both in their country and abroad. Now that Pirapakaran has had a direct shot at H.E.Blake and his diplomat colleagues, I hope, the next time he gets the urge to slate our government, he will instead also tell Pirapakaran, "stop shooting, start talking".

74

WHAT DOES TERRORISM COST?

(The Island, 28th Mar.2007)

The public have been bombarded recently in the media with the question "What Does Peace Cost?" In fact, in my view, peace does not cost anything. Let me explain. Take any person walking on the road any where any day in Colombo. What does peace mean to him? It means his ability to get about his business of the day without hindrance. His business of the day usually involves his freedom and opportunity to earn a living, support his family, educate his children, have enough to eat and sleep the night undisturbed. The cost entailed in this activity is the human condition of having to live with limited resources and our inability to satisfy all our desires, unless of course one belongs to the exclusive and privileged class of Norwegian-Kroner-super- rich. Their resources appear to be unlimited.

In the areas of our country affected by terrorism this peace is not available. This very absence of peace is the horrible cost of terrorism. Restoration of this peace is the primary duty of any government and all true citizens are expected to support the measures taken to end terrorism.

The rhetorical answers in the advertisement are that peace cost us "truth", "sacrifice", "understanding", "love", "acceptance", "human value", "tolerance" and "forgiveness". This is absurd. Every man and woman, everyday in life fully enacts all the above values of life by the sheer fact of getting on with his/her life to the best of his/her ability given the human condition and its limitations. Most of us work with and in association with others to earn a living. This cannot be done and the objective of the work cannot be accomplished without sacrifice, understanding, accepting of human value, tolerance and forgiveness. There is love behind all these emanating from the love of oneself to love of the family members, and our fellow associates at work and at play, and in general, love for all that exist. Thus peace does not cost us anything, but this peaceful life is shattered the moment terrorism strikes. Even the mere threat of terrorism turns our lives topsy-turvy. Our positive well-being is immediately affected physically, socially, psychologically and spiritually. The costs entailed by terrorism are enormous. All democratic norms of life are anathema to the terrorists.

Therefore the question should have been "What does terrorism cost?" It not only costs lives but also everything we associate with our normal way of conducting our lives. I perceive a hidden agenda behind this media splurge. In asking the wrong question and supplying the wrong answers, it is perhaps the intention, to brainwash us into thinking that peace at any cost is worthwhile. The hidden message is appease the terrorist, give him what he wants and we shall have peace. Let us not talk about terrorism or the terrorist and the mayhem he proliferates, because the terrorist is a protected species!

At first glance, the advertisement appears to convey the message that peace is too costly. Therefore by implication it is better to allow the conflict to continue. This situation is what the conflict-resolution brigades want. They can then ply their trade ad multos annos and enjoy the luxury life on a feather-bed of Kroners, Euros, Swiss Francs, Sterling Pounds and US Dollars. What a cynical lot they are!

There is another aspect to these advertisements other than the wastage of funds which could be better utilized. The advertiser is perhaps unable to raise the question of terrorism because it then involves the open identification of the terrorist and the wreckage he has directly and indirectly caused in this country. There is no rhetoric or quibbling possible here, because the people know who the terrorist is and are aware of all the death and destruction caused by him. Should he embark on identifying the terrorist and the desolation he has caused so far, then this advertiser would inevitably have to condemn the terrorist and seek to recommend measures to counteract the activities of the terrorist. He will have to lend open support to actions taken by the government to check violence, to isolate and combat the irrational and unacceptable ideology of the terrorist. This course of action might militate against the conditions of foreign funding of the advertiser. Thus we seem to have a proxy brain-washing campaign to persuade us to believe that peace at any cost is what suits this country. These perverse advertisements are aimed at weakening our resolve to fight terrorism in all its forms. To this extent the advertisements serve to lend moral support to the terrorist, to denigrate the achievements of our armed forces, and to encourage the terrorists to prolong the agony of the nation.

The advertiser is telling us that the pursuit of ending terrorism and restoring peace in the country is costing us too much in terms of sane human values. Therefore the suggestion is that we halt our pursuit and agree to the terms proposed by the terrorist. The fact is all our human values have been already overthrown by the terrorist a priori, and the government's efforts to restore them are at best, a posteriori—ie. after effects.

A democratic nation is beset with problems when fighting terrorists as it has to abide by the standards set by the International Humanitarian Law. It has to respect and give due weight to Human Rights of all individuals. The terrorist is under no such constraints, he will in fact exploit this situation to achieve his objectives. Thus we have had terrorist artillery fire directed at the army from the vicinity of churches, hospitals and schools. We have had the heinous crime of Tamil people being used as shields against army fire in response to the initial attack by the terrorist. The terrorist has no scruples, and his supporters totally ignore his aberrations together with the fact that the soldiers too have Human Rights, even though they are engaged in combating terrorism. All these are costs of terrorism deliberately ignored by the advertiser by asking the wrong question and supplying the wrong answers.

The United nations Security Council Resolution of 1373 unanimously and unequivocally condemned the 9/11 attacks on US soil and expressed its determination to prevent all such acts of violence. It called upon the member states to take action to prevent and suppress all terrorist acts. It called for cooperation in the exchange of information regarding actions of terrorist persons or networks, traffic in arms and explosives, use of communication technologies and possession of weapons of mass destruction. Why did the UN bother to exert itself to this extent? It is because the cost of terrorism is totally unacceptable to the nations of the world. It is no less so to a small nation like Sri Lanka.

Let me repeat, peace is not costly, but maintaining peace when faced with armed terrorists is very costly. Fighting terrorists who use state of the art weapons and equipment without any scruples is very expensive in terms of men, materials and money. Nevertheless no nation can live with terrorism. It has to be ruthlessly put down by taking extraordinary measures like the Patriot Act in USA, Prevention of terrorism Act in UK, and the Prevention of Terrorism Act in Sri Lanka. True patriots will seek to cooperate with these measures to rid the land of terrorists, and not resort to subversion by posting all sorts of hindrances under the guise of Human Rights, and have the soldiers' arms tied behind their backs when fighting the terrorists.

It is indeed true that we are "one people, one nation, and one country". The conclusion derived from this is that, if anyone tires to fracture this unity by force of arms, then he should be severely dealt with without any mercy. The advertiser would not venture this far, because, I suspect, his sincerity is questionable and his sympathies lie elsewhere than the country and its people.

ALL PARTY PARLIAMENTARY GROUP FOR TAMILS (APPG)

The Island 21st may 2007

20th May 07.

Hon. Simon Hughes MP,
House of Commons,
Westminster Parliament,
London SW 1

Dear Mr. Hughes,

ALL PARTY PARLIAMENTARY GROUP FOR TAMILS (APPG)

I have read the speech you made in House of Commons (HC) on the above topic with great interest. Though I disagree with the entire speech, for brevity I would like to confine my attention here to a handful of issues. I hope you will give it the kind consideration it deserves as you are an ardent advocate of audi alteram partem.

At the beginning of your speech you admitted that you are "sympathetic to the Tamils' case", that you visited late Mr. Balasingham (for consultations?), that "you attended Tamil events at Trafalgar Square" and now you are arguing in HC for the "unbanning of the LTTE in UK and EU", given these facts and sentiments, it would be foolish and reckless for anyone to regard you as anyone other than "a supporter of the Tamil Tigers" and that you "take the terrorists' view" solely as the only version that matters. In my view you have allegedly sold your soul to the Tigers and the terrorism they perpetuate all over the world including the UK. You chose to ignore the various illegal rackets the LTTE are engaged in the UK including extortion by physical threats.

In your speech you totally ignored the interests of the many Sinhalese as well the Sri Lankan Muslims and non-Tiger Tamils in your constituency as well as in Sri Lanka. This is an outrageous partisan approach. How could you be anyone other than "a supporter of Tiger terrorism"? Hence many Sri Lankans together with the "the Sri Lankan government and officialdom" are justified in considering you as an ardent supporter of the LTTE.

You pay high tribute to the Norwegian government. If they had been so efficient and competent how come the Peace Process has failed? Why not ponder a while on the part played by the Norwegians vis-à-vis the part played by the Senator Michel in the Northern Ireland case. The good American Senator was strictly impartial and maintained scrupulously the trust of all stakeholders in the conflict. The Norwegians on the other hand were partial to the LTTE and have been caught secretly supporting the LTTE financially and militarily. They have lost the confidence of the Sri Lankans at large. They have become part of the problem and yesterdays men with a tainted record in Sri Lanka as well as middle-east. They should resign and give way to an honest and impartial peace-broker.

You quoted that 13% of the population of Sri Lanka to be Tamils giving the impression that all these people lived in the conflict zone of north and the east of the country. This is a blatant untruth. Nearly half of the indigenous Jaffna Tamils are today living all over the country where there is no military conflict of any kind. They have fled from the thraldom of the LTTE's tribal land where there are no freedom of speech, no freedom of association and now no freedom of movement. Yet the long arm of extortion of the LTTE has been extended to blight their peaceful life in the south of the country. This is the primary cause of abductions of the prosperous Tamils in Colombo and the suburbs. They have to pay the warlord Pirapakaran his due no matter where they lived, Southwark and Bermondsey notwithstanding!

You bemoan the fact that Buddhism was given the foremost status in the country. Perhaps you are sadly ignorant of our 2500 year long history of our country. Nevertheless let me remind you of what your ancestors who stole the sovereignty of this country did in 1815. In that year they signed a Convention with the Kandyans in the name of His Majesty George 3rd. The fifth article of that document reads as follows: ***"The Religion of the Buddha professed by the Chiefs and the inhabitants of these provinces is declared inviolable and its Rights, Ministers and Places of Worship are to be maintained and protected"***. This particular article was severely criticized at that time by the Evangelists in England. Governor Brownrigg conceded that he had to allow this article in order to pacify the Buddhists and to effect the stealthy conquest of the country. This pledge to protect Buddhism was later broken by him in his proclamation of 1818 (art16), after the bloody suppression of the Kandyan rebellion of 1817/18 by the imperial British. You appear no different to the colonial marauders of the bygone British Empire in trampling down the hallowed traditions and history of the people of this country. Even the die-hard colonialists acknowledged the primacy of Buddhism in this country because that was the prevailing fact at that time. This situation has not changed today as you accept yourself that more than two-third of the population is Buddhist.

You appear to be averse to Sri Lankan and Indian politicians trying to win the votes of the nationalists. Your hypocrisy is too patent here. By making this speech in HC are you also not trying to win the votes of the Eelamist Tamils in your constituency?

You trace the beginning of our troubles to the disenfranchisement of Indian Tamil workers in the plantations of the hill country. Do you not know that one must have the franchise in the first place for disenfranchisement to take place. Those plantation Tamils were migrant workers imported from India by the British planters who stole the lands of the Kandyans. They were no different to the migrant workers in England. Have you granted all those migrants to England the franchise? The very onerous conditions imposed and prevarications your government resorts to are all calculated to deter migrants obtaining the British citizenship. I respect the sovereign right of Britain to determine who becomes a British citizen. Should not the same right be extended to other sovereign nations? Incidentally by importing the Indian workers the British created and left behind intractable problems for us. We have not resorted to Idi Amin's pogrom of expulsion, we have now enfranchised those Indians, a fact you failed to acknowledge.

While pretending that you are not prescribing solutions you manage to do just that. Let me quote "Sri Lanka must give self-government to the Tamils where they want it". Our government will no doubt have its appropriate reply to all those British MPs who pontificate solutions for country's terrorist problem while they unilaterally and resolutely condemn in Parliament the July 7 London bombings. You are giving hypocrisy a bad name! In any case your hidden agenda to dismember the country surfaced when you said that "if later the Tamil people voted for independence in a free election that would be a separate issue.......The world would have to accommodate that through proper international recognition processes". You have condemned yourself by your own words in the eyes of all non-LTTE Sri Lankans. You are, in my view, a separatist and an Eelamist. You are shamelessly making use of the freedom in your august HC to promote the vivisection of this country.

Finally a few reminders: it is the LTTE who walked away from talks on the peace process. It is the LTTE who wants an ethnic enclave and cleared the areas under their control of all non-ethnic Tamils. The Muslims and Sinhalese in Jaffna were thrown out with only the clothes they were wearing at that time. It is the LTTE who prevented voting at the last election under pain of death. One voter had his hands chopped off. It is the LTTE who eschews democracy and slaughters all Tamils who stand for democracy and therefore have a dissenting voice. It is the LTTE who have enforced no-go areas. Even the SLMM are not allowed access to their areas. The ceasefire agreement was broken by the LTTE just two weeks after signature. To-date they have violated it more than 7000 times, the latest is the arms ship sunk by the Maldivians.

You have projected the settlement in Northern Ireland as a good example to follow. Indeed it is. The three crucial factors that contributed to this peace settlement are the renunciation of violence by the IRA, the verifiable decommissioning of weapons and the recognition of the legitimacy of the Ulster Constabulary. I am bewildered as to why you fail to urge these three salutary conditions on the LTTE. If tomorrow the LTTE decides to follow IRA's example, peace will arrive the next day. Don't you think that you should urge the LTTE to follow the example set by the IRA?

You are badly wrong to think that the many Tamils in UK expect to return to the Eelam paradise one day to live under the ruthless dictatorship of Pirapakaran. Your colleague, the deputy mayor is unlikely to give up the congenial comforts of wall-to-wall carpeted and centrally heated house, two or more family cars, avenues of opportunity in education of her children and the vast amount of money she earns for the arid and desolate lands in the Wanni. She, like many of her kind in UK, is fighting a proxy war in which her children are safe in Britain while the children of poor Tamil parents are deprived of all education and conscripted by the LTTE to be trained as killers and suicide bombers. Peace will come to this country only when the peace-breaker is brought under control as your police have done in the case of the British terrorist outfit. Would you promote the cause of those terrorists? No. Then why do you promote by your overtly partisan speeches the cause of the terrorist LTTE? I hope to contact you when in England this summer. Thanking you for reading this short note.

Yours truly,
Durand Appuhamy.
Millewa Niwasa, 12/283 Mirigama Road,
Dawatagahawatha, Negombo.

76

PROPOSALS ARE FOR DISPOSAL

(The Island, 23rd May 2007)

Before I make my brief comments on the SLFP's constitutional proposal let me draw the attention of the reader of esteemed newspaper to problems connected with both the federal and devolution forms of government

The Quebec state had its election on the 26thof March 2007. The Liberal Party lost its majority and was reduced from 72 seats in the state legislature to 48 seats, a recently formed party—Action Democratique Du Quebec (ADQ)—came second with 41 seats, earlier it had only 5seats and the separatist party—Parti Quebecois-- came third with36 seats, earlier it had 45 seats. On the face of it the separatists appeared to have lost, but appearances are deceptive. The newly emergent ADQ under Mr. Mario Dumont is seeking more autonomy for Quebec on a platform of "affirmation without separation". What this really means will come out if and when ADQ becomes part of the coalition government.

What is of relevance here is the fact that even after so many years of a fully federal government in Canada the separatist problem remains unsolved. Therefore the valid question is how could it solve our separatist problem compounded as it is with unbridled terrorism?

Here is another sort of problem faced by federalists when it comes to fairly sharing the limited resources of the country. In India the sharing of the waters of river Cauvery has become a very virulent contentious issue. Even awards made by independent commission on this issue have been condemned as unacceptable by the three southern states of India including Tamilnadu. A similar problem has arisen in federal Australia. Three states—New South Wales, Victoria and South Australia-- are disputing the relative share of each of the waters of the mighty river Murray-Darling. The central government wants to take over the management of the waters of this river and share it equitably among all three states disregarding the parochial interests of each state. Federalism has failed here too. There are also many other issues failed to have been solved by the federated form of government.

In this respect I would urge the reader to reflect on the fate of Mahaveli waters running through the three Provinces—the Central, North Central and the Eastern—once we have a federal government. The Mavil Aru incident alone is sufficient to send jitters through the spine of our politicians and pro-LTTE NGOs, if they do have spines.

Devolution is no panacea either to a separatist problem. Power was extensively devolved to Scotland. It had its own parliament controlling the affairs of that part of the world. Yet the Labour party that gave devolution as well as ruled Scotland lost power at election on the 3rd of May 07. The Scottish national Party (SNP) headed by Mr. Alex Salmond won with a majority of one seat over Labour Party (47 to 46). The SNP stands for independent, separate and sovereign nation. It has promised a Referendum on the issue by 2010.

What is of significant to us is the fact that the Labour party failed to stem the separatist tide by installing a devolved government in Scotland. Its failure is abysmal in that it was in charge of implementing devolution in Scotland. How could this unsuccessful meddler in our affairs—The British Labour Government or its Parliamentary Committee—suggest let alone prescribe solutions to our problems, having ingloriously and abysmally failed in Scotland? Another country where devolution has failed is Spain. Peace talks with the terrorist group ETA are on hold at the moment. There the Basque province was given asymmetrical devolution, but the problem of terrorism and separatism remains as strong as ever.

With the above examples as our background let us look at few aspects of the SLFP proposals given that these proposals are open for discussion as well as for disposal. The biochemist professor at APRC is expected to throw all the proposals emanating from various parties into the constitutional vat, stir them up properly and then draw out the genie of a viable solution acceptable to the vast majority of the population. Surely in addition to his expertise on biochemistry he will need an Alladin's lamp and its genie as well for this miraculous exercise!

The word "unitary" is absent in the proposal so is the word "federation". But the unitary character is emphatically enunciated in the "supremacy of the Parliament' and the power given to the President to take over a District Council if he is satisfied that there is a failure in the administration of the District. There is a similar provision in the Indian Constitution and it is quite frequently invoked by the President of India. What is necessary here is the definition of the criteria for determining the failure in the administration of the District.

The unit of devolution is the District. This is logically to be expected given the desire to give power to the grass-root level. Contiguous Districts could amalgamate on the basis of a referendum in the Districts. District administration has the merit of preventing secession. The people in the district and its administrators would be within reach of one another and therefore truly attuned to the needs of the area. However, the cost of 30 District Councils could become a heavy burden on the people, and the 30 District Chief Ministers could pull the country in thirty different directions when it comes to developing the country.

A valid accusation is that this district level devolution is much less than what is already given by the 13th Amendment to the Constitution. This amendment gave us the Provincial Council system in 1987. My suggestion is that the Provincial Council system has been a white elephant and a failure. Why persist with a system that does not contribute to the progress of democracy and development of the country? The expectation that this Provincial administration would solve our problem of separatism had not been realized and is unlikely to be realized and has been rejected wholesale by the LTTE. Is it not time to jettison this Indian imposed non-performing system of government and look at other alternatives?

The power given to the President to elect the Chief Ministers of the

Districts is objectionable. He should be elected by the other elected members of the District and approved by the President. The grounds for denying this approval should be laid out in the Constitution.

Together with these thirty Chief Ministers, the President has the power to appoint twenty others to the 75 member Senate. Thus the majority is his people. This cannot be considered as grass-root level democracy, rather it could become crony democracy similar to the non-elected MPs of today. In any case as it stands the Senate appears to be an effete body not justifying the cost and perks that would be bestowed on its members. A second chamber is probably necessary, but it ought to be constituted to promote peace, reconciliation and a wider sharing of power at the centre. This is possible if the majority of the Senators are independent, educated and patriotic and the chamber itself has a good ethnic mix of democratic minded individuals.

The SLFP proposal is ominously silent on the independent commissions that should be appointed under the 17th Amendment to the constitution. This cannot be excused. We need these Commissions for good governance and SLFP should incorporate this into its proposal with improvements to prevent the current deadlocks in the appointment of commissioners and the functioning of the commissions.

Expectations and aspirations are usually higher than what the real situation can satisfy. This is the case today where the expectation and aspiration of the Tamil community appears to border on the impossibility of a separate homeland. Thus no matter what proposals are made the LTTE would outrightly reject them. A separate homeland is the end objective of the LTTE's terrorism. This violence cannot be stopped except by counterterrorism. We cannot all run into bunkers when LTTE's planes drop bombs on us. We need to shoot them down or destroy them on the ground before they embark on their mission to bomb the country.

The rest of the Tamil community as well as the Muslim community have been given the opportunity to scrutinize, discuss and dispose this proposal and the many others made to APRC. They should engage in this exercise with an open mind so as to arrive at a solution acceptable to the majority of all communities in the country. At this point if the LTTE fails to fall in line they will become an irrelevant entity bereft of support of the people. One thing for sure, the government has demonstrated its desire to arrive at a solution by negotiation and this negotiation among all democrats should start now.

77

THE ISOLATION OF LTTE HYPOTHESIS

(The Island, 16th June 2007)

The accepted political wisdom of our times appears to me to be the formulation of a strategy to isolate the LTTE from the Tamil community and the world at large. Almost everybody seems to accept that this can be achieved by installing a federal constitution in Sri Lanka. Thus isolated, it is assumed, that the LTTE will then either fall in line and become a democratic party fully participating in the processes of this new government structure; or simply wither away bereft of the support it enjoys and utilizes now. Hey presto! The national problem is solved for all times! I must admit that the theory of isolation of LTTE is attractive to me too though federation is not my means to achieve that end. In Popperian terms the above hypothesis is falsifiable because the LTTE cannot be confined to isolation just by mere constitutional reforms of any democratic type. This is because the LTTE simply does not accept any democracy of any kind nor can the LTTE survive in a democratic society.

Most Tamil political commentators accept that approximately one-third of the Tamil population in this country is hard-core Eelamists and will remain devoted to LTTE through all thick and thin. Of the rest, half is neutral and will side with the LTTE so long as it is winning and will desert it when the LTTE starts loosing; the remaining half is democratic, and has been anti-terrorist though not averse to fighting for their perceived rights. Thus, if these estimates are correct, then it is quite plausible to accept that there will always be substantial support for LTTE among the Tamil population in this country. In this situation complete isolation of the LTTE is an impossibility. Nevertheless the Tamils in the east recently demonstrated the conditions necessary to make them abandon the LTTE. When the security forces militarily defeated the LTTE and chased them away from their bunkers, the

Tamil people abandoned the LTTE walked miles to get to government areas. And now they are happily returning to their broken homes under the guardianship of the security forces. There is a lesson here for those who advocate the isolation theory via federalism.

The diaspora Tamils are usually the most vociferous and strident supporters of the LTTE. They will use their wealth and contacts to nullify any attempts made to isolate the LTTE. In this age when money can buy support and influence, it is not beyond LTTE manipulators in the western world to install formidable barriers to prevent the isolation of the LTTE. They are doing so now in the UN and EU sub-units and in some state legislatures such as the British parliament These foreign LTTE devotees will find help for their project to save the LTTE among some Sinhala misguided politicians, Sinhala NGOs and some subversive international NGOs. It is quite possible that the LTTE could be even directly funding them to sing on their behalf. They will always find some reason or other to berate the government just when the government is gaining the upper hand over the LTTE.

The LTTE is today a billion dollar business accountable to no one and does not produce profit statements and balance sheets as per prescribed standards of accounting. The agents of the LTTE have their hands in almost every illegal yet lucrative business deal taking place somewhere in the world. Their Funds-Flow Statement, if available, would be the envy of any international legitimate business organization. This availability of funds to run their organization and buy sophisticated weapons alone is sufficient reason why the LTTE will not wither away as expected. As stated above they will simply use these funds to buy and retain support of people that matter in various countries for their Eelam project and continue to fight as long as they have the means to buy the weapons.

The strict social organization of the Tamil society in the Wanni is based on the complete acceptance of the hierarchy of the LTTE. The LTTE has had nearly thirty years to brain-wash everyone there that project Eelam is real and achievable with their support. At the dawn of the day this strict regime of compliance begins with the singing of praises of Pirapakaran at school and ends with military training of adults at twilight. The bonds thus established are not easily broken. As dissent is not allowed, fear of one's life is sufficient to keep the Wanni Tamils firmly tethered to the LTTE. These Tamils cannot abandon LTTE until the de-commission of the arms of the LTTE or the military defeat of the LTTE takes place. The east has amply proved this point.

Would India allow the complete isolation of the LTTE? There are some Indians like Dr.Subramanian Swamy, once a Union Cabinet Minister of India, who boldly tell us that "LTTE is a part of the problem, and cannot be part of any solution" (his book "Sri Lanka in Crisis: India's Options"). But such Indians are few. He advocates three solutions for India to implement in Sri Lanka. One, an Indian type quasi-federation, two, the partition of the Sri Lanka, and three, the merger of Sri Lanka with India. He also argues that India is obligated to disband and eliminate LTTE and the use of Commando force to lift Pirapakaran and Pottu Amman from wherever they are hiding. In my view the de-commissioning of their weapons and the military debilitation, if not defeat, should top the list of practical steps for a solution to our military conflict. With no weapons in their hands to force others to submit to them, the gradual disbanding of the LTTE would inevitably follow suit. Perhaps then, like the IRA, they will become a political force.

There are many Indians in Tamil Nadu who will support the LTTE no matter what a few brave Indian politicians have advocated. This is why we have a continuous flow of illicit aid to the LTTE mostly originating from Tamil Nadu. Most Indian Tamil politicians would subscribe to Narayan's (Indian PM's National Security Advisor) doctrine of keeping Sri Lanka isolated by imposing restrictive prescriptions on our weapons purchases, and Raman's (a retired Indian Official) decree that India "should not help the Sri Lankan government in neutralizing the LTTE's ground capabilities". It is quite plain from the above that there are strong forces in India that will ensure the survival of LTTE and prevent it from being isolated from the Tamil people. Their agenda are not only inimical to Sri Lanka, but are also very dangerous to the long term survival of Akhand Bharat! (indivisible India).

As the "Political Watch" of the Sunday Island reminds us "in 1987 the Indian sponsored Provincial Councils system was accepted by every Tamil group other than the LTTE. A Tamil government was formed in the North and the East. At that time the LTTE was isolated with the entire world supporting the peace deal. Despite all the isolation the LTTE stood their ground and through sheer intransigence, managed to have their own way. Today Indo-Lanka Accord is no more, but the LTTE is still around. Trying to defeat the LTTE by isolating it, is a joke".

Given the reasons above, the hypothesis that LTTE can be isolated by the offer of a federal solution to the present conflict, is untenable. Hence the exasperating question, what then is the solution? The solution is manifest in what happened in the eastern province. There the LTTE was militarily defeated and chased out of their bunkers. The Tamils ran away from their homes and from the LTTE's dictatorship. Now they have returned home trying to rebuild their lives as free citizens of this country. There is peace there now despite efforts at disruption by LTTE cadres. This then is the solution. The defeat of the LTTE in the eyes of the Tamils under their control is what is required to isolate the LTTE from the Tamils. Though some might argue that military defeat of the LTTE is not possible and that they will resurrect themselves even after the defeat, yet eternal recurrence is not one of the attributes of any terrorist organization anywhere in the world. All of them usually go to the graves with their leader. In any case what I am arguing for is the perceived defeat of the LTTE in the eyes of the Tamils, who hitherto considered the LTTE as their saviour/messiah leading them to the paradise of Eelam. The virility of the LTTE is the force of its weapons and the willingness to use them indiscriminately. This is also the Achilles heel of the LTTE. The security forces are right to pursue the objective of irreparably damaging the LTTE's military strength in the eyes of the Tamils under their control. Our forces should supplement this by targeted information blitz on the very many failures of the LTTE including the fact that even after twenty-five years Pirapakaran has singularly failed to win the war and establish Eelam.

Does this mean that we should give up our search for a political solution? No. The APRC should spend more time on arriving at a definition of the problem first and then seek a solution based on the democratic principles of freedom and rule of democratically promulgated law. There is now a surfeit of solutions but no real perception of the problem!

78

SHUT UP AND PUT UP

(The Island 12th July 2007)

It is time that all those acolytes of LTTE who berated our security forces and kept telling the world that the terrorist LTTE cannot be defeated, to shut up and put up or else decamp to Mullaitivu and await the arrival of the security forces there. Thoppigala has been cleared of the Tiger scourge and the people in the Eastern Province can now think of a settled life there.

It is very urgent now that as soon as displaced people are settled, a proper census be conducted, the electoral register be updated and the necessary measures be taken for the conduct of free and fair election. It is of paramount importance that the government demonstrates to the world that democracy prevails now where once tyrannical dictatorship of Pirapakaran oppressed the people. It is also time to tell the Co-Chairs that they have to support this shift towards democracy or else they remain badly exposed as fraudulent preachers of democracy and Human Rights.

I congratulate our security forces and all our valiant soldiers. They have shown that they are imbued with true grit and unfailing patriotism unlike some of our politicians scrounging on the state treasury living parasitical lives. I have no doubt they will go forward for greater victory and freedom if given a free hand.

Finally I again request the Pereras, Rupasinghes, Wickramasinghes and Foreign Ambassadors and High Commissioners to desist telling us that the LTTE cannot be defeated. They can and will be defeated if our soldiers are allowed to do what they have plainly demonstrated they are capable of doing. Any propaganda against our security forces will not stick anymore.

The settlement of the political problems of the country by negotiation will, no doubt, be made easy once the terrorist problem is ended. The Tiger on the run would want a respite and this will soon be obtained for him by Godfather Soldheim by announcing "Peace Process Talks". Is this not pathetic and predictable partisanship?

79

DEVOLUTION REVISITED

(The Island, 24th Sept.2007)

The deliberations of the APRC seem to have reached a state of dreamtime with no significant output to-date other than the Reports of Experts and the occasional squeaks by the chairman of the APRC. These Reports only highlighted the vast cleavage that existed among our constitutional cooks, many of them appeared ever eager to turn out a palatable dish to appease the terrorists and to win substantial power and perks for the political elites at the expense of the voters.

If one were to believe the political commentators in the media, the trend now appears to be towards some sort of devolution of powers within a unitary constitution and to move away from a federal set up. Even though we have sadly failed to define and identify the problem to which devolution is adduced as a remedy, yet it is pertinent to look at devolution at least as a means to overhaul the glaring inadequacies in our present constitution.

In this respect the eminent lawyer H.L.de Silva has lucidly argued **(in The Island of 6th and 7th Sept.)** the case for "operating with a genuine spirit of commitment the constitutional scheme that became law with the enactment of the Thirteenth Amendment in the Northern and Eastern Provinces in each unit separately (and not as a merged unit) in order to observe its strength and weaknesses as a viable system of government, ensuring as a first step that all undemocratic and violent moves to derail it are suppressed with a firm hand and a true opportunity is given for the free expression of the genuine desires and wishes of the people".

Given that the Thirteenth Amendment is already the law of the land it is sensible to implement it to the full at least in the Eastern Province after complete restoration of peace and a free and fair Provincial Council election there. I would go further, and embody in the Provincial Council Constitution the principles of Recall and of direct democracy where many key decisions on local police, local tax, education and health are taken at local level via local referendum if necessary like in Switzerland. The government should let go its firm hand on the subjects mentioned above and let the people govern themselves. This will be a perceptible change in the way provincial government is conducted. The people in the Province will really have a direct voice in the way the government business is conducted.

The Provincial Council system has become a white elephant precisely because the powers given to the Councils have been usurped by the central government. They are, at the moment, merely dollar guzzling institutions providing the opportunity to many of the local politicians to enrich themselves by plundering the treasury. The local people have no voice in the many matters decided on by local politicians mainly for their personal benefit or for the benefit of their cronies. Direct democracy with the Right to Recall will obviously act as a deterrent to the blatant abuse of powers by local politicians. They will be forced to do things for the benefit of the people as decided by the people. This is indeed a political solution where communalism will be replaced by the citizens acting as equals in society for the benefit of the society in which they live, work and play. The discriminating labels such as Sinhalese, Tamils and Muslims will have no place in local politics. These will be replaced by issues that concern the progress and development for all the people in the Province.

Peace is essential for this scheme to succeed. The LTTE's presence in the east has been eliminated though stray LTTE cadres are likely to attempt to disrupt normal life there. The frequently reported presence of armed personnel should also be neutralized by the government. All those who can prove the ownership of land and property should have them restored to them subject to security requirements. The owners of land and premises taken over by the security forces should be adequately compensated. These are basic social conditions necessary for the satisfactory functioning of direct democracy. Otherwise partisan politicians will exploit even minor deficiencies to derail any settlement. An example is the shrill voice of TNA politicians that Tamils are forcibly deprived of their lands in order to create Sinhala ghettos in the east. This argument is totally untenable, given that many Tamil ghettos are daily sprouting all over Colombo, especially in Wellawatte. Negombo and Chilaw and other towns being so colonized and the right to do so is not disputed here. (see Art. 14.1 as pointed out by Mr. H.L.de Silva). Why this alarm and sensitivity when and if only the Sinhalese are involved?

The Thirteenth Amendment was based on the Indian constitution and had the blessing of the Indians as well as other local political parties. Therefore all those commentators as well as politicians calling for an "Indian model constitutional settlement" surely cannot oppose what has been proposed here. What they might be afraid of are the powers given to the central government in the Concurrent List especially the power of the Central government to suspend the Provincial government and directly run the administration of the province. The fact is that in India this has happened nearly one hundred times since independence without any perceptible difference in the government of the country. This mechanism was used to get rid of inefficient and corrupt local Indian administrations resulting in subsequent better government of the local state.

Given the protracted armed conflict in our country and the unfortunate attempt at Unilateral Declaration of Indeopendence by Mr. Perumal in 1989, it is imperative that the central government retains the power to dismiss a local administration on grounds specified by the constitution. Devolution and federal set up have inherent in them the germs of separatism Let me illustrate this with two recent examples where devolution and a sort of federal administration had not stopped the drift to separatism.

The first is Scotland. There is no language, religion nor even economic deprivation problems between the Scots and the English. Eleven billion pounds a year is transferred from London to Scotland and the London MPs have no say in how this money is spent. But Scottisn MPs in Westminster can vote on measures that affect only England.

Scottish universities levy no tuition fees. On average pounds 4138 per primary school pupil was spent in Scotland as against pounds 3684 in England in 2005/6. In the secondary school the figures were 5771 pounds in Scotland and 4638 pounds in England. Medical care in Scotland is tangibly better than in the south. When devolution was handed over to the Scottish Parliament in 1998, Donald Dewar, the then Labour First Minister exclaimed that devolution was "an event not a process". George Robertson another senior Scottish Labour politician asserted that devolution would "kill nationalism stone dead". They were badly mistaken. Devolution has in fact set rolling an unstoppable bandwagon under the control of Mr. Alex Salmond towards separatism and independence. He expects to win the Referendum on separatism in 2010.

Mr.Alex Salmond is the leader of the Scottish National Party demanding independence and separatism for Scotland by ending the 300 year old political union of Scotland and England. He won the Scottish election in May by one extra vote and became the Chief Minister in Scotland. On the one hundredth day in power he published a White Paper proposing a Referendum for independence in 2010. Far from putting the lid on separatist Scottish nationalism, devolution has opened the Pandora's box of political uncertainty and turmoil in UK.

Immediately Salmond is demanding a plethora of powers for the Scottish parliament. The most important among them is the power to raise taxes and reduce corporation tax. The outlook appears to be that more powers will be transferred now and later on until Scotland is an independent state in all but name awaiting the seal of legitimacy by referendum. This no doubt is a prospect awaiting Sri Lanka. This is one valid reason why the central government needs to retain powers over the Provincial council.

The second example is Belgium with a 10.4 million people having six separate parliaments, some of whose members and functions overlap. All these elaborate arrangements of devolution and official recognition of languages (Flemish, French and German) were designed to stop separatism and the disintegration of the country. Belgium has had a long running animosity between the Flemish in the north and the Francophones in the south. Today the crisis has reached breaking point. Alas many Belgians appear to agree that their country's end is nigh.

There is a political crisis at the moment in Belgium. The Flemish politician, Mr. Yves Leterme is expected to stitch up a ruling coalition from among the Flemish-speaking MPs. A majority of these MPs believe that the current system of government should be ended and that the Flemish-speaking majority in the north should be made a separate country with a raft of powers transferred from the federal parliament to its regional parliament. As Prof. Robert Deschamps of Namur University put it "transferring the remaining powers over tax and social security would destabilize it (federal government) and empty it of all sense. The federal institutions would simply be replaced by the regional, leading inevitably to the irreversible separation of the country" No wonder the Francophones accuse Leterme of bad faith. In their books Leterme does not care about the country. To him it was "an accident of history" with no value in itself. His real ambition is to lead a sovereign Flemish state. Could this be the eventual fate of Sri Lanka in a Federal set up?

The final note is on the calibre of our politicians lacking the requisite qualities to abide by the rules and the laws of the land. They will be the weakest link in the chain of constitutional arrangement concocted for the country. At the moment do we have statesman-like politicians to implement with care, diligence and even-handed the provisions of a new order of our constitution? I have my doubts.

80

IS THIS THE TWILIGHT OF EELAM?

(The Island, 10th Oct. 2007)

There was a time when the acolytes of the LTTE ably supported by the anti-Sri Lankan NGOs waxed lyrical about the de facto LTTE regime in the North and the East. Those partisan commentators alluded to the Kangaroo courts, the Stassi-like police stations and the extortionist administration in the LTTE gangland as respectable institutions of a nascent state. They argued unabashedly that on the basis of those counterfeit institutions, Eelam should be recognized and legitimized. All I can say to those misguided men/women, especially the Sri Lankan among them, pudet, quia pudendum est (I am ashamed, because it is shameful). Where are those institutions today?

What we need is a radical perception change in the light of the presently available facts in existence in the Northern and the Eastern provinces. The Jaffna peninsula has been under the control of the army for many years now. Innumerable have been the subversive murderous activities by the LTTE to rouse the people against the army. They have all singularly failed. In fact, now the Jaffna folk are co-operating with the security forces there in exposing the Tiger cadres and their arms caches. Even though the lives of the people in Jaffna have yet to return to normal as in the south, these people have come to appreciate the better lives they lead now compared with the indigent hand-to-mouth existence they had when the oppressive LTTE was in control of Jaffna. The shops are open and do sell all sorts of goods the people want to buy. The prices are yet high all because of the extra-ordinary transport costs involved. But as supply of goods stabilize, prices plummet as in recent times.

The schools are functioning normally, exams are held on time, and the children are not under threat of abduction by the LTTE. Forget what the pro and anti-government media say about the situation in Jaffna; just look at the faces of children on their way to and back from school. Those faces speak eloquently of hope and joy predicting the better times to come.

The farmers and other workers are not anymore coerced to pay ***kappan*** to LTTE cadres. The fishermen are gradually allowed to return to their normal fishing grounds and dispose their harvest in the open market at prevailing prices. All religious practices and rituals are conducted without interference. The night curfew and security checks still hold because of the many attempts made by the LTTE to infiltrate and destabilize the relative peace that prevails in the peninsula. The many failed skirmishes at the frontlines at Muhamalai, Nagarkovil and the islands west of Jaffana should have made the LTTE realize that Pirapakaran's vow to retake the peninsular is not even a dream anymore. In Dante's words "a hemisphere of light [has] lit the dark" in Jaffna, and the glorious days of peace and freedom without the scourge of terrorism cannot be far away from the blighted people.

The eastern province has been cleared of LTTE, but they have left behind the problems of land mines and internally displaced people. The resettlement of these people is taking place rather too slowly for the likings of many. Nevertheless the problems are enormous, the rebuilding and reconstructions cannot be done overnight, but that the resettlement is taking place according to "international standards" as accepted by UN Agencies is a tribute to the government as well as the INGO officials engaged in this thankless job there. The INGOs have yet to internationally protest against the callous planting of land mines by the LTTE in the villages to maim and kill the civilians.

The fact however is that the LTTE has lost out forever their strongholds in the east and will forever remain barred from entering this province, let alone, revive their much flouted illegitimate administrative set-up there. During the liberation struggle the Tamil people voted with their feet to abandon the custody of the LTTE and fled to the government controlled areas for protection and sustenance. Would these people be willing to be enslaved by the LTTE again? The loss of the entire eastern province together with the proposed capital and harbour of Trincomalee is irreversible and irreparable to the cause of Eelam. The fading twilight on Eelam has started yielding to the engulfing darkness to obliterate the LTTE and its Eelam paradise forever.

The government cannot, however, allow the east to be a prey of gun-totting individuals parading as new saviours of these liberated people. Our security forces have achieved a remarkable victory in the east, therefore they alone should be the guardians of these people to gently push them towards a responsible democratic way of life.

The LTTE is now confined to two districts—Killinochchi and Mullaitivu— a sparsely populated shrub jungle landmass covering about 6000 square kilometers with about 300,000 to 400,000 indigent and impoverished people. That these economically deprived people can provide the men and material necessary to pursue a long military campaign against the army is open to question. The LTTE's dependence on foreign help is indispensable. This avenue has been effectively blocked by the recent scuttling of LTTE's ships in the high seas by the navy. Our navy has been a remarkable success in preserving the territorial integrity and sovereignty of the nation and will, no doubt, continue to render this valuable and critical service to the nation.

The LTTE has also seriously suffered by the arrests of its functionaries in USA, England, France, Australia and Canada. These were principal men and women who raised funds and financed the purchase of arms and ammunition for the LTTE. They are now out of business and their bank accounts have been frozen. There are still others, but they do not enjoy the freedom to act as they did before. They have to do whatever they do clandestinely and therefore less effectively. In the meanwhile their far-away beneficiaries have got to improvise on many things including arms and ammunition for the fighting cadres. On top of this there are now anti-LTTE diaspora Tamils quite active not only in the field of propaganda, but also in exposing the clandestine LTTE operators in the western countries.

Discounting propaganda plants in the media by interested parties, it is a well known fact that Pirapakaran is an ailing man. Inflicted as he is with Insulin dependent Diabetes, hypertension and related kidney problems, one cannot expect him to endure for long the tremendous pressures of fighting a war day-in-and day-out. He is bound to succumb to stress sooner than later like most mortal men. As he is Eelam now, when he departs, Eelam will collapse. It is this fear that has led to the jockeying for positions within the LTTE hierarchy. Any new leader will, of necessity, have to be ruthless in eliminating his rivals and this in-fighting will lead to the disintegration of the LTTE.

Finally in the south of the country we now have a government with able and willing security forces ready to fight the LTTE to the finish if needs be, as well as the determination to arrive at a political solution to the conflict. Though I remain unconvinced, the recent "repositioning" of the UNP as regards the envisaged constitutional settlement appear to lead to congruence with the stand taken by the President. If the UNP is genuine in their new conversion on the way to the ***Pola,*** then it is quite possible to arrive at an agreed proposal to end the conflict. We remain with bated breadth.

Nevertheless the fact remains that the LTTE has been decisively defeated in the east and has been now quartered and quarantined to a small area of the country. Given the fanatical nature of the LTTE cadres a frontal confrontation would lead to bloodbath and untold misery for the few civilians living there. Instead, as is being done now, the security forces should pick on them piecemeal on many fronts, while the SLAF selectively pummel the war assets and hiding places of top LTTE men/women. Simultaneously supporting propaganda to the civilians should urge them to abandon the LTTE as they did recently at Silavaturai. It is my surmise that the demise of the LTTE is nigh and inevitable.

The Eelam delusion has run its course to a futile finish. It is said that when "one person suffers from a delusion, it is called insanity", that exactly is the status of Pirapakaran; "when many people suffer from a delusion, it is called religion", that is why some Tamils made Pirapakaran the Sun-God and worship him to-date. The time has come for us now to imagine with John Lennon a Sri Lanka without LTTE and Pirapakaran, and exert all our energy to make it happen. I am liable to be charged and convicted of presumptuous optimism for what I have written above. I do not mind, for I prefer to join the Carmina Burana chorus and sing loud and clear, "ecce gratum et optatum ver reducit gaudia: purpuratum floret gratum, sol serenat omnia. Iam iam cedant tristia" (Behold the pleasant and longed-for spring brings back joyfulness, violet flowers fill the meadows, the sun brightens everything, sadness is now at an end).

81

CROUCHING TIGER TO FLYING TIGER, WHAT NEXT—ROCKETING TIGER?

(An Unpublished Article)

On the 4th of Apr. AL Jazeera TV reported that an Australian army officer had been arrested for stealing a rocket. In the light of this news item my question above has some relevance. Why would anyone wish and risk stealing a rocket if it was not intended for use either by himself or by some one else? There may not be any connection between this army officer and the LTTE, but we do know that there are many wealthy Australian Tamil Tigers who would dearly love to get their hands on a rocket and ship it to Mullaitivu for use by their God-King, who is now on the run – his cadres are today desperate fugitives in the east of the country.

When old Soviet Union broke up there were many discarded rockets available for destruction in the many states that broke away from the Soviet Union. But not all of them were destroyed. The impoverished scientists who created these lethal weapons hid them hoping to sell them to illegal arms merchants. These are still available for purchase by arms dealers. KP (Pathmanathan) the arms commissar of the LTTE, would be quite interested to obtain these rockets. His problem would be not only the transportation of the rocket itself, but also the delivery system of the rockets and the training required for its correct handling and targeting. These problems are not insurmountable. The LTTE could have expatriate cadres trained abroad or as had happened previously, obtained the services of foreign mercenaries.

My intention in raising this prospect is not to create alarm among the populace, but to make us aware that from the Tiger perspective, this is their natural progression. It is therefore urgent to seek and destroy all air assets and his very ability to mount any air attacks in the future. The excellent work of the navy destroying his arms shipments and his Sea Tiger bases are also part of this vital process. In short the LTTE should be made effete and ineffectual by the destruction of as many war assets as possible. Our Embassies should be alive to the possibility of efforts to purchase rockets, rocket delivery systems and the hire of rocket scientists abroad.

There is a discernible change of strategy in the military campaign of the LTTE. Having suffered repeated losses in the east, the LTTE is on the run in the east with just a toe-hold in Thoppigala. They have not only lost a vast amount of territory but also, and most importantly, lost their stranglehold on the Tamil people of the east. These Tamil people were their source for their manpower for fighting cadres as well as slave labour. They also provided taxes from their meagre earnings. Land empty of people cannot become the Eelam paradise of Pirapakaran. His claim to be the "sole Representative" of the Tamils becomes meaningless and spurious given that the Tamils in the east have abandoned him in droves and have sought refuge and new lives in the government controlled areas. So it is to be expected that he will resort to desperate measures to win back the Tamils, to boost the morale of his remaining cadres and to persuade the gullible Co-Chairs that he is still in the business of founding his evil empire. He is bound to resort to any measure to advance even one step both nationally and internationally.

The significant change in LTTE attacks is in the present targeting of civilians. First we had the mindless mortar attack on Tamil civilians at Morrakotchchenai and Santhiveli near Batticaloa. Eight died including children. The Anti-War Front has not protested yet. Then followed the brutal killing of six Sinhala Tsunami Aid-workers engaged in the completion of a Childrens' Home in Mailambaveli near Eravur. The Anti-War front is still asleep. Then followed the Koddawattuwan bus bomb blast that killed sixteen bus passengers on their way to Badulla. The Anti-War front appears to have gone into a coma. As the army cannot be blamed for any of these murders, the Anti-War Front remains silent exposing their bias towards the LTTE. This trend of slaughtering the civilians, I expect, will continue. Anywhere a large crowd is present, would likely to be targeted by the LTTE.

The LTTE will also try their hand at staging spectacular destructive events. The bombing of Air Force was just one such event. They won world attention by that attack. The Co-Chairs have not condemned it and many others have remained silent over it. Do we therefore need the approval of these mute Tiger sympathizers before we destroy those air assets of the LTTE?

It is alleged that a patriotic Lankan (was it a Sinhala?) snake saved us from another purported attack on an oil installation. The snake killed the Tiger cadre on a reconnoitering mission near the oil installation. The other soft economic centers would also be on their list of items to be destroyed. Large crowds at social and religious functions could also become targets for the bloodthirsty LTTE. To prevent LTTE engineered carnage of any sort, the government has got to do what it is doing at the moment and fine tune its intelligence gathering on the activities of the LTTE and Tiger devotees in our society. The society as a whole should stay alert and observant of what is happening in and around their environment.

Given LTTE's search for lurid sensational massacres, a rocket would ideally fulfill their multi-faceted objectives. A rocket could carry not only explosives but also weapons of mass destruction. It need not be a ballistic missile. If it can travel just one hundred miles south of Mankulam and crash on land anywhere south, the devastation would be unimaginable. As a nation we would be in a situation similar to Japan post Hiroshima and Nagasaki A-bomb blasts. Pre-warned is pre-armed. The security forces need our support so that this scenario would never become a reality.

The government too has got a lot of things to do. It should get the displaced people in the east settled in their homesteads as speedily and as humanely as possible. The reports that these hapless people are ill-treated by government functionaries should be investigated. Having liberated them from brutal oppression of the LTTE, what purpose does it serve to harass these people any further? These Tamils should be also involved in the rebuilding effort and made to realize that they and their children do have a future.

The government should also prepare the ground for a free and fair election in the east no sooner the resettlement of the people is complete and the electoral register is updated. People power in a free election would deal the deathblow to the LTTE in the east and go a long way towards maintaining this country in one piece. The triumph of democracy in the east would be the harbinger of better times for the Tamil people in Jaffna and the Wanni. In this climate new structures of government could be evolved to satisfy the aspirations of all people in this country.

The momentum of democratic activity could lead to regime change within the LTTE itself making it an indecent irrelevancy. Bereft of the support of Tamil people, controlling a daily diminishing extent of mostly unproductive land and deprived of sufficient weapons, the LTTE would end up a spent force rightly blamed for all the troubles endured by the Tamil people. So let us be optimistic that the end to our agony is at hand.

As regards the rocketing Tiger there is no need to alarmed. We have had the worst. Airport attack, Central bank attack, Maligawa Attack, Bus and train attacks have all been endured with great forbearance and the country goes about its daily business regardless. This then is the spirit and courage that we as a nation should evince in the face of all Tiger outrages.

[This article was written during the Thoppigala battle. It was not accepted for publication by the newspapers.]

82

A COUNTRY FOR 80 MILLION TAMILS

(The Island, 18th Dec. 2007)

The supremo of the LTTE, Vellupillai wants a country exclusively for 80 millions Tamils, now living spread all over the world. He, of course, would be the self-elected President and Prime Minister of that country! Before proceeding any further, I am reminded of what Lewis Mumford wrote in 1961 in his book "City in History": "that each historic civilization begins with a living, urban core, the polis, and ends in a common graveyard of dust and bones, a Necropolos or a city of the dead; fire-scorched ruins, shattered buildings, empty workshops, heaps of meaningless refuse, the population massacred or driven into slavery". This is almost the present spectacle of the Wanni gangland over which Velu reigns supreme, and that too would be the fate of his greater Eelam with 80 million Tamils if he does manage establish such a country. That Velu is vanity begot and created sick to extol vain pursuits is quite evident.

Velu is, to my mind, a socially dangerous freak of the universe. His malignant aggression, evinced by his destructiveness and cruelty, is not merely a defence against a threat, but is characteristic of this man. Killing and cruelty have become to him pleasurable activities by themselves needing no external stimuli. He pays homage to death by exercising absolute control over the minds and bodies of his cadres, and by daily dispatching them to certain death either as suicide cadres or frontline soldiers. He is incessantly seeking to transform living humans into corpses and destroy for the sake of destruction. How can such a man rule over others except by bullet and terror? An appropriate appellation for his death dealing organization should be "LTTE Murderers Inc."

This absolute control over his cadres and other hapless Tamils under him appears to have infused in him the delusion of omnipotence. This is the reason for his demand for an unattainable greater Eelam for 80 million Tamils. He would next "want the moon" like ***Caligula*** in Albert Camus' play. The figure, 80 million is a figment of his mind. He could not prove this figure.

There are nearly 60 of his 80 million Tamils living in their own country under their own leaders exercising their semi-autonomous political life together with their language rights, and enjoying their cultural life in Tamil Nadu. The overweening arrogance of Velu cannot accept that as satisfying condition of a large majority of Tamils. He wants them all to live under his jackboots owing absolute allegiance and obedience to him. Would any of the Tamils now living in cast-bound Tamil Nadu want Velu as their undisputed leader? Perhaps only a few like Vaiko would want Velu and the greater Tamil Eelam. Other present democratic leaders of Tamil Nadu would not want Velu, the low caste foreigner in their midst as their leader. The powerful Tamil brahmins would reject him wholesale. The fact, however, is that Velu is so ambitious in his own mind and maniacally egotistical in his thinking, that he is calling on all these people to come under his absolutely oppressive suzerainty.

In making this demand, Velu is launching a frontal onslaught on the Union Government in New Delhi and the present Constitution of India. He wants the dismantling of present-day India. Given the many fissiparous active forces in India, this mischievous and ominous call should be taken seriously by India. India needs to revisit its 16th Constitutional Amendment passed by Nehru (in 1963) against the DMK separatists. Velu has also attacked India on other grounds including the Indo-Lanka Accord in his 27th Nov. speech. Mighty India knows what should be done. But will it move a finger?

Most Tamils now living in the western world would not abandon their newly acquired life styles to return to Velu's Eelam. Both materially and socially all these people are well-off beyond their dreams. Would any of them swap their high octane life for a miserable life of slavery and destitution with no freedoms and Human Rights of any kind? Perhaps Velu is dreaming of a situation where the international community would promulgate a present-day Balfour Declaration (this created the modern-day Israel) creating the greater Eelam centered in Sri Lanka. His expectation is that, the Diapora Tamils will then flood his country to make it the newest country to join the UN with a flag full of bullets and a snarling tiger's head. This is the impossible dream for which he has sacrificed hundreds of innocent humans and is determined to continue this obscene violent oblation. His bloated ego needs "an object of devotion to be the focal point of all his strivings and the basis of all his effective—and not only proclaimed—values" (Erich Fromm: The Anatomy of Human Destructiveness). This is his brand new country--the greater Eelam. He would not lay down his life for it, rather, he would kill others or have others killed for it.

In Sri Lanka itself, Velu is now restricted to a very small area of the country with hardly any natural resources. It is mainly a parched area in the north of Sri Lanka full of thorny shrub jungle, where the people eke out a meagre existence from dry land. He has direct control over 3 to 4 lakhs of people, most of whom are dependent on government handouts for their daily sustenance. This population is diminishing at accelerated velocity due both to emigration to government controlled areas, and unforgivable deaths due to his war with the GoSL. A few others live on the salaries and pensions paid by the government. Almost all of them are dependent on the government for their medical needs. The education of their children too is directly dependent on the government to the extent permitted by Velu and his cadres. For, Velu requires these children to fight his war than to grow up as educated valuable citizens of the country. In short, if the government so wishes, it could throttle the life in Velu's tiny eelam by withdrawing all support it now gives to the people living there. That it has not done so is because it knows that they live there under coercion and that they are not all supporters of the LTTE. They are still citizens of this country in dire need. Given this precarious predicament Velu's vision of grandeur lording over a greater Eelam smacks of a brain gone mad beyond redemption. The most suitable remedy for this malignity is a swift regime change in this renegade part of the country. Any GoSL pursuing this policy should be supported wholeheartedly.

There are quite a few lakhs of Tamils living outside Velu's control in the areas south of Sri Lanka. Once greater Eelam is founded, Velu expects them to return to his greater Eelam. Any straw poll of Tamils taken any time any day on any street on Colombo will drive a missile through this unfounded grand vision. In spite of the occasional difficulties and confrontations these Tamils have with the security forces, they will not abandon their comparatively comfortable lives to return to indigent hell hole of Velu. These Tamils are economically, socially and politically well-off. They can get their children educated without sacrificing them to the Sun God. They can protest without fear against the government whenever necessary. They can take their grievances to the Supreme Court and obtain relief. They can get their politicians to stage protest campaigns in the well of the Parliament itself whenever necessary. They can also marshal sympathetic press and electronic media and other civil and religious organizations on their behalf to obtain relief for any unmitigated grievances. All these actions are not possible nor allowed under Velu in his tribal land. Therefore these Tamils will not give up their present lives. Moreover quite many of them did abandon their native north decades before the present armed conflict and their roots are firmly established wherever they now live in the south of the country. To them greater Eelam is a hollow meaningless vision not an attractive proposition beckoning them to prosperity and peace. As they did in 1983, they will not move nor be shifted. This is the reason for the vast investment in buildings by Tamils all over the main towns in the south Sri Lanka.

It is quite clear that Valu wants to tear off Tamil Nadu from India and join it to the Northern and Eastern province of Sri Lanka to found his greater Eelam. If the Malaysian authorities are correct that their Tamil trouble-makers have connection with LTTE, he would be also angling for a portion of that country too, so that his present-day Wijenagar empire would be his undisputed domain. This is truly an unattainable dream of a mad man, and could have been left as idle prattle, but for the fact, that this mad man has got arms, ammunition, death-dealing fanatical cadres and suicidal Black Tigers to pursue his dream. He has to be halted by dealing with him in the same way he deals with others. He is as dangerous to south Asia as Hitler was to Europe.

83

NAKED UNHRC INTERVENTION AD AETERNAM

(The Island, 29th Dec. 2007)

It is axiomatic that Sri Lanka should not be allowed to be the playground of the UN Human Rights Commissioner (UNHRC). We should do our best to put right whatever failures we have had on Human Rights issues in our own convincing and transparent way. In this respect, I suggest the establishment of a mobile Human Rights Police Force exclusively to investigate and to bring to justice the culprits. There should also be especially designated lawyers in every main town to assist this Police force. Further, I would also suggest a Special Human Rights Tribunal, under the aegis of the Supreme Court to dispose of the Human Rights cases as expeditiously as possible and not allow cases to drag on for years. I hope Minister Samarasinghe will take note of my suggestions.

In case the UNHRC does establish its office in Sri Lanka, will it depart from our shores having accomplished its projected task/s? This is the point I want to explore in this short note.

It is likely to be naked intervention ad aeternam (to eternity). The predatory intention of interfering in almost all activities of the government, besides purely Human Rights issues, had been flagged by the various pronouncements of the Commissioner Ms. Louise Arbour. An example being her intention to probe "issues of discrimination and exclusions, gender inequalities, the low participation of women in public and political life, the rights of migrant workers and press freedom". Mind you, feminism started in the west and still flourishes there because of the perceived gender discriminations prevalent there. Therefore Ms.Arbour should have started her probes there first!

In a way almost all legislative and executive activities of the governments in power could have some bearing on the Human Rights of the citizens. Thus her self determined and promulgated remit is really unlimited. This is why UNHRC's stay in this country will not only be entrenched but will also be permanent and its activities will be extended and expanded over and above the issues which prompted the intervention in the first place. It is likely that UNHRC will invent new areas for investigation as they go along so that their stay will have no termination. Are we prepared to accept this situation?

In any case, having monitored the alleged infringements of Human Rights, what else could the UNHRC do? Will they be in a position to put a stop to these alleged abuses as this would be the rationale for their existence in this country. No, the UNHRC will be a spectacular failure in this respect, as it will not have any enforcement powers. Rather, initially, they will invent cases to demonstrate the failure of the government to condemn it as a "failed state", so that a Kosovo type intervention could take place, effectively substituting UN government for Sri Lankan government elected by the people of the country. At most UNHRC will become another ineffective and expensive score-keeper like SLMM. Surely the many anti-Sri Lankan NGOs are now doing this job anyway, so why should we need another glorified effete body to do the same work? Is it to find excuses to punish the government of the day and the people of this country by slinging at us unsubstantiated allegations of Human Rights violations?

At the point of initial entry the UNHRC will set its own agenda with probably a verbal agreement. If the government had the presence of mind to insist on a written agenda/ agreement, it will be cleverly crafted so that the ambiguities would lend themselves to many interpretations and conclusions. This will be a deliberate ploy to expand UNHRC's activities into areas of social politics ad libitum (at pleasure). From experience we do know that whatever country the UN entered, there they remained for ages without solving the problems they were expected to resolve. Sri Lanka will be no exception, and once here, the UNHRC will find many issues and new ones at that, to intervene and therefore remain here forever and a day.

According to The Island of 21st Dec.07, Cambodian authorities have branded the UN Human Rights envoy (Mr.Yash Ghai) as an unacceptable arrogant official. He has "heaped criticism on the government for alleged rights violations and called the judiciary 'a perversity'". The Cambodian government has accused him of focusing only on the negatives and ignoring the government's efforts to address human rights concern. Rings familiar, does it not? The Prime Minister, Hun Sen has vowed never to meet this envoy.

There are also the personal monetary interests involved for the personnel of the UNHRC and its local crony NGOs. With their dollar salaries and dollar per diem allowances, they could live luxury lives like lords of the manor, in expensive hotels in a country with benign weather, and have their children educated in well known public schools and prestigious universities at home; the contrast being, engaging in Human Rights work in a god-forsaken country in Africa or dangerous countries like Iraq or Afganistan. It is patently clear that job security and survival are potent factors that will motivate the UNHRC men/women to perpetuate their "jobs" in Sri Lanka sine die (without end). I have no compunction in asserting that once the UHHRC is in our country, it will not depart unless we throw it out bodily. Which government will have the gumption to do that, given our indebtedness to many international organizations?

This reminds me of what happened to the Kandyans in 1815. They invited the British to enter their country to get rid of the local king who had become a tyrant. The job was done but an Agreement was signed to enable the British to stay put in the Kandyan kingdom indefinitely and impose their rules and laws on us. They did so with impunity for the next one hundred and fifty years!! "The Kandyans used to inquire when the English intended to return to the maritime provinces. 'You have now' said one, 'deposed the king and nothing more is required, you may leave us'. The local (English) administration was a foreign yoke and was regarded with aversion by all classes and ranks of the people" (Henry Marshall: A General Description of the Island). This will be the fate of UNHRC. The country and its hapless citizens will remain entrapped by the UNHRC on one side trying to condemn our country as a "failed state" and the Tamil Tiger terrorists on the other.

The conclusion is clear, keep the UNHRC away from our shores and deal with Human Rights infringements in an effective manner in our own way.

84

LIFE AFTER THE ABROGATION OF CFA

(The Island, 22nd Jan. 2008)

The vociferous noises and lamentations against the abrogation of CFA came from the UNP, the anti-national NGOs and some western countries with vested interests. They have predicted doom and gloom on Sri Lanka as a result of this abrogation. This remains to be seen, though hard times ahead cannot be denied. They also predicted Armageddon when the army took on LTTE in Mavil Aru and chased them out of the east, but this did not materialize. These NGO Jeramiahs did not see nor hear the doom and gloom that prevailed in the country while the CFA existed. The country should move on leaving these mercenary soothsayers to bark for their dollars and kroners in Lipton roundabout. They are yesterday's conflict-resolution amateurs, who miserably failed in their avowed objective of resolving the conflict in the country, even after spending millions on seminars and meetings in five-star hotels both in Sri Lanka and abroad! They will now try to manoeuvre the fall of government in order to stop the army's drive to end Velu's terrorism in the country. This should not be allowed to succeed.

There are many unacceptable clauses in the CFA as pointed out by many commentators (self included) from the time it was signed in 2002. The CFA badly compromised the territorial integrity of the country by providing for the demarcation of the country, by recognizing the LTTE's terrorist army, and by allowing greenhorn foreigners to arbitrate and decide on the demarcation of the territory between the sovereign government and a terrorist outfit. There was no "safety net" here. Instead the CFA entrapped the legitimate government of the country, forcing it to yield not only territory but also de facto exclusive power over that territory to the terrorist LTTE. We are now not saddled with this odious agreement any more. We have at last regained our true independence and sovereignty. Many benefits as well as obligations follow from this annulment of the CFA.

Because of the CFA, many foreigners arrogated to themselves the power to interfere in our affairs. They made pilgrimages to the Wanni to pay obeisance to the LTTE and for consulting the LTTE without any reference to the government. On return from the Wanni these foreigners made ex-cathedra statements on the conflict mostly favouring the LTTE and to debilitate and demoralize our legitimate security forces. This cannot happen anymore nor should it be allowed to happen. The Foreign Office should take the necessary steps to prevent this happening. The fact that Co-Chairs had requested from the government open access to LTTE in the Wanni, is evidence enough that the government now has the option to deny that access and to impose conditions for the privilege. However, this power should be exercised with caution without jeopardizing our good relations with the world outside.

The Co-Chair status for some countries have no foundation for their existence any more. These countries should be reminded in no uncertain terms that Sri Lanka is an independent country and should be treated that way. That their genuine efforts and advice would be considered in depth, but the decisions on any of them would be entirely based on furthering the interest of the country. In short, the CFA gave them the opportunity to interfere in the internal affairs of the country, the CFA is now buried, it follows therefore, that these countries should also stop poking their noses into our affairs. If they do, they should be told to stop it and we should marshal our friends in the UN to complain against such unwarranted interference. Here we have a good example of how once we allow foreigners to get involved in the affairs of the country, they persist and try to impose their agenda on us, even after we take the necessary steps and follow the accepted procedures to terminate their services. So keep the foreigners out of our affairs, all trespassers should be bundled out of the country.

The facilitation function of Norway should be stopped forthwith. The fact is they have failed in their effort to bring peace to this country because of their overtly partisan approach to peace-making. Their former Prime Minister, Mr.Jagland did admit recently in The Aften-Posten newspaper, that their failure in all the peace efforts they engaged in, was due to their arrogant approach to the problems, and that this arrogance was fuelled by the petro-dollars. Norway will not like this situation and will endeavour to use its influence with other Nordic countries and the EU to hurt Sri Lanka economically by resorting to all sorts of trade restrictions and anti-Sri Lanka resolutions in UN bodies. Our Foreign Office has to be vigilant as well as pro-active on an overtime basis, to both anticipate as well as counter the strategies of an offended and vindictive Norway. Norway is unlikely to retire hurt and wounded. It would be planning a come-back even by manipulating our greedy MPs with petro-dollars to topple the present government and then offering its services as the saviour of the country. Anathema to them!

The country was entrapped by the promise of 4.5 billion dollars loan to partition the country between the LTTE and the rest, giving the LTTE a totally disproportionate area of the country as well as the sea. The fact that we have lived and survived without this loan is ample proof that we can continue to do so in the future. In fact, if these creditor-nations are genuine in their desire to help the country, they do have an excellent opportunity here and now in the eastern province. They can help in the material rebuilding and development of this province and the establishment of strong local democratic institutions there. Why have they not come forward? Could it be that such a move would militate against their hidden agenda as regards the future of this country?

There is now only one army and one nation. Anyone else claiming the existence of another country within Sri Lanka protected by another army has neither the right nor the legitimacy to exist. No country in the world would allow such a situation. Therefore the GoSL should take all measures necessary to eliminate this parasitical menace. I have full confidence that our security forces have the ability and capacity to accomplish this task, notwithstanding the outcry from some foreigners, diplomats and anti-national NGOs that LTTE cannot be defeated. Temporary set-backs would not deter our determined security forces. The nation should lend full support to this urgent and monumental task by refraining from strikes, and bearing up with understanding the temporary economic cost of war. The jumbo cabinet should also lend support by surrendering at least half their salaries and perks. After all our ministers are all very rich persons, surely at least for once, for the sake of the country, they could lead the way by this not so big a sacrifice for them.

The government too has many obligations to fulfill resulting from the abrogation of CFA. The foremost duty at the moment is the restoration of democracy and rule of law in the liberated eastern province. It appears that armed gangs rule and near anarchy is prevailing there. This is completely unacceptable. The gangs should be disarmed, the police should take over and the thugs should be brought to book. All the sacrifices made by the army to liberate it from the LTTE will become futile if another section of terrorists takes control of the same. This is now a handle for the nosey-parkers of the UN to beat us into submission for their foothold in the country.

Local election in the eastern province is evidence of prevailing democracy only if it is held under peaceful conditions without intimidation and fear for one's life. The reports coming from the east are indicative of a violent atmosphere leading to a corrupt and rigged election. If this happens the government will totally fail to convince anyone that the fight against the LTTE is the liberation of the Tamil people. Whereas, a democratically elected and functioning local government would be the unassailable evidence of government's good intention and effort to bring about peace in the country.

The other obligation of the government is the assurance of safety of Tamil people living elsewhere in the country. This is a very difficult job given the level of infiltration of the LTTE in the south. Extra sensitivity should be brought to bear in the hunt for terrorists and laid down procedures should be minutely and scrupulously followed, and if mistakes are made a sincere apology with compensation should be made. Most Tamil citizens of this country know that the LTTE is making use of them without their consent every time they explode a claymore bomb in the south. We do need these people to be on our side if we want to successfully defeat the LTTE.

The government also has obligation to protect the rest of the population and do everything possible to lighten the economic burden likely to fall on the people due to the ongoing conflict. All abductions and Human Rights violations should be hunted down and justice should be meted out to the thugs involved. All foreign junkets by the President and ministers should be ended. The anti-corruption unit should be given the power to initiate inquiries on its own without reference to it by others. It should be set a bi-annual objective and failure to achieve it should automatically trigger a change of personnel. The tax system needs to be reviewed not only to reduce or abolish taxes that burden the people but also to bring into the tax-net all those who have been so far unfairly exempt from taxation. The burden of taxation should be borne equitably by the people of this country. This will enable at least the reduction of taxes on some essential goods and services. Hard times are ahead. For the sake of the country we should grin and bear it and look forward to making our country non dependent on foreign loans and aid that come with humiliating strings attached. The fight is on not only in the Wanni but also in the south. The country expects the government and its Ministers to lead the way.

85

WHAT MAN HAS PUT TOGETHER MAN CAN ALSO RENT IT ASUNDER

(The island, 6th Feb. 2008)

With the help of lethal weapons and a fanatical hard core of LTTE cadres, Velu did put together an illegitimate administration of sorts in some parts of our country. He had Gestapo-like police stations, Kangaroo courts, extortionate fiscal system and an atrocious educational system to brainwash the young. He also had an army, navy and a couple of small planes. His acolytes in Sri Lanka and abroad claimed that this was a de facto state and demanded recognition and legitimacy for this all-apparent oppressive dictatorship of a ruthless despot. Ranil, as PM of this country, accorded this privilege to Velu by signing the CFA. Ranil had mortgaged the future of country to which he had no rightful claim without any effort to consult the wishes or the desires of the people or their representatives. This was the beginning of a journey to absurdity for the country, while, for Velu, it created the golden opportunity to advance and enhance his claim for Eelam. A jubilant Velu probably hailed us "vive le fous"(long live the nuts)!! Not we, but the UNP of Ranil did richly deserve this harangue!!

However, the edifice put together by Velupillai Pirapakaran was a very dangerous one. If it was allowed to stand and be reinforced by his murderous cadres, the consequences would have been calamitous for the country. The nation-state of Sri Lanka would have collapsed. We would have had two states in perpetual armed conflict and foreign interlopers dictating and determining our destiny. Therefore Velu's efforts had to be thwarted and his mini-state had to be demolished. Removal of Velu will bring us peace to the extent that the guns he wielded will fall silent, but more importantly, there will then prevail suitable ambience for concluding with all concerned citizens a lasting peace.

The abrogation of CFA was one of the necessary demolition jobs. This abrogation gave the message to the world that we are not prepared to co-exist with a terrorist rag-bag and share this country with them unconditionally. By the same token we have demonstrated that the LTTE and Tamil citizens are two separate entities, and that, if any political accommodation is required, it will be with the Tamil citizens of this country in a manner agreeable to all communities in this country. The LTTE will then have to join the crowd as another interested and reformed party.

The other consequence of this abrogation is the elimination of institutional terrorism in this country. This necessarily entails the defeat of the LTTE which is the fount of all terrorism in this country. The multi-front attack on LTTE positions on land and sea combined with aerial bombardment of all LTTE's military assets are, in my view, the right approach to the demolition job on hand. In this process, if GoSL is lucky enough to eliminate the LTTE hierarchy and Velu himself, then the demise of Eelam would be a certainty. This is the compelling reason for the full support we should extend to our forces. They have done it in the Eastern province, they will certainly do it in the Wanni probably much sooner than expected. The ratchet effect of defeat after defeat on many fronts would be the total collapse of the morale of the many hastily trained unwilling fighters among the LTTE cadres. It is not beyond reason for us to expect them to simply put down their weapons, walk out of their bunkers one day and surrender to the GoSL forces. In this respect, it is the duty of our army to encourage defection by suitable propaganda in the Wanni. This is a notable failure on the part of the Government's propaganda institutions. This is the opportune moment to engender disaffection among the LTTE cadres.

Earlier the GoSL security forces had reclaimed the vast Eastern province from LTTE's grip. It was here that Velu was intending to establish his capital city with the necessary deep water harbour and probably an international airport at Hingurakgoda. This part of his dream house has collapsed together with all the infra-structure of his courts, police stations, revenue departments and inhuman Gulag-type cells and prisons. The people under his thraldom voted with their feet, abandoned him, and are now on their way to building their democratic institutions. Over 800 candidates, some of them probably terrorists of yesteryear, are prepared to participate in the democratic process of local elections which, given the recent violent past, could be physically dangerous to the candidates. It is the duty of the government to create the environment for a free and fair election by disarming all those with arms. A free and fair election and fully functioning local government in the east would not only deal a death punch to the LTTE's Eelam, but would also demonstrate to the world, that democracy can prevail against terrorism. The world should support this born-again democratic exercise undertaken in very difficult circumstances.

Another counter punch to LTTE's terrorism is the political arrangements necessary to bring to an end the festering wounds caused by the demands for satiation of aspirations and elimination of grievances. This is an impossible exercise. Aspirations of anyone, minority or not, can be staked up as high as high heavens, therefore no country in the world has even attempted to satisfy the political aspirations of minorities within their borders. The same is true of tiny Sri Lanka. Some grievances can be mental formations. Until and unless those afflicted with these mental aberrations are themselves prepared to seek a suitable mental remedy for those afflictions, little can be done by others to cure them. Outsiders can only submit persuasive arguments, substantiated wherever possible with facts, to help these people to disabuse themselves and accept reality for what it is. Thus for instance, economic deprivation and under-development, educational handicaps and lack of job opportunities are not piled upon the Tamils only, they are also the lot of a vast number of Sinhalese and Muslims living all over the country. Peace is necessary for economic development, and this development would lead to all-round advancement of all citizens. Therefore while the army is doing its job, the authorities should put together a political plan for installation at the termination of the armed conflict. It would be inexcusable on the part of any political party not to engage in this exercise.

For the moment the 13th Amendment to the Constitution together with the Provincial council system has been proposed as a solution by the APRC. I have strong reservations on this proposal for many reasons. A discussion of these reasons will lead to a long digression away from the objective of this essay. But for practical purposes, I do accept the fact that this is now part of the law of the land, and as democrats, we have got to abide by the law of the land. It is from this perspective I would urge the political players to consider this body of law already available and ready to be implemented.

Given the fact that the now functioning Provincial governments in the south of the country have failed us and have become white elephants to the tax-payers, there is no guarantee that this same system will be successful in the north and the east. Nevertheless, with hindsight experience of the failures of Provincial councils in existence, the new councils could be better adopted to serve the needs of the people. Therefore it is worth a try.

As required, a free and fair referendum after the guns fall silent, will decide the question of merging the two provinces and will provide the opportunity to think out of the box created by the colonial British, and recast the provinces based on the needs of the people of the area. The creation of ethnic ghettos will only serve diabolical agendas of the racists among us. Segregation based on race or religion of people will lead us to future trouble and should be avoided at all costs. Shia, Sunni and Christian enclaves have not saved Lebanon, the respective demagogues are at one another's throats tearing apart the country at the same time. Similarly the alienation of crown land to the provinces will have to be implemented with due care for the generations still unborn. The unborn future millions of Sri Lankans cannot be deprived of land to live and earn a living in any part of the country of their birth. The delegation of police powers needs to be done on a graduated scale, so that the few frustrated yet active LTTE cadres, if any, would not use these powers to stage a come-back.

It is unwise to appoint politicians as advisors to the Governor of the northern Province. Politicians, by and large, are self-serving corrupt persons. They corrupt even the best of systems set up to serve the people. Therefore the Governor should be given a free hand to elect a very limited number of qualified and experienced persons, not necessarily politicians, to help him in the rebuilding and development of the province until such time that elections are held for the local and provincial councils in the north.

Let me end by quoting the Tamil sage Valluvar " money and means, time, place and deed; decide these five and then proceed" (675) "It's a country which has souls of worth; unfailing yields and ample worth" (731) Thirukkural.

86

COULD YOU BECOME A CITIZEN OF NOWHERE?

(The Island, 4th Mar.2008)

The thunderous answer, I expect, would be 'no way man'. Yet the reader would not be surprised to be told that there are Sri Lankans in and outside the country working towards this end and to enrich themselves in the process of disembowelling the country. They are the modern traitorous collaborators working for dollars, dispatching secret documents to their foreign panjandrums, full of debatable and doctored information to crucify the country on trumped up charges of Human Rights violations. Thus recently, The Human Rights Commission of Sri Lanka (HRCSL) was demoted from Status "A" to Status "B" based on the reports submitted to the International HR Commission by a coterie of Sri Lankan NGOs, only five of them were properly registered with the Director of NGOs, ten with Registrar of Companies and seventeen of them were non-entities with no legal recognition for operation in Sri Lanka. The protests and representations of HRCSL itself were ignored. It is a great tribute to our democratic freedom, however defective, that we allow these vultures to ply their perfidious trade. It is traitorous acts of this kind that has made the Serbs of northern Kosovo citizens of nowhere today. The same fate awaits the Sinhalese and Muslims in the east if we allow separatism in Sri Lanka.

Before proceeding I need to explain why I consider all our citizens not engaged in terrorism or underhand NGO work to be true patriots, with warts and all, of this country. We are all contextual individuals. We belong to a family, a school, a professional organization, a club a church or temple or a mosque. We work in association with others. We have varying degrees of loyalties to each of these organizations. Encompassing all is "the nation conceived as a project, a project somehow or other brought to birth in the past and carried on so that a morally distinctive community was brought into being which embodied a claim to political autonomy in its various organized and institutionalized expressions" (Alasdair Macintyre, Moral and political philosopher). As patriots we are committed to a particular way of linking our past which has conferred on us a distinctive moral and political identity beckoning us to perpetuate it in the nation that is ours, and for international recognition, project it to other nations. We owe unconditional allegiance to this project and shoulder unavoidable responsibility to make it flourish forever no matter the difficulties encountered on the way. This is true patriotism.

Patriotism is not allegiance to a particular leader or a form of government. Patriotic allegiance is conditional upon that leader and the government fulfilling the expectations of the patriots as stated above. At this tragic moment in our history, LTTE's terrorism is engaged in frustrating and destroying this ***"project Sri Lanka"***. This government is determined to eliminate this terrorism. It is therefore right for all patriots to support the government in this hazardous exercise, and all others who secretly plot to subvert the efforts of the government, are by definition, traitors and enemies of Sri Lanka. The use of force against the political sovereignty and territorial integrity by the LTTE is naked aggression and the government is justified on two counts, in violently responding to this aggression. The first is self-defense by the victim and the other is law enforcement by the victim. Only the state has the "monopoly of the legitimate use of physical force within its territory" (Max Webber). From this it follows that only the state has the exclusive right to protect its citizens from any infringement of rights by the use of violent means. It is proper for any nation to join in this effort and not intervene to stop it. Given the terrorist nature of the LTTE, the least other nations could do, if they cannot not help us, is to refrain from interference in our endeavour to eliminate terrorism in this country.

This is where I am against all those false missionaries preaching to us the old colonial doctrine (see below) of "responsibility to protect" or R2P. In recent times, the NATO went into Serbia after having destroyed the infra-structure of that country by indiscriminate bombing, with

R2P in one hand and the machine gun in the other. This venture today appears to have ended by appeasing the separatist Hashim Thraci, (once a condemned terrorist of the West and now the PM of Kosovo), by creating Kosovo as an independent and sovereign state, against the provisions of the UN Charter and the Resolution 1244 of June 1999 reaffirming the territorial integrity and sovereignty of the Balkan states. This unilateral declaration at one stroke made Serbs still living in north and south Kosovo, citizens of nowhere, as they do not recognize their independent new country and its citizenship, and as they are deemed by the Muslim Kosovans of the new country to have lost their old Serbian citizenship. This could well happen to our country to our Sinhalese, Muslims in the east and the Tamils in the south, if we allow interlopers with vested interests and probably in the pay of LTTE into our country. The NGOs clamouring for UN intervention in our affairs are our fifth column saboteurs and collaborators in the project to destroy Sri Lanka. They stand condemned as their end-game is probably the creation of Eelam with Velu as PM and Predident!

The Portuguese came to this country to save our souls. But they plundered, pillaged and slaughtered our ancestors and forcibly occupied a part of the country for nearly one hundred and fifty years. The Dutch came to protect us from the depredations of the Portuguese. They too ravaged and exploited the resources of the country and waged war on the Kandyans. They too forcibly occupied a part of the country for another one hundred and fifty years. The British followed the Dutch. Governor North in 1815 actually invoked the R2P doctrine in his declaration of war on the Kandyans. The war, he declared "was for the deliverance of the Kandyan people from their oppressors and for offering protection to every Kandyan who was prepared to welcome their deliverers" (Emmerson Tennent, An Account of the Island, p.89). The British too plundered, pillaged, slaughtered men, women, children and animals and used scorched earth policy to subdue the unwilling Kandyans. They too forcibly occupied the country for another one hundred and fifty years. With such stark lessons of history staring at our faces, it would be wholly irresponsible and totally unacceptable to allow any international interloper to step into our country with the ostensible intention of engaging in R2P work.

There are probably persons in eminent positions in international institutions and multi-national companies sitting in secret conclaves deciding the fate of vulnerable countries. They first send their hit-men/women to get the selected country graded as a failed state in economic terms. Then with the help of local collaborators they fish for information to condemn the country as having failed to maintain even the minimum of Humanitarian Laws and Human Rights. By this time their contacts in the networks are activated to usher in Resolutions in the UN for physical intervention in the country concerned on the basis of R2P. All these become easy if the victim country is already in the throes of armed struggle against a terrorist outfit as in Sri Lanka, and if this terrorist outfit has already infiltrated the cabal deciding the fate of the country. The LTTE has excellent contacts in high places and are also well known for buying influence as was exposed in their attempted bribing of US government Agents. The first step was taken as regards Sri Lanka last year. There were many persons publicly proclaiming that Sri Lanka was a failed state even though the economy was growing at 7% according to the Central Bank. Even if you reduce this figure by half, it was still a better performance than many countries in the world including some in the EU. This propaganda has not petered out because the government keeps borrowing dollar funds in the commercial market at high commercial rates. The government certainly needs to rein in its desire to guzzle dollars.

The second phase of Human Rights violations is in full swing now even though it has yet not been proved that the government was directly connected with any of the allegations. The manufacture of such evidence becomes easy once R2P Offices are established in this country under the UN mandate and beyond the control of our legally constituted institutions. I suspect a well hatched conspiracy is being enacted not only to stop our efforts to eliminate LTTE's terrorism, but also to vivisect the country and hand over a large part of it to Velu. The government should be firm in its determination to keep out the false R2P missionaries and mercenaries.

What can the ordinary people do to protect our country? One, whatever job you are doing now do it well so as to be satisfied that you really earned your day's wage. Second, abstain from unnecessary strikes at work places. Third, do not indulge in gossip or believe in gossip as regards our armed forces. Fourth, help our armed forces in whatever way possible and within your means when called upon by the authorities. Fifth, be vigilant at all times as the LTTE is stalking us at all times in the most unexpected places. By doing these five simple things you are furthering the cause of project Sri Lanka and to that extent you are a true patriot.

87

"THERE IS NO MILITARY SOLUTION" - GO TELL THAT TO NATO

(The Island, 3rd Apr. 2008)

I might also add "go tell that to President Sarkozy of France" for, he will be sending additional French troops to Afganistan soon! Every conflict has a solution however long it takes. That end is the very end of the conflict itself. The World wars, the Korean war, the Vietnam war, the Vietnam war against Cambodia's Pol Pot, the Peruvian war against the Sandanista did have the end of defeat for the enemy and was followed by the restoration of peace. Why prevent Sri Lanka from following a similar course especially when the government, the majority of citizens and the soldiers are yearning for the defeat of the terrorist LTTE and the dawn of peace in the country?

Can our NGO Dollar hungry bosses justify the invasion of northern Iraq by Turkey, a member of twenty-one nations NATO, with NATO supplied arms and kill Kurds if there was no military solution to their problems? If there is no military solution why is NATO fighting in Afganistan even after Al Queda extended an invitation to talk peace? If there is no military solution why are the allied forces fighting in Iraq at enormous cost in men, material and money? It is not a matter of friendly war games in these two countries. It is a paramount urgency to kill as well as debilitate the perceived enemy before he kills others. It is also propelled by the desire to impose a solution economically and politically favourable to the invaders of both Afganistan and Iraq. We saw this starkly illustrated in Kosovo.

The province of Kosovo within Serbia had an ethnic and a religious problem which degenerated to a terrorist problem. The UN and NATO forced the Serbians to talk peace with Kosovars. It took them nowhere and Kosovo was brought under UN control, but as terrorism continued unabated, the Serbs fought back with equal ferocity. NATO then ignored all niceties of diplomacy, flouted international law and guarantees of territorial integrity, and cast aside the UN itself, and unilaterally resorted to a military solution. NATO bombed Serbia continuosly for over two months into submission. It destroyed roads, bridges, communication centres and TV networks, schools, hospitals and government buildings and factories. It killed many Serbian civilian citizens. It captured the perceived enemy, the Serbian President Mr. Milosovic. In short this military adventure was a success and had the eventual solution in the unilateral declaration of independence of Kosovo from Serbia. Economically this solution was favourable to NATO as oil from the Caspian Sea could be routed through Kosovo and access was now available to exploit the vast mineral resources in Kosovo. Politically, as a new ally of NATO, Kosovo could be pitted against Russia if and when necessary, as evidenced by the huge US army base being constructed and expanded in Bondsteel within Kosovo. So who says there is no military solution to problems? Is it the case that military solutions ought to be pursued and are acceptable only if executed by NATO and the EU? No, the rich and the mighty are not the sole inheritors of this planet.

Vellupillai Pirapakaran believes in a military solution, and in fact, he recently announced that he will obtain a Kosovo-type solution for his Eelam. One ought to accept his obdurate consistency in resorting to both terrorist and military action to create his dream Eelam. Velu appears to be convinced that the profits to be won by war outweigh the risk and losses to be incurred. The government, however, cannot accept this loss and is forced to face the danger and endeavour to eliminate it. As far as we know the NGOs, the INGOs, the Foreign VIPs and other Human Rights Hypocrites have yet to tell him directly that there is no military solution, that he should lay down his arms and seek negotiation. Only Mr. Anadasangaree has directly and publicly told him that there is no military solution and that he should seek peace by laying down his arms. This advice has been ignored by the warlord. Given this situation why should a democratically elected government not meet force with force and defeat the enemy?

Nearly two centuries ago a savant advised his countrymen that all those who desire peace should prepare for war (Qui desiderat pacem, praeparet bellum). This applies most cogently to the modern world as it is beset with insidious terrorism on all fronts. The objective of the present military campaign of the government is simply the defeat of LTTE terrorism in our land. It is clearly not directed at Tamils. This is verifiably true, because the Security Forces are engaged in mortal combat only in the areas under the control of the LTTE. The Tamils living elsewhere live as normal a life as other Sri Lankans, enjoying the same social benefits of free education and healthcare and suffering the same economic hardships. The majority of the people, the entirety of the security forces and the government of the day do believe that the LTTE can be and ought to be defeated and guns ought to be silenced first for peace to emerge. There can be no peace so long as Velu controls land and retains armed cadres ready to kill and destroy property at his behest. The eastern province is an outstanding example of prevailing peace after the LTTE guns have been silenced. It is on the road to normality through the residual debris of post LTTE terrorism.

It will certainly take time for the eastern province to revert to democratic normality by way of elections to local bodies. In the meantime we should expect demands and posturing for positions of power and prestige by various interested parties based on communal ethnicity. One can only advise our misguided politicians that the economic and social development of the eastern province is for all persons living there and therefore cannot be confined to one ethnic community as against another. This was the sectarianism we had under the LTTE. This was what our soldiers got rid of at great sacrifice of their lives and limbs, therefore we simply cannot go back to this decadent state of affairs. The local eastern politicians should grab this opportunity to usher in a political culture de novo wherein every one counts. This process will be greatly helped if the TMVP cadres do surrender their weapons voluntarily and are then provided security by the government.

I do believe that there is a military solution to our terrorist problem. Military force is necessary to eliminate terrorism and the persons prosecuting terrorism in our country. I do accept that our Security

Forces have the capacity, ability and the motivation to defeat the LTTE as they did in the eastern province. Once this is achieved, there will be the suitable ambience and space available to initiate a political arrangement that will satisfy, if not all the people all the time, at least most of the people most of the time. This is the democracy of everyman as practised everywhere.

In the case of Serbia/Kosovo the NATO acted as the prosecutor, judge, jury and executioner in punishing the Serbs for the mistakes of their politicians. We see a similar posturing taking place in the case of Sri Lanka's mortal combat against, as per FBI, the most ruthless terrorists in the world today. The arbitrators of our fate have been the NGO and the INGO supported countries in the EU. They are holding the Democles Sword of Human Rights and the colonial doctrine of Right to Protect over our heads to punish our country economically by withdrawing the privilege of GSP+ for our Apparel Manufacturers. Unfortunately the Human Rights situation in Sri Lanka did deteriorate and did provide the opportunity for these counterfeit moralists to take the country to task. Now the situation has vastly improved and many impartial institutions are in place and active to improve as well as prevent the flagrant infringement of Human Rights of people. No recognition has been accorded to these improvements, or any allowances made for the plight of the people blighted by terrorism. We have been repeatedly warned that there is no military solution to our problem and the military campaign against the LTTE should be stopped. As pointed out above, these very same countries do have military campaigns and ignore the Human Rights of the people of the countries they have invaded. This is the disgraceful hypocrisy of some of the rich and powerful nations in the west. They will certainly add to their crime of snobbish arrogance and uncaring irresponsibility if they do withdraw the GSP+ to the thousands of indigent women workers in the Garment industry in Sri Lanka. What has the EU got to gain by punishing ordinary working women just so to appease the LTTE which they have condemned and banned as a terrorist organization?

88

QUESTIONS FOR Ms. BENITA FERRERO-WALDNER

(The Island, 9th Apr.2008)

9th Apr.08.

Ms. Benita Ferrero-Waldner,
EU External Relations Chief,
EU HQ,
Brussels

Dear Madam,

QUESTIONS FOR Ms. BENITA FERRERO-WALDNER

As EU's External Relations Chief, thank you for your condemnation of the suicide attack which killed Minister Fernandopulle and fourteen civilians and injured many other bystanders. The Sri Lankan newspaper readers did, however, note that you failed to make any mention of the well known source of this suicide attack, let alone condemn that source by name. That name is LTTE, in case it is absent in your vocabulary. We also noted that you failed even to make a request that these murderous activities should stop forthwith.

As on many previous occasions, again you wanted the government to negotiate for a political solution This is easily said than done and thus the following questions for your considered answer:

1) Could you tell us how the government can negotiate with LTTE who have walked out of negotiations on flimsy reasons? When they did walk out in Geneva why did the EU fail to urge them to get back to negotiating?

2) Could you tell us what we have got to negotiate on when the LTTE wants nothing but a separatist Eelam? Have you by chance

persuaded them to give up Eelam so that negotiation is possible?

3) Is it your view that we should negotiate Eelam? The vivisection of the country? The surrender of a disproportionate part of the country to the terrorists you failed to name in your condemnation?

4) Can we know the political settlement EU expects us to negotiate? Or should I say, wants to impose on Sri Lanka? Would this not be undemocratic, and against the Human Rights of all the citizens of Sri Lanka?

5) Why is NATO fighting in Afganistan without negotiating a political settlement with Taleban and Al Queda? Have you also publicly advised the EU members of NATO to negotiate as you frequently do in the case of Sri Lanka?

6) How come that thousands of soldiers from EU countries are bombing and killing Iraq citizens without negotiating a settlement? Is this not contrary to the wishes of the citizens of those same EU countries?

7) Have you publicly advised Israel to negotiate with Hamas in Gaza rather than bomb and kill those Palestinians?

8) Why do you always keep badgering and pestering the government even when it gets hit badly by the LTTE? Why no such needling of LTTE the perpetrator of mass murder?

9) The Austrian citizens recently held vigil all over Austia to expiate themselves from the shame and blame for allowing the fatherland to be gobbled up by Hitler and the Nazification of the people and to express their firm determination never to allow such a thing to happen again. What then is wrong when we Sri Lankans take up arms to fight the fascist LTTE and the Tamil Hitler and take all measures to prevent the same downfall and ravage of the country as was experienced by Austria?

10) Unlike NATO in Afganistan, and the Allied forçes in Iraq, Sri Lankan forces are not fighting in a foreign country. We are fighting for our democracy, our Human Rights and the preservation of our

country as one and only Sri Lanka. What exactly is wrong in this our struggle against LTTE terrorists?

I have many more questions but I shall stop here as you are probably busy trying to repair the damage done to international law and the UN itself, by the despicable and disgraceful conduct of EU in Kosovo.

This letter will reach you in the near future and I hope you will kindly oblige me the answers.

Yours truly,

Durand Appuhamy. (Sri Lanka)

(Needless to say, no answers were tendered)

89

LIFE, LIBERTY AND PROPERTY

(The Island, 12th June 2008)

From very ancient times most political philosophers have accepted life, liberty and property as fundamental rights of man. Some considered them to be the solid foundation of the capitalist system. It is my intention to explore the concept of property in this short article while casting a passing glance at life and liberty in Sri Lanka.

The right to life begins at conception in mother's womb. Though some might dispute this statement, I take it as a convenient starting point for this essay. Once conceived, the baby has the right to unhindered life till natural death. The baby should be given the opportunity to develop its personality to lead a satisfying life to itself and the society. Education, training and ethical behaviour in society become crucial to this important project.

There are many laws in our country protecting the lives of individuals. The flaws stare at us at the enforcement level of these laws. Mexico City is supposed to be the abduction capital in the world with one abduction taking place every ninety seconds. Yet it is not headline world news because almost all abductions are for ransom by criminal gangs, and because the Mexican police force has been successful in catching the criminals. We too have many abductions and kidnappings in this country. Many of them are by criminal gangs looking for easy ransom. Only a few have been caught so far. Some abductions have been attributed to the Security Forces without any substantiating evidence except the flimsy circumstantial evidence of "this could not have happened without the cooperation/knowledge of the Security forces". Nevertheless, many people have disappeared into thin air after having been abducted by unknown persons all over this country. Whether the government or the Security Forces are directly involved or not in these abductions, the government will be held responsible to the extent that it failed to give protection to these victims, and also because it has failed to catch the culprits and free the victims. The accusing finger will ineluctably point at the Security Forces. Thus the accusation that a sense of impunity prevails will stick so long as the government fails in its primary task of protecting the lives of its citizens. It is right that we rave and rant against the government for this dereliction of its duty by the citizens. A Special Anti-Kidnap Task Force is a dire necessity to solve these crimes urgently. Until then, the government will remain accused and under deep suspicion.

In another realistic sense there is no right to life for anyone in this country. So long as Vellupillai Pirapakaran (VP) is alive. He can kill anyone at his will and fancy with impunity as he had been doing for the last thirty years. His ears are deaf to protests. Bogus Human Rights activists in Sri Lanka and the many foreigners trading in Human Rights simply ignore the depredations of VP. There are no dollars to be extracted from castigating a terrorist who is only a militant in their parlance. The cost-free rhetoric of ritual condemnation by these self-appointed high priests of Human Rights only encourages VP to commit more beastly crimes against humanity.

There is liberty of sorts in this country. There is liberty to live wherever you want in this country except in the LTTE gangland. There is liberty to engage in trade, industry and profession of one's choice. There is freedom to practice one's religion without hindrance. However, the freedom to express one's opinion has become a conflict zone. This is all the more so where opinions concern the military operations against the LTTE. So long as the government remains a democracy, then freedom of expression is imperative aspect of life. At the same time as the government is involved in a "do-or-die" battle against a ruthless terrorist outfit to preserve the country in one piece, there ought to be some restraints on full freedom of expression. I would suggest that journalists carefully weigh the following factors before broadcasting their opinions/facts. (1) Will LTTE gain advantage over the army by the revelation? (2) Will the revelation demoralize the soldiers? (3) Is the revelation actually a fact or a mere slanderous and libelous opinion? (4) What has motivated the revelation? (5) Is there an alternative course of action where corruption and abuse of power are involved? and finally, (6) is it necessary for the public know what has been revealed at this moment in time? and in what way would the public benefit by the revelation?

A confrontational press is most necessary in a democracy in normal times. But it becomes a potent instrument to flay the government in times of national conflict as in the situation today. Therefore, some restraint is called for on the part of the journalists and it is incumbent on the government to bring to book all those involved in attacking and killing the journalists. Political thugs and goons cannot be allowed to act as censors of freedom of expression.

Private property is necessary for the development of the autonomy, the ethical personality and the capacity for responsible agency of al individuals, even though, Pierre-Joseph Proudhon regarded it as theft. He probably foresaw the accumulation of ill-gotten wealth of some of our politicians and their cronies! It is probably true to assert that the ownership of private property "has a great moralizing effect on the individual owner. It promotes virtues like responsibility, prudence, and self reliance; it gives him a place to stand in the world, a place where he can be confident that his freedom will be recognized and respected; and it affords him control of at least a minimum of those natural resources access to which is a necessary condition of his agency".(The Right to Private Property by Jeremy Waldron). In theory private property is a system of rules governing access to and control of tangible and intangible resources. It is a bundle of rights ranging from ownership and possession to derivation of income from and the freedom to sell or gift the property to another person.

Man also has an ineliminable core of self-interest which he is not easily prone to sacrifice for the greater good of others. His rights in this case become "the extent of egoism he can proclaim against the community without moral embarrassment". In a free society he will use this right to accumulate property/ wealth out of proportion to his needs. It is this aspect that prompted Marx to state "in your existing society, private property is already done away with for nine-tenths of the population; its existence for the few is solely due to its non-existence in the hands of these nine-tenths" (Communist Manifesto). This proposition is debatable. The fact is that even in little Sri Lanka there are a few extremely rich persons controlling vast resources, while the vast majority are living hand to mouth in a perpetual struggle for survival on a daily basis. To me this situation is morally obnoxious. Our taxation system needs to be overhauled to bring about a fairer allocation/distribution of resources and wealth without killing the incentive to aspire to the status of wealth and privilege.

Hegel suggested that the pauperized rabble tend to nurture hatred of the rich, the society and the government. Such men loose the sense of right and wrong, of honesty, and self-respect. This situation should be remedied by the government. The Eastern Province today is in a similar predicament. The IDPs there need the wherewithal to survive in a hostile environment where facilities for a dignified existence are virtually non-existent. It is opportune that the government has shifted a large amount of funds for the development of this province. It must now pursue diligently that plans are executed on time and development benefits the people tangibly in employment, in income generation and sustained revenue for the families and other institutions. The objective should be that the easterners have ample opportunities to earn a decent living, educate their children, build their homes and enjoy leisure activities of their choice.

The Eastern Provincial Council has a very onerous job. It has to build the Province from ashes left by the separatist conflict. It has to bind together the hitherto separatist forces of communalism and religious bigotry. It has to have within its folds sincere men whose actions will be transparent. There cannot be egotistical pursuit of personal cult and one community favouritism at the expense of others. The eastern leaders should eschew all forms of violence and firmly affirm the right of everyone to life, liberty and property. This will by itself promote peace.

It is appropriate to end this essay with a quotation (from Rawls' Theory of Justice). "It is no injustice in the greater benefits (wealth) earned by a few provided that the situation of the persons not so fortunate is thereby improved. The intuitive idea is that since everyone's well-being depends upon a scheme of cooperation without which no one could have a satisfactory life, the division of advantages (wealth) should be such as to draw forth the willing cooperation of everyone taking part in it, including those less well situated". I hope the political leaders in the Eastern Province are willing learners.

90

SHOULD THE SECURITY FORCES FIGHT LTTE TO THE FINISH?

(The Island, 26th Aug. 2008)

The government and the security forces are under tremendous pressure from most western nations and the LTTE sympathetic INGOs, local NGOs and Mr. Kumar David (in The Sunday Island, 17th Aug.) to stop the current campaign against the LTTE and start negotiations with the LTTE, despite the fact that all previous negotiations have been futile, and only helped the LTTE to rearm, reorganize and re-launch vicious attacks on our security forces and the civilians. In this context the question above is pertinent and requires a deeper analysis taking into account the prevailing thinking on war and how a war should be conducted against a sub-state terrorist outfit.

Let me start by admitting that war is horrible. In addition to horrific deaths and ghastly injuries to human beings, it causes the devastation of the environment and leaves in its wake traumatic psychological fissures that would linger for years to come. Indeed I do agree with every word of the American civil war General William Tecumenseh Sherman, who was reported to have said, "I am sad and tired of war. Its glory is all moonshine. It is only those who have neither fired a shot nor heard the shrieks and groans of the wounded who cry aloud for blood, for vengeance, for desolation. War is hell". Yet this same General carried out a scorched earth campaign during his infamous march through Georgia, because he wanted to expedite the end to the civil war.

The current campaign against the LTTE is justifiable and ought to be fought to the finish. My reasons are based on the just war theory of Jus ad Bellum (JAB) coming down to us from St. Augustine, Aquinas, Suarez, Hugo Grotius, Michael Walzer and others. LTTE's "aggression is morally as well as physically coercive---- it is singular and undifferentiated crime because in all its forms, it challenges rights that are worth dying for"(UN General Assembly Ruling on Aggression 3314/1974). Legitimate violent defence against aggression by a democratic government should take into account and fulfill many stringent conditions before embarking on lethal defence to protect its sovereignty and territorial integrity. A terrorist gang will, of course, ignore all conditions. Let us examine these conditions below.

1) "Only a legitimate authority should declare and wage war". No matter the defects in our brand of democracy, it is quite evident that our government is one elected by the people and therefore legitimate. It has not formally declared war because it is not fighting another country. It is campaigning against a terrorist gang that has subjugated a section of the people and gained control over some territory with fire power and is an imminent threat to all the citizens and the country. This condition therefore has been fully complied with by the government and our security forces.

   Vellupilai Pirapakaran (VP) has no legitimacy whatsoever. Therefore all his actions as well as that of his cadres are illegal, criminal and totally unacceptable and ought to be resisted and undone.

2) "There must be just causes for going to war". The government has plenty of reasons for going to war. Separatism and possible bifurcation of the country would goad any country to take up arms to defend its territorial integrity. Just look at what is happening in Kasmir and the north-eastern states of India and the recent happenings in Ossetia. In addition to this threat, our country suffered terrorism and physical attacks on non-combatants on a vast scale all over the country. Mavil Aru was the turning point. Its closure by LTTE denied water to thousands of people. Any government would have taken the necessary measures to restore the water supply and save its people from dire sufferings drought conditions would have imposed on them. This was the immediate just cause that led to the present conflict.

VP violated both Human Rights and Humanitarian laws by deliberately depriving the people of water and access to water. He stands guilty of attempting mass murder of those farmers who could not have lived long without life-giving water.

3) "War must be the last resort". This present military campaign was indeed the last resort by this government. It did attempt peace talks in Geneva. LTTE simply walked out of negotiations. The government did tolerate vicious mortal attacks on its security forces, the Army Chief, Secretary for Defence and civilians working in the paddy-fields, sleeping at home and traveling in buses. War was imposed on it by the LTTE.

   VP had been mollycoddled by the previous UNP government, some Western nations and their envoys in Colombo, and the NGOs. VP had come to assume that he could with impunity commit murder and mayhem anywhere in the country. He arrogantly assumed that he was invincible and that his cadres were superior to the armed forces in combat. He was itching for battle to prove this point and win Eelam by inflicting a famous defeat on the army. Wither his overweening pride today?

4) "There must be reasonable prospect of success". This condition needs no explanation. Success was achieved by the security forces in the Eastern Province. Today the government forces have achieved considerable success in their forward march towards Killinochchi and Mullaitivu (K&M), the sanctum sanctorum of LTTE. A word of caution is necessary here. In many of my previous articles I have alerted the country to the possibility of the use of crude WMD (weapons of mass destruction) by the LTTE. This was based on the fact that many highly qualified Chemists and Bio-Chemists in many western Universities are covert LTTE supporters and took the opportunity to travel to Sri Lanka during the infamous CFA. At the same time there were TV programmes in many western countries of the possibility of crude WMD attacks on major cities. Now that Karuna Amman too has referred to this possibility, one hopes that the army too has taken account of this and has counter measures at hand. Given the fact

that LTTE has been forcefully congregating the Wanni Tamils in K&M as human shields, any use of WMD there would be likely to kill more Tamils civilians than government soldiers. This will not matter to VP as killing is his profession. He is likely to use his planes to drop these chemical/biological weapons on civilian towns in the south and put the blame on the army with the help of Sinhala NGO kottiyas.

5) "There should be proportionality between the defensive violence used and the offensive violence caused". This condition pertains to jus in bello or whether the war is conducted in a justifiable manner. So far one cannot notice any asymmetry in the campaigns. LTTE's air raids have been fewer but more spectacular than the air raids of the SLAF. The latter has confined its attack on specified LTTE's war assets, bunkers, boats and assembly points of cadres. All these are legitimate targets in war. The use of crude U-Boats and land mines gave the LTTE an advantage over the army. The land mines will remain a crime against generations of Tamils still to be born as they will be the people who will live in those killing fields and will become the limbless and lifeless victims.

The allegations against the army of killing civilians in Trincomalee and Sampur still remains to be proved. Public investigation of those incidents points to the intention of punishing the culprits if proved guilty. Nevertheless, the whole of the Eastern province was captured with minimum of civilian casualties by the army.

Here I must draw the attention of the reader to the way the Allied forces and the Americans conducted their Second World War, keeping in mind that they are among those who preach Human Rights to us and keep telling us to stop the war and negotiate with the terrorist VP. The Germans laid siege to Leningrad in Sept. 1941. More than a million Russians civilians were estimated to have died of starvation and disease by the time the siege ended in 1943. Churchill resorted to terror bombing of Hamburg, Berlin and Dresden, thousands of civilians (estimated 800,000) died and a larger number were severely wounded. In early 1940s Prime Minister Churchill defended his action by proclaiming that "the bombers alone provide the means to victory"(quoted by Walzer in Just and Unjust wars). In March 1945 President Truman ordered a massive incendiary raid on Tokyo which turned the city into an inferno and killed more than 100,000 civilians. He then followed it up in August with the atom bombs on Hiroshima and Nargasaki. He defended his action on TV by stating "we have used it to shorten the agony of war". The Japanese too pillaged, murdered and raped the Nanking Chinese on a massive scale. This is a raw wound on the side of the Chinese to-date. Our army has not employed such war crimes. They in fact exposed themselves to mortal danger in order to safeguard the lives of the citizens in the Eastern province and win the war without any civilian casualties.

6) "Right intention should motivate the need to wage war". As far as I can see the objectives of the present military campaign are (a) to defeat LTTE's terrorism for good, (b) to liberate the people and the lands under their control, (c) to restore democratic local government in K&M districts and (d) to negotiate a long term constitutional settlement to our political problem. All these are in the spirit of the Bhagavad Gita which admonished us to "prepare for war with peace in mind" (2.38). St Augustine in Bk. X1X of his City of God, wrote that "wars are waged with peace as the object, even when they are waged by those who are concerned to exercise their warlike prowess, either in command or in actual fighting. Hence it is an established fact that peace is the desired end of war. For every man is in quest of peace, even in waging war, whereas no one is in quest of war when making peace". Hugo Grotius also asserted that "the unabated desire and invariable prospect of peace to be the only end for which hostilities can be lawfully begun". This is what the Sri Lankan nation expects from its security forces. Hopefully this eventuality will soon become a reality thanks to the supreme sacrifices of our valiant security forces.

Finally it could be possible that LTTE cadres engaged in the last moments of a hopeless battle would be awaiting a surrender that could never come given the mentality of VP. They should be treated with magnanimity and given hope to live normal lives in a peaceful post LTTE world. Thus negotiations, not with VP, but with other responsible Tamils should take place once LTTE is substantially defeated and K&M are brought under army's control. If VP is caught alive, a very unlikely event, he should be tried for war crimes in addition to the many murderous crimes he has committed.

[Disclaimer: From the above, in case readers conclude that I am a mouthpiece for the government, No, I am not, I do not belong to any political party or any NGOs or INGOs. I am a concerned ordinary citizen totally against LTTE's brutal terrorism. I do sincerely believe that our Security Forces are doing the right thing for the country and we should all wholeheartedly support them].

91

A JUST END TO A JUST AND SUCCESSFUL\ MILITARY CAMPAIGN

(The Island, 27th Oct. 2008)

The call on the LTTE cadres to surrender by Lt.Gen. Fonseka was opportune and well-timed. The several objectives behind it are the speedy end to the conflict, the avoidance of unnecessary killing of our youth, the avoidance of destruction of property, the flora and fauna of the country. The capitulation of the LTTE leaders and the political settlement of the many problems would inevitably follow the end to this vicious conflict and after the restoration of law and order. In the meanwhile, it is quite possible that the LTTE would take all necessary measures to isolate their fighting foot-soldiers from all information concerning the surrender and the modes of surrender. Therefore it is incumbent on the army to get the message to those isolated and insulated cadres in the bunkers who would be living in a world of blissful ignorance. As causing disaffection is also part of the strategy of fighting the enemy, one hopes the army would rain the conflict areas with Tamil leaflets giving information on surrender.

Surrender would be no easy matter even though most of the ordinary cadres are conscripted and unwilling fighters. Potential LTTE mutineers and deserters will have to bide time waiting for the opportunity to walk out without jeopardizing their lives. For, they are sure to be shot on sight by the other fanatical LTTE cadres. All those who survive this mortal conflict and their fellow citizens would want to affirm that Sri Lanka is different and better, for the army's victory and the defeat of the LTTE.

It is the conventional view that the only true aim in war is the total destruction of the enemy's forces in the battlefield. Clausewitz would want "the overthrow of the enemy". In a just war there are legitimate ends to war and once these are attained, the war should be stopped.

Further fighting would be beyond the limits of justice and reason. All who are killed beyond this point would have died in vain. The way the war is terminated can determine much about the subsequent peace. Therefore it is right that we give thought to how and when we should terminate the current military campaign.

Vellupillai Pirapakaran (VP) is a man with whom a compromise peace is impracticable and unthinkable. The evil nature of his Eelamism is outside the moral world of bargaining and accommodation. The criminality inherent in the very core of his aggression threatens the very lives of all citizens, the political independence and territorial integrity of Sri Lanka. Therefore unconditional surrender of VP and his other leaders of Eelam should be demanded. This means that the government, like the Allied Governments in WW11, would not negotiate with LTTE leaders and would have no dealings with them of any sort, "except to instruct them about the details of orderly capitulation" and legal chastisement for the LTTE leaders. It also means the elimination of and non recognition for any LTTE authority and the political and physical reconstruction of the Wanni and the induction of democracy therein. If unconditional surrender is not forthcoming, then the military campaign should be pursued to the bitter end.

VP and his henchmen are the pompous scheming guttersnipes. They have perpetrated yet another slaughter of defenceless non-combatants in Anuradhapura on the 6th of Oct. This was a totally repugnant crime and unnecessary carnage. The LTTE authors of this as well as the numerous other crimes must be made to pay. They should be judicially punished after local and international legal processes.

The capture of Killinochchi would expedite the fall of Pooneryn and Elephant Pass. That, in my view, would be the moment for negotiation on terms of surrender and termination of the conflict even though such a step, at first glance, looks preposterous and even immoral as the enemy has not yet been completely crushed. I advocate this step because we are not fighting an enemy foreign nation but some of our own misguided citizens, and we have got to go on living peacefully with them in the post VP world. It is true that many of the ordinary Wanni citizens might have been helpers of the LTTE and would have worked for them in various capacities, and their children would be among the fighting LTTE cadres. Their complicity cannot be condoned. Yet the other view also needs to be taken into account before we demonise the Wanni citizens. They were under the thraldom of the LTTE where dissent meant brutal punishment and death. We have seen the dungeons and the iron and barbed-wire cages, the brutal instruments of unabashed torture and agonizing beastly killings. Those Wanni citizens were the oppressed and suppressed people without relief for the last twenty-five years. Therefore they should not be subject to further suffering by their new liberators. Magnanimity is the virtue of the victor.

As the conflict progresses adversely against the LTTE there will be some leaders among them who will realize the futility of further killing and destruction. There will be other Karuna Ammans among the Wanni LTTE cadres who still command the respect and regard of the ordinary fighters. Such men/women might not be morally respectable or untainted. All that is required of them at this point in time is the sincere motive to end the conflict. They are the ones with whom the army should parley to bring about the end to the conflict and obtain their help to hunt down VP and his henchmen.

The Wanni non-combatant citizens are today placed in a perilous situation of grave vulnerability by the LTTE. Their pathetic predicament is the responsibility of the heartless LTTE. This is also a good example of moral depravity of the LTTE as it takes for granted that morality does not apply to LTTE, but it applies with full force to the GoSL. The Tamil citizens are used as innocent shields against the army. In doing this the unscrupulous LTTE is exploiting the adherence of the scrupulous to moral standards, that is, the moral prohibition against the killing of the innocents and damage the reputation of the army even when accidents occur in which innocents get killed. The Sri Lankan army has done better than what the Germans did in Leningrad. The German army did not allow the trapped Russians in Leningrad in 1941 to escape when they laid siege to that city. Our army has laid out safe escape routes and designated safe assembly areas in the Wanni for the citizens. This humanitarian gesture has been ignored by the international acolytes of the LTTE. Field Marshall Von Leeb who commanded the German army in Russia at that time even gave orders to shoot the civilians who attempted to escape the siege. Such men have already surfaced from among the LTTE as related by the recent escapees (by boats) in the Mannar district. I hope the Germans in Colombo will remember the skeletons in their cupboard and recognize and accept the good intentions of our government and stop taking punitive measures by stopping aid to the country on unsubstantiated flimsy accusations. I also hope that the Indian government will realize that our army has taken adequate measures to safeguard the cornered Tamil citizens which their army has failed to do in both Kashmir, Nagaland and in Assam. The Indian government stands accused today of failing to provide protection to the citizens against jihadi terrorists in general and protection to Christians against the wave of violence seen in Orissa and Karnataka since Aug. 2008. India is plagued with terrorism even in Delhi. It is taking unprecedented steps to eliminate the Indian terrorists, yet it appears that the Indian government is making use of proxies to stop us fighting the terrorist LTTE within our country. The pledges it gave at the SAARC summit to fight terrorism appears to be hollow and insincere. This is duplicitous diplomacy of the highest order.

Once the army has taken adequate and sufficient measures to resist further aggression, restore peace in the conflict areas then the settlement should be directed towards all-out disengagement, demilitarization, and decommissioning of all arms by the LTTE. This then would be the justice in the settlement of our conflict.

One should not forget the fact that once the conflict is terminated the civilian population should be left in a position to contribute to an independent political life for themselves. This may not be immediately possible as they have been reduced to a nomadic life just now. Thus their resettlement would take priority. There will be political vacuum in the Wanni for some time. This must be carefully handled so as to avoid the reemergence of exLTTE cadres in responsible positions. On the other hand if such persons have completely and publicly eschewed separatism and armed rebellion and criminally untainted, then it will not be risky to entrust them with the rebuilding the areas and reinstating democracy there. Their involvement in the new political life based on democracy and rule of law will be a positive contribution towards enduring peace.

As our valiant and courageous tri-security forces espy the defeat of the LTTE this side of the horizon and as the nation's expectation of the end of the conflict is eagerly awaited, one is reminded of what Michael Walzer said about terrorism: "I doubt that terrorism has ever achieved national liberation---no nation that I know of owes its freedom to a campaign of random murder---although terrorism undoubtedly increases the power of the terrorists within the national liberation movement" (Terrorism: A Critique of Excuses). The LTTE terrorists have played out this power to exhaustion. They have been outplayed and outgunned by the army. This message needs to be conveyed to the isolated and insulated LTTE cadres in the frontline. They should be assured of a better life than the abject destitution of a hopeless life in the bunker. Time is fast approaching to call a halt to carnage and revert to peaceful days and peaceful lives for both our soldiers and the conscripted LTTE cadres, and keep at bay the international interlopers with secret agendas in our national affairs.

92

FAILED SAVIOURS OF FAILING STATES

(The Island, 6th Nov. 2008)

Not long ago there were many false prophets, especially of the NGO fraternity, proclaiming in the media that Sri Lanka was a failed and/ or a failing state. They then projected themselves as our saviours and argued with might and main that Sri Lanka had become an eminently suitable candidate for R2P (responsibility to protect), and that Human Rights vultures should be sent to Sri Lanka to strip the country clean of all vestiges of independence and sovereignty. One of the criteria used to judge this country was the undefined, supposed to be "deteriorating economic status" of the country. Those prophets did choose to ignore that many countries in the world did suffer severe economic problems due to hike in petroleum products and many prosperous western countries were beset with strikes against hikes in prices of all sorts of goods including food. Have we not survived this crisis now? Why are these NGO Cassandras gone silent now? Is it the fact that Sri Lanka has now become a successful state all of a sudden?

Of course, we do have another major problem on hand and that is the campaign to eliminate LTTE terrorism. Those false prophets attributed our economic problems to our military campaign too. Our saviours were also keen to put a stop to this successful military campaign as a means to salvage the country from the status of a failed state. In this, their hidden agenda was the not-so-hidden intentions to help the LTTE to regain the lost momentum to fight the army. I do not deny the high cost of fighting a war. But the unbearable higher cost of not fighting terrorism would ultimately be the loss of the very country we cherish and now live in. The end-objective is worth the short-term cost we incur now.

The Dollar-fattened NGO eggheads always implicitly accepted that political liberalism and economic free trade prevalent in the western capitalist democracies were the best suited for our country. To them these two assumptions were the true pillars of human rights and democracy. They are beyond learning the fact that each country needs to attain its own equilibrium in democracy according to its own culture and mores. What is right for and works in one country may not be appropriate for another country and another people, especially if that country has had a recorded history, economic, social and religious culture stretching over thousands of years.

The much worshipped western democracies are today embroiled in financial crises of staggering proportions. By the aforementioned criterion of "deteriorating economic status", quite many of them are failing, if not, failed states almost going bust. An initial random roll-call would include Iceland, Hungary, Poland, Georgia, Argentina and Pakistan. International Monetary Fund has rushed in to mobilize a "Special Fund of Several Billion Dollars" to stave off sovereign defaults and to prevent a domino collapse across the world.

The bastions of capitalist democracy and free trade have been shattered and the snobbish citadels within those bastions, the crème-de-la-crème of financial institutions, have spectacularly collapsed. Thus the US, UK, France, Germany and Japan have mounted billions of Dollars worth of rescue to stave off disastrous financial collapse of their economy. Japan is even getting ready to make money handouts to its citizens. In all those countries the governments have abandoned free trade and resorted to full and/or partial nationalization of some of the foremost banks. Tax-payers money has been poured in to rescue capitalism even though the High Priests of capitalism are not sure whether a cure would soon ensue.

I am reminded here of Marx's Manifesto wherein he wrote: "The bourgeoisie……has put an end to all feudal, patriarchal, idyllic relations…. It has resolved personal worth into exchange value, and in place of the numberless indefeasible chartered freedoms, has set up that single, unconscionable freedom—Free Trade". Having imposed this cultural revolution, liberal capitalist economics and ethics were foisted on us as an ideal. The greedy pursuit and accumulation of ostentatious wealth was enshrined as the ultimate objective of man's endeavour.

Human Rights were advocated as necessary freedom to attain this obnoxious objective. Now the buzz-word is not Human Rights, not Free-Trade, it is Regulation, euphemism for Nationalization.

My gripe, however, is that, (1) are we not witnessing a spate of failing states? And (2), would nationalization not violate the hitherto enjoyed Human Rights of some conspicuous actors in the economy? So where are our local NGO saviours of failing states? Why have they failed to take to Lipton Circus to enact their usually comic drama calling for R2P and Human Rights Monitors to all the above-mentioned countries? The answer my friends, is that they are all cowards and betrayers of this country. The failing states are their true friends who feed them with dollars to run down our country, to directly and indirectly help the terrorist LTTE and eventually divide this country. They remain exposed and condemned.

93

OUR OPEN SOCIETY AND ITS ENEMIES

(The Island, 3rd Feb.2008)

A society where the prevailing form of government is democratically elected and is accountable and responsible to the electors is prima facie an open society. "A society in which individuals are confronted with personal decisions" is known as an open society. In this society there is social mobility by competition among its members. Every individual is free to pursue his desired career, make economic gains and move up the social ladder. Whatever the faults, a democratic country is considered as an open society mainly because the citizens of that country do exercise freedom and have many personal rights making them all constitutionally equal. There is freedom of critical thought and discussion in all spheres of human activity. Such freedoms are considered as indispensable preliminaries to acting wisely. This open society will have constitutional as well as institutional barriers against the exploitation of man by man. "Our modern open societies function largely by way of abstract relations, such as exchange or co-operation". Most contacts and dealings are at arms length via the phone, internet and paper contracts. Face to face contacts are still there but minimal. The new faith of the open society is "the faith in man, in equalitarian justice and in human reason". Only such a society has the potentiality to fulfill man's desire for personal enhancement, satisfaction and at least a modicum of happiness.

A closed society "resembles a herd or a tribe in being a semi-organic unit whose members are held together by semi-biological ties— kingship, living together, sharing common efforts, common dangers, common joys and common distress". Tribal exclusiveness prevails in a closed society and therefore this society will seek to shut out foreign influences which are condemned as inferior and degenerative. Universalistic humanitarian principles will be taboo but will be replaced by anachronistic tradition, old virtues aimed at arresting social change. Criticism and dissent have no place in this closed society. The tribe is everything and the individual is nothing, the collective stands higher than the individual. North Korea and the erstwhile tribal land of Pirapakaran are closed societies both in the literal as well as intellectual sense. The latter practiced romanticized gangsterism while the other extols the collectivist ideology above everything else. Closed societies are usually headed by tyrannical dictators who will suppress all dissent ruthlessly. A closed society is an outdated zoo with cages full of almost perfect monkeys.

Sri Lanka is no five-star democracy but it still is an open society even though there are many institutional imperfections, avoidable waste, untold human suffering due largely to corruption and parasitical life of the elite, many of whom are openly engaged in the crudity of money-grabbing, and of late, the homicidal efforts also have been engineered to arrest change by deliberate attack on the freedom of expression. It is still an open society, despite the mortal combat with a murderous closed society led by VP.

Who are the enemies of our fledgling open society? First and foremost has been the closed society of Pirapakaran(VP). Thankfully this danger is being physically eliminated by our courageous and valiant security forces. All Sri Lankans should remain forever grateful to the security forces for this liberation from the terrorists. We should stop giving prominence to VP, the gangster, after his capture or demise. He deserves to be treated only as a war criminal and a serial killer. We should turn our attention towards his closeted acolytes among the politicians, the Sinhalese managed NGOs and some foreign managed INGOs. They will seek to rob us of our victory over terrorism by peddling various seemingly attractive post conflict solutions. Without exception all their solutions would, if closely examined, turn out to be recycled sugar coated demands of VP aimed at bifurcating the country, if not immediately, in the future. They are certainly the behind-the-lines enemies of our open society. I challenge these dollar NGO mercenaries to take a hard look at the way people of all ethnicities live next to one another, love one another and work in co-operation as well as in competition in many major towns of our country. These people evince closer understanding, integration of interests, a life of common dependence and common sacrifice. There is no devolution or constitutional settlement here. They live as Sri Lankans, in Sri Lanka and for Sri Lanka while maintaining their individual ethnic identities. This is the live answer to our NGO pundits. Replication of this situation in conflict-torn areas should be urgently considered and relentlessly pursued.

Many Jaffna men and women live harmoniously and in peace in almost all areas of the country in the south. Why is such a mixed harmonious life not possible in Killinochchi, Paranthan, Mullaitivu and Jaffna peninsula? If racism could be discarded when traveling down to and settling down in Wellawatha, so it could be jettisoned at the Jaffna railway station or KKS harbour or Palaly airport itself. Peace is living with other fellow beings without strife and conflict. Exclusive enclaves lead to suspicion, jealousy and accusations of discrimination and favouritism of one over the others. A new north and east with many Wellawathas and Kotahena-like suburbs and villages in conflict cleansed areas would surely pave the way for all of us to be Sri Lankan first and whatever else after.

Then there are some foreigners with self-fabricated fancy theories such as R2P, Failed States and manufactured Human Rights Index. They wrap themselves with the fabric of Human Rights to dupe the unwary. These are identifiable enemies of our open society. Their secret objective is the destabilization of our country. They should not be allowed to operate in our country. The foreign saboteurs among them should be deported forthwith and the indigenous men and women should be arraigned for treason if this is possible.

The Rule of Law governs an open society. The law of the country is normally legislated and promulgated by a democratically elected body and is enforced by legally established agencies such as the Courts of Law and the Police department. Decisions and declarations made by the Courts are part of the law of the land and ought to be obeyed first, and then contested, if necessary, through the appeal procedure.

All who disregard any determination of the Court of Law do become enemies of the open society. Their disobedience makes the country lawless, the society inequitable and creates a section within society with impunity to do whatever pleases them at the expense of others. They are wreckers trying to dismantle the very foundations of open society to usher in totalitarian dictatorship.

Religious bigots are another batch of enemies to open society. They not only try to prevent others from practicing their religions, but also try to enforce their religion and religious ethos on unwilling others. Economic inducements to convert the destitute and poor peasants are unacceptable. Equally resorting to heavy-handed law to prevent such conversions could only lead to more intractable problems. Toleration which is the hallmark of open society could be replaced by contentious division and conflict. We have in Sri Lanka, a religious section who wants to arrogate to their religion and ethnicity all victories of our security forces. They deliberately ignore the many patriotic Malays, Muslims, Tamils and Christians in the security forces that have died for the country and continue to die for the country. Now that Mullaitivu is under government control, I like to remind these bigots that in 1996 in a desperate attempt to save Mullaitivu, 275 elite commandos under the command of Lt. Col. A.F. Laffir were heli-dropped near Alampil under heavy fire from the LTTE, who had by then entered the army camp. Although wounded he led the attack from the front and died fighting the LTTE. Such brave men in our security forces who belong to minority communities stand insulted by our religious bigots. The President was right to call the victory by our security forces as victory of the whole nation. This in no way diminishes the major contribution expected of and actually and admirably made by the majority ethnic community in fighting the terrorists. Religious fanaticism in whatever form has a corroding effect on open society and should be scotched at the earliest as the President did immediately after the fall of Killinochchi by claiming it as the victory of the whole nation.

There cannot be an open society without freedom. Without freedom every man's place in life, his civil and social rights and duties together with the security of earning his living would be determined by the status of his birth. I agree with J.S.Mill that without freedom, there will be no scope for spontaneity, originality, genius, for mental energy and for moral courage. Society will be crushed by the weight of collective mediocrity.

The spirit of an open society is the freedom for open discussion, criticism and compromise. A free press, a free radio and TV are therefore necessary for the open society to thrive and progress. These institutions act as barriers to the imposition of one man's will on another. Therefore any physical extra-judicial attack by anyone on these agencies and its personnel is simply unacceptable. Such mindless scoundrels should be hunted down and suitably punished. They are all morons unable and unwilling to articulate and sustain their point of view in the public domain. Such men are both misologists (haters of arguments) as well as misanthropists (haters of men) fit only for living in a closed society. Every law is an infraction of freedom, nevertheless, laws should maintain maximum degree of non-interference compatible with minimum demands of social life. It is the sacred duty of any democratic government to act as the indefatigable watchdog to maintain this frontier un-invaded not only by itself but also by others. Failure here on the part of the government would be the death knell to open society. (All quotations are from Sir Karl Popper's book; "The Open Society and its Enemies").

94

A LOOKBACK THAT PROVOKES ANGER

(The Island, 23rd Mar. 2009)

I know it is easy to be wise after the event. Nevertheless there are aspects in the political life of the country that need to be forever kept in focus and continuously projected on the face of our mercurial politicians and forgetful people. Given below are only a couple of acts of insanity committed by our politicians in the recent past, vis-a-vis the LTTE. Their recall does make one angry. These events are exhumed here from our recent tragic history so that repetition of the same would be avoided at all times in the future.

Bloody strife and ruthless terrorism has torn this country asunder over the past three decades. Our gallant security forces would soon help us to close this dark chapter in our history. Then it should be celebrated by all Sri Lankans, especially the Tamils, because they suffered the most under the LTTE. I shall certainly celebrate it with a bottle of Bollinger and drink to the health and prosperity of our security forces. Let us also be aware that there are a few politicians, anti-Sri Lankan NGOs and some foreigners making preparations to denigrate this great victory and write it down disparagingly in their own twisted terms. Woe be unto them!

We now deserve a land of hope and glory. We do have men and women to deliver to us this state of serendipity Just look at the exemplary dedication the soldiers have evinced and their indomitable courage to overcome all obstacles to deliver the country from terrorism. Such traits of character applied to the politics of this country should surely yield the peace and prosperity we all yearn for this country and its long suffering citizens. Politicians take note. It is time you either do or depart.

The "peace process" concocted by partisan Norwegians was imposed on the country and our Security Forces as if it was the new Ten Commandments to be obediently observed by all except the LTTE. This importation of greenhorn Norwegians and the freedom given to them to literally determine the destiny of the country by ambiguous and equivocal agreements were inexcusable acts of folly of our arrogant political leaders. They ignored our history and the depredations of foreigners for over five hundred years in our country. If appropriate punishment is not possible under our present constitution for these failed leaders, the minimum available is to banish them from politics and deny them any opportunity for leadership in this country. One is already in this state of doldrums, and I hope the other will soon be dumped there by his political party. He rightly belongs to political oblivion.

The most obvious solution to our terrorist problem was to fight it to the finish. This was deliberately set aside in favour of many paper solutions purporting to give de facto and de jure recognition to the terrorist gang. Many hours of deliberation at great expense was expended all over the world and as the saying goes it was viperam nutricare sub ala (to nourish a viper in one's bosom). The terrorist took full advantage of this to fully establish their bogus credentials as "freedom fighters" and "sole representatives of Tamils" in foreign capitals, to establish their international offices and to organize the Tamil diaspora to fund their murderous projects in the country. So began Pirapakaran's (VP) ambitious fortress-Wanni-Eelam-project, the forced conscription and brainwashing of Tamil youth and the acquisition of many lethal weapons and crude aerial bombers, a fleet of ships and trawlers with under water crude U-boats and chemical weapons, all necessary to guard and protect his fortress and his dictatorial regime. If the obvious solution had been pursued vigorously and relentlessly from the very start, VP would not have been in a position to do any of the things he had done to-date. Alas, instead, our political leaders preferred to build devolution castles in the air ably supported by the Norwegians, and anti-Sri Lankan NGOs. From what we see and know of Wanni now, it is quite clear that one more year of this futile pursuit would have been sufficient for VP to establish his Eelam in Sri Lanka. This does make one angry, does it not?

Our political leaders also systematically debilitated our security forces by uncritically adopting the false propaganda that LTTE was invincible. The corollary was the deprivation of appropriate arms and ammunition to the security forces with the attendant degradation of their morale to fight the enemy. Ultimate humiliation was forced on our military men and women when they were made to act as odd-job workers to the LTTE. To have made these noble soldiers the guardians of the terrorist LTTE, menial porters at the airport for the LTTE, chauffeurs of the LTTE transporting them in expensive vehicles according to their wishes, and providing helicopter transport to venues for their war counsels, were all inexcusable and unpardonable acts of callous irresponsibility towards those soldiers, who were prepared to die for the country fighting against the very same terrorists. Those political morons should even now plead for pardon from those soldiers.

See what these same security forces have achieved today. With new leaders, clear objectives, fresh motivation and unfailing commitment they have knocked the stuff out of the LTTE. They were heavily burdened with thirty to forty kilos backpack, soaked from head to foot, mud splattered all over, had to carry their heavy weapons and its ammunition through all kinds of man made and natural jungle obstacles facing the bullets and landmines of the enemy. This was and is indomitable courage, absolute devotion to duty and country, and admirable display of bravery for all times to come. Tottenham Hotspur football club's motto audere est facere (to dare is to do) suitably applies to our valiant soldiers. Should we not remain always grateful to them?

One top politician once castigated the head of our navy when he reported to him the sinking of a LTTE ship. The very same navy today rules the waves around Sri Lanka. It has knocked out the LTTE's sea capability effectively even sailing as far away as over 1500 nautical miles from our coastline and effaced systematically the importation of arms by the LTTE. It still engages the LTTE as and when they emerge from their hidden coves on to the open sea. It has ensured the safety of sea lines of communication and our harbours. It will soon take on the onerous duty of safeguarding the vast exclusive economic zone. Again proper leadership, motivation and dedication to duty surmounted the bullets, suicide boats and under-water scooters to render our island's safety, security and integrity.

Our relatively small air force too has co-ordinated and collaborated with the ground forces and the navy to thwart LTTE's offensive infiltrations and to bomb their centres of control and command. The well-hidden underground bunkers of top LTTE cadres that we see today are obvious testimony to the efficiency and accuracy of air strikes and the fear those LTTE cadres entertained towards our air force. They too were ridiculed by pro-LTTE acolytes as being corrupt and incapable of downing the crude LTTE bombers. But our airmen have prevailed, rendered yeoman service, and done their duty to their country. The moral of all these is that one should not put down our soldiers. They are the first and the last line of defence of our country.

What of the future now? Decapitation of the LTTE would deprive it of any guerrilla campaign capacity. LTTE will not have anyone to command and control it. They will not have any geographical space to operate from. The northern jungles are now as well known to the army as to the LTTE. It is most unlikely that the Tamils will support them again, except the few hard core LTTE laymen. Even these would be soon betrayed by the many grieving parents who lost their children to the LTTE. Certainly we will have isolated acts of terrorism for a short while from the LTTE stragglers seeking revenge for their defeat. Continued vigilance will be necessary.

Internationally the country will face hard times from both Tamil Nadu and the Tamil diaspora. These angry men and women will subject the country to all sorts of unjustifiable and unsubstantiated accusations with the object of preventing the country's political, economic and social progress. They will certainly seek to carry on a proxy war in Sri Lanka. They have planted their Quislings in important international bodies to advocate their propaganda. They will have ample funds for this from the prosperous billion dollar international business empire of the LTTE. The battle to dismantle this financial infra structure in foreign lands should begin now and pursued relentlessly in the same way as Al Quieda's finances were frozen and made inaccessible. Our

High Commissioners and Ambassadors should also reach out and pro-actively engage expatriate Tamils to wean them away from further LTTE suzerainty and stranglehold.

It will take time to de-mine, to rebuild, to reconstruct and to rehabilitate the displaced people. In the meanwhile they should be treated courteously and kindly even though some of them have been supporters of the LTTE. They should be infused with hope of a stable and prosperous future, if not for them, at least for their children. Many foreign nations are likely to offer substantial help for the reconstruction of the Wanni. Unlike post Tsunami, this time around the government should enact a plan and ensure that all work conforms to this plan and such assigned work is completed within the specified timeframe. The Nation-Building ministry should be getting ready for this now because a properly supervised application of foreign funds for reconstruction would help to assuage the destitute IDPs and would lead to economic prosperity of the country.

A look at the long-term settlement of our conflict, I shall leave it for another article. For now let me remind our readers that what we have endured is very similar to what our ancestors endured for twenty-one years under Kalinga Magha (1224-1235). Vijayabahu ended it and ushered in peace and prosperity to the country. The evil VP has wrought on the country should be buried with him and we should look forward with hope and joy.

95

THE BIGGEST HOSTAGE RESCUE OPERATION IN THE WORLD

(The Island, 6th Apr. 2009)

It is now as clear as daylight that the LTTE has really and truly taken hostage of all Tamil civilians in the "no-fire-zone"(NFZ). Unable to face the army, the LTTE cadres have now run into the relative safety of this zone and are clearly holding the people as hostage there and have resorted to murdering them if they attempted to escape their captivity. The LTTE cadres are the "sole Murderers (not Representatives) of Tamils"

This is no different to what recently happened at some hotels in Mumbai. The terrorists captured these hotels, held the people therein as hostages and fought the Indian Police and the army for nearly three days before the innocent could be freed, and the beastly terrorist could be eliminated. Many lost their lives and many others survived the deadly ordeal. Without exception, everyone blamed the terrorists for the deaths. The Indian security forces took some flak for taking such a long time to make the rescue.

As it was the government that declared and designated this area in the northeast as "no-fire-zone" (NFZ), it will be called upon by all and sundry supporters of LTTE to abide by its declaration. They will ignore the fact that the LTTE has now shifted some of their heavy weapons to NFZ and are using them without any compunction on the army. We have already seen SAM missiles fired at our helicopters and artillery fire is a frequent occurrence. The army is unable to retaliate in equal measure for fear of killing the civilians. But the rescue of civilians must proceed in the same manner as it was done in Vakarai and Sampur in the east where civilian lives were safeguarded.

With the help of anti-LTTE hostages and surrendering LTTE cadres the army hopefully will obtain the vital information on the hiding places of top LTTE cadres and Pirapakaran himself and then precision bomb the lot out of existence. That will soon end the misery for all even though this inevitably will result in innocent deaths for which the blame should be placed on Pirapakaran himself.

In the meanwhile I salute our brave soldiers for risking their lives to save the Tamil civilians even though they have to fight with small arms and brave artillery and mortar fire from LTTE. As the Bible says "greater love hath no man than this, that a man lay down his life for his friends" Our soldiers are today engaged in the most dangerous and the biggest hostage rescue operation in the world. When it is all over, as it will soon be, I shall hail our soldiers as the men of this century even though there is a long way to the end of this century. Their selfless sacrifice to save the Tamil civilians should be indelibly recorded in our history and acknowledged by the world at large notwithstanding the few men/women in high positions at the UN who are hostile to Sri Lanka and sympathetic to terrorist LTTE. [The Island newspaper and self were the first to use this headline, other media copied it thereafter].

96

"WITHOUT A SONG AND A DANCE WHAT ARE WE?"

(The Island, 3rd June 2009)

In the Sunday 24th the English newspapers, there were many commentators preaching to the readers that we should restrain our celebrations of the victory over the evil forces unleashed on us by a megalomaniac. I like to tell these emotionally castrated writers that they should take a dip in the Beira lake so that its bacteria filled waters at least will help them to clean their minds, if not their bodies.

The people have put up with untold misery imposed on them by Velu. They have borne with Bodhisathwa patience the atrocities committed on them by Velu over the last thirty years. They, (I mean all communities) have lost their fathers, sons, daughters to the monstrosities of Velu. Quite many people have lost their jobs, properties and all their savings. The future prospects for the people of this country were bleak until this "ogre from the mountain" was completely destroyed together with his goons. This is what the President and his Security Forces have achieved. The sense of liberation and gratitude in the people was so overwhelming that it needed the outlet of spontaneous celebration. A Sinhala/Tamil New year together with Dansals thrown in at street parties was completely in order. It was also an instinctive expression of gratitude for the epic victory of the Security Forces.Why should one restrain such joy? Why cannot the people give vent to their emotions in a positive way? Velu with the connivance of Ranil and the West had reduced us all to the status of three-fourth Sri Lankans and was, (going by the quantity and quality of captured arms), probably poised to recruit a mercenary army to completely delete our citizenship and march on to Colombo itself. We were saved from this ignominious fate by our Security Forces. Why should we not rejoice at this monumental achievement? We have and we should rejoice to our hearts' content.

The commentators have missed completely the heartbeats of the common Sri Lankans by leagues.

It is true that many Tamils failed to join in the celebrations but probably chose to silently mourn the death of a monster. This is their democratic right. An enlighten few at Wellawatha, Jaffna Trinco and Batticaloa did take to the streets to celebrate the passing away of the same monster. This is the future way to go. There cannot be any mental ghettoes of narrow racism in any of us anymore. The Tamils have got to take their due places in all national celebrations and as they were the most affected by Velu's oppression, they had all the reason to take to the streets as their brethren in Jaffna did. One can only hope that at least in the future the Tamils will start thinking that they are Sri Lankan first and Tamils after and be wary of pushing themselves into exclusive racist cul-de-sac. This is the lonely road to nowhere and ruin. If in doubt, ask the IDPs in Kadirigamapura.

The message to the newspaper killjoys and spoilsports is that expressing one's joy in street parties is not triumphalism aimed at further flogging the vanquished. It is Milton's message that "the brazen throat of war had ceased to roar/ All now was turned into jollity and game/ to luxury and riot, feast and dance" (Paradise Lost, X1),Pedestalled in triumph I am of course quite happy to sing out loud together with the Group ABBA "without a song and a dance what are we?" And, "thanks for the music" dance and Kiribath. [As usual some spoilsports did criticize this spontaneous expression of joy and relief. I think they were mistaken. Even today the west commemorates the end of the European wars even though the participants are not among the living to celebrate.]

97

CHANGE WE HAVE AND CHANGE WE MUST

(The Island, 7th July 2009)

Senator Obama became President of USA by playing on the word "change" during the election. Americans are still debating, many months after his election, whether any real "change" has taken place in the American society, the economy and politics. Our President and our Security Forces have delivered the "change" we wanted and badly needed. We are now one country without terrorism and terrorists' claim to separatism. I am reminded here of Edmund Burke's truism "a state without the means of some change is without the means of its conservation" (Reflections). This change to conserve our country and its territorial integrity will come in the form of new arrangements (constitutional or otherwise), once the immediate needs of the Tamils victimized by the now defunct LTTE terrorists have been sorted out.

Before everything else, I hope, the proponents of political change will make an effort to examine critically the welter of conflicting claims, grievances aspirations and interests and make a prioritized list of them. This attempt to understand and define the problem would facilitate the solutions. Such solutions need not necessarily be a change of the constitution. Only when we clearly define our problems, only then can we proceed to offer genuine and acceptable cures for the perceived wrongs in our society. Preferably the APRC should have endeavoured at least to make a list of the knotted issues before looking for solutions.

No matter how elegant the new formulation, as it is man-made, it will always have some defects. I leave them for our many constitutional experts, who are a dozen a penny, to sort them out. I am here more concerned with the weakest link in the chain—the humans who have got to implement the change for the benefit of all citizens.

We the citizens have got to change too. Presidential fiats cannot abolish the physical existence of the minority and majority communities in any country. Our minorities have had their own value systems, language, beliefs, customs, conventions, habits and practices transmitted over centuries to successive generations. They therefore will identify themselves with such community culture for security and emotional satisfaction. Should we not accept this for what it is? What is paramount is the prevention of a new Velupillai transforming this attachment into xenophobia, an exclusivist and expansionist doctrine seeking absolute control over geographic territory and over all the members of the Tamil community. How could we achieve this? We need to actively promote a truly genuine nationalism that captures and expresses, as Hegel would call it, the Volksgeist or the true character of our nation. A nationalism that would increase the cohesion of the nation. We need a nationalism that "metamorphoses the subjects into full-fledged citizens" (Geertz: The Interpretation of Cultures). The type of nationalism I have in my mind is "the sentiment of belonging to a community whose members identify with a set of symbols, beliefs and ways of life, and have the will to decide upon their common political destiny" (Guibernau: Nationalisms). We do display such absorbing nationalism at international cricket matches. Now we do need to transfuse this sentiment to other national events. One example of it occurred in Galle in December 2008 Tsunami Remembrance get-together under the guidance of a Deputy Minister (Hon. Hemakumara Nanayakara) and the organizational expertise of an ex-diplomat (Mr. Walter Fernando). One hundred torch-bearers from each community (Hindhu, Muslim, Buddhist and Christian) followed by large croups of people gathered at the Galle Fort for the Commemoration. The significance of this gathering was that they were not only expressing national solidarity, but also were displaying national identity of the kind we should promote. They were enacting in Renan's terms the experience of "having suffered, enjoyed, and hoped together" (Renan: What is a Nation?).

Our nation-state is multi-ethnic, multi-lingual, multi-religious, and multi-cultural. Our world is one where the political and the national unit cannot be congruent or homogenous. We need a nationalism that allows and vindicates the right to be different while maintaining the over-arching identity with the nation. This is an arduous yet not an impossible task given the space created by the defeat of the terrorists.

Our multi-ethnicity is a matter of perception. In reality we are a hybrid nation. Many inter-ethnic marriages still do take place. According to the beliefs in the two main religions, one who died as a Sinhalese today could be born a Tamil tomorrow. As humans there are no differences in our physical appearance or intellectual capacity, even though some racists do believe in the superiority of intellect of the man from the north! What is factual is that we are all born in this country, live in this country and therefore owe allegiance to this country. This is what the new nationalism should emphasize. This is the change we urgently require.

It is true that we have two different indigenous languages. This should be considered a plus factor. While Sinhala is confined to this country only, Tamil has many adherents all over the world. By giving equal weight to both languages in this country, we share in the advantages of a greater coverage of the Tamil language. We should use our languages to learn our civic national catechism, in which all of us will be imbued with all the duties expected of us: from defending the state, to paying taxes, working and obeying the laws. The change required here is that, like in Switzerland, we have got to become multi-lingual citizens. Tomorrow's citizens should be given all the opportunities to learn each other's languages. Others, especially those government officials who come in contact with the public, should take a leaf out of the efforts the President makes to learn and speak in Tamil. Perhaps spoken adult language lessons over the national TV could help to bridge the present gap.

Our multi-religion and multi-culturism are only skin deep. The close connection between popular Buddhism and Hinduism is too obvious for any elaboration. The Christians and the Muslims do not share the beliefs and practices of others. Nevertheless amicable co-existence is apparent in that at least some Muslims and Christians do participate indirectly in Buddhist and Hindu festivals in places like Kataragama,

Kandy and Anuradhapura. St. Anthony's feast at Kochchikade, Colombo and the Madhu catholic festivals do attract people of all faiths. Our religions, songs, dances, literature, poetry and theatre should not be promoted as ethnic events. They should be projected as Sri Lankan arts and culture. Transposing Lord Macaulay's Minute of 1835: "we have to create a class of persons, Sri Lankan in blood and colour and Sri Lankan in taste, in opinions, in morals and intellect". This is another change we need to usher in at the earliest opportunity.

This kind of nationalism has the capacity to create common identity among a heterogeneous people as most of the citizens would have accepted and adopted as their own, the symbols and rituals associated with that nationalism. The identity that ensues from genuine non-partisan nationalism will endow on every citizen the right to decide upon their common political destiny. It makes possible meaningful relationships with others as we shall live and work with a common culture. It will "situate" a person as he will now be identified with an entity recognized by the nations of the world.

Our flag is our national symbol and our national anthem is the ritual connected with our flag. Both demand the highest respect. Given that "the nation is the result of a daily plebiscite" (Renan), we need to constantly re-enact our identification with them. For, "it is by uttering the same cry, pronouncing the same word, or performing the same gesture in regard to some object that the individuals become and feel themselves to be in unison" (Durkheim: Elementary Forms of Religious Life).

Underpinning all these is the need that we do have a society where opportunities are available to all to progress in education. Employment is a matter of suitable qualification and/or skill. A society where freedom of expression exists together with the freedom to live anywhere in this country according to one's wishes and the demands of the job. This is the responsibility of the government in power. Failure to create this environment will be disastrous, as the new nationalism will be stillborn and the old divisions will re-emerge to destroy our society. A lean and mean government has become a necessity to usher in the changes and promote relentlessly the new nationalism of national identity. Rampant corruption and lawlessness militate against new beginnings.

Identity politics or the politics of ethnicity was killed off at Nandikadal. Minority politicians who peddle these blatantly racist ideals should not be allowed to function in our new society. They should be persuaded to change from such damaging enterprises to more profitable and beneficial ideals of progress and unity of the people and nation. Similarly there cannot be any exclusivist enclaves in this country which now is one land, one country and one people. Just as much as no one grudges at Tamil settlements in Wellawatha, Kotahena, Wattala, Kandy and Negombo, no one should be alarmed at Muslims and Sinhalese settlements in Killinochi, Mullaitivu or Jaffna peninsula. This land belongs to all born here and live here. Let us live and let live.

Today we live in a globalized world. The foreign Tamils, inimical to Sri Lanka, are all bent to destabilize our society by using the pervasive global technology, currency markets and stock exchanges and the international media. We need to counter this by reactivating our true nationalism as the legitimizing ideology and by articulating our set of all inclusive values and the right of our people to decide our political destiny. Those foreign Tamils have no stake anymore in this country which they abandoned for their material wealth and prestige. They should seek their homelands in the countries where they have found their domestication.

98

THE MATTER OF SECURITY OF THE NATION

(The Island, 14th Oct. 2009)

I must admit that I too often wondered, why GOSL could not set free or settle all those LTTE-victimized people, (I do not accept the term IDPs), now in temporary camps, who have been screened and found to be civilians with no active connection with the LTTE. The main reasons given by the GOSL, among others, are that de-mining has not been completed and that the security of the nation makes it paramount for the screening to be completed too. Indeed, if one thinks deep enough, these two reasons are valid as well as sufficient to explain the delay in settling the LTTE victims. It must be pointed out that, as of now, the GOSL has started to resettle people in cleared lands to the west of A9 road. The GOSL has also published advertisements calling on relations of LTTE victims to apply for guardianship of the same. The response, so far, has not been very encouraging!

On the first point the government has been guilty of not properly publicizing the slow, dangerous and arduous work of de-mining. It is true that recently remote controlled machines have been used to churn up the land to expose the mines for safe disposal. Presumably these machines can only be used in open fields and not in small cottage and homestead gardens of small areas and wooded and forested lands. These require human hands and dogs to clear the land foot by foot until every inch is clear. The vicious minds of the LTTE did oftentimes net-work many mines together but left them scattered over several feet. In some cases they were also connected with a time-lapsed trigger to hidden claymore mines away from the area examined.

After these elaborate clearing operations are completed, the UN Agency will be expected to inspect the area and declare it cleared and safe for people to inhabit that land. GOSL should have given extensive publicity to this dangerous work necessitated by the wonton and callous mindset of the LTTE. They knew that they were burying mines in lands belonging to Tamils and most of the intended victims would be Tamils. No one,-- the UN, Foreign Governments, INGOs, NGOs or TNA-- castigated the LTTE then, when they resorted to this outrageously murderous conduct. Now all these born-again-moralists are impatient and are quick to find fault with the GOSL for delay, and even accuse the GOSL as pursuing a deliberate policy of delaying mine-clearance as a punishment of the Tamils. TNA has attributed to GOSL other racially motivated objectives for the delay. Would these do-gooders accept responsibility for deaths and injuries to people, if tomorrow, the GOSL settled these people in lands and buildings without any proper de-mining and bomb clearance? No, they would not, such is their duplicity. We should, however, thankfully acknowledge the active cooperation extended to us by some international mine-clearing organizations and the Indians in this onerous task.

There is also question of where to settle these people when it is well-known that their houses are roofless and wall-less, some are booby-trapped and their wells are destroyed or poisoned by the retreating LTTE. Further easy access roads to even these houses have been destroyed by the LTTE in their desperate effort to halt the advancing army. Can these do-gooders restore these properties overnight for resettlement of the people? No.

I do place the blame on the government's propaganda body for failure to broadcast to the people and the world the enormity of the work involved and the many thousands of man-hours needed to clear even a small plot of land. It is not too late to pictorially apprise the world that this dangerous work is being done day in and day out at the risk of lives of dedicated teams of people both Sri Lankan and foreign.

Before examining the second reason given by the government, we have got to identify Sri Lanka's many enemies. There are some rich and influential foreign governments who openly pose as our friends yet behind our backs work to keep our country perpetually conflict ridden. They use their dominance in international bodies to obstruct our way to progress and prosperity. The top functionaries of such governments will not be averse to help born-again Tamil insurgents in our country. Then there are the economic refugee Tamils now settled down in various foreign countries for good. They have no intention of returning to Sri Lanka or their Eelam utopia now or in the future. I call them foreign Tamils. [It is incorrect to call them diaspora Tamils. The term diaspora applied to the dispersed Jews who were expected to return one day to the land of Jerusalem and found Israel. This the Jews did]. No way will the materially prosperous Tamils in the west would give up their comfortable lives and return to toil in the arid Wanni to found Eelam. They would rather employ proxies to do this dirty work to de-stabilize Sri Lanka. They are ardently pursuing this task now via internet and by buying for cash influential and high profile persons to bad-mouth Sri Lanka with the help of the LTTE's cash mountains, available to them in the western capitals. They too will want to resurrect separatist forces in the country via the remnants of the LTTE now disguised as civilians. This is likely to be a long drawn out fight which the present and future governments should learn to counter and cope with, giving no quarter to these foreign Tamils.

Within the country we have many enemies too. There are some in the TNA—Politicians, who still entertain the achievement of separatist Eelam by stealthy political means. They still talk about exclusive Tamil Eelam. Their offers for cooperation should be closely scrutinized for both problems now and potential problems in the future. We also have fifth columnists in our NGOs and INGOs. The top men/women in these organizations are the Judases who will betray the country for the proverbial thirty pieces of silver (dollars?). At the moment, together with some journalists and newspaper personnel, they are very active trying to gather "evidence", or rather, manufacture it, to vilify the country and our valiant security forces. They too probably hope for the day when LTTE terrorism will raise its ugly head to slaughter innocent civilians again. When and if this happens you will not hear even a whimper of protest from these NGO wallahs!!

Within the camps now housing the LTTE-victimized Tamils there are various categories of enemies. There are the people who were employed by the LTTE in various capacities in civilian work as well as military projects. They have to be identified and assessed and evaluated in terms of their commitment to peaceful life now and their potential to drift back later to insurrectionary behaviour. Closely allied to these people are the families of deceased cadres or the Mahaveerer families. Rehabilitating these die-hard families would be no easy task. Nevertheless, they need to be identified, separated and closely monitored.

There would certainly be many LTTE cadres who actively fought our security forces. Some of them could be conscripts with no stomach for Eelam. Some of them could be loners or joined together in secret cells, harbouring anger and hatred and waiting for an opportunity to avenge the deaths of their colleagues. Our police have been able to pick up some of them not only from within the camp but also from towns in the south of the country.

The process of screening such dangerous men/women would take many man-hours of patient work. First there is their identification by more cooperative LTTE colleagues and eliciting from them as much information as possible about the suspect. Then there is the tracing of their parents and relations, if still among the living, to establish not only the background but also the fact that the person in question has been an active LTTE cadre. Finally the suspect himself would be questioned carefully to confirm the facts already known from other sources and to elicit other yet unknown information about him and others. He/She will also have to be evaluated for the prospects of rehabilitating him/her as a peaceful citizen, so long as the suspect was not implicated in some dastardly criminal act like the murder of civilians. My description is very brief yet one can imagine the time even this investigation will take and the number of persons it will involve to establish the fact that the suspect was really and truly an active brainwashed LTTE cadre. For easy comprehension, now apply this procedure to not 300,000, but just 1000 persons in the camp to initially arrive at the time involved in screening them and then multiply by 300 to gage the time required to screen the entire LTTE-victims in the camp. In short screening too is a time consuming job with no short cuts. No risks can be taken here as these LTTE cadres are very dangerous terrorists who could cause irreparable harm in society.

Here again the GOSL's publicity machinery is gravely at fault in not explaining to the people the slow and careful work involved in screening camp occupants. Just spilling out statistics of identified LTTE cadres in no way explains the delay and the patient work involved.

The army exhibited a vast array of lethal weapons captured from the LTTE at BMICH. Even though this was only a very small fraction of the total amount, it really was an amazing experience even to look at them and one that caused chilling fear when one considered the end objective of all those weapons. Velu truly had the whole of Sri Lanka in his aim but for our brave soldiers. I strongly urge the army to use the Galle Face and exhibit All the weapons captured to date for the whole world to see. A terrorist with this sort of weapons could not be a peaceful man. Those who believed him were all morons.

Almost everyday the army is digging up large caches of LTTE buried arms from all over the Wanni. It is likely that there are many more such hidden lethal weapons still to be discovered. If, as is suggested by the LTTE sympathizers, we free the camp inhabitants without any screening, it is almost certain that these hidden treasures of the LTTE would find their way into the arms of these men/women, and we would soon have a battle again on our hands, and the security of the nation would be thrown into jeopardy. These new insurgents/terrorists would also have the support of the enemies of our country as listed above. This then could be the new secret agenda of our enemies, and the reason for their unabated agitation to free the LTTE-victims in the camps. Screening, investigation, identification and separation of cadres must be pursued to the finish. The threat to the nation is real and cannot be allowed to raise its head again. In the meanwhile, all those established to be victimized civilians should be allowed to go back to their homes if that is their wish, provided their home areas have been cleared of mines. The government should expedite this process and continue to rebuild the infra-structures like roads, water supply and electricity while these people are living in their houses.

99

WHO OWNS WANNI?

(The Island, 14th Oct. 2009)

Many spectacular and amazing events have taken place in Wanni and now many significant events contributing to the welfare of our country are taking place there. Some narrow minded TNA politicians, having ignored what has happened, and what is now happening in Wanni, are already beating the racist drum trying to claim an exclusive Tamil enclave in Wanni. This is the reason for the above, otherwise, absurd question.

According to The Island newspaper (12th and 13th Sept.), the TNA MPs, with hardened racist mindset, have alleged that the government "wants to change the Wanni's demography by settling at least 30% Sinhalese in Kilinochchi and Mullaitivu districts. There is a plan to change the demographic pattern in the Wanni area so that there is no such thing as a Tamil province". The above alleged accusation was made at a meeting with the visiting Tamil Nadu politicians by TNA MPs. My immediate response at that time was, so what? Why should we not change? Many Sinhala provinces are no more exclusively Sinhala anymore.

The government panicked, condemned it as "a barefaced lie" without an iota of truth in it. Earlier a government Minister had already said at a press conference that his government "would not in any way try to change the ethnic ratio in the northern and eastern provinces". I am dismayed with this stance, and I do strongly disagree with the government's position on this matter for reasons given below.

The antidote to the above segregationist policy came from Western Provincial Member C.Y.P. Ram. He said that the Tamil Nadu politicians were "of the opinion that they (LTTE-victimized Tamil in camps) should be allowed to live among their Sinhala brethren in any part of the country so that communal harmony would be guaranteed" (13th The Island). True indeed!! He lives among the Sinhalese and Muslims and others, and has first hand experience of harmonious social, economic, and religious intercourse of Tamils with others, and the peace that prevails benefiting all communities. Experience has been his best teacher.(Usus est optimum magister).

No matter the various theories about the original people of this island, I like to refer to Emmerson Tennent (a Colonial Secretary) who toured this country in Aug. 1848 and later wrote a book on "Ceylon, An Account of the Island". He noted that the Wanni was a desolate place with only a few remote villages, some of them controlled by Wannichies. The rest of that country was wild jungle wherein marauding bandits roamed spreading death and destruction. What I wish to point out is the fact that not long ago there was no settled population in Wanni and the few who lived there did pay annual tribute to the king in Kandy. It is the Tamil politicians who manufactured the concept of "Tamil Wanni" to the detriment of Tamils as well as the country after many Tamils drifted there in relatively recent times, including the estate Tamils planted there by the Norwegian "Red Barna". This highly divisive myth needs also to be discarded forthwith, and exposed as a poisonous brew to kill off all efforts at reconciliation and rehabilitation of people. The Wanni belongs to all the people in this country. This irrefutable communal ownership has been emphatically and irretrievably established once and for all times by our security forces in recent times.

I am concerned here only with the common land under the control of the government and its policy on settling people on this land. The government cannot be blamed if it pursues a policy of ethnic dilution in its land settlement policy. I strongly advocate such a policy because our Constitution permits any Sri Lankan to settle down anywhere in the country and pursue his avocation without any hindrance. The government minister referred to above, seems to have forgotten that he has sworn to protect and abide by the provisions of the Constitution. Is he not advocating a foolish segregationist policy?

Of course, in actually settling people on land, first preference should be given to landless people in the area, no matter their ethnicity, after that, some fair and justifiable scheme should be adopted for the rest. A blank refusal to settle people because they are Sinhalese or Muslims (ie.Non-Tamils) would be systemic discrimination outlawed by our constitution. The Tamil politicians who want this discriminatory policy should ask themselves what would happen to the landless and houseless Tamils if the same policy is applied favouring the Sinhalese and Muslims in Wellawatte, or anywhere else in the country. On the basis of our Constitution settlement of people on vacant land should not be purely on grounds of ethnicity.

Ethnic dilution has already taken place in Colombo and other towns. This has not brought about strife and conflict. What we do see instead is the harmonious co-operative endeavour to overcome the difficulties of daily life and lead a life of humanly achievable contentment. This in turn creates more opportunities for the entrepreneurs among us. In the playing fields we see children of various ethnicities engaged in friendly competition to win a trophy. In the high street we see business competitors of various ethnicity, living cheek by jowl, plying their trade without killing each other. In the professions too there is severe competition for clients and the clients choose their professionals ignoring their ethnicity. This intermingling benefits all. If this was not true then the Tamils would have deserted these ethnically diluted towns long ago. On the contrary what we witness today is an unending inflow of Tamils from the north and east into these towns, even after the end of the military conflict in the north and east. The opportunity for advancement for anyone lies within a mixed society.

The emergence of another Pirapakaran from such a mixed society is a near impossibility. In Colombo north we do have a Tamil politician who vigorously pursues the interests of Tamils and is an outspoken ardent advocate of everything Tamil. It is important to note that he operates within the parameters of democratic norms and rule of law. He cannot go beyond this boundary as his constituency is a mixed one where a large contingent of Tamils live. These Tamils would not want their representative to embark on the disastrous road of extremism and break the cosy relationship they now have with their neighbours, clients and customers of other ethnicity. Such a venture will result in conflict, if not, hostile ostracism. This reasoning is also valid for any ethnically diluted province in the north and the east whether it be Omanthai or Killinochchi. I strongly believe that we should have non-segregationist, ethnically mixed areas all over our country. If the Tamils can live and prosper in mixed societies in Colombo, Kandy, Wattala, Negombo and many other towns, there is no earthly reason why they cannot do so in Killinochchi, Mullaitivu and Pranthan!!

Our resources are severely limited. Our political representatives have to bargain with the Central Government to obtain whatever development funds due to their provinces. Their bargaining power will be enormously enhanced when our representatives have behind them not just one community but members of all communities in the island. The inherent dynamics of a diluted and stable ethnic community is social coherence, cooperation and peace. This should indeed be the future vision of our society.

Finally I would like to ask the TNA politicians and UPFA minister why did we send our Security Forces scouring all over Wanni? Was it not their mission to demolish root and branch the crude exclusively Tamil eelam of Pirapakaran? Did they not satisfactorily accomplish this task and free the victimized Tamils incarcerated by the maniac Pirapakaran? Our security forces have comprehensively cleared the Wanni towns, jungles, beaches and riversides, at great sacrifices to themselves, of all traces of the myth of exclusive Tamil eelam. There is no going back to this era anymore. The peace momentum our security forces have generated demands inclusive societies everywhere, especially in the Wanni. Once the current resettlement process is over, the process to change the ethnic mix of our society should be actively pursued so that we could all truly claim the right to live anywhere in this country. Where there is freedom [to settle down], there is my fatherland, (ubi libertas, ibi patria).

IS TNA BORN-AGAIN LTTE?

(The island, 29th Mar.2010)

Like many Sri Lankans, I am thoroughly disappointed with the current election Manifesto published by the TNA. This Manifesto, in my view seeks to perpetuate the irrational policies of the defeated LTTE. A thirty-year armed confrontation to win their demands, did only take the LTTE to decimation on the shores of Nandikadal lagoon and the Tamil people to abject destitution and IDP camps. This fact and the lessons ensuing from it appear to have escaped the framers of the TNA Manifesto. One can only hope that the long-suffering Tamil people, to whom their living conditions, livelihood, health, security and education are the most urgent needs, will have the courage to reject the demands in this infamous Manifesto, and vote for the candidates who proclaim the vision of reconciliation, hope for the future prosperity in conjunction with and in combination with all other citizens of this country.

In short the TNA Manifesto states the following: (1) Merger of the North and the East and the power sharing arrangement to this unit. (2) Devolved power over land, finances, law and order and socio-economic development. (3) Power to attract and employ foreign funds without interference from the Central Bank or the National Treasury. (4) A federal political solution with power for self-determination. And this should be acceptable to the Tamil speaking Muslims. The President in a recent interview with the Straits Times was forthright in rejecting all these demands. Therefore the TNA like the LTTE is on a collision course with the present government. Surely this is not what the country or the LTTE-victimized Tamil people want in the post LTTE era.

To me the items 2 and 3 are susceptible to negotiation as proper safeguards can be devised against abuse as well as discriminatory use of such powers. We already have the Indian government more or less directly helping the Eastern Province in socio-economic development, subject to the supervisory overview of the government. Similarly devolved powers over law and order too could be allowed to be exercised with constitutional and institutional controls. The police force in the autonomous Scotland could be an example to draw up suitable safeguards against the abuse of this power by the provincial authorities. Obviously these (land and finances) are matters for detailed negotiation by those knowledgeable in those subjects.

To me the sinister demands appear to be 1 and 4. They are the haunting echoes of the LTTE's siren call for homeland and Eelam. Given the present context, the merger of North and east is really impracticable and unattainable. The mixture of races in the east will not accept the dominance of the Jaffna Tamil in that province. They have already had the bitter experiences of what that dominance entailed over the past thirty years. Would they like to go back to that kind of discriminative regime even if there are no guns now to enforce such an oppressive system? The Muslim and the Sinhala votes in the East in the coming General Election would, I expect, correct the aberration in the Presidential election and are likely to prove me right that they have no truck with the TNA. In fact it would not surprise me that many Batticaloa Tamils too now want reconciliation, prosperity and growth rather than confrontation and an ever deteriorating social and economic situation for themselves and turn away from TNA. I believe that their urgent needs are not what the 1 and 4 in the TNA manifesto seeks to obtain.

I regard with utmost suspicion TNA's call for self-determination to the merged North and the East. Internal and external self-determination is simply a spurious distinction to deceive the people. The end-objective of both is the same. Long ago comrade V.I. Lenin (in his ***Right of Nations to Self-Determination***) came to the "conclusion that self-determination of nations means the political separation of these nations from alien national bodies and the formation of an independent national state". He further emphasized that "it would be wrong to interpret the right to self-determination as means anything but the right to existence as a separate state". Any other interpretation of self-determination by various "spin doctors" would be mere meaningless semantics and an attempt to deceive the people. Many provisions in the UN Charter do not admit the right to self-determination by minorities that will fragment/bifurcate an already existing member state of the UN. The UN Resolution 1514 (of 14thDec.1960) ended with a categorical provision; "any attempt at the partial or total disruption of the national unity and the territorial integrity of the country is incompatible with the purpose and principles of the Charter of the United nations".

I have cited the above ideas on self-determination because I suspect that TNA is here following what Mr. Balasingam in the halcyon days of LTTE advocated. Here is what he said at the now infamous Vanni News Conference (10th April 2002). "By self-determination, we mean the right of our people to decide on their own political destiny. It can also mean/apply to autonomy and self-government. If autonomy and self-government is given to our people, then also we can say that internal self-determination is to some extent met. So self-determination entails autonomy and self-government. In the extreme case, in the last resort, it means secession". Later in the Tamil Guardian (see quoted in The Island 6th June 2002) he explicitly argued the LTTE's right to "Tamil homeland and the right to ***national self-determination***", not internal self-determination anymore!. He had been deliberately equivocal in order to hide the fact that self-determination was separatism. He mixed this up with autonomy to make it palatable to the citizens of the country. This is what, in my view, the TNA is also attempting to do. They want to deceive the people into thinking that the self-determination of the merged unit will not lead to separatism but only to autonomy. They appear to have forgotten that our soldiers marched from Mavil Aru in the east to Mannar in the west and doubled back to Nandikadal in order to defeat once and for all the separatism of the LTTE. As the President has already said the short answer to TNA should be NO MERGER, NO SELF-DETERMINATION. This is the verdict expected from the Tamil people who have already traversed this via dolorosa (way of sorrow) only to be bitterly disappointed and end up as impoverished hostages and penniless IDPs. The current TNA is not prepared to learn from recent events and it is time that it too is replaced with persons who think Sri Lankan first and Tamil or Hindu thereafter. I hope the current split in the TNA will lead to this eventuality.

APPENDIX : A brief history of recent significant events in the dealings with the LTTE.

1990 Feb. President Premadasa held peace talks with LTTE at the Hilton hotel. After acquiring a large stock of weapons and a large sum of money from the government on the pretext of fighting the Indian-installed Tamil National army, the LTTE resumed its attack on our military. President Premadasa was assassinated by the LTTE on May 1st 1993.

1994 Oct. the newly elected President Mrs.Kumaratunghe initiated peace talks with the LTTE. Her Secretary Mr. Balapatabendi led the government's peace delegation. It collapsed after four rounds when the LTTE launched attacks on our navy in Trincomalee.

2001 Dec. The general election was won by Mr. Ranil Wickramasinghe's party. He had declared during the election campaign that he would resume peace talks with the LTTE.

2002 Feb.22nd Mr. Wickramasinghe signed the Norwegian brokered Ceasefire Agreement (CFA), without consulting his Cabinet of Ministers, without debating it in Parliament and without the knowledge of the sitting President, who alone had the power, according to the Constitution, to declare war or conclude a peace-deal.

2002 Mar.2nd The first Sri Lanka Monitoring Mission (SLMM) chief retired Norwegian Army General Trond Fruhovde arrived in Sri Lanka.

2002 Peace talks were held in Thailand and Norway on Sept 16th, Oct. 31st and Dec. 16th.

2003 Peace talks were held in Thailand, Germany and Japan on Jan. 6th, Feb 7th and Mar.16th.

2003 Apr.21st LTTE withdrew from peace talks on the pretext that it was not invited for reconstruction talks held in Washington on the 14th of April

2003 June 9th Tokyo donor conference when the $4.5 billion loan was pledged for reconstruction of devastated war-torn areas.

2003 Oct 31st Interim Self Government Authority (ISGA) proposals were handed over to the government by the LTTE.

2003 Nov. 4th President Mrs. Kumaratinghe took control of the Ministry of Defence and PM Ranil and Norway withdrew from peace talks on the 13th and 14th of the same month.

2004 Mar 6th Karuna broke off from the LTTE with nearly 5000 LTTE eastern cadres. On April 8th UPFA won the general election.

2004 Dec. 26th Tsunami devastated the coastal areas of our country. The LTTE took the opportunity to press for control of rebuilding of the tsunami destroyed areas under their control. On June 24th the Post Tsunami Operational Management Structure (PTOMS) was signed.

2005 Nov. 19th Mr. Mahinda Rajapakse was elected President. In December he was greeted with claymore attacks in Jaffna and on our soldiers. In one instance nearly 150 of our soldiers were killed and there were attacks on our navy.

2006 Feb. 7th agreed to new peace talks. This was held in Geneva on 22nd and 23rd of February. On the 20th of April LTTE officially pulled out of peace talks indefinitely and continued to attack civilian targets. There were further attempts made to revive peace talks but were rejected by the LTTE on flimsy grounds.

2006 May 29th EU proscribed the LTTE and froze all LTTE assets in member countries.

2006 July 21st LTTE closed the sluice gates of Mavilaru reservoir and cut off the water supply to nearly 15,000 villagers in the government controlled areas. This was the beginning of the end of LTTE.

2006 Oct. 28th and 29th last ditch attempt was made to resume peace talks but broke down due to disagreements over the reopening of the A9 highway. The government then decided to chase the LTTE out of the eastern province and free nearly 35,000 civilians held as human shields by the LTTE.

2008 Jan the CFA was finally jettisoned by the government.

2009 May 18th/19th LTTE was finally vanquished on the shores of Nandhikadal lagoon and more than 300,000 Tamil hostages were rescued by our security forces.